C++ Object Databases

David Jordan

ADDISON-WESLEY

An imprint of Addison Wesley Longman, Inc.

Reading, Massachusetts ● Harlow, England ● Menlo Park, California
Berkeley, California ● Don Mills, Ontario ● Sydney
Bonn ● Amsterdam ● Tokyo ● Mexico City

The publisher offers discounts on this book when ordered in quantity for special sales. For more information, please contact:

Corporate & Professional Publishing Group
Addison Wesley Longman, Inc.
One Jacob Way
Reading, Massachusetts 01867

Library of Congress Cataloging-in-Publication Data
Jordan, David. 1957-
    C++ object databases : programming with the ODMG standard / David Jordan.
        p.   cm.
    Includes bibliographical references and index.
    ISBN 0-201-63488-0 (alk. paper)
    1. Object-oriented databases. 2. C++ (Computer program language)
I. Title.
QA76.9.D3J67 1998
005.75'7—dc21   97-41576
                                                                    CIP

  Copyright © 1998 by Lucent Technologies

ISBN 0-201-63488-0
Text printed on recycled and acid-free paper.

2 3 4 5 6 7   MA   00 99 98 97

2nd Printing December, 1997

C++ Object Databases

Programming with the ODMG Standard

David Jordan

The Addison-Wesley Object Technology Series

Grady Booch, Ivar Jacobson, and James Rumbaugh, Series Editors

[http://www.awl.com/cseng/otseries/]

David Bellin and Susan Suchman Simone, *The CRC Card Book*

Grady Booch, *Object Solutions: Managing the Object-Oriented Project*

Grady Booch, *Object-Oriented Analysis and Design with Applications*

Dave Collins, *Designing Object-Oriented User Interfaces*

Bruce Douglass, *Real-Time UML: Developing Efficient Objects for Embedded Systems*

Desmond F. D'Souza and Alan C. Wills
Objects, Components, and Frameworks with UML: The Catalysis Approach

Martin Fowler with Kendall Scott *UML Distilled: Applying the Standard Object Modeling Language*

Martin Fowler, *Analysis Patterns: Reusable Object Models*

Peter Heinckiens, *Scalable Object-Oriented Database Applications:*
Design, Architecture, and Implementations

Ivar Jacobson, Maria Ericsson, and Agenta Jacobson
The Object Advantage: Business Process Reengineering with Object Technology

Ivar Jacobson, Magnus Christerson, Patrik Jonsson, and Gunnar Overgaard
Object-Oriented Software Engineering: A Use Case Driven Approach

Ivar Jacobson, Martin Griss, and Patrik Jonsson
Software Reuse: Architecture, Process and Organization for Business Success

Wilf LaLonde, *Discovering Smalltalk*

Lockheed Martin Advanced Concepts Center and Rational Software Corporation
Succeeding with the Booch and OMT Methods: A Practical Approach

Thomas Mowbray and William Ruh
Inside CORBA: Distributed Object Standards and Applications

Ira Pohl, *Object-Oriented Programming Using C++*

Terry Quatrani, *Visual Modeling with Rational Rose and UML*

Yen-Ping Shan and Ralph Earle, *Enterprise Computing with Objects:*
From Client/Server Environments to the Internet

David N. Smith, *IBM Smalltalk: The Language*

Daniel Tkach and Richard Puttick, *Object Technology in Application Development* Second Edition

Daniel Tkach, Walter Fang, and Andrew So
Visual Modeling Technique: Object Technology Using Visual Programming

To my wife, Tina,
my children, Jennifer and Jeremy,
and my parents, John and Lorrie.

Table of Contents

References 441

Index 443

Foreword

It has been my pleasure to work with Dave Jordan for some years now. Without his contributions to the ODMG over these years, the ODMG C++ binding as well as many of the other ODMG chapters would have been much weaker. In this book Dave has once again demonstrated high standards for readability and unambiguous accuracy in technical writing.

The book describes how to write object database applications in C++, but it also provides an excellent overview of object database systems, an explanation of the contrast between relational and object database system approaches, a concise description of the OQL query language and ODMG object model, and some insight into the performance and features of different object database products. This book should be useful to anyone in the industry using or contemplating the use of object database products, particularly where multiple database products are involved.

To understand Dave's contribution in this book and to ODMG, it is important to realize that in any standards group the primary goal of the vendors must be to make sure that their companies can implement a proposed standard in a timely and efficient way. The programmer's goal of a simple, unambiguous, and consistent standard gets insufficient attention. It is in these areas that Dave has made significant contributions to the ODMG and to object database technology, and in this book Dave has provided what the programmer needs in working with the ODMG interface. These contributions require dedication to the common good of forwarding an industry and technology. I firmly believe that without the help of people like Dave a good technology would be all but lost by now. The demonstration that there is support for a standard approach to object databases has brought this industry hundreds of millions of dollars a year and has brought programmers a technology that enables hundreds of new application domains. This book provides an excellent overview and a comprehensive description of this technology from a programmer's perspective.

Rick Cattell

Preface

It seems I was destined from the beginning of my career to be involved in object database technology. My academic advisers unintentionally led me toward the technology. Mike Warren, my undergraduate psychology professor, got me interested in both semantic network modeling and computer science. Upon graduation in 1979 I took a job with NCR Corporation in Dayton, Ohio, and pursued my M.S. in computer science at Wright State University. At NCR I worked with network model databases and was on a team that ported UNIX to an NCR machine. Along with my adviser at Wright State, Bob Dixon, I became interested in object technology when Smalltalk-80 was introduced; we worked on several object-based projects.

When I completed my master's degree in 1983, I took a job with AT&T Bell Laboratories in the UNIX System Development Laboratories at Murray Hill, New Jersey. I was very fortunate to have Tom Cargill as my mentor. Tom was developing a debugger called pi (process inspector) in a new programming language being designed by Bjarne Stroustrup. Knowing C and wanting to use object technology, I began learning C++ in 1984.

Early in 1985 I transferred to the Bell Labs site in Columbus, Ohio, where I still reside. Our project was to develop a factory engineering application for managing circuit pack designs and the processes used to manufacture the packs. I was responsible for the database schema design and also served as the C++/OOD facilitator on the project. I began reading about a new technology called object databases. CAD/CAM was one of the original application domains to use object databases. The technology appealed to me, because it combined my interests in objects and databases and was applicable to the project I was working on. Just a handful of commercial products were available, and they were based on special-purpose proprietary languages that integrated database functionality. It seemed that the technology would not gain very much market acceptance unless a more mainstream, general-purpose programming language was used.

At OOPSLA '85 I met Tim Andrews of Ontologic, which had a commercial object database product called Vbase. The company had its own object language called COP, which was C with object and database extensions. I encouraged Tim and others at Ontologic to abandon COP and use C++ instead. We considered establishing a joint business relationship between Bell Labs and Ontologic to co-develop a C++ object database product, but Bell Labs wasn't interested. Ontologic developed the C++ product anyway, and I served as a member of its Technical Advisory Board. Ontologic released the first commercial C++ object database product in 1987. I tried to convince my project members and others at Bell Labs to use the technology, but they were reluctant because of a lack of standards and the absence of major players in the marketplace.

In 1992 I learned that Rick Cattell had organized a consortium of object database vendors, called the Object Database Management Group (ODMG), to define standards for object databases to be adopted by all the vendors. At last! A standard interface supported by all the vendors would lead to market acceptance. Each vendor had selected several people to serve as reviewers of the standard. Joshua Duhl, the Ontologic ODMG representative, selected me to be a reviewer. In 1993 Rick Cattell invited me to become the ODMG C++ Editor.

I was ecstatic. Rick had offered me an incredible opportunity. The ODMG had just released its 1.0 specification. I joined the ODMG and have served as its C++ Editor for releases 1.1, 1.2, and 2.0. Implementations of the standard are now available from many of the vendors.

This book describes object databases using the ODMG C++ and Object Query Language (OQL) interfaces. It can serve as an introduction to object database technology and as a reference for anyone using an implementation of the ODMG standard.

The Audience for This Book

This book is targeted toward software developers who are knowledgeable about object design and C++ and want to learn about object databases. Managers are encouraged to read the book *Object Databases: The Essentials*, by Mary Loomis. Other books are available that cover more technical details of object database implementations. Rick Cattell's book *Object Data Management* is an excellent reference.

The Role of Object Database Vendors

By design, this book does not directly discuss any particular vendor or implementation. Aspects of implementations change over time as architectures adapt to advancements in computer environments and the demands of users. Other books that discuss implementation aspects of object databases have become outdated as the technology has advanced and matured.

I chose not to compare the vendors directly. As ODMG C++ Editor, I need to maintain a good relationship with the vendors. If I had compared the vendors directly I would probably have gotten every vendor upset with me. People tend to react more to negative statements than to positive ones. Every implementation design decision has both positive and negative side effects. Application developers have biases based on their system requirements that guide their choice of the best architecture for their needs. Readers who want to understand the feature differences among the vendors should obtain a copy of *The Object Database Handbook: How to Select, Implement, and Use Object-Oriented Databases* by Doug Barry.

A Quick Tour of the Book

This book is divided into four parts. Part I covers object database modeling. The first chapter provides an introductory example to give you a feel for what it is like to develop a complete application with a C++ object database. Chapter 2 shows how to open a database, begin transactions, and commit transactions. The object modeling facilities found in an object database environment are covered in Chapters 3–9. The ODMG 2.0 standard serves as the interface. No vendor-specific interfaces are covered, although some aspects of various implementations are discussed.

Part II covers the Object Query Language, which has been adopted by the ODMG as the standard query language for object databases. It is assumed that you are not already familiar with OQL, so the OQL chapters read like a language reference manual. Object databases have historically been weak in their query language support, especially compared with relational databases. Some object database vendors have implemented their own variations of SQL access; each vendor maps the object model to SQL differently, resulting in a loss of application portability despite the use of the same query language. OQL is a powerful query language for objects, and its implementation by all the vendors will greatly enhance the acceptance of object databases. Those vendors who have not yet implemented OQL are driven by market demand for SQL support. If developers want query language standardization for object databases, they should insist that vendors support an OQL implementation.

Part III discusses the various architectures used by object databases. Rather than rewrite their systems from scratch, most ODMG implementers place an ODMG interface on their existing architectures. There are many differences among the vendor architectures, something that can affect the suitability of a vendor's product for a particular application. Understanding these differences is important when you're deciding among the product offerings. Performance is also covered here, because the performance characteristics of an object database are often derived from its underlying architecture. Part III concludes with a discussion of the schema representation.

Part IV examines relational and object-relational databases, contrasting them with object databases. There is also a discussion of object support in the 1996 draft version of the ANSI SQL3 document as well as some musings about the future of each of these technologies with respect to Java.

The appendices have a different style from that of the body of the book. Appendix A contains the declarations of classes used by the book's examples. Appendix B and C are a complete reference to the ODMG 2.0 C++ interface. Because implementations available in the marketplace were still based on the ODMG-93 1.2 interface, I have noted the differences between the releases so that you can use this book with either release. Appendix C is devoted to the metaclasses introduced in ODMG 2.0. These classes are used by an application to access a description of a database's schema. An overview of these classes appears in Chapter 16.

Acknowledgments

I would like to thank those who provided me with software used in the writing of the examples. François Bancilhon of O_2 Technology and Dirk Bartels of Poet Software contributed their implementations of the ODMG-93 release 1.2 standard. Richard Patterson of Microsoft provided me with a Visual C++ 4.0 compiler, and Chris Tarr of ObjectSpace provided an STL implementation.

I gratefully acknowledge the time and effort of those who reviewed drafts of this book. ODMG members that reviewed the book include Sophie Gamerman at O_2 Technology, Richard Jensen at Persistence Software Inc., Raymond Lai at Versant Object Technology, Olaf Schadow at Poet Software, and Ken Sinclair at Object Design, Inc. Other reviewers include Donna Autrey, Carter Glass, Howard Lee Harkness, Tina Jordan, Brian Kernighan, Ed Schiebel, and Kathy Stark. I also greatly appreciate the time and effort Martin Fowler spent assisting me with the UML diagrams. Very special thanks go to my friend Dennis Leinbaugh, who not only reviewed the book several times and provided extensive editorial comments but also served as a professional colleague to bounce ideas off of during the writing process. I would also like to thank the team at Addison-Wesley, including Katie Duffy, Marina Lang, Pamela Yee, and Jacqui Young. A special thanks also goes to Betsy Hardinger who served as copyeditor, this book and future writings will benefit greatly from the things learned from her editorial comments. Finally, I would like to extend my sincere appreciation to Mike Hendrickson and John Wait of Addison-Wesley for giving me the opportunity to publish this book.

Part I:
Object Database Modeling

Chapter 1
An Introduction

When you're using a C++ object database, *a single object model is shared by the database and the application.* The application's C++ class declarations serve as the schema definition, allowing C++ developers to work in a familiar language and modeling environment. A database interface is provided that seamlessly integrates with the application. Developers do not need to define the application's model in both C++ and a separate database language and modeling framework. Nor do they need to define a mapping between the application and the database model. A single, extensible type system is shared by both the application and the database. This shared model is a primary characteristic of an object database and the source of much of its value.

This chapter leads you through the process of creating an application using an object database. You will learn how to do the following:

- Define a database schema
- Create new object instances in the database
- Associate a name with an instance and then access the instance by name
- Establish relationships among instances
- Access related instances via navigation
- Modify an instance
- Delete an instance

Complete applications are shown performing these operations using standard C++ syntax. These basic operations are required by all applications when accessing a database.

I use the interface of the Object Database Management Group (ODMG) standard in this chapter and throughout the book. The ODMG is a consortium of object database vendors and users that are defining standard application interfaces for object databases, and each of the vendor members is committed to supporting the interface in its products. I have served as the C++ editor of the ODMG since 1993. Some of the vendors have already released implementations. A complete description of the ODMG classes is found in Appendix B and C; you are encouraged to reference them as needed.

1.1   An Example Application

The sample application is used to manage lists of gifts to be given to people. The object model consists of two classes: GiftList and Gift. A GiftList models a set of people and the gifts they are to receive. There can be multiple gift lists. The GiftList class maintains a singly linked list of Gift objects. Figure 1.1 illustrates the classes and their relationship.

This book uses the Unified Modeling Language (UML) notation. There is a one-to-many relationship between GiftList and Gift: each Gift instance is associated with one GiftList instance, and each GiftList instance can have multiple Gift instances associated with it.

Assume that the classes are declared in the header file giftlist.hxx:

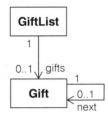

Figure 1.1 GiftList and Gift class relationship.

```
class Gift {
friend class GiftList;
friend ostream & operator<<(ostream &, const GiftList &);
public:
                              Gift(const char *fn, const char *ln,
                                        const char *gift,
                                        unsigned long c);
                              Gift();
friend    ostream &          operator<<(ostream &, const Gift &);
friend    istream &          operator>>(istream &, Gift &);
private:
          char               first_name[16];
          char               last_name[16];
          char               gift_descr[30];
          unsigned long      cost;
          Gift *             next;
};

class GiftList {
public:
                              GiftList(const char *n,
                                        unsigned long b);
                              ~GiftList();
friend    ostream &          operator<<(ostream &,const GiftList &);
          void               addGifts(istream &);
private:
          char               name[20];
          unsigned long      budget;
          Gift *             gifts;
};
```

The Gift class contains the name of the person receiving a gift, a description of the gift, and its cost. A singly linked list of Gift instances is maintained, with the head of the list in a GiftList instance. Gift contains a pointer called next that is used to reference the next element on the list. The GiftList class has a pointer named gifts that contains the address of the first element on the list or 0 if there are no elements. A GiftList instance also has a name and a budget, which should not be exceeded. These are normal classes that any C++ application could declare. An instance of one of these classes is *transient*, which means that it exists only during the execution of the application process in which it is created and is not stored in the database.

A class definition file contains the constructors for these two classes.

```
#include <giftlist.hxx>

GiftList::GiftList(const char *nm, unsigned long b)
: budget(b)
{
    strncpy(name, nm, 19);
    name[19] = 0;
}

Gift::Gift(const char *fn, const char *ln,
           const char *gift, unsigned long c)
: cost(c)
{
    strncpy(first_name, fn, 15); first_name[15] = 0;
    strncpy(last_name, ln, 15);  last_name[15] = 0;
    strncpy(gift_descr, gift, 29); gift_descr[29] = 0;
}

Gift::Gift()
: cost(0)
{
    first_name[0] = 0; last_name[0] = 0;
    gift_descr[0] = 0;
}
```

The constructors initialize their data members.

Examples in the book use the C++ iostreams library. Most C++ programmers are familiar with this library, which should be available with all C++ environments. The operators operator<< and operator>> have been overloaded for the ostream and istream classes to provide stream output and input, respectively. They are used in the examples to read initialization data and to output the values of instances.

Suppose we decide that instances of these classes should be stored in an object database. We need to make a few changes to these classes to make them persistence-capable. *Persistence* means that the object is stored in the database and persists beyond the execution of an application process. The instances of a persistence-capable class can be stored in the database.

First the application must create a database. The database vendor provides either a command or a graphical interface for this purpose. The ODMG standard does not dictate how a database is created; the procedure is different with each vendor. In ODMG, each database has a name. Assume we create a database called *Gifts* using a vendor-supplied tool.

Next, we define a schema. In a C++ object database, the database schema is derived from the C++ classes declared in the application. A utility called a *schema capture tool* reads the application's header files, which are used to generate a schema. The schema capture tool may also generate additional code that must be linked into the application. Figure 1.2 illustrates the procedure and components involved in compiling an object database application.

We must make a few changes to the C++ classes before we can run the schema capture tool. In ODMG a class attains persistence by being derived from the base class d_Object. All ODMG C++ classes have a name prefixed with d_. Gift and GiftList must be derived from d_Object.

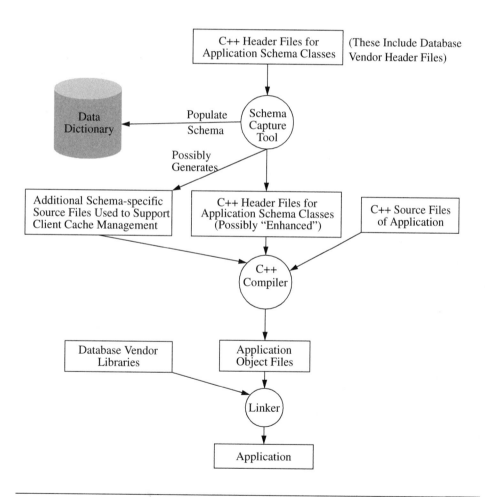

Figure 1.2 Application compilation procedure.

A pointer can contain the address of an object in memory, but that address value is meaningless to another application process. Thus, you cannot simply store the value of a pointer in the database and expect it to be usable by another application. ODMG defines a smart-pointer class called d_Ref<T> to represent a reference to an instance of class T. Instances of this class can be stored in the database and used to reference database objects. The class T must be derived from d_Object. The d_Ref<T> class has an interface similar to a pointer. To store instances of our classes in the database, we must change the pointers to type d_Ref<T>.

These changes are the only ones required to Gift and GiftList to make them persistence-capable; they are highlighted in the following code in bold. Assume the vendor has provided a header file, called odmg.h, that contains declarations of the ODMG classes. This header must be included before we use ODMG classes. Namespaces were not prevalent in compilers when the ODMG standard was designed. When enough compilers support namespaces, implementations will place their types in a namespace called odmg. Namespaces are not used in this book.

```
#include <odmg.h>

class Gift : public d_Object {
friend class GiftList;
friend ostream & operator<<(ostream &, const GiftList &);
public:
                              Gift(const char *fn, const char *ln,
                                       const char *gift,
                                       unsigned long c);
                              Gift();
friend   ostream &           operator<<(ostream &, const Gift &);
friend   istream &           operator>>(istream &, Gift &);
private:
        char                 first_name[16];
        char                 last_name[16];
        char                 gift_descr[30];
        unsigned long        cost;
        d_Ref<Gift>          next;
};

class GiftList : public d_Object {
public:
                              GiftList(const char *n,
                                       unsigned long b);
                              ~GiftList();
friend   ostream &           operator<<(ostream &,const GiftList &);
```

```
            void              addGifts(istream &);
private:
            char              name[20];
            unsigned long     budget;
            d_Ref<Gift>       gifts;
};
```

Both classes are now derived from d_Object and use a d_Ref<T> instead of a pointer to refer to an instance. These class declarations are ready to be input into the schema capture tool. The member gifts of GiftList and next in Gift were not explicitly initialized in the original constructors for these classes. As a pointer, the value would have been garbage after initialization of the containing object. But the d_Ref<T> class has a null constructor that initializes the instance to a null value. The Gift and GiftList constructors will automatically invoke the d_Ref<T> null constructor, because the members are not explicitly initialized.

Once the capture tool has been run and the schema has been defined, an application can insert objects into the database—in our case, Gifts. To perform operations on objects in the database, we use two ODMG classes: d_Database and d_Transaction. All application interaction with a database must be enclosed in a *transaction*, which is represented by an instance of the d_Transaction class. We use d_Database to open a database. An instance of an application class can be given a name that is unique within a database. The name can easily be used by another application to access the object. The d_Database class has operations to name instances and to access them by name.

The following application creates a persistent instance of GiftList and gives it a name.

```
    #include <odmg.h>

    d_Database db;
    const char * const db_name = "Gifts";

    int
    main(int argc, char *argv[])
    {
        db.open(db_name);        // opens the named database
        d_Transaction tx;
        tx.begin();              // begins a database transaction

        char *name = argv[1];
        unsigned long budget = atoi(argv[2]);

        GiftList *giftlist = new(&db,"GiftList")
                                    GiftList(name, budget);
```

```
db.set_object_name(giftlist, name);

tx.commit();             // commits the transaction
db.close();              // closes the database
return 0;
}
```

The code assumes that the application has the proper number and type of parameters. We declare an instance of d_Database named db globally so that it can be accessed by all functions in the application. The new operator is called; it has been overloaded in d_Object to take a pointer to a d_Database instance. This call creates a persistent instance of GiftList in the database associated with the variable db. The next line uses db to associate a name with the Gift-List instance.

This is the complete application. The two lines of code highlighted in bold are all that is required to create and name the instance. The application need not use an embedded database language such as SQL. No mapping is required between the application and the database representation of the object. The application must be linked with the database vendor's libraries and with some object files generated during the schema capture process.

Now let's write an application to access a GiftList instance by name and print it to the standard output stream.

```
#include <odmg.h>

d_Database db;
const char * const db_name = "Gifts";

int
main(int argc, char *argv[])
{
    db.open(db_name);        // opens the named database
    d_Transaction tx;
    tx.begin();              // begins a database transaction

    char *name = argv[1];
    d_Ref<GiftList> giftlist = db.lookup_object(name);
    if( giftlist.is_null() ){
        cerr << "No gift list with the name ";
        cerr << name << endl;
        return -1;
    }
    cout << *giftlist;  // this one line is replaced in
                        // subsequent transactions
```

```
        tx.commit();             // commits the transaction
        db.close();              // closes the database
        return 0;
    }
```

Subsequent examples in this chapter use this same `main` except that the line printing the `GiftList` instance is replaced. The `d_Database` member function `lookup_object` returns a reference to a named instance. If the name does not correspond to an object in the database, a null reference is returned. The variable `giftlist` of type `d_Ref<GiftList>` is declared and initialized with the return value of `lookup_object`. The member function `is_null` is a Boolean function. ODMG has a type `d_Boolean` with values `d_False` and `d_True` (zero and nonzero, respectively). The function `is_null` returns true if `giftlist` has a null value or returns false if the reference refers to an instance of `GiftList`.

If `giftlist` refers to an instance, the next line writes the object to the standard output stream. The `operator<<` requires a reference to a `GiftList` object. The reference is obtained by applying to `giftlist` the dereference operator (`*`) of `d_Ref<GiftList>`. This same syntax would have been required if `giftlist` had been a pointer to the object instead of a `d_Ref<GiftList>`. The call to `lookup_object` returns only a reference to an instance and not the instance itself. This dereference operator causes the object to be accessed automatically from the database and instantiated in the application. No software is required of the application to map the object from the database into its C++ representation.

The `GiftList` class has a member function called `addGifts`. It reads one gift per line from an input stream until `EOF` is reached. Each line contains the information needed to initialize a `Gift` instance.

```
    void
    GiftList::addGifts(istream &is)
    {
        Gift *gift;
        mark_modified();
        while( is.peek() != EOF ){
            gift = new(&db, "Gift") Gift();  // creates a Gift
            is >> *gift;              // initialize from istream
            gift->next = gifts;       // put at head of list
            gifts = gift;
        }
    }
```

This function modifies the `GiftList` object. Before an object from the database can be modified, a call must be made to `mark_modified`, which is defined in the base class d_Object. This is the only code the application must add. As before, the new operator is passed the address of db so that the Gift instances are created in the database. The function mark_modified does not need to be called for newly created instances. The assignments to the gifts member of GiftList and the next member of Gift establish a relationship among the instances in the database. The addGifts member function could be enhanced to refuse to add a gift if it would exceed the budget of the gift list.

We won't repeat the function main here. Assume the previous definition of main except that the line

```
cout << *giftlist;  // this one line is replaced in
                    // subsequent transactions
```

is replaced by the following line:

```
giftlist->addGifts(cin);
```

The variable giftlist invokes the addGifts member function. The operator-> is defined in d_Ref<GiftList> to return a pointer to the GiftList instance. Like operator*, this function instantiates the GiftList instance in the application's memory before returning a pointer to it.

Note that the application has not named every individual Gift instance. Often, only a small percentage of the objects are named. Once a primary object such as the GiftList instance is accessed by name, the related objects are accessed by navigating among object references.

We use the stream output operator to verify that the Gift instances have been added to the GiftList. The operator<< is overloaded to output a GiftList instance.

```
ostream &
operator<<(ostream &os, const GiftList &gl)
{
    d_Ref<Gift> gift;
    os << gl.name << " " << gl.budget << endl;
    for( gift = gl.gifts; !gift.is_null(); gift = gift->next)
        os << *gift;
    return os;
}
```

The for loop navigates through the Gift instances associated with the Gift-List instance. Navigation among instances via an object reference such as d_Ref<T> is the primary means of accessing related objects in an object database.

We must also write code to delete a `GiftList` and its associated `Gift` instances from the database. A destructor performs this processing.

```
GiftList::~GiftList()
{
    d_Ref<Gift> gift, giftn;

    for( gift = gifts; !gift.is_null(); gift = giftn ){
        giftn = gift->next;
        delete gift.ptr();
    }
}
```

The C++ `delete` operator requires a pointer to an instance. The `d_Ref<T>` class has a member function called `ptr` that returns a pointer to the referenced instance. The `operator->` function is used to access a member. If you require only a pointer to the instance, call the function `ptr`.

The same `main` function is used for the delete transaction. The line

```
cout << *giftlist;   // this one line is replaced
```

can be replaced with the following code:

```
delete giftlist.ptr();
```

The function `ptr` is called on the `d_Ref<GiftList>` instance to get a pointer to the `GiftList` instance. When `delete` is invoked, the `GiftList` destructor is called and deletes each of the associated `Gift` instances. Then the `GiftList` instance is removed from the application memory and the database.

We have shown how to use object references to instantiate instances in the application. A large application may have many references to the same instance. The object is instantiated in the application when the first such reference is dereferenced. The object database knows which objects have been instantiated in the application. There will be only a single instantiation of an object in the application. All subsequent calls from other references to access the same instance return a pointer to the one instantiation, and no database access overhead is required. This capability provides a major savings in application development costs and run-time overhead.

Object databases are characterized by their support of *database transparency.* Because a type system is shared by the database and application, objects can be mapped between the two in an unobtrusive manner. The database is much less visible to the application than it is with other database technologies. Application complexity and development costs are reduced when developers understand and manage only a single data model instead of managing several models and the mappings among them.

The C++ object model serves not only as the schema but also as the database interface. As applications iterate over collections and dereference object references, database processing is performed "under the covers." Applications appear to be navigating among memory-resident objects when actually the traversal operations are also causing database retrievals if the object is not already in the application. But this activity is hidden from the application.

The database software maintains an *object cache* for the application, and this promotes database transparency. The object cache is a region of memory in the application that contains the database objects that have been accessed by the application. When an application intends to change an object, it calls the function `mark_modified` defined in `d_Object`.

The application need not propagate the updates to the database. When an application commits a transaction, the database software automatically writes to the database the objects that need to be written. This approach can substantially reduce application development costs. Libraries that modify objects can be developed and used without the need for a mechanism to coordinate with the applications using the library.

1.2 ODMG: Object Database Standardization

Until recently, no industry standard existed for object database technology. Each vendor had its own proprietary interface. The underlying architectures are also very different. Without a standard interface, an application is dependent on the market success of the chosen vendor. Vendors of object database products are relatively small, and companies dependent on a vendor could be severely affected if the vendor encounters financial difficulties. That's why many development organizations have been reluctant to use the technology. Standardization of application interfaces will reduce vendor dependence and increase application portability, reducing the risks of adopting the technology.

The ODMG standard has several interrelated components. An ODMG implementation is required to support only a subset of them. At a minimum, the vendor must support one language binding (C++, Smalltalk, or Java).

ODMG defines an object model that provides a set of object modeling primitives to be used by the application. The other components support the constructs defined in the object model. The model contains a discussion of the properties that can be associated with an object, including attributes, relationships, and operations.

The model supports single and multiple inheritance and concrete and abstract classes. (Concrete classes can have instances, and abstract classes cannot.) You can define extents to contain all the instances of a class. Instances of a persistence-capable class can be either transient or persistent.

The ODMG object model is not described in this book, but all its modeling components are covered. The ODMG C++ and OQL language interfaces support the object model, and these interfaces are covered in detail. If you are interested in a complete description of the ODMG object model, you are encouraged to obtain the latest published ODMG specification. The ODMG web site at www.odmg.org can also be accessed to learn more about the ODMG organization and standard.

An Object Definition Language (ODL) is defined and serves as a language to define object database schemas that are independent of an application programming language. ODL is a superset of the Object Management Group's CORBA Interface Definition Language (IDL), and ODL supports the modeling capabilities defined in the ODMG object model. ODMG extensions support constructs such as relationships, which are needed in a database environment.

ODMG implementations can use ODL as the basis for schema definition. ODL serves as input to populate the database data dictionary and to generate C++ class declarations for use by the application. ODMG does not specify how ODL is mapped into C++ class declarations; the C++ representations of ODL will differ among vendor implementations. Thus, use of ODL for schema definition will not be portable across ODMG implementations. Few vendors, however, plan to use ODL for schema definition, opting instead to use the C++ class declarations defined by the application programmer. Historically, developers have preferred to let the schema be derived from their class declarations. For these reasons, ODL is not covered in this book.

If mappings were defined from ODL to each application programming language, ODL could be used to provide a single schema-definition facility that could generate appropriate class declarations in each application programming language. But ODL lacks language constructs that developers want to use, so the resulting declarations won't be sufficient for many applications. The best ODL can provide is the least common denominator of language features among the supported languages.

The Object Query Language is defined by the ODMG. OQL provides excellent declarative access to objects in an object database. It directly supports the object paradigm: operations, relationships, inheritance, polymorphism, and so on. Chapters 10 through 13 discuss the capabilities of OQL.

ODMG release 2.0, published in 1997, specifies application programming language bindings for C++, Java, and Smalltalk. The 2.0 release corrects a few problems found in release 1.2, but it consists primarily of new collections, extents, and metaclasses. This book focuses explicitly on C++ object databases and ODMG release 2.0. A complete definition of the ODMG 2.0 C++ interface is provided in the appendices. Implementations of the ODMG 1.2 C++ interfaces are available, and release 2.0 implementations are forthcoming. For this reason, all the code examples in this book are based on the 1.2 release.

We are at the dawn of a new era in object databases. In 1996 the vendors began introducing commercial products based on the ODMG standard. Before the standard, each vendor offered only a proprietary interface. Standardization will expand the market. Relational database vendors have enjoyed a long period of market acceptance, largely because of the SQL standard, but this situation could flip-flop. Relational database vendors are developing object-relational products, which differ quite a bit from object databases. Even though the ANSI SQL committee is defining SQL3—a standard for objects in relational databases—each vendor is releasing its own proprietary object interface. The result will be a lack of standardization in the object-relational market. A document that defines a standard is meaningless unless multiple suppliers provide interfaces that conform to the standard. Chapter 17 discusses SQL3 and other aspects of incorporating objects into relational databases.

Chapter 2
Databases, Transactions, and Exception Handling

Applications often need to store objects in a database so that other applications can access them. A database provides both long-term storage and coordination of access by multiple applications. An object stored in a database is said to be *persistent*. Its lifetime extends beyond the scope of a single application process. Objects that exist only during a single process are *transient* objects.

An application process accessing a database usually interacts as the client of a *database server process* (see Figure 2.1). Multiple application processes can interact with the database concurrently. The database server coordinates access among the clients. It maintains a *database cache* that contains data from disk that is being accessed by applications. An object database also maintains a *client*

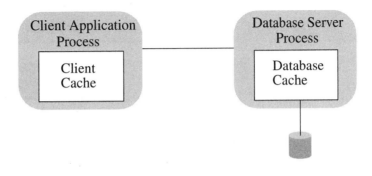

Figure 2.1 Database client-server architecture.

cache in the application process. A client cache is unique to object databases; other database technologies, such as relational databases, do not provide client cache management. Some of the characteristics and benefits of an object database derive from its having a client cache.

An application usually needs to access multiple objects from a database. These objects can reside in the same database or can be dispersed among several databases. Some object database implementations allow a set of databases to be centrally coordinated and managed; such a set of databases is referred to as a *database group* in this book. Figure 2.2 illustrates a database group that comprises four separate databases containing objects. Usually an object can reference any object in the same database group, as shown in Figure 2.2. Each vendor has its own terminology for a database group, such as *federated database* and *database network*.

All access to objects in a database is performed in the context of a *transaction*. A transaction is initiated by an application process, which performs a logical group of operations against objects in the database(s). The set of operations is treated as an atomic operation; either *all* or *none* of them is performed.

Some applications use *threads* (supported in ODMG release 2.0) to execute multiple code sequences within a single process. A thread can be associated with at most one transaction at a time, but a transaction can have multiple threads

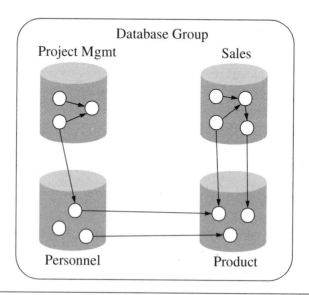

Figure 2.2 Database group.

associated with it. An application can therefore have multiple concurrent transactions. Each thread can have its own transaction, or more than one thread can cooperate in the same transaction context. It is also possible for a thread to switch from one transaction to another. There are many situations in which threads are useful to an application.

Problems can occur while an application is accessing objects from a database or committing a transaction. Examples include hardware failures or the inability to communicate with other processes or machines. Or a resource required by the database software, such as memory or storage space, can become exhausted. Lock contention can occur if two or more applications try to access the same data.

The database software needs a way to notify the application that a problem has occurred. Error conditions are represented by *exception* objects. The standard exception handling mechanisms of C++ are used in the ODMG interface.

Each of these topics is covered in detail in this chapter. It presents the ODMG interfaces for databases, transactions, and exceptions, followed by a complete application that uses the facilities.

2.1   Database Access

The ODMG standard provides a specification for accessing a single database. Implementations can support access to multiple databases, but the standard does not require it.

Before an application can access objects in a database, it must be opened. Each database is identified by a name. The ODMG class d_Database has a member function called open, which is passed the name of the database to open. An enumeration called access_status is passed to indicate the access mode to be used.

Suppose an application maintains salary information in a corporate database called Personnel. The following code opens the database.

```
d_Database db;
db.open("Personnel");
```

The function open has a second parameter of type access_status with a default value of d_Database::read_write. To prevent any other application from accessing the personnel database while this application has it open, you should explicitly specify an access of d_Database::exclusive.

```
d_Database db;
db.open("Personnel", d_Database::exclusive);
```

Instances of `d_Database` are not persistent, and they must be declared by the application. A database must be open before a transaction is started. Once the application has finished performing transactions on a database, it must be closed by a call to the `close` member function.

2.2 Transactions

A transaction has several characteristics, which can be denoted by the acronym ACID. A database transaction should support each of these characteristics.

- Atomicity
- Consistency
- Isolation
- Durability

Atomicity requires that either all or none of the operations included in the transaction is reflected in the database. These operations often have interdependencies, and performing only a subset of them often compromises the overall intent of the transaction.

Consistency requires that a transaction transition the database from one consistent state to another, preserving its semantic and physical integrity. The database implementation should ensure that consistency is maintained at a physical level and should guarantee atomicity. Much of the semantics needed to determine data consistency cannot be expressed directly in the database specification; it must be managed directly by the application. The application must assume accountability for maintaining the semantic integrity of the object model. It should not alter objects in ways that place them in an inconsistent state. Applying encapsulation when you define classes helps prevent this alteration.

Isolation requires that each transaction appear to be the only transaction manipulating the database even though other transactions may be running concurrently. A transaction should not see intermediate results of other transactions that have not committed. This principle is related to the need for each transaction to be atomic. For a transaction to see a subset of another transaction's updates could present an inconsistent view of the database because of interdependencies among the updates. The other transaction may also abort, in which case none of the updates that may have been accessed will be part of the committed state of the database.

The highest level of isolation is attained when all the transactions executing are capable of being *serialized*. This state is achieved if the database contents that result from a set of concurrent transactions are the same as the contents that would result if those transactions had been executed in serial order with no concurrency.

A high degree of isolation can limit the amount of concurrency that can be achieved. An application that can tolerate a reduced level of isolation in exchange for a higher degree of concurrency can allow *dirty reads*. These let a transaction access a modification made by another transaction that has not committed. The other transaction may abort, in which case the value obtained from the database would not reflect a consistent database state. The nature of the application determines whether this reduced level of isolation is acceptable.

Durability implies that committed transactions are resilient in the face of failure conditions. Once a transaction successfully commits, the updates are guaranteed to be reflected in the database despite any failures that may occur after the commit. Durability implies that the database can be recovered in the event of system or media failure. The database state should reflect the updates of all transactions that committed successfully before the failure.

2.2.1 The `d_Transaction` Class

The ODMG `d_Transaction` class provides a typical set of transaction operations. As with the `d_Database` class, its instances cannot be persistent. They serve to group a set of operations initiated by an application. All operations performed on persistent objects must be enclosed within a transaction. The same `d_Transaction` instance can be used repeatedly for consecutive transactions.

A transaction is started with a call to `begin` after a `d_Transaction` instance is created; the constructor does not automatically start a transaction.

```
d_Transaction tx;
tx.begin();

// perform operations on objects in the database...

tx.commit();
```

When `commit` is called, all the persistent objects that have been created, deleted, or modified during the transaction are committed to the database. All the objects are removed from the application cache, and the locks acquired by the transaction are released. If the application prefers to retain the objects and their associated locks in the cache and commit the current changes to the database, `checkpoint` should be called.

Calling `abort` releases all the locks acquired by the transaction, and none of the changes is applied. If a transaction is active and the destructor for its d_Transaction instance is called, it is aborted. This implies that the transaction is aborted if the d_Transaction instance is a local variable and there is a return from the function without a call to commit. This arrangement also applies if the d_Transaction object is declared in a function that lies between a function that throws an exception and the function that catches it.

2.2.2 Two-Phase Commit

If an application has a transaction that manipulates objects in multiple databases, each database must be able to commit successfully. If one or more databases cannot commit, the databases may be left in an inconsistent state.

A *two-phase commit* process is used to ensure that all the databases participating in a transaction are updated properly. Essentially, a subtransaction exists for each database in the transaction. The two-phase commit protocol instructs each database to determine whether its updates can be committed. A prepare command is often used to indicate this phase. Once the database servers have responded, if all of them indicate that their subtransactions can commit successfully then the second phase of the commit instructs each database server to commit the transaction. If any of the databases encounters a problem during the prepare step, the entire transaction is aborted. This handshaking ensures that if all the transaction operations cannot commit, none of them will.

2.2.3 Thread Operations

An application can have multiple threads accessing the database, but each thread must be associated with a single transaction. The d_Transaction class has a function called join, which joins the current thread to the transaction. A thread can disassociate from a transaction by calling leave. If join is called on a d_Transaction instance A but the current thread is already associated with a different d_Transaction instance B, a leave operation is implicitly performed on d_Transaction instance B before the thread is joined to d_Transaction instance A. A thread can determine which transaction it is currently associated with by calling the static function current defined in d_Transaction.

The database software provides each transaction in the application with its own transaction context, as if each one were initiated in a separate process address space. All the transaction ACID properties are preserved for each d_Transaction object in the application. Some existing implementations, however, have a separate cache region for each transaction in progress. An application should not allow threads of different transactions to share any database objects, because the results are likely to differ among implementations.

2.3 Exceptions: Handling Failures

The ODMG standard uses C++ exception handling mechanisms. An instance of the ODMG class d_Error, derived from the exception class defined in the ANSI/ISO C++ library standard, is thrown when an error occurs. It contains state information describing the error. Each distinct error has an error number referred to as the *kind* of error; the type kind is defined in d_Error. Functions are provided to set and get the kind of error. Appendix B provides a complete description of the d_Error class and each kind of error.

You can provide additional information about the error by invoking one of several operator<< functions, which append the information to a string. These functions take one of several common types; the complete list is provided in Appendix B. The application can call these functions repeatedly. Each time the exception is caught and rethrown, an application handler could add relevant information.

The error information string can be accessed by calling the member function what, a virtual function defined in the base class exception. This function is defined in the ANSI/ISO C++ standard for accessing a description of an exception.

2.4 A Complete Application Transaction

The following main routine illustrates each of the steps required to open a database, begin a transaction, and catch any exceptions that may be thrown.

```
#include <odmg.h>

d_Database db;

main(int argc, char *argv[])
{
    int ret;
    d_Transaction tx;

    try {
        db.open("Personnel");
        tx.begin();
        // perform transaction
        tx.commit();
        db.close();
    }
```

```
catch(d_Error &err){
    cerr << "DB error " << err.get_kind() << " ";
    cerr << err.what() << endl;
    ret = -1;
}
catch(exception &e){
    cerr << "exception " << e.what() << endl;
    ret = -2;
}
catch(...){
    cerr << "unknown exception\n";
}
return ret;
}
```

An application would usually have a `try` and `catch` block in `main` to handle errors, but the database open or transaction operations can be performed in other functions called by `main`. For brevity and illustrative purposes, they have been placed in `main` here. It is up to the application developer to determine where to place `try` and `catch` blocks.

The ODMG standard does not specify the names of header files. In this book, the file name `odmg.h` is assumed to contain all the needed ODMG declarations. Each vendor provides its own header file names for its ODMG implementation. It's a good idea to localize these differences in your application header files and include the necessary header files for your vendor implementation.

Chapter 3
An Overview of
Object Database Modeling

The object paradigm gives us a rich framework for modeling a problem domain. Encapsulation, inheritance, and polymorphism provide many benefits that facilitate development throughout the project life cycle. For its part, an object database provides long-term storage of objects and coordinates concurrent access. Application development benefits greatly when we use the same modeling paradigm for both the database and the application.

C++ applications need not use an object database; they can use a different database technology such as relational. But the database would not be aware of the object modeling information. It would be aware only of the underlying object implementation, which is at a lower level of abstraction. Developers would need to map the application's types from its object model to the database's model and type system. Maintaining both models and a mapping between them is a significant burden.

C++ object databases support the capabilities of the C++ language for defining object models and types, and the application's class declarations serve as the definition of the database schema. The application need only define a single model in a single language to be shared by both the application and the database.

In this book it is assumed that you are familiar with object modeling and C++. Some topics are presented here from a database perspective, so their descriptions may differ slightly from those in object design texts.

The entity-relationship (ER) data model is used in this book as a basis for explaining object database modeling. It is used in the industry as the basis for object methodologies as well as database schema designs. Most developers reading this book will already be familiar with either the ER model or one of the object methodologies, although this background is not required for them to understand the material.

This chapter introduces the constructs of the ER data model. Many kinds of objects are found in an object model. They often serve in a role related to one of the ER modeling constructs, which serve to delineate several categories of types. Some of the behavior of a type is derived from its membership in a particular type category. The chapter concludes with a discussion of abstraction, which should be used by types in each type category to provide an atomic interface and hide the complexities that result from the aggregations in the underlying implementation of a class.

3.1 The Entity-Relationship Data Model

The ER data model was introduced by Peter Chen in 1976. As one of the most popular approaches for defining an application data model, it has been enhanced over the years. As object-oriented technology gained acceptance, the ER data model was extended to include object concepts. The object modeling primitives in most object methodologies are derived largely from the ER model.

An ER model can help guide the design of the logical and physical database schema. The *logical* schema defines the entities, attributes, and relationships of the problem domain, whereas the *physical* schema is concerned with storage representation and access mechanisms. ER has been used by applications that employ hierarchical, network, and relational database technologies. The ER model is a solid foundation on which you can define application data models in a manner largely independent of the underlying database technology.

The ER model is used both for modeling objects in the application and for designing a database schema. Moreover, with an object database the application object model is the specification of the database schema. Thus, ER concepts provide a common foundation for describing object database models.

3.1.1 ER Modeling Primitives

An application ER model is modeled in terms of the following:

- Entities
- Relationships
- Attributes

Objects can be used for modeling these ER model constructs.

An *entity* is any *thing* that needs to be modeled. The definitions of entities and objects are intertwined. Texts on ER modeling describe an entity as an object, and texts on object modeling describe an object as an entity in the problem domain. *Webster's* describes both *entity* and *object* as "*things*" and *Roget's* treats *entity*, *object*, and *thing* as synonyms. Novices in object technology often ask, "What is an object?" The answer is to explore the "*things*" that need to be managed by the application, which often turn out to be the objects that the application must model: people, places, inanimate objects, concepts, events, and so on. Entities are the most common form of object modeled in applications.

A *relationship* is an association between two or more entities. It is important to understand how entities are interrelated, because much of a system is devoted to maintaining such relationships. Examples include the spousal or parental relationship, the relationship between an employer and an employee, and the association between a product and its parts. Objects are also used to represent relationships.

Both entities and relationships can have *attributes*: properties or characteristics associated with an entity and a relationship. An attribute has both a name and a type. The type of an attribute is called a *domain*. Simple domains include types such as integers and strings. A `Person` entity might have attributes to represent a name and address.

A class can also serve as a domain type. For example, an instance of a class `Date` can be used to represent the date of birth of a `Person` entity. Each domain represents a particular abstraction, and its interface should provide a set of operations that supports the abstraction. For example, a number of common operations are performed on dates.

ER models have historically focused only on data attributes. Object models place more emphasis on the operations of the interface representing the abstraction. The data attributes have played a secondary role, because they are typically encapsulated in the implementation and are not accessible components in the object interface. In an object database model, both the attributes and the operations must be defined.

3.1.2 Similarities among Database Models

Each database technology (network, relational, and object) has different terminology for the mechanisms it provides to represent ER models. Table 3.1 maps the constructs and the terminology used by each technology. By understanding this mapping, you can apply what you know about one technology to the others. This mapping is also useful when you must migrate a specific model from one database technology to another.

Entity-Relationship	Database Technology		
	Hierarchical/Network	Relational	Object
entity (type)	record type	table	class
entity storage	file	table	extent
specific entity	record	row/tuple	instance
entity identifier	primary key	primary key	object ID
attribute	field	column	member
relationship	link	foreign key	object reference

Table 3.1 Similarities among database terminologies.

3.2 Type Categories

Each entity, attribute, and relationship in the ER model of an application is represented by a type. When the object-oriented paradigm is applied, many of these types are represented by objects. Consider Figure 3.1, which illustrates an object and encapsulation. The object provides a set of operations that represent its abstraction. These operations insulate the users of the object from the internal implementation, often an aggregation of data components.

Every type, whether an object or a primitive type such as int, establishes a context for its subcomponents. For example, a simple type such as an integer consists of an aggregation of bits. Operations are defined for manipulating the bits in a manner that supports the integer abstraction. The value of an instance of a type is derived from the collective values of its components. The validity of a component value is often based on the role of the component in supporting the value of its containing type.

Figure 3.1 Encapsulation of an object.

The values of the components are often interdependent, and the need to under-stand these interrelationships introduces complexity. The containing type should maintain the values of its own components. The logic needed for this task should be localized in the operations defined for the type. For example, a class that repre-sents a date domain type has operations that embody the notion of a date. You can perform date arithmetic, comparison, and so on. The code that uses the date class does not need to understand how the date is represented internally (its internal components and interrelationships). The term *semantic integrity constraint* refers to mechanisms that maintain such interdependencies when data is modified, and the object paradigm uses encapsulation for maintaining semantic integrity. Encap-sulation reduces complexity by localizing and minimizing the code that needs to understand and maintain the component interdependencies.

An applications object model consists of a set of types, and each type typi-cally serves in the role of one of the ER constructs. Each ER construct consists of an aggregation of components. The components of a domain are usually one or more primitive C++ types, although a domain can contain instances of other domain classes. A class is usually defined for each entity in an object model and consists of an aggregation of one or more attributes, each attribute having a partic-ular domain type. A composite entity has instances of other entities as its compo-nents.

Each ER modeling construct represents a *category of types*. Some of the func-tionality of a type is derived from its role as an entity, relationship, or domain. Certain characteristics are common to every type that represents a domain; the same is true for entities, collections, and composite entities. The following sec-tions provide high-level descriptions of the different type categories. A later chap-ter is devoted to each one. Each type category has operations that are supported by all its types. These operations represent, metaphorically, basic transactions that applications perform when manipulating instances of the type.

3.2.1 Entities

Most object methodologies focus on the design of objects that represent the entities in the problem domain. In an object database, the entity objects are the unit at which both persistence and identity are attained. The `Gift` and `GiftList` classes used in Chapter 1 are examples of entities. A flight reservation system would have entities to represent planes, airports, passengers, and flights. A class would be defined for each of these entities.

A persistence-capable class can have instances stored in the database and accessed by multiple application processes. Instances of persistent classes can also be transient, and this means they exist only within a single application process. The object database literature and vendor documentation usually refer to the entity objects simply as "objects" or "persistent objects."

Every persistent instance of an entity class has a unique object identifier, which is used elsewhere in the database to reference and access the instance. The object identifier is separate from the attributes. It is *immutable*—that is, it cannot be changed by an application. Persistent instances are sometimes called *denotable objects*—that is, they can be denoted (referenced) elsewhere in the database. Persistence and identity distinguish entity classes from types in the other type categories. Object identifiers are covered in Chapter 6.

An entity's properties, including attributes, relationships, and operations, are implemented by the data and function members of a class. Each data attribute has a name and is an instance of a particular data type. Similarly, each operation is a member function with a name, parameters, and a return type. An entity should control modifications to the values of its attributes, which may depend on the values of other attributes in the entity. The class representing the entity is responsible for maintaining its overall abstraction value. It establishes the context that determines the valid values for the attributes in its implementation. Entities are covered in Chapter 5.

3.2.2 Domains

The term *domain* refers to the category of types that serve as the data types for attributes and the return types of functions. An attribute does not have an object identifier and cannot be referenced directly in the database. An attribute attains persistence by being embedded as a member within a persistent object.

Most texts on object-oriented programming do not use the term *domain* to refer to an attribute data type, but that definition is used extensively in database texts. The term *domain* also is used extensively in books on set theory and abstract algebra, which serve as the theoretical foundation for many aspects of database technology.

A domain can be either a single primitive C++ type, such as `int`, or a class composed of its own set of attributes. The database vendor may provide a set of useful domains, such as date, time, money, and so on. Developers can also define application-specific domains to represent things such as phone numbers, Social Security numbers, and bitmap images.

In relational database normalization theory, a relation is in first-normal form only if all the underlying domains are *atomic*. To be atomic implies that it cannot be decomposed. Any aggregation in the implementation is not visible in the interface. Each abstraction in an object design should be atomic. A class, for example, has both an interface and an implementation, and the implementation often consists of an underlying aggregation of components. But the class interface should hide the implementation and represent the abstraction. Even a simple domain such as an integer is an aggregation (of bits). The integer abstraction provided by the language is atomic even though the underlying implementation is not.

Encapsulation can be used to render a user-defined domain type atomic even if its implementation is an aggregation. This concept is a central theme in this book. It applies to types in every type category and should not be specific to domains. Domains are covered in Chapter 4.

3.2.3 Collections

A *collection* represents a set of zero or more values of some type. Lists, arrays, and sets are examples of common collections. A collection is represented by a class that is parameterized based on the type of element it contains. The C++ `template` feature is used for defining collection classes. A template parameter indicates the type of element in the collection.

Collections play a vital role in object databases. For example, an attribute can consist of a collection of values of some type. Collections also are used to represent relationships among entities that have a cardinality greater than one (one-to-many and many-to-many). Collections also serve as a way to access all the instances of a class. The collections defined in ODMG are persistence-capable. They can be stand-alone, persistent objects that have identity, or they can be embedded in an entity object to serve as an attribute's domain type. Collections are covered in Chapter 7.

3.2.4 Composite Entities

Another type category is the *composite object*, or *composite entity*. Some authors refer to this type as a *complex object*. A composite entity is one that has a composition or aggregation of other entity objects in its implementation. These other objects are called *subobjects* and may themselves be composite entities. Some object methodologies call them *object containment hierarchies*.

A composite entity manages the existence and interdependencies of its component subobjects, which are said to be *existent-dependent* on the composite entity. This means that when a composite entity instance is deleted, all its subobjects are also deleted. Composite entities are covered in Chapter 9.

Composite entities are common in CAD/CAM applications, where a design contains many interrelated subcomponents. For example, an object model of a Boeing 747 airplane would consist of instances of many classes. The plane would be represented by an instance of a composite entity called `Plane`. Operations that pertain to the plane as a whole would be defined as member functions in the `Plane` class. A subassembly such as a wing, cockpit, or fuselage would be represented by a composite entity instance that would contain a set of interrelated component parts. Often, you need a large, complex part hierarchy to represent a complex design. Managing the interrelationships among the components is a significant aspect of the application's functionality.

3.3 Aggregation, Abstraction, and Atomicity

A major focus of this book is the relationship among aggregation, abstraction, and atomicity as they relate to the entity, domain, and composite entity type categories.

A composite entity is an aggregation of entities. An entity is an aggregation of attributes of specific domains, and domains are aggregations of other types. The types in each of these categories represent an abstraction, and the implementation of the abstraction consists of an aggregation of components. The aggregation and the interdependencies of the components create complexity. Encapsulation reduces the complexity and provides an interface for the type that corresponds to the abstraction. The operations in a type's interface should hide the aggregation in the underlying implementation.

The progression of aggregation and containment from domains to entities to composite entities is shown in Figure 3.2. Composite entities are represented by rounded rectangles. Their components can consist of entities and other composite entities. Composite entities provide a set of operations that are used to manage the interrelationships among the component entities, which are represented by circles. Their components consist of domain instances, represented here by various shapes (types) labeled with a *D*. The types at each level of the hierarchy should use encapsulation to hide their underlying implementation, thereby reducing the complexity of the model.

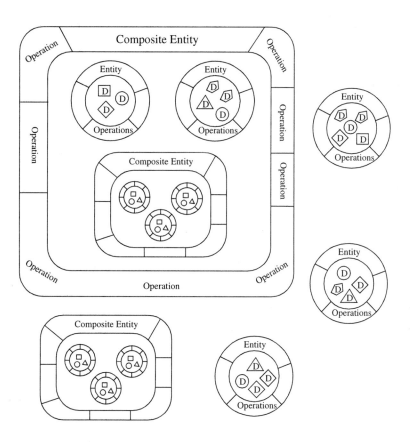

Figure 3.2 Containment hierarchy of type categories.

Chapter 4
Domains

Domains are the most primitive types stored in a database. Entities and relationships usually have a set of attributes, and domains serve as the data types for these attributes. Each attribute is an instance of a given domain type. Domain types usually are not capable of persistence, although there are some exceptions. An instance of a domain type attains persistence by being embedded within a persistent object. Many different types can serve as a domain in an object database schema. Application developers can define their own domain types when they use an object database; they are not restricted to the domains supplied by the database vendor.

This chapter first describes the limitations of other database technologies in adequately supporting the domains that applications need. We then examine the characteristics and categories of domains. Finally, the ODMG domain types are described, and the chapter concludes with a discussion of C++ types that are not supported by implementations.

4.1 Domains in Other Database Technologies

Other database technologies (hierarchical, network, and relational) provide a fixed set of domains. The following domains are most commonly supported.

- Integer
- Decimal number
- Floating-point number

- Character string (fixed and variable-length)
- Bit string (fixed and variable-length)
- Date
- Time
- Timestamp
- Binary large object (BLOB)

These data types are the ones supported in the SQL92 standard. The attributes in the application object model must be represented by one of these vendor-provided types. An application that uses an SQL database and requires a type with different semantics or representation must decompose the application type into one or more of these primitive types. Some complex attributes must be represented by multiple rows in a secondary table; a join operation would be needed to access these rows.

The functionality of these data types resides in the relational server. The language used by the application usually has its own types, which correspond to the database types to some degree. The database vendor usually provides a mapping between the database types and the corresponding data types in the application. Operations performed on the database domain types are expressed in SQL and are performed only in the relational database server. The applications use the capabilities of their language's native types to manipulate domain instances in the application. The database and application types often have different functionality, something that increases complexity for the application.

Some database types (such as date and time) do not have a corresponding data type in the application. The application must extract the values of the abstraction (such as month, day, and year) that can be represented by its data types. It defines a representation for the database type and uses these values to initialize an instance.

Applications may need to represent a type that is not supported by the database. It must be built on top of the basic types supported by the database, and a mapping must be defined between the two representations. The mapping and associated semantics are known only by the application software; the database does not model the application abstraction, because it cannot provide a corresponding interface using its tools, such as query languages and report writers. Even though the application may define a rich object model and type system, the query language user must interface at the lower implementation level, which does not reflect the abstractions in the object model. The semantics are unclear, causing the schema to be more complex. This situation is similar to writing a program in a high-level language such as C++ and then debugging it at the level of the assembly language.

Vendors of relational databases attempt to address some of these type representation issues by supporting a *BLOB* data type. A BLOB provides storage for variable-length binary data. Applications typically use a BLOB to store things such as images, audio, video, or graphics data. A BLOB also works as a "storage bin" for non-normalized data that cannot be represented effectively in relational tables. No semantics are associated with a BLOB; the data must be interpreted by applications. The only operations supported for a BLOB are the getting and setting of its value.

BLOBs carry various restrictions. They are potentially huge; if BLOB updates are recorded in transaction logs, the logs can rapidly exceed their capacity. Therefore, some systems do not record changes to BLOBs in transaction logs, resulting in a loss of transaction semantics. Instead, applications often store the data directly in the file system, storing only the file name in the database. Developers are then responsible for providing transaction properties. Some database systems allow only one BLOB column per table, an approach that is inconvenient if the entity has several attributes that are best represented by a BLOB. Extra tables must be created, one for each BLOB.

4.2 Domain Categories

The categories of domains are based on varying levels of aggregation and encapsulation.

* Primitive literal types
* Composite types
* Abstract data types

These categories and the corresponding ODMG types are discussed here. C++ object databases allow most types supported by C++ to be domains.

All domains have an implementation that is an aggregation of components, either bits or other domain instances. A type representing a date is considered atomic even though it contains several components: year, month, and day. Similarly, a string is considered a domain type even though it is represented as an array of characters. These components are values of the abstraction; the representation of the implementation may be entirely different.

The first-normal form rule of relational databases states that all domains must be atomic; alternatively, it could state, "Each domain should represent an atomic abstraction." This rule is also considered a good object design practice. As long as a domain's interface is atomic, its implementation can be nonatomic if encapsulation is used to hide the implementation's aggregation. Applications may need to store data in a non-normalized form to meet performance requirements. Vendors of relational databases have been forced to support the storage of non-normalized data.

4.2.1 Primitive Literal Types

C++ provides a set of primitive literal types, including the following.

- `char` (signed and unsigned)
- `short` (signed and unsigned)
- `int` (signed and unsigned)
- `long` (signed and unsigned)
- `float` and `double`

The operations that can be performed on instances of these types are provided by the compiler and machine environment. You cannot use encapsulation to specify user-defined operations for these built-in types.

A *pointer*, another primitive C++ data type, is used to contain the memory address of an instance of a particular type. Pointers are not supported in the ODMG standard, although some vendors support them. Some vendors allow pointers that reference persistent objects to be stored directly in the database; others allow pointers to reference only transient data. Applications that use pointer attributes are not portable among ODMG implementations. Pointers are discussed further in section 6.1.7.1.

The C++ Boolean data type `bool` was added to C++ after the ODMG published its release 1.2 specification. The `bool` type is not yet prevalent in compiler implementations. Many ODMG functions return a logical Boolean value of true or false. The type `int` is used in ODMG releases 1.0–1.2 as the type for a Boolean value. An integer value of 0 represents the Boolean value false, and a nonzero integer value represents the Boolean value true. This convention has been used in C and C++ for decades. In ODMG release 2.0, the interfaces have been changed to use the ODMG `d_Boolean` type, which has values `d_True` and `d_False`.

4.2.1.1 ODMG Primitive Types

ODMG supports a subset of the C++ primitive types. Table 4.1 shows the `typedefs` that are provided in ODMG implementations for the supported data types.

The types `int` and `unsigned int` are not included in the ODMG interface. The size of an `int` is based on the word size of a machine. Existing machine

Type	Size	Description
d_Char	8 bit	ASCII character
d_Octet	8 bit	No interpretation
d_Boolean	Not defined	d_False and d_True
d_Short	16 bit	Signed short integer
d_UShort	16 bit	Unsigned short integer
d_Long	32 bit	Signed integer
d_ULong	32 bit	Unsigned integer
d_Float	32 bit	IEEE Standard 754-1985 single-precision floating-point number
d_Double	64 bit	IEEE Standard 754-1985 double-precision floating-point number

Table 4.1 ODMG primitive literal domains.

architectures have integer word sizes of 16, 32, or 64 bits in length. If you're using an object database in a multimachine environment that involves more than one word size, you cannot transfer an `int` across machines and preserve its value, because some machines may use fewer bits than others. If the application will never operate in such an environment (a risky assumption these days), it may be possible to use an `int` with some implementations.

The types defined in Table 4.1 originate from the Interface Definition Language (IDL) of the Common Object Request Broker Architecture (CORBA) standard. These types have the same range and interpretation on all platforms. To achieve heterogeneity, some ODMG implementations require that these types be used instead of their equivalent C++ types. Some implementations allow the use of standard C++ data types such as `long`, and others do not. Applications are more portable and more likely to support heterogeneity if these types are used.

4.2.2 Composite Types

A composite type contains multiple data members that are directly accessible. A `struct` or `class` with public data members is a composite type. A *structure* is an aggregation of data members that is grouped for some semantic reason. Composite types do not use encapsulation.

Most C++ programmers use classes instead of structures so that they can use encapsulation and inheritance. But structures are needed when you're interfacing with legacy C software. A structure itself can contain nested, embedded structures. Attributes can be nested to an arbitrary depth, although some implementations may have some restrictions.

A C++ array, which can be declared as an attribute of a persistent object, can be considered a composite type that has indexed access to its elements. Arrays are built-in collections provided by the programming language. Standard C++ syntax is used to manipulate arrays. The `Address` structure defined next contains some arrays of characters. Some object database implementations do not support multidimensional arrays, and the ODMG standard does not require such support.

The following types are composite types:

```
struct Address {
        char             street[40];
        char             city[20];
        char             state[3];
        char             zip_code[6];
};
struct Point {
        int              x;
        int              y;
};
class Rectangle {
public:
        Point            origin;
        int              width;
        int              height;
//      operations
};
```

The `Rectangle` class contains a member of type `Point`, itself a composite type. The `Rectangle` class is considered a composite type here because of its public data members.

4.2.3 Abstract Data Types

A class can be defined to implement an abstract data type (ADT) that represents an abstraction. The word *abstract* used here is not meant to imply an abstract base class as in C++ but rather a user-defined type that represents an abstraction in the problem domain. The ADT provides operations that embody the abstraction being represented, maintaining a consistent abstraction value as the object is altered from one value to another. The operations maintain the semantic integrity and internal consistency of an instance.

An abstract data type is distinguished from a composite type, because encapsulation presents an interface that embodies an atomic abstraction. The implementation may be a complex aggregation of components, but it is not accessible.

ADTs are provided by either the database or the application. One commonly supported ADT is a date. Applications often have their own abstract data types that must be stored and managed in the database. An object database allows these types to be defined and used in the schema.

4.2.3.1 Collections

A collection is a kind of abstract data type and is required by most object models. Various kinds of collections can be defined to support operations and behavior, and they vary in performance characteristics. You should choose a collection type based on its expected usage requirements. Most of the original C++ libraries consisted of collection classes.

Collections can serve as the domain type of an attribute. They also serve other purposes, such as defining relationships, accessing the set of all instances of a class, and in query processing. Chapter 7 discusses collections in detail.

4.2.3.2 Embedded Persistent Objects

Most object database implementations allow any type to be used for an attribute, including a persistence-capable class that is used as a domain. In that case, however, the instance loses its object identifier and cannot be directly referenced elsewhere in the database.

4.2.3.3 Other Examples

Some data types are applicable across many application domains. A binary coded decimal (BCD) data type, for example, is common in some application models. Another data type, perhaps based on the BCD type, could represent an amount of money.

Applications often have their own types that are not known by the database management system software. They can serve as the type of an attribute when an object database is used. Other database technologies have historically not allowed such an extensible typing system for attribute domains. Such flexibility is one of the advantages of an object database.

4.3 ODMG Domain Types

ODMG defines a set of classes to represent common domain abstractions. These classes support the C++ canonical form, which includes a default initialization function (null constructor), copy constructor, assignment operator, and destructor. They also support functions specific to their abstraction.

Probably every data model has string attributes. ODMG defines a string class called d_String, which supports only the minimal set of operations needed to store strings in the database. It is not intended to be used as a general string class with extensive string manipulation operations. This approach is unfortunate. Market demand is likely to force the vendors also to support the string classes defined in the ISO C++ standard.

ODMG also supports the following classes to represent date and time abstractions. Appendix B has complete definitions of these classes.

- d_Interval

- d_Date

- d_Time

- d_Timestamp

Instances of these domain classes can be stand-alone transient instances or can be embedded as attributes of persistent objects. This chapter provides examples of their use as stand-alone transient instances, and persistent objects and their attributes are covered in Chapter 5. Whether an instance is stand-alone or embedded, its behavior is the same.

These classes were defined before the ANSI/ISO C++ standard libraries were released, so there is some overlap. The ODMG types are implemented in multiple programming languages. Market demand will likely force the object database vendors also to support the classes defined in ANSI/ISO C++ libraries.

4.3.1 The d_String Class

The d_String class represents a variable-length string. A d_String instance can be initialized with a character array, another d_String instance, or nothing (which initializes the instance to a null string value).

```
d_String    nullString;                          // null constructor
d_String    composer("Mozart");
d_String    popArtist("Michael Bolton");
d_String    singer(popArtist);                   // copy constructor
d_String *  favorite;
```

```
composer = "Beethoven";                    // assign with char *
favorite = new d_String("Richard Marx");
popArtist = *favorite;                     // assign with d_String
```

The d_String class does not directly support the C++ iostreams interface, but stream insertion and extraction operators could be defined as follows:

```
istream &operator>>(istream &is, d_String &s)
{
    char buffer[256];
    is.width(256); // limit to a max of 256 chars
    is >> buffer;
    s = buffer;     // illustrates assignment with char array
    return is;
}

ostream &operator<<(ostream &os, d_String &s)
{
    os << (const char *)s;
    return os;
}
```

As shown in operator<<, a function is provided that converts a d_String to a const char * so that the internal string value can be accessed.

Comparison operators compare a d_String with either another d_String or a C++ character array. A member function gets the length of a string, and operator[] accesses a character at a specific index in the string. The following function changes each lowercase letter to uppercase.

```
void makeUpperCase(d_String &s)
{
    register unsigned long i;
    register const unsigned long len = s.length();

    for( i = 0; i < len; i++){
        char c = s[i];
        if( isalpha(c) && islower(c) )
            s[i] = (char) toupper(c);
    }
}
```

Persistent classes that require a string attribute can use either the d_String class or a character array. A character array has a fixed size, whereas a d_String instance can contain a string value of varying length.

```
class Employee : public Person {
{
        char                gender[2]; // "M" or "F"
        d_String            email_address;
}
```

Attributes, as components of entity types, are discussed in Chapter 5.

To support a string of an arbitrary size, the object database implementation stores the contents of the string outside the object. This approach can result in some degree of overhead, although it is often minimal. With a character array the data is directly embedded in the object, so there is no secondary data to be retrieved and managed. Thus, a character array is often somewhat faster. A character array may be a better alternative if the string value is small and varies little in size and value.

4.3.2   The d_Interval Class

The d_Interval class represents a duration of time and is also used with the other time-related classes to support arithmetic operations. An instance can be initialized with day, hour, minute, and second values. A day is the largest unit of time that can be specified with d_Interval, because the number of days varies with larger time units (such as months and years). The following function inserts the interval components into an output stream.

```
ostream &operator<<(ostream &os, d_Interval &i)
{
    os << "Interval(" << i.day() << " days ";
    os << i.hour() << " hrs ";
    os << i.minute() << " mins ";
    os << i.second() << " secs)";
    return os;
}
```

This function illustrates use of the functions that provide the components of the abstraction value. The member function is_zero can be called to determine whether all the time components are zero.

The C++ canonical form and a full suite of comparison and arithmetic operations are supported. The d_Interval class supports non-normalized input, normalizing the time components when they are accessed. For example, after all the following lines of code have been executed, all the d_Interval instances will have a value equal to a day and a half (36 hours).

```
    d_Interval int1(1,12);           // 1 day, 12 hours
    d_Interval int2(int1);           // same as above
    d_Interval int3(0,36);           // same as above
    d_Interval int4(0,24,12*60);     // same as above
    d_Interval int5(0,12);           // 12 hours
    d_Interval int6(6);              // 6 days
    d_Interval int7;                 // all zeros
    d_Interval int8(0,-12);          // -12 hours
    d_Interval int9(2,-12);          // 1 day, 12 hours

if( int5 < int1 )
    int5 *= 3;
if( int1 == int2 )
    int6 = int6 / 4;
if( int1 + int2 == int3 * 2 )
    int7 = int1 * 2 - int2;
int8 = d_Interval(6) - 3*int9;
```

The expression in each `if` statement is true. Instances of `d_Interval` are often used when arithmetic is performed on instances of `d_Date` and `d_Timestamp`.

4.3.3 The `d_Date` Class

The `d_Date` class supports a date abstraction consisting of a year, month, and day. If an instance is initialized with no arguments, it has the value of the current day. A static function called `current` returns a `d_Date` instance with the current date. The `date` components are passed to the constructor as follows.

```
    d_Date      today;       // initialized to current day
    d_Date      birthday(1959, 6, 16); // year, month, day
```

Suppose an attempt is made to initialize an instance with an illegal value such as

```
    d_Date      badDate(1996, 13, 2);
```

This attempt throws an exception of kind `d_Error_DateInvalid`. To avoid this exception, the static Boolean function `is_valid_date` is provided to verify the validity of the values.

The year, month, and day components of the abstraction can be accessed. The following function inserts a date value into an `ostream`.

```
    ostream &operator<<(ostream &os, d_Date &d)
    {
        os.width(2);    os << d.month();
        os << '/';
```

```
        os.width(2);    os << d.day();
        os << '/';      os << d.year();
        return os;
    }
```

Weekday, an enumeration embedded in the d_Date class, identifies the days of the week—for example, Monday and Tuesday. An enumeration called Month is used to identify the months in a year—for example, January and February. The class supports the C++ canonical form and a set of arithmetic and comparison operations. The following code calculates various dates.

```
d_Date day;                         // defaults to current day
d_Date today(d_Date::current());    // another means of
                                    // getting current day,
                                    // but less efficient

cout << "Today is " << today << endl;
cout << ++day << " tomorrow\n";

day = today + d_Interval(1);
cout << day << " tomorrow\n";

day = today;
cout << --day << " yesterday\n";

day = today;
day -= 7;
cout << day << " this weekday last week\n";

day = today;
day += d_Interval(7);
cout << day << " this weekday next week\n";

day = today;
day.next(d_Date::Tuesday);
cout << day << " next Tuesday\n";

day = today;
day.previous(d_Date::Friday);
cout << day << " last Friday\n";

int days = today.days_in_month() - today.day();
cout << days << " days until payday!\n";
```

The following function computes the number of days until Christmas. If Christmas has already passed this year, it determines the number of days until Christmas next year.

```
int
shoppingDaysTillNextChristmas()
{
    d_Date today;              // default is current date
    d_Date christmas(today.year(), d_Date::December, 25);

    if( today > christmas ){
        christmas = d_Date( today.year()+1,
                            d_Date::December, 25);
        return christmas.day_of_year() +
                today.days_in_month() - today.day() + 1;
    }
    return christmas.day_of_year() - today.day_of_year();
}
```

ODMG 2.0 added a function that lets you subtract two d_Date instances and get a d_Interval instance. The preceding function is much simpler using this new ODMG 2.0 function.

```
int
shoppingDaysTillNextChristmas()
{
    d_Date today;              // default is current date
    d_Date christmas(today.year(), d_Date::December, 25);

    if( today > christmas ){
        christmas = d_Date( today.year()+1,
                            d_Date::December, 25);
    }
    d_Interval intrvl = christmas - today;
    return intrvl.days();
}
```

You can use the function is_between to determine whether a given date falls between two other dates. The following function determines whether a product warranty is in effect when given the purchase date and the number of months that the warranty is honored. It uses the function addMonths to add a positive number of months to a given date. It must take into account the variable number of days in a month.

```
d_Date
addMonths(const d_Date &d, unsigned int months)
{
    register unsigned int i;
    d_Date date(d.year(), d.month(), 1);

    if( months >= 12 ){        // more than a year of months
        i = months/12;         // get complete # of years
        date = d_Date(d.year() + i, d.month(), 1);
        months -= i*12;        // adjust month by # of years
    }
    for( i = 0; i < months; i++){
        date += date.days_in_month();
    }

// if original date was a leap day, need to adjust day
// for a nonleap year
    int dayofmonth = date.days_in_month() < d.day() ?
                        date.days_in_month() : d.day();
    date += dayofmonth - 1; // set the actual day in month
    return date;
}

int
isWarrantyInEffect(d_Date &purchase, unsigned int months)
{
    d_Date warrantyDate( addMonths(purchase, months) );
    return d_Date::current().is_between(purchase,
                                        warrantyDate);
}
```

A period of time is denoted by start and end dates. A function called overlaps determines whether two periods overlap. Suppose each person has a singly linked list of Trip structures that contain information about the nonoverlapping trips that he or she has scheduled. The list is ordered according to the trip dates.

```
struct Trip {
        Trip(const d_Date &sd, const d_Date &rd, struct Trip *n)
                        : startDate(sd), returnDate(rd),
                        next(n) {}
        d_Date          startDate;
        d_Date          returnDate;
//      other attributes
        struct Trip *   next;
};
```

The `newTrip` function determines whether a new trip can be scheduled. It is passed the start and end dates and a reference to a pointer that references the first node on the list (if the list is not empty). If the new trip time does not conflict with other scheduled trips, it is added to the list (in sorted order) and a nonzero value is returned. If the new trip date conflicts with an existing trip, however, zero is returned.

```
bool
newTrip(d_Date sdate, d_Date edate, struct Trip *&trips)
{
    register struct Trip **tp;
    for( tp = &trips; *tp; tp = &((*tp)->next) ){
        if( overlaps( sdate, edate,
            (*tp)->startDate, (*tp)->returnDate) )
            return false;
        if( sdate < (*tp)->startDate )
            break;
    }
    *tp = new Trip(sdate, edate, *tp);
    return true;
}
```

4.3.4 The `d_Time` Class

The `d_Time` class is used to represent a specific time of day. It is managed internally in Greenwich Mean Time (GMT). Its components are hours (0–23), minutes (0–59) and seconds (0–59.9999). All arithmetic is performed on a modulo 24-hour basis. If an attempt is made to initialize an instance with an invalid value, an exception object of kind `d_Error_TimeInvalid` is thrown.

The null constructor sets the instance to the current time. A static function called `current` returns the current time. Both of the following variable declarations initialize an instance to the current time.

```
d_Time   time1;
d_Time   time2(d_Time::current());
```

The following expression initializes an instance to 3:20 PM in the current time zone.

```
d_Time   afternoon_break(15,20,0.0f);
```

Functions are provided to access the components of a d_Time instance. The following function could be used to output the hours and minutes of the time (we don't print the seconds in this example).

```
ostream &
operator<<(ostream &os, const d_Time &t)
{
    char    fill_char_save = os.fill();

    os.width(2);    os.fill(' ');    os << t.hour();
    os << ':';
    os.width(2);    os.fill('0');    os << t.minute();
    os.fill(fill_char_save);
    return os;
}
```

The function `fill` is defined for `ostream` and either returns the current fill character (if a parameter is not passed) or sets the `ostream`'s fill character to the value passed as an argument.

Embedded in the d_Time class is an `enum` (Time_Zone) to provide names for each time zone. A default time zone is maintained by the class and is initially set to the local time zone. Another function changes the default setting to a different time zone, and another one resets the default time zone to the local time zone.

The d_Time class provides arithmetic functions that use the d_Interval class. A d_Interval instance can be added and subtracted from a d_Time instance. Subtracting one d_Time instance from another d_Time instance results in a d_Interval value.

You can use the equality, inequality, and comparison operators to compare the values of two d_Time instances. A period of time can be denoted by two time values. Several `overlaps` functions can be used to determine whether two periods overlap in time.

4.3.5 The d_Timestamp Class

The d_Timestamp class has both a date and a time component and provides functions to access each of them. The static function `current` returns a d_Timestamp object with the current date and time. As with the other time-oriented classes, arithmetic and comparison operations are provided. Two d_Timestamp instances can also be used to define a period, and several `overlaps` functions are provided. The d_Timestamp class provides more than just a pairing of d_Date and d_Time instances; d_Timestamp instances are treated as a single integrated value with respect to update operations. For example, consider the following code.

```
d_Timestamp ts(1999, 12, 31, 8);
d_Interval hr_18(0, 18);

ts += hr_18;
```

The resulting value of `ts` is January 1, 2000, at 2 AM, likely a chaotic time for many computers and intoxicated people in the world.

4.4 Restrictions on Using Some Types

Some C++ data types are problematic and are not supported by some proprietary implementations. In particular, the following types are difficult because of differences among processors and compilers.

- Unions
- Bit fields
- Pointers and references

Support of these types is not required of ODMG implementations, and their use is not portable. Let's look at the aspects of these types that make them problematic.

4.4.1 Unions

A C++ `union` defines a storage unit that can contain a value that is of one of several specified data types. A `union` holds the value of only one of these types at a time.

```
union multi_type {
        double          float_val;
        d_Ref<Amount>   amount;
        unsigned short  smallInt;
};
```

The amount of storage used by an instance of `multi_type` is based on the type having the largest storage requirements.

A `union` is used when there is concern about storage overhead and a value of only one of the data types is needed at a time. To determine which type of data is currently being stored in the `union`, you use a *type flag*. In the following declaration, the member `valueType` will contain a value used to determine the type of `value`.

```
class MyClass {
        multi_type          value;
        int                 valueType;
//      other attributes
};
```

This flag (`valueType`) is checked before a value is accessed in the `union`.

```
void
process_MyClass(MyClass *mp)
{
    switch(mp->valueType){
    case 1:
        // use mp->value.float_val
        break;
    case 2:
        // use mp->value.amount
        break;
    case 3:
        // use mp->value.smallInt
        break;
    }
}
```

The application knows that `valueType` defines the type of the `union` value. The application is responsible for setting the type tag when a change occurs in the type of value stored in the `union`. Encapsulation should be used to enforce this.

The data types declared in the `union` may have different binary representations on different machine architectures. To the database, the `union` is just a set of bits. When an object containing a `union` is brought into the application cache, some data types may require either a mapping to a different binary representation or cache management (in the case of the `d_Ref<Amount>` and `d_String` types).

This requirement poses a problem for the database software, which has no way of determining the type of the data. Some implementations provide a means for the application to tell the database which type the `union` contains. A *union discrimination function* is defined by the application for each `union`. When the `union` is moved into and out of the application cache, the database calls the union discrimination function to determine which type of data is stored in the `union`. Or the database may require that an integer value from 1 to N be associated with the `union` types, the integer value corresponding to the declaration order of the types in the `union`. The application may need to specify an appropriate integer member that the database knows to examine.

4.4.2 Bit Fields

The binary representation of bit fields varies among machine and compiler environments. A database implementation may support bit fields and guarantee their correctness in a homogeneous environment (with the same compiler, operating system, and processor), but they are less likely to work if any of these elements varies.

4.4.3 C++ Pointers and References

Embedding C++ references in persistent objects is also problematic. For example, the following class has a member called `city` that references an instance of class `City`.

```
class Address {
        City &              city; // example of a C++ reference
// other attributes
};
```

ODMG does not support C++ pointers or references as attributes of an object stored in the database. A C++ reference cannot be stored in the database and used to refer to a persistent object; it can be used to reference only transient data. But because the address of transient data is not valid across process boundaries, C++ references are not very useful in an object database environment. The `d_Ref<T>` class should be used in persistent classes instead of pointers or references.

4.5 Closing Comments about Domains

Virtually any C++ class can serve as a domain type in an object database. This is one of the advantages of object databases over relational databases. But vendors of relational databases are beginning to add object capabilities, and it turns out that the easiest way to incorporate objects into the relational data model is to define new object types to serve as domain types for columns. Chapter 17 will cover this technique in more detail.

Domain types are typically not persistence-capable on their own. Instances of domains attain persistence by being embedded in other classes that are persistence-capable. The entities of an application's information model are usually represented by persistence-capable classes. Chapter 5 discusses these classes in detail.

Chapter 5
Persistent Entities

The entities of the problem domain that are managed by an application are usually represented by classes. Instances of these classes usually need to be persistent and accessible from multiple application processes, a capability provided by a C++ object database. Of the type categories found in object database models, the entity type category supports persistence and object identity.

This chapter discusses how to declare persistence-capable classes. The basic operations of creating, reading, modifying, and deleting instances are explained. The chapter concludes with some comparisons between object databases and relational databases.

5.1 The Entity Abstraction

A primary task during the analysis phase of a project is to discover all the entities in the problem domain that need to be modeled. A class is defined for each entity to be represented in the application.

An entity consists of a set of properties that also must be determined during analysis. These properties include attributes (of some domain type), relationships (with other instances), and operations. They are represented by data and function members in the classes. Each data attribute is of a specific type referred to as a domain (covered in Chapter 4).

Entity instances often are related to other instances in the object model. The relationships are included in the class declarations. Special objects, provided by most of the object database implementations, are embedded in the classes involved in the relationships. These special objects are discussed in Chapter 8.

Operations are also associated with entity classes and are implemented as member functions. They should provide an interface that embodies the entity's abstraction and should perform all modifications to instances. Encapsulating the implementation localizes the semantics and minimizes the amount of software that needs to understand the class implementation.

Entities often have IS-A relationships with other entities, and these relationships are represented in C++ by inheritance relationships among classes. IS-A stands for the *is a kind of* relationship between two things. For example, a butterfly is a kind of insect, and a car is a kind of vehicle. Inheritance is used in C++ and other object-oriented programming languages to represent these IS-A relationships. C++ object databases directly support the inheritance relationships declared among C++ classes. The application can use both abstract and concrete classes.

5.2 Making a Class Persistent

In a C++ object database, the application's C++ class declarations serve as the definition of the schema. This is one of the fundamental advantages of an object database.

5.2.1 The d_Object Base Class

When an application uses the ODMG interface, a class must be derived (directly or indirectly) from the ODMG d_Object base class so that its instances can be stored in the database.

The following code declares a class Person to be persistence-capable by deriving from d_Object.

```
class Person : public d_Object {
public:
        d_String            last_name;
        d_String            first_name;
//      other properties of a person
};
```

Inheritance relationships can also be defined among persistence-capable classes.

```
class Employee : public Person {
public:
//        properties of an employee
};
```

Because `Person` is derived from `d_Object`, `Employee` is also persistence-capable.

5.2.2 Instances

Because `d_Object` provides support for persistence, many people incorrectly assume that all the instances are automatically persistent. Instances can be persistent or transient, although the transient instances will include the overhead of the data members of `d_Object` required to manage a persistent instance. The specific `new` operator that is called to create an instance determines whether it is persistent or transient. The three `new` operators are discussed in section 5.4.

Each persistent instance has an *object identifier* that is used to reference the object. The identifier is associated with the instance until it is deleted. The object identifier is immutable; it cannot be changed by the application. Only the attributes can be changed. Changing an attribute value does not affect the identity of the object, in contrast to a relational database, in which identifiers are stored in columns.

The `d_Ref<T>` class is used to represent an object reference. When a `d_Ref<T>` instance is stored in the database, it contains the object identifier of the referenced object. Chapter 6 discusses `d_Ref<T>` in detail.

5.3 Properties

The properties of a class include the data members and the function members. A property has a name and a type (domain). You can use the `public`, `private`, and `protected` access control specifiers of C++ to control access to the class properties. The public interface of a class should be a set of operations that represents the abstraction being modeled.

5.3.1 Data Attributes

Data attributes are used to describe the characteristics of the entity being modeled. Attributes do not have their own object identity and cannot be referenced elsewhere in the database.

An object establishes a *context* in which its attributes reside. The attributes provide implementation values to support the abstraction value of their containing object. The object's context governs which values are valid for each attribute. It establishes many of the associated semantic integrity constraints.

The data attributes of an object should be declared `private`. The word *should* reflects good object design policy. Implementations do not require this approach. Data members could be made `public` but with a resulting loss of encapsulation. Operations defined for the object would then control all modifications to the attributes. The operations are responsible for maintaining the semantic integrity of the object.

5.3.1.1   Static Data Members

In C++, a `static` data member of a class has only one copy that is shared by all instances of the class. The `static` member has class scope; it is not contained in each instance. These members are not stored in the database but instead reside in the data section of each application process that includes the class.

5.3.1.2   Transient Members

Some object databases allow a data member to be declared to be transient; it exists in the object while in memory, but it is not stored in the database. These transient members are useful when data is directly associated with an object and is needed by most of the transactions, but it does not need to be stored in the database. The data may be needed when computations are performed during a transaction but is not valid in the context of another transaction. The syntax varies among vendors. Some of them treat all pointer data members as transient attributes. Others require the attribute to be preceded by a keyword specifier such as `transient`. ODMG does not support this feature.

For example, suppose that a user interface `Form` class is being used to display an object's attributes in a window. A `Form` object is associated with each `Person` object. Given a `Person` instance, it may be convenient to reference the associated `Form` object directly.

```
class Person : public d_Object {
//       other members of Person
transient Form *             _form; // transient keyword is vendor
                             // extension, not ODMG or C++
};
```

The schema capture tool that parses the C++ class declarations would find any transient attributes and would note that they should not be stored.

5.3.2 Operations

The public operations should provide an interface that represents the abstraction being modeled. They are responsible for maintaining the semantic integrity of an instance, knowing which alterations are valid. These operations can be considered "minitransactions" defined for an object. In fact, each transaction that is identified during analysis to operate on an instance should be defined as a member function.

Public operations can also be used to implement *derived attributes*, a property of an object that is computed versus one that is stored. The value of the derived attribute is often based on the values of other data attributes. The term *derived* here does not imply inheritance. For example, the `Person` class may define an `age` operation.

```
d_UShort
Person::age() const
{
    d_Date today = d_Date::current();
    d_UShort years = today.year() - _birth_date.year();
    if( today.day_of_year() < _birth_date.day_of_year() )
        --years;
    return years;
}
```

Some operations may be direct mappings of data attributes, providing *get* and *set* behavior. But other operations may perform computations with the data attributes and return a value, essentially defining derived attributes. If both stored and derived attributes are accessed via operations, there is no syntactical difference in access. The user of a class need not know which functions return stored versus derived attributes. The *functional data model* defined in some database books uses this approach. It provides a lot of flexibility by allowing the class implementation to change without affecting users of the class.

If all access occurs via operations, you can add functionality to an operation to be executed whenever a call is made to access the attribute, providing a *trigger*-like operation. Derived attributes and triggers are often supported in other database technologies. Class operations provide the right mechanism to support these capabilities in an object database.

5.4 Creation

Instances are created by invoking the `new` operator. Three `new` operators are defined in the ODMG standard as members of the `d_Object` class. They must be provided, but implementations can include additional operators to take advantage of vendor-specific features. The specific new operator used to create an instance determines whether it is transient or persistent. Once created, a persistent instance cannot be made transient nor can a transient instance be made persistent.

5.4.1 Creating Transient Instances

There are two ways to create a transient instance using the ODMG interface. All local variables of persistence-capable classes are transient. For example, the following function declares an instance of the Person class as a local variable.

```
void
recruit()
{
    Person candidate;
    ...
}
```

The local variable candidate is not stored in the database.

Two forms of the new operator can be used to create a transient instance. Assume that a class called Employee has been defined by the application and derived from the class Person. The following code creates two transient employees.

```
Employee *emp1, *emp2;
emp1 = new Employee();
emp2 = new(d_Database::transient_memory, "Employee")
                  Employee();
```

The first new operator uses the standard syntax for new, taking no additional parameters. It creates a transient instance, as do all other new operators called without arguments in the C++ application. The second new operator has an argument that is a pointer to a d_Database object. This pointer is used to indicate in which database the new object should be placed. This function can be used to create either transient or persistent instances. The public static data member in class d_Database, called transient_memory, is used to indicate that the object should be transient. If the first argument to new had been a pointer to an open database, the instance created would have been persistent and placed in that database.

Some vendors need to know the type of an instance when it is created. Unfortunately, this information is not automatically available inside the new operator, so it had to be included in the call to new so that all the vendors could support the standard. All vendors support the ODMG new operators that require the name of the class. The vendors that do not require the class name may provide additional new operators that are more convenient, but the software will not be portable to some implementations.

5.4.2 Creating Persistent Instances

You can use the following new operator to create persistent instances. Using the previous Employee class, the following code creates a persistent instance.

```
d_Database db;  // assume this points to an open database
Employee *emp3 = new(&db, "Employee") Employee();
```

The d_Database instance must refer to an open database. This new operator is the same function used in the previous example to create the transient object referenced by emp2. In this call, a pointer to an instance of d_Database referring to an open database is passed to new. This new operator lets you create both persistent and transient instances.

5.4.3 Clustering Instances

If a set of related objects is frequently accessed, it is advantageous to group the set physically in the database. Clustering hints can be provided when an instance is created. *Clustering* is an optimization technique that applications can use to reduce the number of disk transfers and the amount of client and server cache memory required to access the objects. In some architectures it can also reduce client-server communication overhead. In implementations that map blocks directly from the database cache into pages of the client, clustering reduces the amount of client memory required. If you increase the ratio of objects needed by the application relative to the number of required pages, you will reduce the number of pages necessary to contain all the needed objects.

ODMG provides an interface to specify that instances should be clustered.

```
Employee *emp4 = new( emp3, "Employee") Employee();
```

The new object referenced by emp4 will be clustered in the same database and "near" the object referenced by emp3, which was created in the previous example.

The nearness that can be specified varies among the implementations. It can be a page, segment, class, or database. Vendors can provide other interfaces that support specific clustering capabilities, but they are not portable among ODMG implementations.

Some implementations provide clustering automatically; the application need not specify clustering when an object is created. Automatic clustering can be based on the class of the instance or on its relationships with other objects.

5.5 Initialization at Creation

Two forms of initialization are used for an object in an object database. When an object is first created, its attributes must be initialized. In C++, constructors perform this task on all objects created in an application. The second form of initialization occurs when an application process first accesses an object in the database that was created earlier by another application process. But the object is now being instantiated in the client cache of a new application process. This is called *activation* and is covered in section 5.7.

Constructors serve the same purpose in a C++ object database that they serve in other object programming situations. An application can define as many constructors for a class as needed. Attributes that are not provided with initial values should be initialized to a null value. It is recommended that a null constructor be defined for user-defined domain types in order to initialize the instance to a null value.

For example, our `Person` and `Employee` classes can have the following constructors. Recall that we added a member `_form` that references transient data used to display the object in a user interface.

```
Person::Person(const char *fname,const char *lname,d_Date bd,
          const struct Address &addr, const char *phone)
     :   _first_name(fname), _last_name(lname),
         _birth_date(bd), _address(addr)
{
    strncpy(_phone_number, phone, 10);
    _phone_number[10] = 0;
    _form = new Form();
}

Person::~Person()
{
    delete _form;
}

Employee::Employee(const char *fname,const char*lname,
           d_Date bd, const struct Address &addr,
           const char *hphone, const char *ophone,
           const char *email, d_Float sal)
```

```
                :   Person(fname, lname, bd, addr, hphone),
                    _office_phone(ophone), _email_address(email),
                    _salary(sal)
         { }
```

5.6 Deletion

With an object database, an object is not explicitly deleted by an application until it is deleted from the database. The removal of an object from the client cache is called *deactivation* and is covered in the next section. When an object is deleted, the destructor is called if it has been defined. It performs any cleanup that is needed to maintain data integrity, including things such as deleting secondary objects managed by the object. This process is called *delete propagation*.

Two deletion mechanisms are available in ODMG. Objects can be deleted either by using the C++ `delete` operator or by using the `delete_object` operation defined for `d_Ref<T>`. The `Employee` objects pointed to by `emp3` and `emp4` could be deleted from the database this way:

```
    d_Ref<Employee> empRef(emp3);

    delete emp4;
    empRef.delete_object();
```

You can use the `delete` operator if the application has a pointer to an object that needs to be deleted. The pointer must be initialized to the memory address of the object in the application cache; the object must already be in the cache.

If the application has only a reference (`d_Ref<T>`) to an object, you can use the member function `delete_object`. When called, the object may or may not be in the cache. To execute the destructor, the instance must be activated in the cache.

Once the destructor has executed, the object is removed from the application cache. If the transaction commits successfully, the object is deleted from the database; if it aborts, the object will continue to exist in the database, as will other persistent objects that may have been deleted by the destructor. Transient instances are usually not affected by transaction activities.

The destructor in `d_Object` is defined as a virtual function, so you can use a base class pointer or reference to delete an instance of a derived class. For example, a `d_Ref<Person>` instance may refer to an `Employee` instance. Invoking `delete_object` will appropriately call the `Employee` destructor.

If the class does not have a destructor and the instance is not in the cache, the object may not need to be activated when it is deleted. Similarly, some implementations provide a mechanism to delete an object without invoking the destructor. This technique may provide performance benefits. In some circumstances it may be acceptable to skip destructor processing and avoid the overhead of activating the object in the application cache. The application must determine whether any processing must be performed if the object is not in the cache. If such processing is required, this mechanism is not appropriate.

Calling the `delete` operator or `delete_object` removes the instance from both the application cache and the database. In some situations an application may want to free cache memory by removing an object from the cache but not from the database. This approach is common for applications with transactions that operate on a set of objects so large that not all of them can fit into the cache at the same time. Once the application is finished manipulating some of the objects, they can be removed from the cache so that memory is available for other objects.

ODMG does not provide a mechanism to remove an object from the application cache without removing it from the database, although some proprietary interfaces support this capability. An application can mark objects as *unpinned*, allowing the database software to implicitly swap the object out of the application cache when cache space is needed. Issues related to cache management are discussed in Chapter 14.

5.7 Activation and Deactivation

As objects are accessed from the database by a transaction, they move in and out of the application cache. This movement is called *activation* and *deactivation*.

When an object is activated, you may need to perform some initialization of transient data. When an object leaves the cache, you may need to perform some deinitialization of the object. Memory may need to be dynamically allocated when the object enters the cache and freed when it leaves the cache. Deactivation may occur when the transaction commits or when the object is swapped out of memory.

Figure 5.1 illustrates the activation and deactivation of an object. The applications represent different application processes accessing the same object during its lifetime; time is shown progressing from left to right. The first application creates a new persistent object; when it commits, the object is deactivated and stored in the database. The second application reads the object, causing it to be activated in the cache. At transaction commit, the object is deactivated and written to the database (if it has been modified). The final application (on the right) accesses the object, causing it to be activated, and then deletes it. When the object is deleted, it

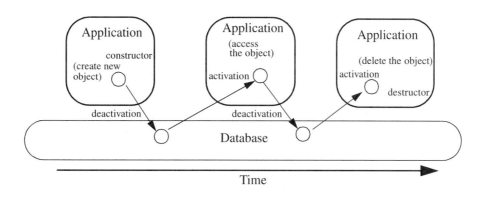

Figure 5.1 Process of activation and deactivation of objects.

is neither deactivated nor written to the database; instead, it is removed from the database.

5.7.1 The `d_activate` and `d_deactivate` Functions

The `d_Object` virtual functions `d_activate` and `d_deactivate` are called by the database software when these events occur. Any functionality that the application needs to perform should be placed in these functions.

The application may want to perform other processing when an object is activated, such as bringing related objects into the application. This processing could be performed in `d_activate`. Or activation and deactivation of an object may necessitate the refresh of a graphical user interface managed by the application.

When you're using C++ in a nondatabase environment, the constructor and destructor should operate in a coordinated fashion, in particular when dealing with the allocation and deallocation of secondary data structures. The constructor is called when an object is created, and the destructor is called when it is deleted.

The `d_activate` and `d_deactivate` functions serve a similar role when a persistent object moves into and out of the application cache. These functions handle any transient initialization of data or other processing needed by the application. The persistent data members do not need to be initialized when the object is activated. Their values are stored in the database, and they are initialized automatically by the database implementation. But transient members need to be initialized. When an object is deactivated, any transient memory it allocated and managed must be freed. Otherwise, memory leaks will occur. The symmetry of these operations is important for effective memory management of the object.

Suppose the object depicted in Figure 5.1 is an instance of `Employee`, which is derived from class `Person`. Also assume that the `d_activate` and `d_deactivate` virtual functions are defined for both classes. The order of execution for the constructor, destructor, `d_activate`, and `d_deactivate` functions is as follows.

```
Application 1 starts
    Person::Person              application creates Employee
    Employee::Employee
    Employee::d_deactivate      called at commit time
Application 2
    Employee::d_activate        Employee object is accessed
    Employee::d_deactivate      called at commit time
Application 3
    Employee::d_activate        Employee object is accessed
    Employee::~Employee         object is deleted
    Person::~Person
```

Notice that `d_activate` and `d_deactivate` of class `Person` are not being called. The database software simply invokes the virtual function, which calls the virtual function defined at the deepest level in the instance's inheritance hierarchy. The database software does not call each `d_activate` and `d_deactivate` function in an inheritance hierarchy as the compiler does for constructors and destructors. Because of the role these functions play in object cache management, it is recommended that applications emulate the constructor and destructor behavior in their implementations of `d_activate` and `d_deactivate`. Thus, each derived class `d_activate` function should first call its base class `d_activate` function, and each derived class `d_deactivate` function should finish with a call to its base class `d_deactivate`.

```
void
Employee::d_activate()
{
    Person::d_activate();
//  perform activation processing for Employee
}

void
Employee::d_deactivate()
{
//  perform deactivation processing for Employee

    Person::d_deactivate();
}
```

In C++, the constructors of embedded objects are invoked before their containing object's constructor is executed. Similarly, their destructors are called after the containing object's destructor. Embedded objects are not explicitly activated and deactivated by the database software; only their containing persistent object has calls made to its `d_activate` and `d_deactivate` functions. If embedded objects need to have activation-type functionality executed, the application should define member functions for the embedded types and explicitly call them from within the containing object's `d_activate` and `d_deactivate` functions. If an object is added as a member or base class, these functions may need to be altered to include a call to an appropriate function.

The function `d_deactivate` is not called for objects when `checkpoint` is called for the `d_Transaction` object. When a checkpoint is performed, the states of the objects in the application cache are committed to the database but remain in the cache for further manipulation by the application.

The process of object initialization during activation and deactivation has varied among vendor implementations. Some vendors do not have architectures that support this type of processing. Others use an approach different from the one adopted in the ODMG standard. Developers should be aware that some of the initial ODMG implementations may not strictly conform to this aspect of the standard. It is important to understand, then, how the implementation you're using handles activation and deactivation.

5.7.2 Activation Implementation Issues

Data is often embedded in an object that is used by the compiler to implement some language mechanisms. This data can have different values from one application to the next. It must be initialized before any application software, such as `d_activate`, can be called.

To implement polymorphism in C++, virtual functions use a *vtbl* pointer that is contained in each instance. A single vtbl pointer is generally used when a class uses single inheritance; multiple vtbl pointers are often used in classes that use multiple inheritance. A vtbl pointer points to a virtual function table associated with the class of the instance. The vtbl pointer introduces complexity for object database implementations. The address of a class's virtual function table will vary across applications. The vtbl pointer is initialized by constructors when an object is initialized. The compiler performs this initialization automatically in the code it generates for a constructor. But with an object database, an application-visible constructor is called only when an instance is first created, and not when it is activated. When an object is activated, the vtbl pointer must be set to the appropriate address for the application. Some implementations explicitly set the vtbl pointer to the proper address when an instance is activated. Others execute a special constructor defined by the database so that the constructor initialization code generated by the C++ compiler sets the vtbl pointer value to the proper address.

A virtual base class presents similar issues, because many implementations of virtual base classes embed a value in each instance that has either the address or offset of the virtual base class instance within the object. This location can vary among C++ compilers. If it is an address (as opposed to an offset), it depends on the address of the containing object in the client cache.

5.8 Instance Modification

When an object is activated in an application cache, the database software implicitly acquires a lock, usually a read lock that allows shared access. If the application intends to modify the instance, the member function `mark_modified` must be called just before the alteration. This member function does not need to be called when an object is created or removed from the database. The ODMG standard does not state what happens if the application modifies an object before calling `mark_modified`. The resulting behavior varies among implementations, so the function should always be called first. If the application does not call `mark_modified`, any changes made to the database are not guaranteed to be detected and written at transaction commit.

Even though the purpose of calling `mark_modified` is to notify the database that the application is going to modify an object, many (but not all) implementations use this call to indicate that a lock should be acquired, usually a write lock. Thus, calling `mark_modified` could be considered an explicit call to lock the object. Some non-ODMG implementations provide a function that allows an application to acquire a specific type of lock on an object.

Many virtual memory operating systems let you control the read/write access privileges of a process's memory on a page or segment basis. Some object database implementations use this capability to control object access. When an object is first accessed, the page containing the object is mapped into the application with read-only access. When the application attempts to write an object on a page, an operating system trap occurs (because the page is write-protected by the operating system). The object database implementation catches and handles the trap. An attempt is made to acquire a write lock for the page. If the lock is acquired, the access protection of the page is changed so that the application can continue execution and modify objects in the page. Implementations using this approach do not require applications to call functions such as `mark_modified` for locks to be acquired properly. But to be portable among ODMG implementations, the application should call `mark_modified`.

If encapsulation has been used for a class and if all the data attributes are `private`, only its operations can modify the state of the object. Operations that do not modify the object should be declared as `const`; the compiler can then enforce the read-only nature of the function. Operations that modify the object should call `mark_modified` before altering an attribute. If this approach is used consistently, the application software using the class does not need to call `mark_modified` directly.

```
void
Person::newAddress(struct Address &addr)
{
    mark_modified();
    _address = addr;
}
```

When `mark_modified` is called, the database implementation ensures that if the transaction successfully commits, the value of the instance at commit time is written to the database. Implementations often maintain a flag, called a *dirty bit*, to note what has been modified. The implementation may set the dirty bit at a granularity greater than an individual instance. The database software keeps track of the instances that have changed during a transaction, and, when the transaction commits, the database software writes the modified objects to the database. The application does not need to propagate updates to the database.

This technique results in a substantial savings in development costs. When applications use other database technologies, they must explicitly propagate the state of all modified objects to the database. The application must know which objects need to be written to the database. It must also write software for each class to write its instances to the database. This requirement can involve a substantial amount of software that the application does not need to write when using an object database.

5.8.1 Concurrency Control

There are two forms of concurrency control: *pessimistic* and *optimistic*. Developers are most familiar with pessimistic control, the more common form. The ODMG specification requires support only for pessimistic control, but vendors can also support optimistic control. What is the difference between the two types?

Both pessimistic and optimistic concurrency control perform locking and check for lock contention. They differ in *when* these activities are performed during a transaction. Each is optimized for a different lock contention scenario. Pessimistic control assumes that lock conflicts are likely, whereas optimistic control assumes they are not likely. With pessimistic concurrency control, locks are acquired just before read or write access of the object, and lock contention is checked immediately. With optimistic concurrency control, locks are acquired and checked for contention only during the transaction commit. With pessimistic control, the application knows sooner whether or not there is contention. It works best when there is a likelihood of contention, whereas optimistic control works best when contention is unlikely. Some vendors support both forms, usually with minimal impact on the application software.

Lock contention occurs when a transaction attempts to acquire a lock that is incompatible with an existing lock. Read locks are compatible but write locks are incompatible with both read and write locks. When lock contention is encountered, an application can either wait until the lock is released or can receive an immediate error return. C++ exceptions are often used as the notification mechanism. For implementations that allow the application to wait for a lock to be released, the application can often specify the period to wait.

5.9 Other Operations

Many kinds of operations can be performed on persistent objects. The behavior of these operations differs depending on whether the object is a simple or a composite object. With a composite object, some of the operations are propagated to the subordinate objects.

When an object contains references to other objects, a decision must be made whether the operation applies only to the current object or applies also to the referenced objects. An operation that is applied only to the current object is called a *shallow operation*. If the operation is applied to the referenced objects, it is called a *deep operation*. Often, composite object operations are deep.

5.9.1 Assignment

An assignment operator can be defined for a persistent object. Attribute values are typically assigned from one object to another. The object identifier associated with an object is never assigned to another object. If the object contains references to other objects, a decision must be made whether only the reference value is assigned (*shallow* assignment) or the referenced object is assigned (*deep* assignment).

5.9.2 Equality

The equality of two entity objects can be evaluated. They are usually considered equal if all their respective attributes are equal. If the object contains attributes that are references, it must be decided whether the equality is based on the references being equal (*shallow* equality) or the referenced objects being equal (*deep* equality). Two object references may not be equal (they refer to different instances) and yet the instances they reference are equal.

5.9.3 Comparison

A natural ordering exists among the instances of some entity classes, usually based on the values of attributes within the objects. Comparison operations are much more common for domain types than for entity types. The less-than operator can be defined to establish an ordering among the entity instances, usually by applying the less-than operator of the attribute types. Often, an application may want to establish many different orders among entity instances. The single set of comparison operators available in C++ may not be adequate for an application's requirements.

5.10 Some Comparisons with Relational Databases

In a relational database, an entity in a model is mapped to a table, which is defined via a `create table` statement in SQL. The entity's attributes are represented by the columns in the table, and the name and type of each column are defined in the `create table` statement. An entity instance is placed in a row of the table.

Inheritance relationships among the entities cannot be declared among the tables. Applications can model and manage inheritance relationships on top of a relational model, but the database does not know they exist.

The relational database does not provide an interface to map instances of entity classes between their database and C++ object representation. All database access, both read and write, is performed on a column basis. When possible, a mapping is provided between the database's representation of a column data type and a corresponding type in the application programming language. But the database implementation dictates which programming language data type is used. Either the application or an object layer on top of the relational interface must provide a mapping at the entity level.

With an object database, the entire instance (all attributes) are brought into the application. It is not possible to access a subset of the attributes. With a relational database, it is easy and natural to access a subset of the attributes.

A relational database is not aware of the instances in the application and doesn't support an application cache. The application is responsible for knowing which objects need to be written to the database. The application must make explicit calls to the database to provide new values for modified attributes. Should the application update all the attributes? Or should it keep track of which attributes have changed, updating only those columns? Should updates be propagated to the database as they occur, or should they be retained and performed at transaction commit? The application developer must make many decisions and implement a lot of software to handle the propagation of updates to the database. With an object database, these things are handled automatically, reducing development costs substantially.

Relational databases do not support encapsulation at the application level, because they do not know about the application's object model. Nor do they provide object-level access. With SQL, all data attributes (columns) are directly accessible. If access control on tables is needed, *views* are defined to limit the columns that are accessible. Users are granted permission to access either a base table or a view. Views are also used to create derived columns via SQL expressions. Thus, views provide a means of attaining some degree of information hiding in a relational database. But there are often restrictions with the use of views. For example, it is usually not possible to update a column of a view.

Columns of a row can be directly altered via the SQL `update` command. Some relational databases let you specify semantic integrity constraints, which are checked at transaction commit to ensure that any changes leave the entity in a logically consistent state. The application first makes the alterations, and then the validity checking is performed at transaction commit.

This approach differs from the one used with an object database. The application defines explicit operations to perform all attribute changes and ensure that valid state changes are made. The knowledge needed to make valid state changes is built into the operations that make the changes. Only the class designer and implementer can alter the attributes directly. This arrangement leads to a higher level of data integrity.

Chapter 6
Object Identification

The primary technique for identifying an object in an object database is to use an object identifier. Another approach is to associate a name with an object. The name consists of an ASCII string with a value determined by the application. An application can then access the object by name.

One or more attributes of a class can serve as a key, which is used by some object databases to locate an object. An application can specify that it wants to access all the objects that have attributes whose values satisfy a constraint often expressed by a query predicate.

Many objects model things that exist in the real world. They may already have associated identifiers, referred to as real-world identifiers, that are different from object identifiers. You can establish object names or keys and then map the real-world identifier to the object in the database.

This chapter covers the various methods for identifying an object. It concludes with some comparisons with relational databases.

6.1 Object Identifier

The primary means of identifying an object is via its object identifier. The database assigns a unique object identifier to each object instance when the instance is first created. The object identifier is not an attribute of the instance; its value cannot be changed by an application.

The database implementation is responsible for generating unique object identifiers. They must be unique so that they will map to a single object. But they are unique only within a given scope, typically either a database or database group. ODMG specifies an interface only for single database access. So an object identifier must be unique within a database, but implementations can expand this scope. Two separate database environments may have an overlap in the object identifiers generated by the database. Objects that must reference one another via object identifiers must exist in the same identifier scope.

In ODMG, an instance of `d_Ref<T>` is used to reference an instance of a class `T`, which must be derived from `d_Object`. It may also contain a reference to an instance of any class publicly derived from `T`. When instances of `d_Ref<T>` are stored in the database, they contain the object identifier of the referenced object. While a `d_Ref<T>` is in memory, its value can be the object identifier or can reference other cache data that contains the identifier. Applications cannot access the actual representation of the object identifier, which varies significantly among vendors.

The following code shows how to declare a reference to a `Person` and an `Employee` instance.

```
d_Ref<Person>        person;
d_Ref<Employee>      emp;
```

A class `d_Ref_Any` can contain a reference to an instance of any class derived from `d_Object`.

```
d_Ref_Any            aperson;
```

Only a subset of the operations available for `d_Ref<T>` can be performed with a `d_Ref_Any`. You must convert a `d_Ref_Any` to a `d_Ref<T>` for operations that require the type of the referenced instance. When the conversion is complete, type checking is performed at run time to ensure that the object is an instance of `T` or a class derived from `T`.

These classes provide a *smart pointer* facility whose interface is syntactically and semantically similar to that of a pointer. Operators are overloaded to provide behavior similar to that of a pointer with the same syntax, such as the dereference operators `->` and `*`. Within these functions, additional database processing is performed. Most of the existing proprietary interfaces use smart-pointer classes similar to `d_Ref<T>`.

The `d_Ref<T>` object reference supports inheritance and polymorphism in the same manner as C++ pointers. Suppose a base class `B` has a derived class `D`. A `d_Ref<B>` can reference an instance of any class derived from `B`, including `D`. The instance can be referenced without regard to its actual type. In this way, you can have *polymorphic references* in the database.

```
class Person : public d_Object {
public:
                              Person(const char *fn,const char *ln);
          const char *      first_name() const;
          const char *      last_name() const;
//        other attributes
};
class Employee : public Person {
          /* definition of Employee */
};
```

The following code creates an instance of `Employee`.

```
    d_Database db; // assume this is initialized to an open db

    d_Ref<Person> person = new(&db, "Employee")
                              Employee("Tina", "Strouble");
```

The variable `person` contains a reference to an instance of `Employee`. As with the use of a pointer, the application can access only `Person` attributes and not `Employee` attributes. However, virtual functions can be called using the variable `person`, and the function appropriate for class `Employee` is invoked.

The dereference operation is one of the fundamental operations in an object database. The `->` and `*` operators defined for `d_Ref<T>` can be used to invoke the operation.

```
    person->last_name();         // used more frequently
    (*person).first_name();
```

The `->` operator returns the address of the object in the application cache. The `operator*` function returns a C++ reference to the object. If the referenced object is already in the application, these operators simply return a pointer or reference to the object. The implementation may need to perform some lookup processing. If the object is not in memory, it is retrieved from the database and placed in the application cache.

Some object database implementations allow C++ pointers to be stored in the database and used as references to objects in the database.

```
class Person : public Employee {
          Person *          spouse;          // and other attributes
};
```

Using pointers makes a database more transparent than using the d_Ref<T> class does. In particular, it can ease the migration of existing legacy C and C++ data structures into a database environment, because they already use pointers to reference transient data. Using pointers for database references has been a hotly debated topic within the object database community, but only some vendors support them and consequently they are not supported in the ODMG standard.

6.1.1 Initialization and Assignment

There are several ways to initialize an instance of d_Ref<T> or d_Ref_Any. The null constructor initializes the reference to a null value. A d_Ref<T> can be initialized with one of the following.

- d_Ref<T>
- d_Ref<D> for any class D derived from T
- T *
- D * for any class D derived from T
- d_Ref_Any

Thus, the following declarations are valid.

```
d_Ref<Person>        person;
Person *             p = 0;
d_Ref<Employee>      employee;
Employee *           e = 0;
d_Ref_Any            any;

d_Ref<Person>        p1(person);
d_Ref<Person>        p2(p);
d_Ref<Person>        p3(employee);
d_Ref<Person>        p4(e);
d_Ref<Person>        p5(any);//requires type check at run time
```

Likewise, you can assign an instance of one of these types to a d_Ref<T>.

```
d_Ref<Person>        p6, p7, p8, p9, p10;
p6 = person;
p7 = p;
p8 = employee;
p9 = e;
p10 = any; // requires type checking at run time
```

Some initializations and assignments are not valid because of the inheritance relationships among the classes. For example, the following lines of code are illegal conversions among references.

```
d_Ref<Department>    dept;
Department *         d = 0;

// the Department class is not related to Employee class
dept = employee;     // illegal
employee = d;        // illegal
// Employee is derived from Person, a derived class reference
// cannot reference a base class object, the same as pointers
employee = person;   // illegal
employee = p;        // illegal
```

If an invalid initialization or assignment is performed with a reference, a d_Error_TypeInvalid exception object is thrown.

As with pointers in C++, the type checking for some of these invalid initializations and assignments is performed at run time instead of compile time. This may vary among implementations. Some template limitations have prevented classes such as d_Ref<T> from providing the same compile-time type checking, available for pointers, that takes inheritance into account. Member template functions, recently added to C++, let you define a smart-pointer template class that allows compile-time type checking of such conversions. As this language feature becomes generally available, implementations should use it to enable more compile-time type checking.

6.1.2 Null References

A database reference can contain a null value. The d_Ref<T> and d_Ref_Any classes have a null constructor that initializes the reference to a null value. You can also set a reference to null by initializing or assigning to it with another null reference or a pointer value of 0. In addition, the member function clear can be used to set a d_Ref<T> or d_Ref_Any to a null value.

There are several ways to determine whether a database reference has a null value. The Boolean function is_null returns true (nonzero) if the reference is null; otherwise, it returns false (0). The ! operator returns true if the reference is null.

The following example illustrates expressions that use these functions.

```
d_Ref<Employee> emp; // assume this is initialized
```

```
if( emp.is_null() ) ...      // ref is null
if( !emp ) ...               // ref is null
if( emp == 0 ) ...           // ref equal to pointer 0
```

6.1.3 Dereference Operations

The dereference operations are used to access an object via a reference. The conversion of a database reference to a pointer is called *swizzling*. The `operator->` and `ptr` member functions of `d_Ref<T>` perform swizzling and return a pointer to the referenced instance. The `operator*` swizzles and returns a C++ reference to the instance. These operators allow a `d_Ref<T>` to have an interface with a syntax and semantics very similar to those of a pointer.

```
void referral(const Person &);
d_Ref<Person>   person;      // assume this gets initialized
d_Ref<Employee> emp;         // assume this gets initialized
Person *        p;

person->last_name();
referral(*person); // passes a C++ reference of the object
referral(*emp); // passes of C++ reference of the base class
p = person.ptr(); // ptr returns cache address of the object
p = emp.ptr();
```

To explicitly access the address of an object in the cache, you must invoke the function `ptr`. Normally, the application can simply use `operator->` to access a member of an object or use `operator*` if a function requires a reference to the object, as shown in the previous code.

Unless an application is sure that a `d_Ref<T>` refers to an object, it should first check whether the `d_Ref<T>` is null. An attempt to dereference a null `d_Ref<T>` with one of these functions throws a `d_Error_RefNull` exception.

Before a dereference operation is invoked, the referenced object may or may not be in the application cache. If it is not in memory, the database software must locate the object in the database, transfer it, and activate it in the application cache. It is entirely transparent to the application whether the object is already in the cache.

These functions may differ in how long the memory address they return is valid. The ODMG standard states the minimal duration, but the address may be valid longer in a given implementation. With all these functions, the address is not valid once the transaction completes (commits or aborts) or the referenced object is deleted.

If `operator->` or `operator*` is used with a particular `d_Ref<T>` instance, the address returned is no longer valid once the `d_Ref<T>` is deleted. Thus, if it is a local variable in a function, the address returned is not valid once this function returns and the `d_Ref<T>` instance is destroyed. Other `d_Ref<T>` instances that refer to the same instance may have returned the address. In this case, the address remains valid until all such references to the same instance are gone. Once all instances of `d_Ref<T>` that refer to a particular instance have been destroyed, the implementation is free to alter the memory address of the object in the cache, even before transaction commit.

If `ptr` is called to obtain the cache address of the instance, the address is valid until the transaction completes or the object is deleted. The deletion of all `d_Ref<T>` instances for a particular `T` instance does not allow the implementation to alter the memory address of the object if `ptr` had been called for one of the `d_Ref<T>` instances. Thus, the address returned by `ptr` is potentially valid longer than the address returned by `operator->` or `operator*`.

6.1.4 Copying a Reference

The copy constructors of `d_Ref<T>` and `d_Ref_Any` perform a shallow copy operation similar to that of a C++ pointer. When a `d_Ref<T>` is embedded within another object and the containing object is initialized or assigned, this shallow copy is performed.

```
class Foo : public d_Object {
        int             x;
        d_Ref<Bar>      bar;
//      other attributes
public:
                        Foo(const d_Ref<Bar> &);
                        // assume no copy constructor defined
};
```

If the application does not define a copy constructor, the compiler automatically generates one that performs member-wise initialization. When one `Foo` is initialized with another `Foo`, both `Foo` instances will contain references to the same `Bar`.

```
d_Database db; // assume this is initialized to open database

d_Ref<Bar>      b = new(&db, "Bar") Bar();
d_Ref<Foo>      foo = new(&db, "Foo") Foo(b);
d_Ref<Foo>      newFoo = new(&db, "Foo") Foo(*foo);
```

But to apply the operation to the object referenced by the d_Ref<T>, the application must specify the functionality explicitly.

```
Foo::Foo(const Foo &f)
: x(f.x)
{
    bar = new(&db, "Bar") Bar(*f.bar);
//   other initialization
}
```

With this definition of the Foo copy constructor, the two Foo instances will refer to different Bar instances. This approach is referred to as a *deep initialization* of Foo with respect to the Bar attribute. Note that Foo may have several different references, and a shallow versus deep decision should be made independently for each reference. The decision made for initialization should also be used for the assignment operation.

6.1.5 Equality

The equality and inequality operators (== and !=) are defined for both d_Ref<T> and d_Ref_Any. Any combination of the following types can be compared for equality.

- d_Ref<T>
- d_Ref<D> for any class D derived from T
- T *
- D * for any class D derived from T
- d_Ref_Any

The equality operator defined for d_Ref<T> can be used to compare a database reference to a null reference.

```
d_Ref<Employee> nullEmp;
if( emp == nullEmp ) ...
while( emp != nullEmp ){ ... }
```

Only a shallow equality operation is performed. Only the object identifier—and not the objects referenced—is compared for equality. This is referred to as *identity equality*. To compare the referenced objects for equality, the references should be dereferenced.

Suppose equality is defined for the `Foo` and `Bar` classes from the previous example. The equality of `Foo` can be based on the value of `bar` (both `bar`s refer to the same instance).

```
int operator==(const Foo &f, const Foo &g)// shallow equality
{
    return f.x == g.x && f.bar == g.bar;
}
```

Or it can be based on the values referenced by `bar`.

```
int operator==(const Foo &f, const Foo &g)// deep equality
{
    return f.x == g.x && *f.bar == *g.bar;
}
```

The application developer must decide which operation is appropriate. If `Foo` is a composite object and the `Bar` instance is a subobject, deep equality is probably appropriate.

In C++, the comparison operators (`<`, `<=`, `>`, and `>=`) can be used to compare pointer values. Semantically, these operations are meaningful for pointers only when referencing data in a contiguous region of memory, as is the case with a C++ array. These operators are not defined for instances of `d_Ref<T>`.

6.1.6 Transparent Access

When an object identifier is used to access an object, several forms of transparent access may occur. They provide many advantages to applications.

An instance of a class derived from `d_Object` can be transient or persistent. Instances of `d_Ref<T>` can be used in memory to reference either persistent or transient objects transparently. An instance of `d_Ref<T>` stored in the database can refer only to a persistent object. A transient object exists only during the execution of the current process and is accessible only in the current process address space. The reference to a transient object is of no use to another application. If a persistent object is written to the database and it contains a `d_Ref<T>` that refers to a transient object, the reference is set to a null value.

When a `d_Ref<T>` is dereferenced, the object is activated in the application cache if it has not yet been activated. The application does not need to know whether it was already in the cache. The application can simply traverse references on an as-needed basis, and the database takes care of activating objects as needed. Consider Figure 6.1. An application can initially access the object labeled C. It then can access object A and then access the collection of object references

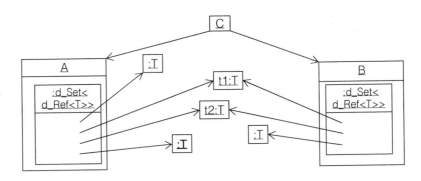

Figure 6.1 Navigation to common objects.

associated with object A. Next, the application can access each of the objects referenced, including the objects labeled t1 and t2. It then can access object B and access each of the objects referenced by the collection associated with object B. The objects labeled t1 and t2 would already be activated in the cache and would not need to be retrieved from the database. The application does not need to know whether objects t1 and t2 are already in the cache. The object database takes care of this cache management automatically. The application will have only one copy of each instance from the database.

This feature contributes to database transparency. The application is provided with the illusion that the entire database is part of the application process. To access objects, no visible calls to the database are necessary. They are hidden within the dereference operation. Application software appears to be accessing memory-resident objects.

Nearly all implementations provide a client-server architecture, in which the database server and client applications can reside on the same or different machines. Many implementations provide client-server heterogeneity; the machines can have different processor and operating system architectures. These implementations allow objects to be accessed on the client machine regardless of the machine architecture used on the server where the object is stored.

Some object databases allow object references to reference instances stored in any database within a database group. The database group provides the scope of uniqueness for the object identifiers. Thus, an object reference embedded within an object in database A may be referencing an object either in database A or some other database B or C in the same database group. In this way, objects can be accessed transparently across databases, as shown in Figure 6.2. This arrangement allows an object model to be stored either in the same database or partitioned among several databases without affecting the object model representation.

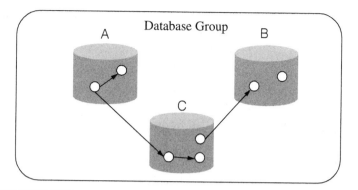

Figure 6.2 Referencing objects in other databases in the same database group.

Software can navigate among objects without needing to know or deal with the complexity of handling cross-database references. They are handled automatically by the database software.

Some object databases allow an object to be *migrated* from one database to another one in the same database group. One important issue is whether the object references are affected by the migration of an object. If the object identifier includes physical location information, the object references will need to be altered to reflect the new database location. Some implementations require that all the current references to the object be changed to reflect the new location. Others allow existing references to access the object transparently in its new database without the need to modify existing references.

6.1.7 Representation and Implementation

The physical representation and implementation of an object identifier is dependent on the database software architecture and differs among implementations. But the application is insulated from these differences. The identifier usually has several logical or physical components indicating the location of the object. The choice of representation affects the implementation of the swizzling operation that maps the object identifier to the address of the object in the application cache.

An identifier can contain any of the following components.

- Database identifier for the current database of the object
- Identifier of the database in which the object was originally created
- Segment identifier
- Page identifier
- Page offset of an object

An implementation will have a subset of these location components. The spectrum of possible representations spans from entirely logical to entirely physical.

An implementation can speed dereferencing by increasing the amount of information about the physical location of an object in an object reference. But it is more cumbersome to migrate an object, because all references to it must be changed. The references can be updated either all at once or individually when each reference is used to access the object. Immediate update of all references can result in significant overhead depending on the number of references.

The representation of an object reference in memory is often different from its database form. The data in a memory-resident d_Ref<T> instance is optimized to provide efficient access to the object if it is already activated. After the object is activated in the application cache, a goal is to attain a speed as close as possible to direct pointer traversal. Another goal implementations have is to minimize the size of the object reference in memory, to keep it as close to the size of a pointer as possible. Its size on disk has been a lesser concern. Essentially the desire is to have the same performance and storage overhead that applications are accustomed to for transient representations of a model.

Figure 6.3 depicts approaches used by vendors to map from an object identifier to an object. The object references are in the far left column, and the referenced objects are on right. The reference in row 1 is a pointer. Each of the other object references is a smart-pointer object, such as d_Ref<T>. The first approach uses a C++ pointer to represent the reference in memory. The other three approaches use an object reference class such as d_Ref<T> to represent the reference; they differ in the reference representation and the way the mapping to the referenced instance is performed. This enumeration of approaches is not intended to be complete nor exactly depict any specific vendor implementation. Some vendors support several approaches. Most of them are unwilling to reveal the exact details of their implementation; they consider it part of their intellectual property. They also consider it to be their competitive advantage, a frequent focal point in their marketing. Novices considering adoption of the technology are often left confused, because each vendor has a different approach and claims it is superior.

6.1.7.1 Pointers: Object Reference Approach 1

The first approach uses a standard C++ pointer to reference a persistent object. Several vendors allow pointers to be used in the database to reference objects. In memory the representation is a standard C++ pointer; on disk the object identifier is stored. Two different approaches are used for handling the pointer in memory. When an object containing a pointer is initially activated in the cache, the refer-

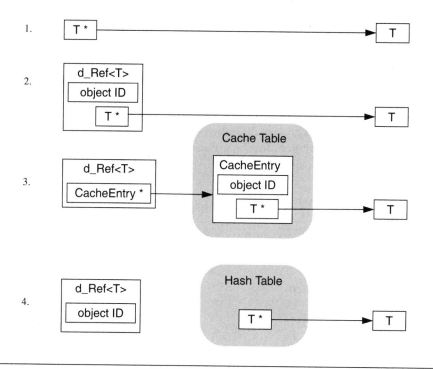

Figure 6.3 Approaches for mapping references to objects.

enced object can be activated immediately or deferred until the pointer is explicitly dereferenced.

With both approaches, the database implementation must first determine whether the object is already in the application cache. If it is, the pointer can be set to the memory address of the object. If the object is activated immediately, it must be brought into the cache, and the pointer is set to the address where the object is activated in the cache.

One drawback of activating the referenced object immediately is that the application may never actually access the object. Each object activated may contain references to other objects, which must also be activated. A recursive-like activation process unfolds, causing a potentially large number of objects to be activated even though they may never be needed by the application.

The activation of the referenced object can be deferred until the pointer is dereferenced. When an object containing a pointer is activated, the object referenced by the pointer is given an address that is not currently in the address space of the process. The pointer is initialized with this currently illegal address. When the application dereferences the pointer, the operating system catches the use of the illegal address. The database implementation handles this memory violation for the operating system and extends the virtual memory address space of the process to include the region of memory where the object is to reside. The object can then be activated in the cache at the chosen address, and the application can then access the object. Notice that this behavior is quite similar to what happens when an application has virtual memory pages that have been swapped out to disk. The database implementation assumes some control of the virtual memory management for the process and treats the database as an extension of the process address space.

6.1.7.2   Object Reference Approach 2

With approach 2, the reference contains both the object identifier and a pointer that holds the address of the object. The pointer is set when the first dereference operation is performed, and the object is activated in the cache. An object can be referenced from multiple places in the application cache. When the referenced object is activated, some implementations can initialize the pointers in all the object references; others set the address when the next dereference is performed. One drawback of this approach is that the size of the reference can be larger than desired.

6.1.7.3   Object Reference Approach 3

With approach 3 the object reference in memory contains a pointer to an entry in a table in memory that contains information about all the objects activated or referenced in the cache. An entry in the table contains things such as the persistent object identifier, the address of the object in the cache if it is activated, the lock status of the object, and other information. If the application cache has multiple references to the same object, each one refers to the same table entry. When the object is first activated, all the references automatically reference the pointer containing the object's cache address.

With this approach, the dereference operation uses the pointer in the reference to examine the cache table entry. The entry indicates whether the object is already activated and has an address. If it has not been activated, it can be retrieved from the database and its address placed in the cache table entry. Once the object is activated, the cache table entry has the address of the object in the cache.

6.1.7.4   Object Reference Approach 4

In the fourth approach the object reference always contains the object identifier that represents the persistent location of the object. Whenever a dereference operation is performed, this value is used to map to the address of the object in the cache. Hash table mechanisms are often used to perform this operation. The mapping from the object's identifier to the cache address is performed with every dereference. This technique uses more overhead than the other approaches. Approaches 3 and 4 provide the flexibility of allowing an object's cache address to change while the application is executing without affecting references. But the application must understand the duration of the validity of the pointers returned from these references.

6.2 Object Naming

A name can be associated with an object in the database. It consists of an ASCII string with a value determined by the application. The name, which must be unique within a database, provides a convenient means for a user to identify an object.

A name is assigned on an object instance basis. There is no requirement that all the instances of a class have a name or that every class have named instances; the application decides which objects should be named. A name can have arbitrary string values. A naming scheme should be devised that best serves the needs of the application.

Often, only a small number of the objects in the database have a name. Once the application has accessed an initial object by name, it traverses object references to find other related objects that are needed. The named object is often referred to as a *root object* or an *entry point object* because of its role in specifying a starting point for accessing a set of related objects.

The ODMG specification provides a single namespace per database. If a name is already in use and you try to assign it to another object, a d_Error_Name-NotUnique exception is thrown.

The set_object_name function in d_Database associates a name with an object. In ODMG-93 release 1.2, an object could have only a single name. If a call was made to assign a name to an object that already had a name, the old name was removed and replaced with the new name. But in ODMG release 2.0, an object can now have multiple names. Each call to set_object_name adds a new name to the object. You can remove all the names associated with an object by passing 0 as the value of the name argument. This technique should be used to delete all the names when an object is deleted, because in ODMG release 2.0 the names are not automatically removed. You can replace the name of an object by calling rename_object, passing the old and new names. A specific name can be removed from an object by passing the value 0 for the new name.

Object Query Language (OQL) allows a name to be used to access an object. To facilitate use of names in OQL, the name should consist only of alphanumeric characters, with no embedded spaces or operators. This practice allows the name to be parsed correctly in OQL. Converting a space to the underscore character "_" is one technique for handling multiword names.

The following example calls an application-written function, create-DBname, that creates a new string whose spaces and non-alphanumeric characters are converted to underscore characters. The code illustrates the naming of a Department instance.

```
d_Ref<Department>
createNamedDept(const char *name, const char *fax)
{
    d_Ref<Department>    dept;
    const char *oname = createDBname(name);
    dept = new(&db, "Department") Department(name, fax);
    db.set_object_name(dept, oname);
    delete oname;
    return dept;
}
```

The d_Database class has a function called lookup_object to map from an ASCII string to a d_Ref_Any. If there is no object with the specified name, a null d_Ref_Any is returned. The following code can be used to access a Department instance, given that its name is in a variable dname.

```
const char *oname = createDBname(dname);
d_Ref<Department> dept = db.lookup_object(oname);
delete oname;
```

If the database has an object with the name referenced by oname but the object is not of class Department or a class derived from Department, a d_Error_-TypeInvalid exception is thrown when dept is initialized. Thus, run-time type checking is performed when dept is initialized with the d_Ref_Any returned by lookup_object.

6.3 Identification Based on Attribute Values

One or more objects can be identified based on their attributes meeting specified value constraints, which are usually expressed in a query language such as OQL or SQL.

Applications may need to perform *associative access* of objects. With associative access, a set of value constraints is specified for attributes and may require that the value of an attribute in one object match the value of an attribute in another object. Associative access is the basis for all object identification, relationship traversal, and query access in a relational database.

Because object references are used to define and traverse relationships among objects, associative access tends to be used less often with an object database. But some applications still require associative access, and the object database implementations provide varying degrees of support. The ODMG OQL query language supports associative access.

6.3.1 Keys

An object can have one or more attributes whose values uniquely identify an instance. These attributes are referred to as the *key* for the object. Database users often access objects by providing a key value. The ODMG standard does not yet support keyed access, but many of the implementations support it.

A key can be simple or composite. A *simple* key consists of a single attribute, whereas a *composite* key consists of multiple attributes. A key can be either a *primary* key or *secondary* key. A primary key is known to be unique for a particular instance of a class. With a secondary key, multiple objects may have attributes equal to the values. A *foreign* key is an attribute used to contain the value of an object's primary key. It is similar to an object reference.

6.3.2 Indexes

An index can be placed on one or more attributes of a class to allow efficient lookup of instances based on their values for those attributes. There is an entry in the index for each instance of the class. Some implementations support an index only on a single attribute; others support multiple attributes. ODMG does not yet support the specification of indexes.

An index usually needs to compare the values of the attribute domain type. But the type may have been defined by the application, and the database software does not know how to compare its instances. Some implementations allow indexes only on primitive data types that the database software already understands. The database must compute a hash value or compare the values of two instances to implement the index mechanism. Some implementations provide a means for the database to gain access to operators defined for the application-defined domain type.

As the number of instances in a class increases, indexes associated with the class must grow. But the growth is usually less than linear, because the index often has an efficient representation to handle multiple instances with the same attribute value.

When the value of an indexed attribute is modified, the index must be updated to reflect the change. There is overhead involved in maintaining an index as the values of attributes change. An index can also take up a considerable amount of space if it contains a large number of entries. A trade-off exists between the performance of lookup versus update because of these index maintenance costs.

6.3.2.1   Hash Indexes

A *hash index* is efficient for locating objects with an attribute equal to a particular value. It relies on a *hash function* that produces a numerical value uniformly distributed over a range of integers. The number is then used as an index into an entry in the hash table. Multiple domain values often get mapped to the same hash entry, so an entry will have multiple values associated with it. Once the entry is located, a search of the entries with the same hash value is required to locate a specific value. A goal in defining a hash function is to have a uniform distribution of hash values for the domain values to minimize the number of domain values per hash value table entry. This approach reduces the time required to locate a specific domain value.

Two functions are needed for any domain used in a hash index. A hash function maps from the domain value to a numerical value used as the hash index. An equality function determines whether the domain value specified in the search equals the domain value in the hash index.

6.3.2.2   B-tree Indexes

A *B-tree index* is optimal either when the values sought lie within a range of values or when the application must perform an ordered traversal of the entries in the index. The performance of many B-tree implementations approaches that of hash indexes. B-trees are also useful when the definition of a suitable hash function is either too complex or impossible. Some implementations support only B-trees; others support both.

An `Employee` class can have an attribute that contains a unique identification number. This attribute could be a primary key, and a hash index would be the most appropriate index. It would also make sense to have a secondary key, perhaps a composite key consisting of the last name and first name of the employee. In this case, a B-tree would be an appropriate index.

6.3.2.3   Class Hierarchy Indexes

An object is an instance of a specific class, which resides in a class hierarchy and may have base or derived classes. An index can be placed on one or more attributes of the class. But there may be instances of classes that are derived from the indexed class. These instances are also considered instances of the indexed class. Should the index contain instances of all classes derived from the indexed class or only instances of the specific class that is indexed? That depends on the types of application requests that are made. A class hierarchy index includes the instances of all derived classes.

6.4 Summary and Comparison with Other Databases

We have discussed several approaches for identifying objects in an object database, including identifiers, names, and attribute value constraints. An object identifier is the most efficient means of accessing an object, and specifying a constraint on attribute values is the least efficient. The database vendors have put a lot of effort into optimizing the access of an object via its identifier. This approach allows applications to use a database reference, d_Ref<T>, to navigate efficiently from one object to another. Furthermore, these references are polymorphic, something that is considered essential in many object designs.

When a user needs to identify a specific object, either a name or a constraint on attribute values is specified. Entities often have attributes that contain identifiers used in the real world to identify instances. During analysis you should determine which objects must be identified directly by users. Then you can use object names and attribute indexes to provide efficient access. Using one identification mechanism does not preclude the use of another; it is possible to use all three approaches. The choice depends on the application and user access patterns.

The identification mechanisms provided by object databases are a superset of those offered by other database technologies. Network databases support *links*, which are somewhat similar to object identifiers. But links often do not support distributed access, and their use is more procedural. They also do not provide the level of database access transparency of an object database.

Relational databases are based on support of associative access. They do not support identifiers or names. The rows of a table in ANSI SQL-92 do not have identifiers, although some products provide a row identifier used to reference a particular row. One or more columns can serve as a primary key for a table, and an index is often placed on the primary key to provide efficient lookup of a row.

An application often has a class that has no associated real-world identifier. With a relational database, you must generate an identifier. With an object database, each object automatically receives an object identifier and you need not generate artificial ones.

The columns of a primary key in a relational database are not treated any differently from other columns in a table, and their values can be altered at any time. Rules and guidelines can stipulate that the primary key not be changed, but users with direct SQL access can change it. Views and security mechanisms must be used to prevent such alteration.

Tables that need to reference a row can contain a foreign key, which can be joined with the primary key to establish a relationship among the tables. The value of foreign key can be used to look up a row in many different tables. But when the join is performed, a specific table must be used. Thus, relational databases do not provide a direct mechanism to support polymorphic references. This function must be emulated by the application in a less efficient manner. This same issue also prevents efficient transparent referencing of rows across multiple databases. Object databases provide much more flexibility in referencing objects in the database.

Chapter 7
Collections

A collection is used to model a set of values of some type. Collections are indispensable in object designs and serve many roles in an object database. They are part of the foundation for the definition of the application's object model and are used to represent relationships among objects in the database. They are also used to return results from a query.

There are many different kinds of collections, each providing its own characteristics. Collections vary in their support for duplicate values, ordering of elements, access of specific values, and iteration capabilities. Common collections include sets, bags, lists, arrays, and dictionaries. There are many operations that all collections support, although their performance may differ.

Operations are provided to insert and remove elements from a collection. Some collections provide operations to determine whether a specific value is an element. Every collection instance has a *cardinality*, which is the number of elements it contains.

An *iterator* object is used to iterate over the elements of a collection. Depending on the collection, an iterator may support forward, backward, and random access of elements. Once an iterator is associated with a collection, it either references a current element or is in an "end-of-iteration" state. Because collections and iterators support elements of a user-specified type, the `template` feature of C++ is used.

When the ODMG began its standardization efforts in 1992, C++ did not have a standard set of collection classes. Many vendors provided collection class libraries, but none was considered the standard in the industry. Each object database vendor had its own proprietary collection classes optimized for persistence. The ODMG defined a set of collection classes, based on the experiences of its members.

In 1994, the C++ standards committee adopted the Standard Template Library (STL). ODMG had already released its ODMG-93 release 1.1 specification. So the ODMG has its own set of collections, which are different from the STL collections. ODMG must also support the Smalltalk and Java languages, and the ODMG collections are meant to be common across the languages. STL is C++-specific, and that prevents it from being the common collections library within the ODMG object model. But STL will become the dominant collection library in the C++ market, and object database vendors have already begun supporting it.

The ODMG C++ interface is gradually including support for STL. In release 1.2, the ODMG iterator class was enhanced to support the STL constant bidirectional iterator interface. The ODMG-93 base class d_Collection was also enhanced to support the begin and end operations found in all STL collections. With these enhancements, STL algorithms can work with ODMG collections. Essentially, the ODMG collections are "iterator-compatible" with STL. This is consistent with the STL design philosophy. With ODMG release 2.0, a significant number of the STL collections are supported. They are listed in the next section.

This chapter discusses the ODMG collection and iterator interfaces. It examines the role played by named collections in the ODMG interface. The use of STL in the ODMG standard is covered, and there is some discussion about the impact of object database implementations on the efficient use of collections. The chapter concludes by explaining how to emulate collections when you're using a relational database.

7.1 ODMG Collections and Iterators

The ODMG collection classes are used to specify the application's object model. They are parameterized based on the type of element they contain. Each of the collection classes is derived from the abstract base class d_Collection<T>. The operations supported by all collection types are defined in the base class d_Collection<T>.

Table 7.1 defines several characteristics of the ODMG collections. Figure 7.1 shows the inheritance relationships among the collections. A complete definition is provided in Appendix B. The d_Dictionary<K,V> class was added in ODMG release 2.0. The elements of the d_List<T> and d_Varray<T> collections are ordered according to their relative position and not their values. The iter-

Collection	Ordered	Allows Duplicates
d_Set<T>		
d_Dictionary<K,V>		
d_Bag<T>		✔
d_List<T>	✔	✔
d_Varray<T>	✔	✔

Table 7.1 ODMG collections.

ator class d_Iterator<T> is defined in the ODMG interface and is used for all collection classes.

The base class d_Collection<T> is derived from d_Object so that a collection can be a stand-alone persistent object in the database. Such a collection has an object identifier and can be referenced in the database. A collection can also be embedded as an attribute of a persistent class. This kind of collection serves as a domain, does not have an object identifier, and cannot be directly referenced. Applications can also have transient collection instances.

ODMG 2.0 supports a subset of the STL collections. These collections are derived from d_Object and are persistence-capable. Their names consist of the ODMG prefix d_ followed by the STL name. The following collections are supported:

- d_set<T>
- d_multiset<T> (similar to a bag)
- d_vector<T> (similar to an array)
- d_list<T>
- d_map<K,V>
- d_multimap<K,V>

Their interfaces are compliant with the STL specification except that they do not support the STL allocator template argument. This is because the object database implementation provides the cache management of the collection, and it can never be overridden by an application. The ODMG 2.0 collections include the d_Object interface.

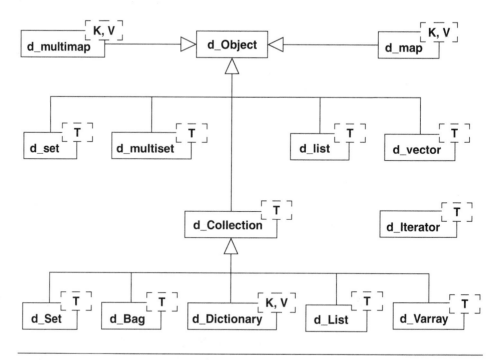

Figure 7.1 Inheritance of collections.

7.1.1 Sets

The ODMG d_Set<T> template class represents a set of elements of type T. A *set* is an unordered collection of elements that has no duplicate values. If a set of integers contains the values (1, 2, 5), inserting a value of 2 into the set will result in the same three elements (1, 2, 5). When a value is inserted into a set, the implementation must determine whether the value is already an element, something that sets are efficient at determining. A set must also be able to determine whether two values of the element type are equal. Thus, the equality operator must be defined for the element type and must be available to the set implementation.

7.1.2 Bags

The ODMG standard has a class d_Bag<T> that supports the bag abstraction. A *bag* is an unordered collection that allows duplicate values. Given the bag of integers (1, 2, 5), a new value of 2 can be added and the bag will contain (1, 2, 5, 2).

7.1.3 Lists

ODMG provides a class `d_List<T>` to support the list abstraction. A *list* is an ordered collection of elements that allows duplicate values. Each element in a list has an index, which determines its relative position. Operations are provided to insert new elements at relative positions within the list. An index operation is provided to access the *i*th element of a list.

7.1.4 Arrays

An *array* is another type of collection supported by object databases. Whereas the arrays of C++ are of fixed length, a variable-length array is usually provided. ODMG defines the class `d_Varray<T>` to support a variable-length array.

Arrays also provide an index operation to access the *i*th element of the array. It usually performs this operation faster than a list does; a list excels at insertion and removal of elements at arbitrary positions. Most implementations also support C++ arrays. But there may be limitations, such as allowing only an array with a single dimension or supporting only a limited set of element types.

7.1.5 Dictionaries

Another collection applications find useful is a *dictionary*, also called a *map* or *associative array*. The `d_Dictionary<K,V>` dictionary class was introduced in ODMG 2.0. A dictionary maps from a key value of one type to a value of another type. Because implementations may or may not allow duplicate key values, dictionaries are often based on hashing techniques or data structures that take advantage of an ordering of the key values. Thus, the key type often must provide a hash function or a function to compare the values of instances. Some dictionaries maintain the keys in order, allowing ordered iteration. A dictionary commonly found in object models has a key of string type that is used to look up a value of some other type, often a reference to an object.

7.1.6 ODMG Collection Element Types

The elements of a collection can be of any type. Domain types are usually supported: primitive literals (`int`, `float`), structures and abstract data type objects, and references (`d_Ref<T>`) to objects. Some implementations restrict element types. Given an object of type `T`, for example, the collection element type may need to be a reference (`d_Ref<T>`) to an instance of the type instead of just an instance of the type `T`. A level of indirection is necessary.

It is common for a collection to contain object references. Suppose a persistent collection contains elements of type d_Ref<T>. During a transaction it may contain references to both transient and persistent instances of T. But only the references to persistent instances can be stored in the database. The ODMG standard does not define what happens to such a collection when a transaction commits. Applications should avoid this situation.

In ODMG implementations, every type T used as a collection element type must support the following operations:

```
class T {
public:
                                T();
                                T(const T &);
                                ~T();
            T &                 operator=(const T &);
friend      int                 operator==(const T &, const T &);
};
```

Except for the equality operator, these functions are the canonical form that all types should support. These functions should be efficient, because they have a direct impact on the performance of collections containing elements of the type.

Many object designs use polymorphism and must store a collection of objects that are of some type derived from a common base class B. The element type should be a reference to the base class B (d_Ref<B>). The actual objects referenced in the collection can be instances of any class publicly derived from B.

7.2 Common Collection Operations

Several operations are common to all types of collections. They are specified in the ODMG d_Collection<T> class. In addition to maintaining the elements of a collection, these operations copy, assign, and test the equality of a collection.

7.2.1 Maintaining the Elements of a Collection

The abstract base class d_Collection<T> provides functions to maintain the elements of a collection. The cardinality function determines the number of elements in a collection. The contains_element function determines whether a value is in the collection. For this function to work, the element type T must provide operator==.

The insert_element function inserts a value into a collection. If the collection is a d_Set<T> that already contains the value, no element is added.

Because d_Bag<T> and d_Set<T> are unordered collections, the new element is not placed at any specific position. A d_List<T> places the new value at the end of the list. Similarly, with a d_Varray<T>, the array size is increased by 1 and the value is placed at the new last position.

The remove_element function removes one element of the specified value, if one exists. Because the d_Bag<T>, d_List<T>, and d_Varray<T> collections allow duplicate values, the element removed is the first one that would be accessed if a forward iteration were being performed. Whenever an element of type T is removed, the destructor is called. If the element type is d_Ref<T>, only the destructor for d_Ref<T> is called and not the destructor for the referenced T instance. The application must remove the T instance if necessary. An overloaded function remove_all removes either all the elements or all the elements equal to a specified value.

When a collection is modified, the mark_modified function is called automatically. This includes the insert_element and remove_element functions described earlier. This action may affect concurrency, because only one transaction at a time can modify a collection.

7.2.2 Collection Copy and Assignment

Each collection class supports the C++ canonical form. The null constructor initializes a collection with zero elements. The destructor destroys the collection object and invokes the destructor for each element, if one exists for the element type.

The copy constructor initializes a new collection using the collection passed as the initialization argument. Every element of type T is copied from the existing collection, invoking the copy constructor of T. Once the copy is complete, each collection has its own copy of each element. But note that if the element type is d_Ref<T>, both collections will be referring to the same T instances. For unordered collections, iteration of the two collections may find the elements in a different order. But the element order is preserved for ordered collections.

When one collection is assigned to another, the destructor is called for each original element of the target collection and the copy constructor is called to initialize each new element.

Copying and assigning collections can be expensive, especially in database applications in which these operations are potentially quite large. The performance depends largely on the cardinality. But it also depends on the element type's efficiency in performing initialization, copying, and destruction, which are applied to each element.

7.2.3 Collection Equality

The equality and inequality operators (== and !=) are defined in the base class d_Collection<T>. Their semantics depend on the type of collections compared. The two collections must have the same element type, but they need not be the same type of collection. For example, it is possible to test the equality of a d_List<T> and a d_Set<T>.

Two collections cannot be equal if they have different cardinalities. The following discussions assume that this condition is evaluated. When an ordered collection (d_List or d_Array) is compared for equality with an unordered collection (d_Set or d_Bag), both collections are treated as unordered. But for ordered collections, the order matters.

Two d_Set<T> instances A and B are equal if they have the same cardinality and if every element in A is equal to an element in B. The d_Bag<T>, d_List<T>, and d_Varray<T> collection types allow for duplicate elements. When an instance B of one of these classes is compared for equality with an instance A of d_Set<T>, if B contains any duplicate element values then B is not equal to A. For A and B to be equal, each element in the set A must be equal to an element in B.

Instances A and B of type d_Bag<T> are equal if they have the same cardinality and if both A and B have the same number of occurrences of each unique value in A. When an instance A of type d_Bag<T> is compared for equality with a collection B of type d_List<T> or d_Varray<T>, A and B must have the same number of occurrences of each unique value in A. Because A is unordered, the order of the elements in B does not affect their equality.

When instances A and B of type d_List<T> or d_Varray<T> are compared for equality, A and B are equal only if they have the same cardinality and if the elements at each position in A and B are equal.

7.3 Iteration

The ODMG d_Iterator<T> class is used to iterate over all the collections. It supports the canonical form; you can initialize an instance with another iterator and perform iterator assignment. The equality of two iterators can also be evaluated.

With ODMG-93 release 1.2, the d_Iterator<T> class supports the STL specification of a constant bidirectional iterator. A constant iterator does not allow direct modification of the collection elements. Both operator++ and operator-- are supported by d_Iterator<T> in their prefix and postfix forms to provide both forward and backward iteration. However, the d_Set<T> and

d_Bag<T> collections do not support backward iteration; a d_Error_-
IteratorNotBackward exception object is thrown.

Several styles of iteration are supported. A member function of class
Department called printProjects is defined in the following code
repeatedly, once for each style of iteration. Department contains a member
projects of type d_List<d_Ref<Project>>. The first two styles presented
are based on the original ODMG-93 specification. The latter two styles conform
to the ODMG-93 release 1.2, 2.0, and STL specifications.

The create_iterator function returns an iterator positioned at the first
element (if the collection has an element). The advance member function
positions the iterator at the next element. The not_done member function returns
true if iteration is not complete.

```
void
Department::printProjects(ostream &os)
{
    d_Ref<Project>        proj;
    d_Iterator<d_Ref<Project> >      pi;

    for( pi = projects.create_iterator(); pi.not_done();
                                        pi.advance() ){
        proj = pi.get_element();
        os << proj->name << endl;
    }
}
```

The get_element function accesses the current element of iteration.

The next member function of d_Iterator<T> dereferences the iterator,
advances the iterator, and tests for the end of iteration, all in a single call. It
returns via a reference parameter the value of the element that was current before
the call to next. It returns true if there is a current element; otherwise, it returns
false.

```
void
Department::printProjects(ostream &os)
{
    d_Ref<Project>        proj;
    d_Iterator<d_Ref<Project> >pi;

    pi = projects.create_iterator();
    while( pi.next(proj) ){
        os << proj->name << endl;
    }
}
```

The `get_element` function should not be used in conjunction with the `next` function. After the return from `next`, the iterator is positioned at the next element, if there is one. Within the while loop, the parameter passed to `next` (`proj` here) should be used to reference the current element of iteration. If a call is made to `get_element` or `operator*` within the loop, the element returned is the element positioned after the element returned by the call to `next`. When the loop is on the last element of iteration, a `d_Error_IteratorExhausted` exception is thrown.

The following implementation of the `printProjects` member function uses an STL style of iteration. The `begin` member function defined in `d_Collection<T>` returns an iterator positioned at the first element of the collection (if it has an element). The `end` member function returns an iterator positioned past the last element. An iterator advanced past the last element is equal to the iterator returned by `end`. The `begin` and `end` member functions were added to `d_Collection<T>` to provide STL compatibility.

```
void
Department::printProjects(ostream &os)
{
    d_Iterator<d_Ref<Project> >      pi;
    d_Iterator<d_Ref<Project> >      pe;

    for( pi = projects.begin(), pe = projects.end();
            pi != pe; ++pi){
        os << (*pi)->name << endl;
    }
}
```

The `operator*` dereference operation is overloaded in `d_Iterator<T>` to access the current element of iteration.

The final style of iteration uses STL algorithms, in particular the `for_each` algorithm. It iterates from an iterator positioned at a starting element until it reaches a second iterator indicating the end of iteration. Each element encountered during iteration is passed as an argument to a function that was specified in the call to `for_each`.

```
void
printName(d_Ref<Project> proj)
{
    cout << proj->name << endl;
}

void
```

```
Department::printProjects(ostream &os)
{
    for_each(projects.begin(), projects.end(), printName);
}
```

7.4 Operations Specific to the Collection Type

Collections usually have some operations that are specific to their abstraction. This section discussions some of the operations specific to each ODMG collection class.

7.4.1 Subsets and Supersets

A set A is a *subset* of another set B if every element of A is also an element of B. Set A could be a subset of B and also be equal to B (A = B). B would be called a *superset* of A. If A is a subset of B but is not equal to B, then A is called a *proper subset* of B. In this case, B is called a *proper superset* of A. Sets A and B are equal only if every element in A is an element in B and every element in B is an element in A.

The d_Set<T> class provides functions to determine whether two sets are (proper) subsets of one another, (proper) supersets of one another, or equal. These functions return a Boolean value of true or false depending on the relationship between the two sets.

7.4.2 Set Operations

Both the d_Set<T> and d_Bag<T> classes support the following set operations using the corresponding operators:

- union +
- intersection *
- difference –

The d_Set<T> class allows these operations to be applied to d_Set<T> instances, and the d_Bag<T> class supports the operations on d_Bag<T> instances. If an application wants to perform an operation on a d_Set<T> and a d_Bag<T> instance, the d_Set<T> instance should first be converted to a d_Bag<T>. The following three paragraphs formally define these operations.

The *union* of sets A and B is a set that contains all the values that are in either A or B. Because a set has no duplicates, the union of A and B has only a single element for each value in A or B. If A and B are bags, the number of elements in their union with a given value is the sum of the number of elements with the value in A and the number of elements with the value in B.

The *intersection* of sets A and B is a set that contains all the values that are in both A and B. Two sets A and B are *disjoint* if they have no elements in common. If A and B are bags, the number of elements in the intersection of A and B with a given value v is the minimum of the number of values of v in A and B. For example, if A and B are bags of integers and the value 7 occurs twice in A and three times in B, the intersection of A and B would have two elements with the value 7.

The *difference* of sets A and B, also called the *complement* of A relative to B, denoted A − B, is the set of all values in A that are not in B. If A and B are bags, for each value v in A, the number of values v in A − B is the number of values of v in A minus the number of values of v in B. Given A = {1,2,2,2,3,3} and B = {1,2,2,3,3,3,4}, then A − B = {2}.

Each of these set operations has five associated C++ functions; they differ in their interface and means of returning the result set. Some of them place the result in one of the original set parameters; others create a new set. Two functions use the operator corresponding to the set operation, and the others use a name. Appendix B defines each function in detail.

7.4.3 d_List<T> and d_Varray<T> Operations

Both the d_List<T> and d_Varray<T> classes support indexed access to their elements. The beginning index value is 0, following the convention of C and C++. You can establish the size of a single-dimension d_Varray<T> instance at initialization or by passing a new size to the function resize. The current size of an array can be obtained by a call to cardinality.

Functions are available to retrieve, replace, and remove an element at a given position. If the index is out of range, a d_Error_PositionOutOfRange exception object is thrown. The insert_element function inherited from d_Collection<T> places the new element at the end of the collection.

The d_List<T> collection provides functions to insert an element at the first or last position or before or after a given position in the list. You can also retrieve or remove the first element and retrieve or remove the last element.

The d_List<T> collection also provides functions to combine the elements of two lists. They vary in definition depending on whether the result replaces one of the original lists or a new list is created. The functions concat and operator+ create a new list that contains the elements of the left operand list followed by the elements of the right operand list. The append and operator+= member functions append the elements of a list operand at the end of a list object. The latter two functions are more efficient, because the result is placed in the list object used to invoke the operation, avoiding the need to return a new list object by value. But if the application does not want to alter the original list, it must use functions that return a list by value.

7.5 **Named Collections and Extents**

Applications often need to access all the instances of a class. This section discusses the two primary approaches used for this purpose.

The ODMG-93 release 1.2 specification requires maintenance of a *named collection* that contains a reference to each instance. Instances need not be referenced in a named collection if the application chooses not to refer to them. A collection can contain references to all the instances or any subset of them. The name of the collection is also arbitrary. The application is responsible for maintaining the named collection. Each time an instance is created or deleted, collections may need to be modified.

The set of all persistent instances of a class is called its *extent*. Many implementations automatically maintain extents. When a transaction creates or deletes instances they are automatically placed in or removed from the class extent. An extent is similar to a table in a relational database. ODMG release 2.0 supports extents.

7.5.1 **Named Collections**

The maintenance of a named collection could be handled in the class constructor and destructor if all instances are to be referenced, as the following example illustrates.

A collection named Depts can be used to contain a reference to each Department instance. The Department constructor would insert a reference into the collection, and the destructor would remove the reference. The Department class would include the following functionality.

```
class Department : public d_Object {
public:
static   d_Ref<d_Set<d_Ref<Department> > > depts();

                              Department(const char *n);
                              ~Department();
// other public attributes

private:
static   const char * const  depts_name;
```

```
static   d_Ref<d_Set<d_Ref<Department> > > _depts;

// other private attributes
};
```

The static member _depts is a reference to a collection named Depts, which contains a reference to each Department instance. When the database is first created, a create_depts function should be called once by an application to create this named collection. A depts function is then called by applications to access this collection.

```
const char * const Department::depts_name = "Depts";
d_Ref<d_Set<d_Ref<Department> > > _depts;

d_Ref<d_Set<d_Ref<Department> > >
Department::depts()
{
    if( _depts.is_null() ) // not accessed yet
        _depts = db.lookup_object(extent_name);

    if( _depts.is_null() ){ // has not been created in DB yet
        _depts = new(&db) d_Set<d_Ref<Department> >;
        db.set_object_name(_depts, depts_name);
    }
    return _depts;
}
```

Each of the Department constructors inserts a reference to its instance into the named collection, and the destructor removes the reference from the collection.

```
Department::Department(const char *n)
: name(n)
{
    depts()->insert_element(this);
//  other initialization
}

Department::~Department()
{
    depts()->remove_element(this);
//  other destructor code
}
```

This approach assumes that all instances are persistent, something that may not always be the case. An application may have a mixture of both persistent and transient instances of a class. Only the application knows which instances are which and where a particular instance should be inserted. In this case, the software that maintains the named collections should not reside in the constructors and destructor of the class.

In this example, a single collection contains a reference for every instance of Department. But it is up to the application to decide which objects should be grouped in a particular collection. An instance can be referenced in as many collections as needed.

7.5.2 Extents

ODMG release 2.0 includes support for extents. Conceptually, an extent for a class T is similar to a d_Set<d_Ref<T>>. It is an unordered collection that contains a reference for each instance of T. An instance of d_Extent<T> is not persistent; it provides an interface to access the persistent instances of T by means of iterators. Instances in the extent that satisfy query constraints, expressed in OQL, can be selected.

An application that wishes to access all the instances in the database of Person and its subclasses would declare the following variable:

```
d_Database *dbp; // assume this references an open database

d_Extent<Person>    Persons(dbp);
```

This variable is then used to access all the Person instances. The d_Extent constructor has a second argument of type d_Boolean that specifies whether to include instances of subclasses. It has a default value of d_True. If the application does not want instances of subclasses to be included, the declaration should be specified as follows:

```
d_Extent<Person>    Persons(dbp, d_False);
```

The extent is maintained automatically by the database, so no insert or remove operations are provided to an application. Whenever instances are created or deleted, the database updates the extent appropriately. Because the application is not directly manipulating the extent, more concurrency can be provided than can be achieved with named collections.

An extent is often maintained for each class in the database. Some instances may never be accessed via their extent, so some implementations let the application specify that only the extents of a subset of the classes be maintained. Avoiding the overhead of extent maintenance can improve performance.

Classes participate in inheritance relationships. Instances are in the extent for their most specific derived class. Some implementations can also place an instance in a base class extent. This arrangement allows the instances of all classes derived from a base class to be accessible via a single extent.

7.6   Other Collection Operations and Considerations

ODMG implementations often provide a superset of the functionality specified in the standard. This is referred to as the *superset rule*. Each vendor had its own collection classes before the ODMG specification. These classes may include some functionality specific to the capabilities of the vendor's product. The vendors will probably continue to support their existing collections and will probably enhance their ODMG class implementation to incorporate the proprietary capabilities. This section describes features that are not part of the ODMG standard but are commonly found in existing implementations.

7.6.1   Access of Referenced Objects

It is common to have a collection containing elements of type d_Ref<T>. When a collection is activated in an application cache, usually only the d_Ref<T> instances are activated and not the objects they reference. But applications usually need to access the referenced T instances.

An application can iterate over a collection and dereference each d_Ref<T> element one at a time. But this approach results in an object-at-a-time activation and transfer of T instances. It can be inefficient and cause excessive client-server traffic. Some implementations let you activate all the referenced T instances together. This technique is more efficient when most of the referenced objects are accessed, reducing transfer overhead and allowing better allocation of cache memory.

7.6.2   Closure Access

An extension to the approach described above (accessing all the objects referenced by a collection) is the support of a *closure* operation, in which all the objects referenced by a particular instance are activated when it is activated. In Figure 7.2, each instance has been given a label to be used in the following discussion. When a1 is activated, b1–b7 would also be activated if a closure operation is performed. Implementations allow you to dereference a specific number of levels; activating b1–b7 would be a single-level closure. In a *complete closure*, all objects reachable via navigation are activated. Applications accessing a composite object often use this facility to access all its subobjects. In the figure a complete closure would activate b1–b7 and c1–c4.

Many implementations that support closure operations perform it on all the references encountered, but it would be useful to activate only a subset of the referenced objects. For example, the application may want only the first collection processed, activating b1–b3. A *path query* is another mechanism that can be used to access a collection of related objects. It specifies a query predicate that has a *path expression* that navigates among a set of object relationships to reach the objects of interest. Part II covers path expressions in more detail.

7.6.3 The Cardinality Magnitude

A collection may contain only a few elements, or it may serve as the extent of a class, containing an element for every instance of T. The cardinalities of collections in the database may vary by many orders of magnitude. You must be careful when operating on very large collections. In some circumstances the collection may have more elements than can fit in the application cache, and the transfer overhead can be prohibitive.

Collection interfaces often give the illusion that all the collection elements are in the cache. But just because the collection is activated in the application cache does not imply that all the elements are also resident. Their activation may be initiated on an as-needed basis. This may occur in logical or physical units, depending on the implementation's underlying cache management and transfer strategies.

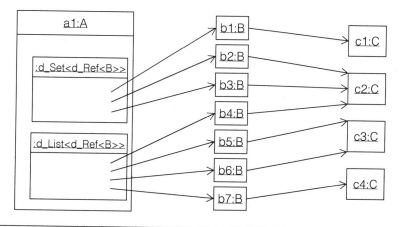

Figure 7.2 Closure.

Some implementations never instantiate a collection in the client cache. The application is merely manipulating a proxy object that sends each operation to the server. These implementations incur minimal activation and deactivation overhead, because the actual collection remains in the server. But individual operations on the collection proxy object require more client-server communication than in implementations that activate the collections and perform the operations locally. There is a cost trade-off between the two approaches. If the application will be performing many operations and the collection is relatively small, activation is more efficient.

Some vendors decided that the interface and implementation of a collection optimized for a small number of elements should be different from one optimized for a very large number of elements. They provide different collections optimized for different cardinalities. The application schema designer must select an appropriate collection based on its estimated size.

Other vendors provide a single interface but different underlying implementations depending on the cardinality. The implementation is entirely hidden behind the collection interface. The collection adapts and changes to an appropriate representation as the collection cardinality changes.

7.6.4 Stand-alone versus Embedded Collections

Implementations may bring all the elements of a collection into the application cache when it is activated in the cache. Depending on the size of the collection, this arrangement can cause both *cache consumption* and *transfer latency.*

Suppose there is a class C that contains a very large set of references to T instances.

```
class C : public d_Object {
        d_Set<d_Ref<T> >   setOfT;
};
```

In many implementations the activation of a C instance also activates the collection and all its references to T instances. The size of the set will affect the time required to activate the C instance.

Only a few applications may need to access the embedded collection, and the others may not want to incur the overhead. An alternative design is for C to contain only a reference to the collection.

```
class C : public d_Object {
        d_Ref<d_Set<d_Ref<T> > > refSetOfT;
};
```

This technique allows a C instance to be accessed without the performance impact of activating the collection. Applications that need to access the collection can explicitly dereference refSetOfT. The collection is probably directly associated with the C instance, especially if it was originally embedded in C. In that case, the application must explicitly delete the collection in the C destructor or it will remain in the database with no references to it if the C instance is deleted. C++ object databases vary in whether they support garbage collection, and the ODMG standard does not require its support.

7.6.5   Collection Modifications

When an application modifies a collection object via one of its supplied operations, the collection operation calls mark_modified. This call is necessary so that the database implementation can acquire a write lock and note that the object has changed. The application need not explicitly call mark_modified for the collection.

There are two situations to consider. If the collection object is stand-alone, its call to mark_modified ensures that the object is saved at transaction commit. But if the collection is embedded inside a containing object, the containing object must have its mark_modified function called. ODMG does not require that the database implementation perform this automatically. If the collection is an embedded member of a persistent instance, the application must call the mark_modified of the containing instance. If all modifications to embedded collections are made by member functions of the containing class, they can make the call to mark_modified.

7.6.6   Collection Optimizations

Object databases have been optimized to provide efficient collection storage and access. In many cases, the collection elements are stored contiguously on disk, minimizing disk transfers and attaining more effective cache use. The collection and its elements can also be transferred between caches more efficiently in bulk form rather than one element at a time.

An ordered collection can have a representation that maintains its ordering on disk, avoiding the need to order the elements when they are activated. With a large collection, this approach can result in substantial savings in overhead.

7.6.7 Collection Indexes

Some implementations let you place an index on a collection. The index contains an entry for each element, allowing an application to find all the elements having a particular value. Normally an index is associated with a class and has an entry for every instance. A collection index potentially has a much smaller cardinality than a class index.

The collection element type may be either a primitive domain or a reference to an instance of a class. For a collection that contains references, such as d_Set<d_Ref<Employee>>, the index is usually placed on attributes of the referenced object, such as Employee. For example, an application may want to find all employees in the collection whose city of residence is equal to "New Albany." A collection index on the city attribute allows efficient access, avoiding the cost of performing a linear search.

If the index is placed on instances that are referenced by the collection, updates to the instances are slower because of index maintenance costs. The index also introduces space overhead.

7.6.8 Cursors

An application using a query mechanism such as OQL usually receives a collection containing the result of a query. The collection is instantiated in the application cache. However, a query may return a very large number of values; the complete set may not even fit in the application cache. And the application may only want to iterate through the collection sequentially and read each element once. In these circumstances it is not possible or not efficient to represent the result by an instantiated collection in the application cache.

A *cursor* provides an alternative. It is essentially an iterator; its interface is quite similar. A cursor iterates over a virtual collection that is not directly instantiated in the application cache. The collection also may not exist in the database cache but simply consist of the result values of a query.

A cursor often allows an application to retrieve groups of values, promoting efficient transfer from the database server. An application can indicate the number of values to retrieve at one time. When more values are fetched, implementations often deactivate the previous batch. The application can iterate over a potentially huge set of values without consuming much of the application cache.

7.7 Implementing Collections in Relational Databases

Most commercial relational databases follow the rule of first-normal form and do not allow a column to contain a non-atomic type. A collection is considered non-atomic and is not supported as a column data type.

7.7.1 Schema Representation

To represent a collection in a relational data model, a table is used that has a separate row for each element. At a minimum, the table must contain columns for the collection identifier and the collection element value. If the element is an aggregate of several values, a column is required for each value. An object with a collection attribute must have a column in its table containing a collection identifier, which is then joined with the table containing the collection elements. The table could store many collections if they have the same element type.

If the collection is ordered, an attribute is needed to establish the ordering. If there are many insertions and deletions into the collection, maintenance of the ordering attribute can be cumbersome and inefficient.

By default, the rows associated with a collection may be dispersed over many disk blocks in the database, creating more disk transfers and increasing cache consumption in the database server. Some relational databases let you define a *cluster* that gathers all the rows in a table that have the same value for a column. Establishing a cluster based on the collection identifier in the collection table allows the elements to be located together in the database.

7.7.2 Indexes

When a collection is represented in a table, an index is usually placed on the column containing the collection identifier. This arrangement allows efficient access of the collection elements. But maintaining an index is expensive in storage space and there is update overhead when row-level changes are made to an indexed column.

An application may need to index the element value. If it is modeling a set that has no duplicates, a unique index placed on both the collection identifier and the element value prevents insertion of duplicate values. It also allows the database to determine efficiently whether a value is in the set.

7.7.3 Application Representation

A relational database does not know about the collections in the application object model. Each element resides in a separate row. If the application needs to instantiate the collection, each element row must be inserted into the in-memory representation of the collection. These insertions involve extra overhead not required with most object databases.

Retrieving an ordered collection from a relational database requires additional overhead. The ordering must be established for the in-memory collection with each application that accesses the collection. You can use the `order by` clause in SQL to access the collection so that the rows are delivered to the application in sorted order. Or the application can perform the ordering when the collection is instantiated and populated. In either case, you incur sorting overhead that can be avoided with an object database.

Propagating updates of a collection object back to the database is cumbersome. The application could alter the database representation each time a modification is made to the collection object in memory. Or all the changes could be performed at transaction commit. Either the application must maintain a list of all changes to be made, or the existing database collection must be removed and recreated. Neither approach is simple or efficient.

7.8 Collection Summary

Collections are a fundamental modeling construct applications use. With a C++ object database, they are also components of the schema definition. Consequently, the implementation can optimize its representation in the database. A knowledge of collection semantics such as ordering helps you to provide a representation that is efficient in memory, in storage, and when transferred. It has a direct static representation that results in improved performance. Object databases have a performance advantage over relational databases in supporting collections.

Relational databases provide excellent support for the dynamic selection of a set of rows based on arbitrary constraints on column values. You can define new sets that were not envisioned during development and specified at schema definition time. Relational databases provide a high degree of flexibility because of their dynamic specification of sets. But this flexibility has an associated computational cost.

Whether an object database or relational database is more appropriate for an application can depend on whether collections must be dynamically specified or whether they can be statically defined when the schema is designed. Most application object models have static, well-understood collections. Such models can realize performance gains with an object database. Other applications require a much more dynamic specification of the groups of data. They may find that a relational database is a better match for their database requirements.

Chapter 8
Relationships

Relationships model associations among objects and can be modeled directly in an object database. Several forms of relationships are supported, some of which automatically maintain referential integrity. Referential integrity exists in a database if every object reference refers to a valid object. In other words, it has no dangling references to objects that have been deleted.

This chapter covers relationships in detail. First, we cover the terminology and then discuss unidirectional and bidirectional relationships along with the relationship interfaces supported in ODMG. A set of scenarios illustrates the relationship behaviors provided by the database implementation when objects are deleted or their relationships are altered.

8.1 Definition and Purpose of Relationships

Relationships are usually first identified during the definition of the application's ER or object model. For many applications, the traversal and maintenance of relationships accounts for a significant portion of the software.

A relationship in an object database is represented by an object with a set of operations. Associations among instances are established, modified, and removed by invoking operations on relationship objects. They maintain the integrity of references at both ends of a relationship.

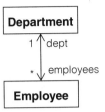

Figure 8.1 Relationship notation.

8.1.1 The Sides of a Relationship

Object and data model methodologies provide a notation for representing relationships. A class in a UML model is depicted by a rectangle. A relationship between two classes is represented by a line that connects them (see Figure 8.1). The classes in a relationship are often referred to as the *ends* or *sides*; a data or function member in each class is used to traverse and access the instances at the other end of the relationship. This member is referred to as a *traversal path*.

8.1.2 The Degree of a Relationship

The number of classes in a relationship is called its *degree*. The most common degree is 2, a *binary relationship*. Object databases provide direct support for binary relationships. A relationship with a degree of 3 is called a *ternary relationship*. Relationships with a degree of 3 or higher usually must be managed by the application. A separate class is often used to represent the relationship itself, and each class in the relationship has a binary relationship with the relationship class.

The following example illustrates a ternary relationship (see Figure 8.2). A department store maintains a wedding gift registry, and the database tracks who

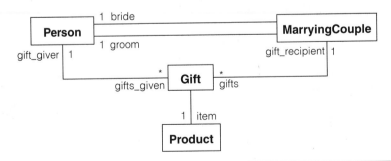

Figure 8.2 Example ternary relationship among `Person`, `MarryingCouple`, and `Product`.

has given specific gifts to a couple getting married. There is an instance of `Person` for each person in the database, whether they are giving or receiving a gift. The `MarryingCouple` class contains references to the bride and groom and the gifts they are to receive. Each person giving gifts has a set of gifts, possibly for multiple couples. A `Gift` class represents the ternary relationship between the couple receiving the gift, the person giving the gift, and the product being given as a gift.

8.1.3 Cardinality

Each relationship has a *cardinality*, which is the number of possible instances at each end of the relationship. The possible cardinalities are one-to-one, one-to-many, and many-to-many. Object models usually have a mix of all three cardinalities. One-to-many relationships are often called *parent-child relationships*. The "parent" object has zero, one, or many "children" objects. A cardinality of many in UML notation is denoted by a *.

A *cardinality constraint* is specified to restrict the number of objects at a given end of a relationship. Both a *minimum* and a *maximum* cardinality are specified if known. It may be a specific number; for example, a bicycle always has two wheels, and a car always has four wheels. Or in our example, there are only two people marrying each other (in most cultures). A constraint may state that an end of a relationship can have zero objects, or it may require that there always be one object. Many application design decisions are based on the cardinalities in the object model.

Cardinality constraints are usually specified in an application's object analysis model. With an object database, the application can specify in the schema whether the end of a relationship has a maximum cardinality of one or many, but facilities are not provided to state that a relationship has a minimum or maximum cardinality of a specific number. These constraints must be implemented by the application, perhaps by calling the `cardinality` function to make sure that a stated maximum has not been reached when adding an instance to the relationship.

8.1.4 Unidirectional and Bidirectional Relationships

Relationships are either *unidirectional* or *bidirectional*. Suppose there is a unidirectional relationship from A to B. A refers to B, but B does not refer to A. The relationship can be traversed only from the A end. Bidirectional relationships are reciprocal; each end refers to the other. If there is a bidirectional relationship between class A and class B, then class A has a reference to B and B has a reference to A. You can traverse from either end of the relationship.

Given a bidirectional binary relationship between classes A and B, from the perspective of an instance of A, the traversal path in B that refers to A is called the *inverse relationship* even though there is only one relationship. The reference in B is often called a *back reference*; it is used to "refer back" to the A instance. The member in B used to traverse to A is called the *inverse traversal path*. This terminology also applies when you're viewing the relationship from the perspective of a B instance.

Consider the representation of a tree structure. The single class TreeNode<T> represents a node in a tree. (Be aware that not all of the implementations support user template classes.)

```
template <class T>
class TreeNode : public d_Object {
        T                               value;
        d_Set<d_Ref<TreeNode<T> > >     childNodes;
};
```

Each node in the tree has a set of references to its child nodes in the tree. This illustrates a unidirectional relationship. A node references its children but not its parent node. It is not always necessary to reference the parent node. If traversals are always initiated from the root of the tree, for example, recursion can be used in the application to keep track of the parent nodes.

You could make the relationship bidirectional by adding a reference to the parent node.

```
template <class T>
class TreeNode : public d_Object {
        T                               value;
        d_Ref<TreeNode<T> >             parentNode;
        d_Set<d_Ref<TreeNode<T> > >     childNodes;
};
```

This technique allows an application to traverse up and down the tree.

8.1.5 Recursive Relationships

Some relationships are recursive. In a tree structure, for example, each node has a reference to its parent node and references to its child nodes. Recursion lets you specify tree traversals concisely. The Person class provides an example:

```
class Person : public d_Object {
public:
        d_Ref<Person>                   father;
        d_Ref<Person>                   mother;
        d_Set<d_Ref<Person> >           children;
};
```

(The data is kept public here to simplify the example.) To access a person's grandfather, you could use the following expression.

```
d_Ref<Person>   person;
// initialize person to reference a Person instance
d_Ref<Person>   grandfather = person->father->father;
```

The member `father` is traversed twice to access the grandfather object. This *path expression* specifies a path through several interrelated objects to access a destination object.

8.2 Relationship Interfaces

A relationship is represented by objects, and operations are used to maintain and traverse the relationship. Both unidirectional and bidirectional relationships are supported.

Figure 8.3 illustrates the classes and relationships used in this chapter. Every department has a set of employees and a set of projects. People in the department work on multiple projects, and projects are often staffed by several people. Each employee may also have at most one office mate, who is represented by the relationship from `Employee` back to `Employee`. This is called a *reflexive relationship*.

These relationships can be represented with either unidirectional or bidirectional mechanisms. The `Department` class could have a set of references to `Project` objects, but then each `Project` object could not have a reference back to its `Department` object. This is a unidirectional relationship. When the schema is designed, you must determine whether navigation of the relationship is required in both directions.

8.2.1 ODMG Unidirectional Relationship Declarations

The following code provides declarations of unidirectional relationships for the object model in Figure 8.3. For a unidirectional relationship, no special relationship object is required. References and collections of references suffice.

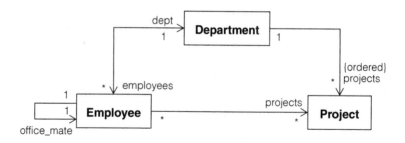

Figure 8.3 Model for unidirectional relationship example.

```
class Department : public d_Object {
public:
        d_Set<d_Ref<Employee> >              employees;
        d_List<d_Ref<Project> >              projects;
};
class Employee : public d_Object {
public:
        d_Ref<Employee>                      office_mate;
        d_Ref<Department>                    dept;
        d_Set<d_Ref<Project> >               projects;
};
class Project : public d_Object {
public:
        d_Date                               completion() const;
};
```

The complete definition of these classes would have other data and function members. The d_Ref<T> class represents to-one relationships, and the d_Set<d_Ref<T>> and d_List<d_Ref<T>> classes represent unordered and ordered to-many relationships, respectively. These classes, introduced in Chapters 6 and 7, are used here to represent unidirectional relationships. The fact that they are used to represent a relationship does not alter their behavior.

Note that the relationship between Department and Employee has traversal paths at both ends, but the relationship between Department and Project has a traversal path only from Department to Project. Both unidirectional and bidirectional relationships are shown here. However, with the relationships declared previously, the application software must maintain the referential integrity among the objects.

Each object in the model that must be referenced by other objects must be a stand-alone persistent object. Thus, the employees collection member of

Department must contain references to employees, d_Ref<Employee>, instead of containing Employee objects directly. If the declaration of employees had been

```
d_Set<Employee>                        employees;
```

then the Employee objects would have been simple structure values embedded in the collection. They would not have been stand-alone objects with identities that could be referenced by other objects in the database.

8.2.2 ODMG Relationship Objects

ODMG defines template classes to represent bidirectional binary relationships that are maintained automatically by the database software. The class d_Rel_Ref<T,MT> represents a relationship with a cardinality of to-one. The d_Rel_Set<T,MT> class represents an unordered relationship, and the d_Rel_List<T,MT> class represents an ordered relationship. The application is responsible for maintaining the order based on the element's relative position in the list. These classes are listed in Table 8.1 with their corresponding base classes. Appendix B describes their interface in detail. All the capabilities of the base class—such as insertion, removal, and iteration over the elements of the collection—are provided in the relationship class. But the operations also maintain referential integrity.

Relationship Class	Base Class
d_Rel_Ref<T, const char *MT>	d_Ref<T>
d_Rel_Set<T, const char *MT>	d_Set<d_Ref<T>>
d_Rel_List<T, const char *MT>	d_List<d_Ref<T>>

Table 8.1 ODMG bidirectional relationship classes.

These relationship classes are used in pairs; the class at each end of a bidirectional relationship must have a member that is an instance of one of these relationship classes. They have two template parameters:

- T: the class at the other end of the relationship
- MT: the name of a string variable that identifies the member in T that is the inverse traversal member of the relationship.

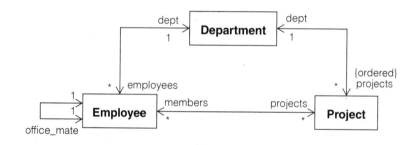

Figure 8.4 Bidirectional relationship model.

The best way to explain how to use these classes is to redefine the relationships in the previous example.

Figure 8.4 shows the bidirectional relationships that are used in the rest of the code examples in this chapter. Consider the relationship between Department and Employee. The Department class has a member employees that refers to instances of Employee, and the Employee class has a member dept that references a Department instance. In the declaration of employees, the second template parameter, _dept, is a string that contains the value "dept". This string refers to the dept member of Employee, which is the inverse traversal member. Similarly, in the declaration of the dept member of Employee, the second template parameter, _emps, is a string that contains the value "employees". It refers to its inverse traversal member, the employees member of Department. The traversal members at both ends of the relationship refer to each other.

The following declarations of the classes use the relationship objects.

```
extern const char _officeMate[];        // Employee <-> Employee
extern const char _dept[], _emps[];     // Employee <-> Department
extern const char _proj_dept[], _d_projs[];// Department <-> Project
extern const char _members[], _projs[]; // Employee <-> Project

class Department : public d_Object {
public:
        d_Rel_Set<Employee,_dept>       employees;
        d_Rel_List<Project,_proj_dept>  projects;
};
class Employee : public d_Object {
public:
        d_Rel_Ref<Employee,_officeMate> office_mate;
        d_Rel_Ref<Department,_emps>     dept;
        d_Rel_Set<Project,_members>     projects;
};
```

```
class Project : public d_Object {
public:
        d_Rel_Ref<Department,_d_projs>   dept;
        d_Rel_Set<Employee,_projs>       members;
};
```

The variables are initialized in a code file (.c, .cxx, .cpp).

```
const char _officeMate[]    = "office_mate";// in Employee
const char _dept[]          = "dept";    // in Employee
const char _emps[]          = "employees";// in Department
const char _proj_dept[]     = "dept";    // in Project
const char _d_projs[]       = "projects"; // in Department
const char _members[]       = "members";  // in Project
const char _projs[]         = "projects"; // in Employee
```

Each traversal member used in a relationship has an associated string variable that contains its name. This variable is used as the second template parameter when the inverse traversal member is declared at the other end of the relationship. The two ends are associated by having each end refer to the other via its second template parameter.

The second template parameter MT is declared to be a const char *. It is not a type template parameter but instead is a value template parameter. The compiler uses the address of the variable to differentiate template instantiations. There can be only one such value for each end of a relationship in an application program. The declarations will not work if the second template parameter is a literal string value. If it were, the address of the literal string would be different in each compilation unit. This could cause the compiler to generate a large number of template instantiations for a given traversal member, but only one should be instantiated.

The object database implementation uses the inverse member specification to associate the two ends so that it can perform relationship maintenance. If one end of a relationship is modified, it can automatically update the other end.

A relationship between two classes is represented by a data member in each class. They are implicitly altered by the relationship objects (d_Rel_Ref<T,MT> and so on) when the application modifies the other end of the relationship. Thus, the database software altering the inverse data member is not in the scope of the class that contains the data member. For example, consider the relationship between Department and Employee. When the dept member of Employee is altered, the database software must change the employees member within Department. But the software that updates employees may not be a member of Department. It depends on where the implementation places the functionality.

Some implementations add member functions directly to the application classes, usually during the schema capture process. If the implementation does not do this, it may require that these relationship data members be declared `public`; this requirement reduces the level of encapsulation. Developers should determine the capabilities of the implementation they are using and design their classes appropriately.

8.3 Referential Integrity Maintenance

The relationship objects introduced in section 8.2.2 perform referential integrity maintenance. When an application modifies one end of a relationship, the other end is updated automatically. Automatic maintenance significantly reduces the chance of programming errors that can cause a loss of referential integrity.

When a modification is made at one end of a relationship, locks are acquired at both ends because both ends must be modified. Most implementations also require that the objects be activated in the application cache when the modification is performed. The locking can become a concurrency issue when the database implementation performs locking at a granularity larger than an object. This issue also exists if the application maintains the relationships manually. Unidirectional relationships may be used instead of bidirectional relationships to avoid the extra locking and attain a higher level of concurrency.

The following sections walk through scenarios that modify relationships among objects. The schema defined in section 8.2.2 is assumed.

8.3.1 One-to-One Relationship Scenario

The first scenario uses the `office_mate` reflexive relationship defined in the `Employee` class. Assume that the following variables are initialized to reference objects in an employee database.

```
d_Ref<Employee>      jennifer;
d_Ref<Employee>      jeremy;
d_Ref<Employee>      brandon;
```

The types of these variables could also be `Employee *`; either type would suffice. A real application program would not have a variable name for a specific person, as we've done here to simplify the discussion. Assume that the reference `jennifer` refers to an employee named Jennifer.

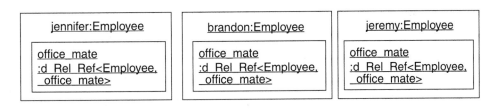

Figure 8.5 No one-to-one relationships.

Suppose that no relationships initially exist among the employees (see Figure 8.5). The variable `jennifer` of type `d_Ref<Employee>` refers to an instance of `Employee`, named jennifer. The object inside each `Employee` instance represents the `office_mate` member. In Figure 8.5 the `Employee` objects have `office_-mate` attributes that do not refer to other employees. They are null.

8.3.1.1 Establishing a Relationship

Suppose we need to make jennifer and jeremy office mates. We can use either

```
        jennifer->office_mate = jeremy;
```
or
```
        jeremy->office_mate = jennifer;
```

Only one end of the relationship is set by the application; the other end is updated automatically by the database software.

After the first line executes, the relationship in Figure 8.6 exists. In this chapter I use the stereotype feature of UML to indicate whether the association has been explicitly set by the application («app») or whether the database relationship objects have altered the inverse member in response to the application («db»). This notation is used throughout the chapter to illustrate the side effects of relationship maintenance. Also, the type names for the objects are omitted in subsequent diagrams to conserve space and allow room for more objects in the figures.

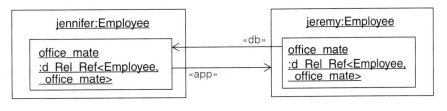

Figure 8.6 Establishing a one-to-one relationship.

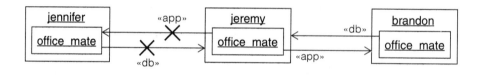

Figure 8.7 Modifying a one-to-one relationship.

8.3.1.2 Modifying a Relationship

Now suppose jeremy and brandon are made office mates. Suppose the application executes the following:

```
jeremy->office_mate = brandon;
```

This code results in the associations shown in Figure 8.7. The `office_mate` attribute of jennifer is now null. By setting the `office_mate` attribute of jeremy to brandon, the following two operations are performed automatically. The application does not explicitly execute them.

```
jennifer->office_mate.clear();
brandon->office_mate = jeremy;
```

Since the application assigned a new value to jeremy's `office_mate` attribute, the UML deletion marker placed on the reference to jennifer is labeled «app».

8.3.1.3 Clearing a Relationship

It is also possible to clear or remove a relationship. Assuming that we have the relationship established in Figure 8.6, executing the following statement sets the `office_mate` reference to null in jennifer and jeremy (see Figure 8.8).

```
jennifer->office_mate.clear();
```

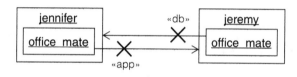

Figure 8.8 Clearing a one-to-one relationship.

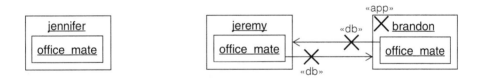

Figure 8.9 Deleting an object in a one-to-one relationship.

8.3.1.4   **Removing a Related Object**

Suppose we have the situation shown in Figure 8.7 and the employee brandon is removed from the employee database. Any bidirectional relationships that brandon is involved in must be updated so that there are no references to a deleted object. The application can execute either

```
        brandon.delete_object();
or
        Employee *b = brandon.ptr();
        delete b;
```

to delete brandon. This results in the situation shown in Figure 8.9. The `office_mate` reference in jeremy is automatically set to null. The value of the reference to brandon is no longer valid, because brandon has been removed from the database. If the reference were not set to null, it would be a dangling reference. An attempt to use a dangling reference causes the exception `d_Error_-RefInvalid`.

8.3.2   **One-to-Many Relationship Scenario**

This section illustrates the effect of modifying one-to-many relationships. Because one side of the relationship is a collection of references instead of a single reference, insertion and removal of collection elements is performed explicitly by the application or implicitly by the database software.

Assume the objects and interrelationships shown in Figure 8.10. The following additional variables are used.

```
        d_Ref<Department>   development, sales;
        d_Ref<Employee>     dana, schaefer, caroline, kristen;
```

As noted before, these are references, and the figures contain the objects that they refer to. Similar to section 8.3.1, the remaining figures in section 8.3.2 will not include the type names to conserve drawing space.

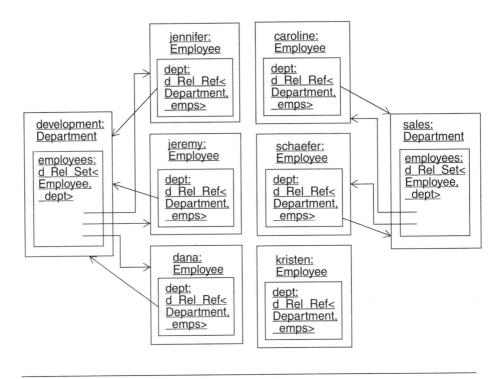

Figure 8.10 Initial set of one-to-many relationships.

8.3.2.1 Establishing a Relationship

Suppose kristen is placed in the sales department. The following line of code establishes the relationship.

```
kristen->dept = sales;
```

After this line executes, not only is the dept reference of kristen set to sales, but also kristen is added implicitly to the set of employees in sales (see Figure 8.11). We could have attained the same result by adding kristen directly to the sales department.

```
sales->employees.insert_element(kristen);
```

8.3.2.2 Modifying a Relationship

Now suppose dana is transferred to the sales department. The application can execute the following statement:

```
dana->dept = sales;
```

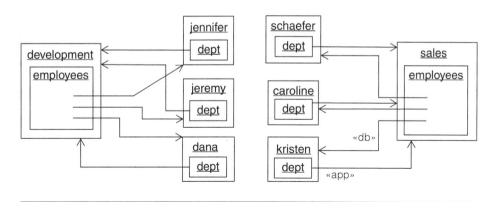

Figure 8.11 Establishing a one-to-many relationship.

Then the database software automatically performs the following steps:

```
development->employees.remove_element(dana);
sales->employees.insert_element(dana);
```

This results in the relationships shown in Figure 8.12.

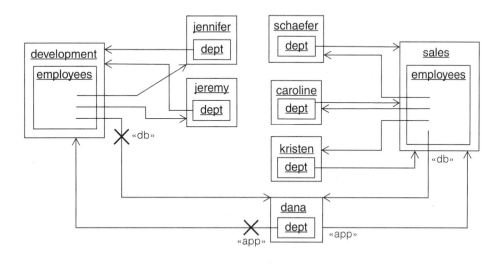

Figure 8.12 Modifying a one-to-many relationship.

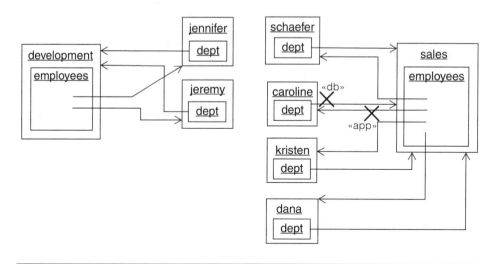

Figure 8.13 Clearing a one-to-many relationship.

8.3.2.3 Clearing a Relationship

Now suppose caroline is removed from the sales department.

```
sales->employees.remove_element(caroline);
```

When this executes, caroline's dept reference is cleared implicitly as in

```
caroline->dept.clear();
```

This results in the structure shown in Figure 8.13.

8.3.2.4 Removing an Object

When an object is removed, all other objects involved in a relationship with it must be updated to remove their reference to it. With one-to-many relationships, different actions are performed depending on the cardinality at the other end of the relationship. To illustrate the effect at both ends of a one-to-many relationship, both a child and a parent object are deleted by the application.

```
development.delete_object();
dana.delete_object();
```

The development object serves as a parent in the relationship between Department and Employee, and dana serves as a child object in the relationship.

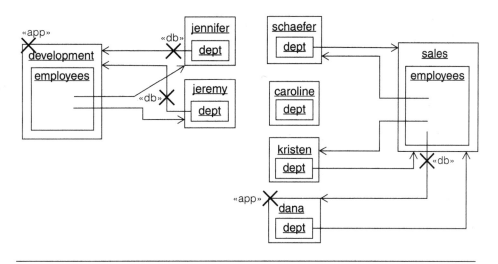

Figure 8.14 Removing objects in a one-to-many relationship.

Figure 8.14 illustrates the result of the application performing both operations to the associations depicted in Figure 8.13. When dana is deleted, the reference to dana in the sales department is implicitly removed. But when the development department is deleted, the dept reference of every object referencing the department is cleared.

8.3.3 Many-to-Many Relationship Scenario

This section examines the effects of manipulating many-to-many relationships by updating the relationship between Employee and Project. Assume the objects and relationships shown in Figure 8.15. The additional Project objects are referenced by the following variables.

```
d_Ref<Project>        gui, database, communications;
```

8.3.3.1 Establishing a Relationship

We now add jennifer to the database project.

```
database->members.insert_element(jennifer);
```

Alternatively, this could have been written as

```
jennifer->projects.insert_element(database);
```

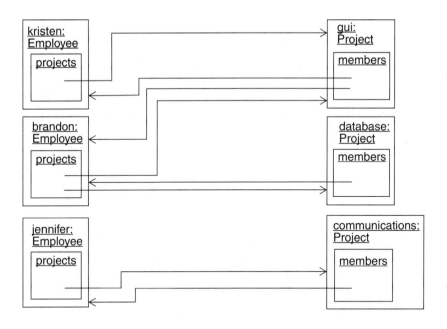

Figure 8.15 Initial set of many-to-many relationships.

Adding a reference on one side of a many-to-many relationship automatically adds a reference at the other end. When the application executes one of these statements, the other one is implicitly performed by the database. This results in the object relationships shown in Figure 8.16.

8.3.3.2 Modifying a Relationship

The d_Rel_List or d_Rel_Set template is used for the to-many end of either one-to-many or many-to-many relationships. With d_Rel_Set, modification of the relationship involves inserting and removing elements from the collection. With d_Rel_List, which supports the positional-related update operations of the d_List class, you can perform more sophisticated operations. In addition to inserting and removing elements at arbitrary positions within the list, you can replace elements at certain positions. The insertion of an element into a d_Rel_Set has already been shown.

8.3.3.3 Clearing a Relationship

When you're clearing a relationship between two objects modeled with the d_Rel_Set class, you must remove an element from the other end of the relation-

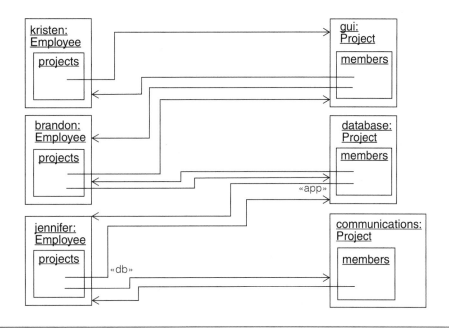

Figure 8.16 Establishing a many-to-many relationship.

ship. Suppose we remove brandon from the database project by executing the following statement.

```
database->members.remove_element(brandon);
```

This results in the changes shown in Figure 8.17. The reference to brandon is explicitly removed from the `members` collection in the database `Project` instance. Implicitly, the reference to the database project is removed from the `projects` collection member in the brandon instance.

8.3.3.4 Removing a Related Object

Now we show the effect of removing an object in a many-to-many relationship. This is similar to deleting a parent object in a one-to-many relationship. Each child object is updated to reflect the deletion of the parent object.

Suppose we complete the user interface development work and the object referenced by gui is removed.

```
gui.delete_object();
```

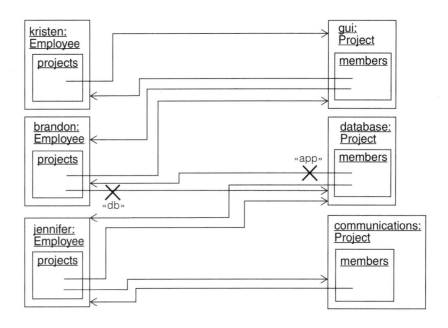

Figure 8.17 Removing a many-to-many relationship.

This results in the object relationships shown in Figure 8.18. Because both kristen and brandon had a reference to gui, their `projects` members are implicitly updated to remove it.

An object may be involved in many relationships with many different classes. When an object is deleted, all references to it in the related objects must be removed. In this last scenario, the related department object would have also been updated, removing the reference to gui from its `projects` member.

8.4 Relationship Traversal and Path Expressions

A relationship traversal path allows an application to navigate to related objects in the database. Both references and collections have been the focus of optimization in object databases, and direct support is provided at a physical level. Their use does not require queries or join processing. Object databases enjoy significant performance advantages over relational databases, which must establish an association dynamically at run time with join processing.

An expression that navigates through multiple objects is called a *path expression*. Given an employee, for example, suppose you want to print information

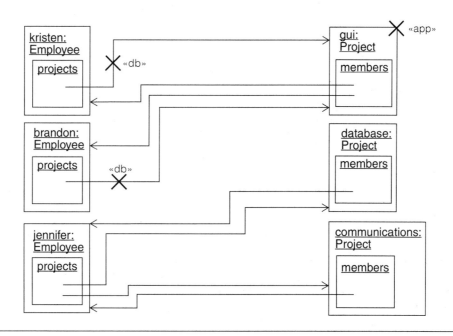

Figure 8.18 Removing an object in a many-to-many relationship.

about the projects that the employee's office mate is working on. Assume that the ostream output operator has been defined for class Project.

```
extern ostream &operator<<(ostream &, const Project &);

d_Ref<Employee>         emp; // initialize this variable
d_Iterator<Project>     projs;
d_Ref<Project>          proj;

projs = emp->office_mate->projects.create_iterator();
while( projs.next(proj) ){
    cout << *proj << endl;
}
```

The expression in bold font is a path expression.

Alternatively, the preceding code could have been written with STL. Assume the following function is defined.

```
void
printProject(d_Ref<Project> proj)
{
    cout << *proj << endl;
}
```

The following STL-style code performs the same functionality as the earlier code.

```
d_Ref<Employee> o_mate = emp->office_mate;
for_each(o_mate->projects.begin(), omate->projects.end(),
            printProject);
```

Some vendors support *path indexes*, which allow an index to include a navigational path. The traversal path is usually specified using query language syntax. The members of the path index can include object references, collections of object references, and even member functions (in one implementation). The final member in the path is usually an object attribute. For example, the following path expression is associated with the Employee class.

```
office_mate->projects->due_date
```

It navigates through both a reference and a collection before terminating at an attribute within the Project class.

When a component of the path is a collection of references, a separate index entry exists for each collection element. A path index allows a query to efficiently find all the objects reachable via a particular traversal path that have an attribute matching a specified value constraint.

Chapter 9
Composite Objects

An object model often contains an object whose characteristics cannot be represented by simple attributes embedded in an instance. These components of the object are best represented by separate objects. If a fixed number of instances of the object were required, they could be embedded, but often a variable number of instances are required. They are considered components of the object even though they are not embedded attributes. The object is called a *composite object* that is composed of *subobjects*. Another name used in the industry for composite object is *complex object*.

Another reason the subobjects must be represented by separate objects is that relationships often exist among the subobjects. The composite object establishes a context for its subobjects and their relationships. The "value" of the composite object is based on its attributes along with the collection values of its subobjects and their attributes and relationships.

Types in both the domain and entity type categories model abstractions whose underlying implementation consists of an aggregation of components. A composite entity is another type category, and it is distinguished by being an aggregation of other objects. These subobjects can be instances of entity classes or can themselves be composite entities. This arrangement allows a multilevel *containment hierarchy* of objects to be constructed.

The term *composite object* is used to refer to the overall abstraction. A specific object, called the *composite base object* in this book, represents the characteristics that apply to the composite object as a whole. The composite base object has a means to navigate to all its component subobjects. The composite base object and all its subobjects are collectively referred to as the *composite object*.

Surprisingly, most object databases do not yet explicitly support composite objects even though the vendors often emphasize that they provide better support for them than relational vendors do. The vendors provide the underlying mechanisms needed to organize a set of related objects, and the applications can use these mechanisms to provide efficient management of a composite object.

9.1 Composite Object Examples

In the example of departments, employees, and projects, each of these objects could be a composite object. The Department class has a set of projects under development and also a set of development processes to be completed for each project. The Department class has a set of Employee objects, but we assume that the employees are components of the entire company instead of the department. If the department is dissolved, the employees are not removed but are reassigned to other departments.

The Project instances associated with a department are considered subobjects of their Department instance. The Project class may itself be a composite object. It may have subobjects representing the process steps required to complete the project. Each process step has an owner and projected and actual completion dates. Figure 9.1 illustrates the relationships among the classes.

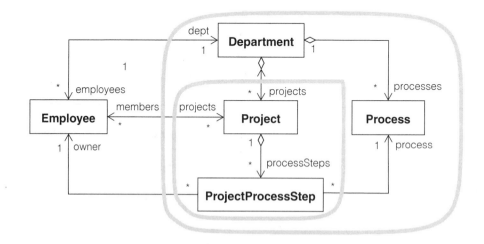

Figure 9.1 Composite object example (Project).

Both `Department` and `Project` are composite object classes. The relationships among these classes could be represented by the following class declarations. The `Department` and `Employee` classes and their relationships were covered in Chapter 8. The `Project` and `Process` classes have instances that are subobjects of the `Department` class. The `ProjectProcessStep` class has instances that are subobjects of the `Project` class.

```
extern const char _dept[], _emps[];        // Employee <-> Department
extern const char _proj_dept[], _d_projs[];// Department <-> Project
extern const char _members[], _projs[];    // Employee <-> Project

class Department : public d_Object {
        d_Rel_List<Project,_proj_dept>   projects;
        d_Rel_Set<Employee,_dept>        employees;

        d_List<d_Ref<Process> >          processes;
//      other members
};

class Employee : public d_Object {
        d_Rel_Ref<Department,_emps>      dept;
        d_Rel_Set<Project,_members>      projects;
};

const char _dept[]          = "dept";        // in Employee
const char _emps[]          = "employees";   // in Department
const char _proj_dept[]     = "dept";        // in Project
const char _d_projs[]       = "projects";    // in Department
const char _members[]       = "members";     // in Project
const char _projs[]         = "projects";    // in Employee
```

Each department has a set of process steps that it performs for each project. The process steps may be different for each department, so each one has its own list. The `Process` class contains general information associated with a process that is not specific to a particular project.

```
class Process : public d_Object {
        d_String         name;
        d_String         description;
//      etc.
};
```

The application does not need to traverse from a `Process` instance to each `ProjectProcessStep` instance associated with it, so a traversal path is not provided. The `ProjectProcessStep` class has a member called `process` that references a `Process` instance. Each project must maintain information about its process steps. Each `Project` instance has `ProjectProcessStep` instances for each `Process` instance in its department's `processes` member.

```
class Project : public d_Object {
        d_Rel_Ref<Department,_d_projs>  dept;
        d_Rel_Set<Employee,_projs>       members;
        d_List<d_Ref<ProjectProcessStep> > processSteps;
// other members
};

class ProjectProcessStep : public d_Object {
        d_Ref<Process>      process;
        d_Date              expectedCompletion;
        d_Date              actualCompletion;
        d_Ref<Employee>     owner; // person responsible for step
// other members
};
```

The `Project` class is considered a composite object, because it manages a set of `ProjectProcessStep` instances. The application accesses instances of `ProjectProcessStep` only via the `processSteps` member of `Project`. The application first acquires a reference to a `Project` instance and then accesses the related `ProjectProcessStep` instances. With this schema, it was unnecessary for the `ProjectProcessStep` class to have a reference back to its associated `Project` instance, because the application would already have algorithmically obtained a reference to it.

9.1.1 Subobjects

A subobject serves as a component of a composite object. An object embedded as a member of another class is not considered a subobject. A subobject can be a simple object or another composite object, so you can construct composite objects consisting of multilevel containment hierarchies of arbitrary complexity.

An object is considered a subobject if it is *existent-dependent* on its composite base object—that is, it cannot exist without its composite object. When an application deletes a composite object, the composite base object and all its subobjects should be deleted. It applies the delete operation to the composite base object. The destructor of the composite base object is responsible for propagating the delete operation to its subobjects.

The `Employee` class is a composite object with subobjects. Each `Employee` instance has information about benefit options the employee has selected,

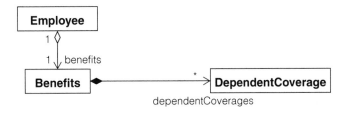

Figure 9.2 Composite object example (`Employee`).

including medical and life insurance, savings plans, and reimbursement accounts for health, child, and elder care.

Suppose that information about each covered dependent must be kept, including things such as their name, date of birth, and amount of coverage (see Figure 9.2). A `Benefits` instance is a subobject of an `Employee` instance, and `DependentCoverage` is a subobject of `Benefits`. However, there is an alternative for representing the relationship between `Benefits` and `DependentCoverage`. The `Benefits` class can have a collection containing an element for each dependent. But instead of the element type being a reference to a `DependentCoverage` instance, it is the instance itself.

```
class DependentCoverage {
        d_String            last_name;
        d_String            first_name;
        d_Date              date_of_birth;
//      health coverage options
};

class Benefits : public d_Object {
// employee benefit information
        d_Varray<DependentCoverage> dependentCoverages;
};

class Employee : public Person {
        d_Ref<Benefits>     benefits;
// all the other members of Employee
};
```

The `DependentCoverage` instances are stored as embedded values within the `dependentCoverage` collection. Because they are not stand-alone persistent subobjects, this association does not qualify `Benefits` as a composite object.

This modeling decision has several implications. The `DependentCoverage` instances cannot be directly referenced by other objects in the database (they are values embedded in the collection). In contrast, the `ProjectProcessStep` instances can be referenced. The `DependentCoverage` instances are activated automatically with their associated `Benefits` instance, whereas the `Project-ProcessStep` instances are not activated automatically. Having references instead of embedded object values implies that more dereference operations must be performed to access the objects. If the implementation acquires locks on an object basis, only a single lock is required for the `Benefits` instance and all its instances of `DependentCoverage`. But separate locks would be required for the `Project` instance and its `ProjectProcessStep` instances. You should take all these factors into account when designing the object model. Choosing one approach over another depends on application requirements.

9.1.2   References to Objects That Are Not Subobjects

An object that has a reference (`d_Ref<T>`) or a collection of references to another object of type `T` is not necessarily a composite object. Many objects that are not composite objects contain references to other objects. Similarly, a composite object that has subobjects may also contain references to objects that are not its subobjects. These referenced objects are not considered components of the composite object and are not affected by operations such as the deletion of the composite object.

The application described earlier has several examples of this. The `Project-ProcessStep` class has a member `process` that is a reference to a `Process` and also has a member `owner` that references an `Employee` instance. Neither of these referenced objects is considered a subobject of the `ProjectProcessStep` instance. Similarly, the `Department` class has a collection of `Employee` references called `employees`. In this object model the `Employee` instances are not subobjects of `Department` even though `Department` is a composite object and has subobjects dealing with its projects and processes.

9.1.3   Composite Base Object

A composite object represents an abstraction that has an associated set of operations. Operations that are specific to the composite object are usually defined within the class of the composite base object. Their implementation often involves manipulating subobjects. The composite base object should appear as an atomic object, representing the composite abstraction being modeled. A goal in defining a composite object is to attain a high degree of atomicity even though the object consists of an aggregation of other objects.

A composite base object often serves as the *root* or *entry point object* for a large set of interrelated subobjects. Vendors use these alternative terms when referring to composite base objects. End users are often allowed to associate a name with a composite object; it is usually associated with the composite base object. Once the composite base object is accessed by name, navigation is used to access the subobjects needed to perform an operation on the composite object.

Subobjects may be given a unique name relative to their composite object, which thereby serves as a *name scope* for its subobjects. The ODMG standard names objects on a database basis, so you could use the name of the composite object as a prefix with the subobject name. Or the composite base object may have one or more dictionaries that map a name to a subobject. You could use these dictionaries as the collection mechanism used to navigate to the subobjects.

9.2 **Physical Organization**

Composite base objects use either unidirectional or bidirectional relationships to refer to their subobjects. It should be possible to navigate from a composite base object to all its subobjects. An application would normally first access a composite base object and then navigate to a subobject, retaining its reference to the composite base object. Therefore you often need not store in the database a reference to navigate from the subobject to the composite base object. Use of a unidirectional relationship may suffice.

Composite objects provide a natural basis for deciding how to cluster (group) and partition (separate) objects in the database. Many object database implementations allow an application to cluster objects. The subobjects of a composite object are often accessed and manipulated as distinct groups, providing a natural basis for clustering. Applications may access only one group of subobjects at a time. It may therefore make sense to cluster the subobjects with a group but to partition each group. This approach may allow a higher degree of concurrency and optimize cache use. When you're deciding whether to cluster or partition objects, you should take into account the existing composite object relationships and the applications' access patterns.

Consider the composite object hierarchy shown in Figure 9.3. Figure 9.4 illustrates depth-first groupings of the subobjects. Groups are illustrated at two levels in the hierarchy. The level at which objects should be clustered depends on the number of objects that can be clustered per block and the level of concurrency that may be necessary at the first level down.

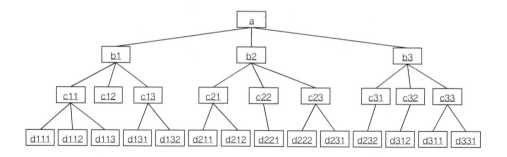

Figure 9.3 Composite object hierarchy.

Figure 9.5 illustrates breadth-first grouping of subobjects. Which of the two clustering strategies works best depends on the patterns of access by the applications.

In the example application, the `ProjectProcessStep` instances could be clustered with their associated `Project` composite base object. Furthermore, the `Project` and `Process` instances could be clustered with their associated `Department` instance. The `DependentCoverage` objects are automatically clustered with their `Benefits` instance if they are embedded within the `dependentCoverages` member.

Applications often manipulate a composite object as a whole. Distinct composite objects are usually partitioned unless they are used together as subobjects of a higher-level composite object.

Ideally, a disk block should contain subobjects only from a single composite object. Clustering the subobjects within a composite object but then partitioning each composite object minimizes the number of disk blocks needed to access a

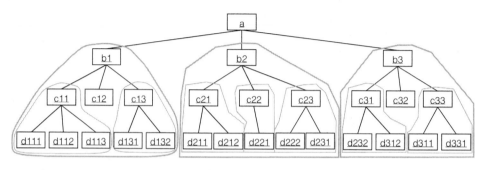

Figure 9.4 Depth-first grouping of subobjects in a composite object hierarchy.

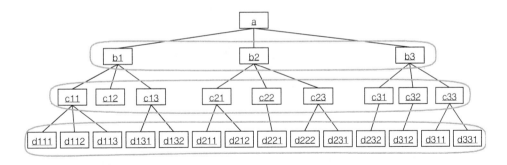

Figure 9.5 Breadth-first grouping of subobjects in a composite object hierarchy.

composite object. If subobjects from multiple composite objects are intermixed, more blocks must be transferred from disk and managed in the database cache.

Partitioning composite objects should increase the amount of concurrency, depending on the implementation's locking granularity. Applications using implementations with page or segment-level locking should make sure that composite objects requiring concurrent access do not have their subobjects intermixed within the same locking regions. Otherwise, applications are likely to encounter deadlock situations as subobjects are accessed.

In the example application it makes sense to partition the Department composite objects. The project or process data for two different departments should be partitioned, because they are not accessed together by one application. This technique will reduce the chance of lock contention between applications manipulating different departments.

The benefits data for an employee may not be accessed very often. It may be more advantageous to have all the Employee instances clustered in the least amount of storage space. In this case it would make sense to partition the Benefits instance away from its associated Employee instance, reducing the amount of database cache needed to access all the Employee instances.

You often need to quickly access a particular subobject of a composite object. Sometimes the application provides direct support for this by using a dictionary that provides a reference to a given subobject based on an identifying value. A path index could also be used to locate a particular subobject.

9.3 Operations

Operations applied to a composite object often result in operations applied to its subobjects. This is sometimes referred to as the propagation of the operation.

Some operations applied to a composite object—such as deletion—must always be propagated to its subobjects.

Some implementations provide a *get-closure* operation to access referenced objects. It can be used to activate all or a subset of a composite object's subobjects. This approach lets you make a single request to the database, transferring the complete set of subobjects as a group versus accessing them one object at a time, a much less efficient operation.

The semantics of common operations—such as the canonical form in C++—must be defined for a composite object. The class designer must decide whether these operations should be shallow or deep. In other words, do they apply to both the composite base object and its subobjects? The functions of the C++ canonical form (copy, assignment, deletion) commonly are deep operations.

A subobject is dependent on its containing composite base object. Thus, when a copy operation implemented by the copy constructor is applied to a composite base object, the operation should create a copy of each subobject. Suppose there are two instances, a and b, of a composite object class. An assignment of b to a would remove the current subobjects of a and make a copy of each subobject of b.

```
a = b;
```

These usually need to be deep operations when you're manipulating composite objects.

But when you design a composite object you may decide that only the composite base object or only a subset of the composite object is affected. Each composite object design requires engineering judgment to determine the scope of a composite object operation relative to its subobjects.

By definition, the deletion of a composite base object should be propagated to all its subobjects. Remember that the composite object may contain references to objects that are not subobjects and should not be deleted. When you design a composite object, you must decide for each reference whether the referenced object is a component of the composite object. The class implementation is responsible for proper management of its subobjects.

The Department, Employee, and Project classes are composite objects in the example application. Their destructors provide the proper deletion of their component subobjects.

```
Project::~Project()
{
    d_Iterator<d_Ref<ProjectProcessStep> > iter;
    d_Ref<ProjectProcessStep> pps;
```

```
        iter = processSteps.create_iterator();
        while( iter.next(pps) )
            pps.delete_object();
    }


    Employee::~Employee()
    {
        if( !benefits.is_null() )
            benefits.delete_object();
    }


    Department::~Department()
    {
        d_Iterator<d_Ref<Process> > iter_process;
        d_Iterator<d_Ref<Project> > iter_project;
        d_Ref<Process>  proc;
        d_Ref<Project>  proj;

        iter_process = processes.create_iterator();
        while( iter_process.next(proc) )
            proc.delete_object();
        iter_project = projects.create_iterator();
        while( iter_project.next(proj) )
            proj.delete_object();
    }
```

Some databases let you propagate locks, although it is not supported in the ODMG standard. The schema designer must determine whether the locking of a composite object implies that the composite base object and all its subobjects must be locked. The database is instructed that when a given object is locked, the lock should be propagated to a set of related objects. The acquisition of the object's lock and the propogated locks must be successful for the application to continue execution. An object indirectly locked due to propagation may itself propagate the lock to other objects. Thus, lock propagation may spread to a large number of objects, limiting concurrency.

Another approach the application can use is to establish a locking policy when accessing a composite object. It could be required that every application first acquire a lock on a composite base object before accessing its subobjects. Locking the composite base object may be treated by the application as an implicit lock on all its subobjects. With some implementations it is then possible for applications to access the subobjects without acquiring locks for them. But this technique works only if all applications follow the policy.

9.4 In Closing

A domain represents the most primitive category of type that can be defined in an object database. It achieves persistence by being embedded as a member of a class that represents an entity. A class representing an entity attains both persistence and identity in an ODMG implementation by being derived from the d_Object class. And finally, a composite object represents the most complex category of type that can be defined in an object database. It defines an abstraction that involves an aggregation of separate persistent entity instances. Domains, entities, and composite objects represent progressive levels of aggregation of data in the database. Encapsulation is used to reduce the complexity that can result in an object model that has multiple levels of aggregation.

This chapter completes the discussion of defining C++ object models for an object database. Part II describes the ODMG Object Query Language.

Part II:
The Object
Query Language

Chapter 10
An Introduction to the
Object Query Language

This part of the book describes the ODMG Object Query Language. The primary goal of OQL is to provide declarative query access to the objects in an object database, supporting the application's object model as defined by the classes in the object database schema.

An OQL query can be specified within a C++ application program, or a user can provide an ad hoc query via a command line, a shell environment, an environment based on a fourth-generation language (4GL), or a graphical user interface (GUI). A 4GL or GUI environment can provide a user-friendly interface for specifying queries and viewing results.

C++ applications often use the direct navigational C++ interface to the database. Early adopters of object database technology often had stringent performance requirements that were not being met by relational databases. A relational database has a single interface to the database: the SQL language. Initially, object databases place greater emphasis on a seamless, tight integration with the C++ language than on query language support. Some of the initial application domains using object databases did not consider query language access to be important. Direct navigational access in C++ met the needs of these initial applications.

But as developers began applying object databases to a broader spectrum of application domains, they recognized that associative as well as navigational database access is needed. Query language support is gaining importance. In a client-server environment, it is advantageous to submit a declarative query to be evaluated on a separate back-end server machine, with only the query results returned to the application. This approach is effective only if the database architecture supports query processing in the database cache. Sometimes navigational access can result in unnecessary transfer of objects from the server to the client. For example, suppose that an application has activated an object. The application may need other objects that are reachable only by performing a multilevel navigation. The intermediate objects in the navigational path may be required only for the navigation. A query specifying the navigational path can be submitted to a database server, which can transfer to the client only the objects of interest. If the application were to perform the navigation, all the intermediate objects in the navigation path would be activated in the application even though it didn't need them. A query language can also provide a better interface for describing associative-type access based on the specification of constraints on attribute values. Again, if the database server can perform query processing, this technique allows only the objects of interest to be transferred.

For an end user, except for the applications that have been written by application developers, the ad hoc query interface is the only other mechanism available. A significant advantage of relational databases is the existence of a standard relational query language—SQL—which can be used in an ad hoc fashion. Users often demand this kind of direct, easy-to-use mechanism for querying and analyzing their data without being dependent on application programmers. Users can avoid the lengthy product development life cycle that's typical of application programs. It saves both time and money.

Chapters 11 and 12 provide a complete description of OQL. Chapter 11 covers the basic expressions and operators, and Chapter 12 discusses how to query collections with predicates. Chapter 13 discusses how to execute an OQL query from within a C++ application.

10.1   The Goals of OQL

OQL was designed by François Bancilhon, Sophie Cluet, and Claude Delobel at O_2 Technology and it has been adopted by the ODMG as its standard object query language. Based on the ODMG object model, OQL supports the object type system defined by the database schema. OQL directly supports the object model constructs of encapsulation, inheritance, and polymorphism as defined in the application model. Both associative and navigational access of the database is supported. OQL provides a superset of the query portion of entry-level SQL-92, which is the common interface supported by relational vendors.

OQL is not intended to be the primary or exclusive interface to the database, nor does it have its own type system to represent the data. It operates within the context of the object model type system defined by the application. In a C++ database environment, the type system is based on the C++ classes that define the schema. In a Smalltalk or Java application development environment, these languages would establish the type system for the database.

This approach is in stark contrast to the one used by relational databases based on SQL. In these environments, SQL and the relational database define the type system and SQL is the sole interface to the database. Mappings must be provided between types known by SQL and similar types in the application programming language.

With an object database, a single, common type system is shared by the database and applications. There is also a high degree of integration with the object-oriented programming language used by the applications, allowing a high degree of interoperability among the applications and query language. For example, OQL allows direct access to the functionality defined in the object model. C++ member functions can be called in OQL to operate on objects in the database.

By design OQL is not computationally complete. It relies on the application, written in an object-oriented programming language, to specify the definition of the functions and object methods to be invoked in queries. Query expressions are composed from a small set of query operators defined in the language.

OQL provides operators only to perform query access of an object database; no update operators are provided to change objects. Allowing direct update of attributes could be considered a breaking of encapsulation. Instead, OQL allows operations defined by the application to be invoked on objects. These operations can update the objects. They can be either C++ member functions or stand-alone functions not associated with a particular class. They can provide the right update semantics based on the object's underlying representation and implementation. Thus, OQL supports the encapsulation defined in the object model, invoking operations defined by the class designer only to alter the object's state. This is exactly what you would expect in an object-oriented query language. The functions are implemented in the same language used to define the object model.

Many application developers working in a SQL environment do not want users to update the database directly; they are concerned about corruption of data. They often restrict the ability to perform updates in the SQL ad hoc environment. Semantic integrity constraints are often used to prevent updates that may cause incorrect and inconsistent changes to data. OQL does not provide an `update` statement as in SQL, but the application can make available in the query environment functions and object methods that perform updates. This approach provides a more direct and explicit means of ensuring data integrity than the approach used in SQL environments.

OQL proponents have adapted the language to gain greater acceptance in the commercial environment, which is dominated by SQL. Some adjustments have made it more compatible with SQL. OQL is fairly close to supporting the ANSI SQL-92 entry-level specification—which is actually SQL-89—the SQL specification that most of the relational products conform to. This similarity should allow existing SQL software and SQL-knowledgeable staff to migrate more easily to OQL. But OQL also offers many capabilities not found in SQL.

10.2 OQL Is a Functional Query Language

OQL is a *functional* query language that is statically typed. Every query expression consists of an operator applied to zero or more operands of a particular type. It returns a value of a specific type. The result type of a query can be any type. By contrast, every SQL query has a result that is a table of tuples. The ability of OQL to return a value of any type allows users to use function composition more effectively when expressing queries.

Type checking is performed when a query is parsed, and an error is returned if there are any typing errors. The OQL environment must have a definition for every type used in an OQL expression. The types are usually defined by the application programming language environment (C++) and database schema.

Function composition is used to construct arbitrarily complex queries. An operand can be either a literal value or another query expression of arbitrary complexity. Every valid query expression is a complete query that can also serve as the operand for another query expression (assuming it produces a value of the right type). This arrangement allows both simple and elaborate queries to be specified.

Suppose an operator F has a single operand of type T_0 and returns a value of type T_1. Also suppose there is an operator G that has an operand of type T_1 and returns a value of type T_2. With function composition, the expression $G(F(t_0))$ is a valid query expression that maps from the value t_0 of type T_0 to a value of type T_2 by invoking operator F with operand t_0 and then invoking operator G, passing the value returned by F.

OQL supports both objects (with database identity) and values (which do not have identity). It supports each of the type categories we have discussed, including domains, entities, and composite objects.

Chapter 11
OQL Expressions and Operators

OQL consists of a set of query operators that can be combined via function composition. Because every valid query expression can serve as an operand for another query expression, elaborate query expressions can be constructed.

OQL is a strongly typed language; each query expression expects operands of specific types and produces a result of a specific type. Type checking is performed when a query is parsed. Sometimes the operand types of a query expression determine its result type. The type of a query expression is derived from the structure of the query expression, the type declarations in the schema, and the types of literals and named objects.

The query operators are described in this chapter and Chapter 12. The description indicates the operator's return type and required operand types. Each example represents a complete query and could also serve as an operand to another query expression.

Some symbolic names are used to represent typed expressions that serve as operands of a query operator. Table 11.1 lists the symbols and their data type. These symbols denote operands in the descriptions of the OQL operators. A subscript is used when more than one expression of a given type is used as an operand. An operand can be either a simple literal value or a complex, deeply nested query expression.

Symbol	Represents OQL Expression
attr	An object attribute
bool	A Boolean expression
char	A single character expression
coll	A collection expression
dict	A dictionary expression
expr	An arbitrary OQL expression
func	A function
i, j, k	Integer expressions
list	A list expression
num	An integer or floating-point number expression
ref	An object reference expression
str	A string expression
T	An arbitrary type

Table 11.1 Symbolic notation.

Given an OQL expression expr, then

```
(expr)
```

is also an OQL expression that has the same type as expr. Parentheses are used to group operations and override the precedence of operators, which are defined in section 11.6.

11.1 Object Access

OQL provides access to objects in the database at the same level of abstraction in which they are defined in the application. The properties of the objects can be accessed, including attributes, relationships, and operations.

11.1.1 Named Objects

As described in section 6.2, a name can be associated with an object in an ODMG object database. The name is a query expression that can be used to access the object. The type of the named object determines the type of the query expression.

The name of an object is a valid complete query expression. Suppose there is a collection object named Depts that contains a reference to each instance of the `Department` class. In C++ the `set_object_name` member function in `d_Database` is used to associate the name with the object. The expression

```
Depts
```

is a valid OQL query that returns the collection object. For OQL to correctly parse a query, the name of an object must consist of a single word (no embedded spaces or operators). For example, the name

```
Network_Architecture
```

could be associated with the `Department` instance representing the Network Architecture Department. These names can be used both as valid complete queries and as an operand to another query expression. The type of the query expression is determined by the type of the named object.

ODMG-93 release 1.2 does not directly support extents, which are the set of all instances of a given class. Thus, there is no default means of performing a query on all the instances of a type, as you would by using tables in SQL. In an ODMG-93 implementation, you can define the equivalent of an extent by creating a named collection containing a reference for each instance of a type. A common naming approach is to use the name of a class (or an abbreviated name, such as Depts) and an ending *s* to imply multiple instances. A query can then use the named object facility to reference the collection of instances in OQL. ODMG release 2.0 supports extents, and OQL implementations will allow a name to be associated with each extent. The name can then be used to access the instances of the class.

The application decides which objects should have a name. As shown earlier, the object can be either a single application object or a collection containing references to many instances. The examples in the following chapters assume several `Employee` instances have names, including the following:

```
ceo
president
highest_paid
smartest
```

The company may have an IQ test, and the employee with the highest score gets the dubious title of smartest employee.

If an application accesses a particular set of objects often, you can create a named collection that contains a reference to each instance. The application can maintain multiple named collections. The set of objects to be processed together is statically specified. This approach results in efficient query processing, because no run-time predicate evaluation is required.

11.1.2   Attribute Access and Relationship Traversal

Given an expression ref that references an instance of type T_1 and attr, an attribute of T_1 of type T_2, the two expressions

     ref->attr   and   ref.attr

can be used to access attribute attr referenced by ref. Both expressions are of type T_2. Either the -> or . operator can be used; they are interchangeable in OQL. They can be used to access an attribute or to traverse a relationship. The attribute can be a data or a function member. If ref references a nonexistent object or contains the null value, an exception is thrown.

OQL does not enforce the C++ access specifiers `public`, `private`, and `protected`. Instead, all class data members are directly accessible. Unfortunately, this arrangement allows end users to access the underlying class implementation directly. An OQL implementation can provide a separate access control facility that could be used to limit a user's access to attributes. The operations in a class's public interface that embody the abstraction being modeled could be made available.

The expression

```
Network_Architecture._budget
```

accesses the `_budget` attribute of the `Department` instance named Network Architecture. The type of the query expression is the same type as the attribute `_budget` (d_ULong).

If an attribute references an object of type T, a query expression using the attribute is a query expression of type reference to T. The query

```
Network_Architecture->_manager
```

is a path expression that navigates from an instance of `Department` to an instance of `Employee` by using the `_manager` member in `Department`.

If an attribute is of type T and T has its own nested attributes, you can apply the . and -> operators repeatedly to access a nested attribute. For example,

```
Network_Architecture->_manager->_address.city
```

is a query expression that accesses the name of the city where the manager of the Network Architecture Department lives. The `Employee` class is derived from `Person`, which contains the attribute `_address` of type `Address`. Class `Address` contains a member called `city` of type `string`. The type of the preceding query expression is a `string`. This query uses a nested attribute, inheritance, and navigation.

11.1.3 Dereferencing

Suppose you have an expression ref that is a reference to an object of type T. The value of the expression ref is an object reference, and its representation will vary among implementations because each has a different approach to representing a reference in the database. Suppose the application needs to access the values of all the data members contained in the object referenced by ref. The expression

```
*ref
```

performs a dereference operation. The result type of the dereference operation is an object of type T, and the result value is the value of each of the attributes of the T instance referenced by ref. This approach is equivalent to use of the dereference operator `*` in C++ when ref is either a pointer or `d_Ref<T>`.

A query expression that uses the name of a named object, as in

```
Network_Architecture
```

actually produces a reference to the `Department` instance. The representation of this reference when you're using OQL within a C++ program would be `d_Ref<Department>`; when you're using OQL interactively, the representation is implementation-specific. To access all the attributes of the department, the dereference operation is used.

```
*Network_Architecture
```

This expression results in the value of the `Department` instance, which consists of all its attribute values.

11.1.4 Null Object References

A query can have an expression that uses an object reference with a null value. The OQL keyword `nil` represents a null object reference value. A query may try to use a null object reference with the operators `.` or `->` or with the dereference operator `*`. The result of such an operation is undefined. The OQL keyword

Operator	Value
`is_defined(expr)`	`true` if expr is defined, otherwise `false`
`is_undefined(expr)`	`true` if expr is undefined, otherwise `false`

Table 11.2 Operators to determine whether an expression is undefined.

`UNDEFINED` represents an undefined value. You can use the OQL Boolean operators in Table 11.2 to determine whether an expression is undefined. The result of using an undefined value as an operand with a Boolean comparison operator (=, !=, <, <=, >, >=) is false. Any other use of an undefined value in a query results in a run-time exception.

11.1.5 Invoking Operations on Objects

You can invoke an operation on an object instance. Specifically, you can call a C++ member function defined in an application class. Query users can be provided an interface that directly corresponds to the abstractions defined in the object model. Unfortunately, some OQL environments lack this feature.

Given an expression ref that evaluates to a reference to an instance of T and an operation oper defined as a member function of type T with no arguments, each of the four expressions

```
ref->oper          ref.oper          ref->oper()          ref.oper()
```

applies the operation oper to the object referenced by ref. The parentheses are optional when the operation has no arguments. Without parentheses, the syntax for invoking an operation is identical to the syntax for accessing an attribute. The type of the expression is based on the return type of oper, and the result value of the expression is the value returned when the operation oper is called. If the function has a return type of `void` in C++, the value of the expression is `nil`. If ref references a deleted or nonexistent object, a `d_Error_RefInvalid` exception is thrown.

If operation oper requires operands and if $expr_i$ are expressions whose types are compatible with the corresponding operand types required by oper, then the two expressions

```
ref->oper(expr1, expr2, ..., exprn)
ref.oper(expr1, expr2, ..., exprn)
```

apply operation oper to the object referenced by ref, passing parameters expr$_i$.

The reference can be declared as a reference to a base class but contain a reference to an instance of a derived class. OQL supports polymorphism when operations are invoked. If the operation oper is a C++ virtual function, the proper function is called based on the type of the object referenced.

11.1.6 Typing an Object Expression

Given an expression expr of type T_1 and a type T_2, where either T_1 and T_2 are the same type or T_2 is derived from T_1, then

    (T$_2$) expr

asserts that expr is an instance of class T_2. This technique is similar to using `dynamic_cast<T`$_2$`>` in C++. It is used primarily for *downcasting* an object reference from a known base class to a possible, but not certain, derived class. A downcast indicates, when a query is initially parsed and type checked, that expr should be treated as an expression of type T_2. At run time the query processor validates that expr is actually an instance of T_2. If expr is an instance of T_2, the result of this expression is a reference to T_2, which can then be used to access a property of T_2. If at run time expr is not an instance of T_2 or derived from T_2, an exception is raised.

11.1.7 Construction of Objects and Structures

An object can be constructed in a query, although it is a transient instance that is not inserted into the database. Given a type named T, with attributes attr$_i$ for i = 1 to n of type T_i, and expressions expr$_i$ such that for each i, attr$_i$ and expr$_i$ are of the same type T_i, then

    T(attr$_1$:expr$_1$, attr$_2$:expr$_2$, ..., attr$_n$:expr$_n$)

defines a new instance of T whose attributes attr$_i$ are initialized by the expressions expr$_i$. Not all of T's attributes are required; those not provided are initialized to a default null value. The provided attributes need not be in the same order that they are declared in C++. A constructor is not called for such an object when it is created. The query user can therefore initialize an object with values that might violate constraints of the class. This is unfortunate, in my opinion. To compensate for this, if an application needs to be able to create an object using a constructor, a function could be defined to perform the operation. The function could then be made accessible in the query environment.

The following OQL expression constructs an instance of `Person`.

```
Person (
    _fname:  "Jerry",
    _lname:  "Gaines"
    _address: Address (
        street:      "1038 Western Branch Blvd."
        city:        "Chesapeake"
        state:       "VA"
        zip_code:    "23309"
    )
    _phone_number:  "8045554309"
)
```

An object of type `Address` is embedded within the `Person` object.

It is also possible to define a new structure in OQL. Given attribute names $attr_i$ and expressions $expr_i$ for $i = 1$ to n, then

$$\texttt{struct}(attr_1 : expr_1, \ attr_2 : expr_2, \ \ldots, \ attr_n : expr_n)$$

defines a structure that contains attributes $attr_i$ initialized with values $expr_i$. The type of attribute $attr_i$ is determined by the type of the expression $expr_i$, T_i. The expression

$$\texttt{struct}(attr_1 : expr_1, \ attr_2 : expr_2, \ attr_3 : expr_3)$$

creates a structure with the following C-like definition:

```
struct {
    T₁    attr₁;
    T₂    attr₂;
    T₃    attr₃;
} value = { expr₁, expr₂, expr₃ };
```

These structures are defined dynamically and they do not correspond to a type defined in the application programming language. They are used in query expressions to produce a multivalued result. Chapter 12 has some examples that use this facility.

The expression

```
struct(title:"Lion King", rating:"G", sales:10000000)
```

creates a structure containing characteristics of a movie. It includes a string attribute called `title` with the value `"Lion King"`, a string attribute called rating with the value "G", and an integer attribute called sales with the value 10,000,000.

11.2 Atomic Literal Expressions

ODMG uses the term *atomic literal* to refer to a simple domain type. OQL has expressions that operate on atomic literal expressions.

11.2.1 Primitive Domain Types

OQL supports the following primitive domain types:

- A null object reference: nil

- Boolean: true, false

- Integer (32 bits)

- Float, consisting of a mantissa and an optional exponent, such as 3.1416 or 31416e-4

- Character, enclosed in single quotes, 'D'

- String, a sequence of characters enclosed in single or double quotes, such as "hello world"

For compatibility with SQL, OQL lets you use either single or double quotes for strings ("hello", 'hello'). But there is ambiguity when a single-character string is enclosed in single quotes. For example, with 'D' it is not clear whether a string or character expression is intended. The context of the expression in the query is used to resolve the ambiguity. To avoid confusion, you should use double quotes for strings.

11.2.2 Arithmetic Expressions

Some unary arithmetic operators are defined for integers and floating-point numbers. They are listed in Table 11.3, where num is an expression of type integer or floating point. The type of the expression result is the type of the operand num.

The integer and floating-point binary arithmetic operators include those shown in Table 11.4. They are of type float if either num_i or num_j is a float. But if both num_i and num_j are integers, the type of the result is an integer. Operator mod does not support floating-point expressions.

Operator	Description
+ num	The value of num
- num	Negation of num
abs num	Absolute value of num

Table 11.3 Unary arithmetic operators.

Operator	Description
num_i + num_j	Addition
num_i - num_j	Subtraction
num_i * num_j	Multiplication
num_i / num_j	Division
num_i mod num_j	Modulo

Table 11.4 Binary arithmetic operators.

11.2.3 Comparison Operators

The binary relational operators return a Boolean value. They include those shown in Table 11.5. These operators can be used with all the primitive domain types: numeric types (int, float), characters, strings, and Boolean (false < true). The operand expressions $expr_i$ and $expr_j$ must be of the same or compatible types (integer and float are considered compatible).

For example, the following query determines whether the CEO makes more than the president of the company.

```
ceo->salary() > president->salary()
```

Operator	Description
$expr_i$ = $expr_j$	True if $expr_i$ is equal to $expr_j$, otherwise false
$expr_i$!= $expr_j$	True if $expr_i$ is not equal to $expr_j$, otherwise false
$expr_i$ < $expr_j$	True if $expr_i$ is less than $expr_j$, otherwise false
$expr_i$ <= $expr_j$	True if $expr_i$ is less than or equal to $expr_j$, otherwise false
$expr_i$ > $expr_j$	True if $expr_i$ is greater than $expr_j$, otherwise false
$expr_i$ >= $expr_j$	True if $expr_i$ is greater than or equal to $expr_j$, otherwise false

Table 11.5 Binary comparison operators.

11.2.4 Boolean Operators

The unary and binary Boolean operators supported include those in Table 11.6. Both the operands and the result are of type Boolean. These operators are listed in the table in the order of decreasing precedence. The not operator has higher precedence than and, which has higher precedence than or. Section 11.6 lists the precedence of all query operators. Given Boolean expressions a, b, and c, the following expressions are equivalent.

```
not a and b or c    is equivalent to    ((not a) and b) or c
a or not b and c    is equivalent to    a or ((not b) and c)
```

You can use parentheses to override the precedence strength of operators. They can also improve the readability of a complex Boolean expression.

Operator	Description
not bool	True if bool is false, false if bool is true
$bool_i$ and $bool_j$	True if both $bool_i$ and $bool_j$ are true, otherwise false
$bool_i$ or $bool_j$	True if either $bool_i$ or $bool_j$ is true, otherwise false

Table 11.6 Boolean operators.

The query optimizer can choose the order these expressions are evaluated within the constraints of operator precedence and groupings via parentheses. If the optimizer expects that one of the operands can be evaluated more efficiently, it can order the evaluation to improve performance. When an `and` or `or` expression is evaluated, the left or right operand may be evaluated first. The evaluation of a Boolean expression can stop as soon as the result is known. With an `and` expression, if the first operand evaluated is false then the result is false and the other operand need not be evaluated. With an `or` expression, if the first operand is true, then the result of the `or` expression is true and the other operand does not need to be evaluated.

11.2.5   String Expressions

OQL supports operations on strings. In Table 11.7, the following apply:

- str, str_i, str_j expressions of type `string`
- char is an expression of type character
- m and n are expressions of type integer

The beginning index of a string is the value 0. The syntax for some of these expressions is identical to that of indexed collections as defined in Table 11.14.

Expression	Result Type	Result Value
str_i || str_j	String	Concatenation of str_i and str_j
str_i + str_j	String	Concatenation of str_i and str_j
char in str	Boolean	True if char is contained in str, otherwise false
str[n]	Char	The $n+1$th character in the string str
str[m:n]	String	The substring of str from $m+1$th character to the $n+1$th character (m <= n)
str like str_j	Boolean	True if the string in str matches the pattern (explained below) defined in str_j

Table 11.7 String expressions.

To create a single string that is the name of the CEO of the company, you can use either of the following expressions.

```
ceo->_first_name || ' ' || ceo->_last_name
ceo->_first_name + ' ' + ceo->_last_name
```

The expression

```
'O' in "Object Database"
```

is true, whereas the expression

```
'O' in "Relational Database"
```

is false.

Given a string expression str that contains the value "object databases offer lots of advantages", the following expression would equal the character 'd'.

```
str[7]
```

The following would equal the string "data".

```
str[7:10]
```

The like operator returns true if a specified pattern of characters exists in a string. The pattern must be a string literal that can include the wildcard characters shown in Table 11.8. The backslash character (\) can be placed just before one of these characters to turn off its role as a wildcard character, as when it must exist in the string. This escape mechanism was introduced in ODMG 2.0.

Wildcard Character	Interpretation
? or _	Matches any character
* or %	Any substring, including an empty substring

Table 11.8 Wildcard characters in a pattern string.

Given the string str defined earlier, the following expression would evaluate to true.

```
str like "object_data*advantage?"
```

If str contains the value "What % of the market?", the following expression is true.

```
str like "*\%*market\?"
```

11.3 Collections

OQL supports collections of elements of an arbitrary type. The collections and their corresponding names in the C++ interface are shown in Table 11.9. The dictionary collection has been added to ODMG 2.0. This section covers the operations that can be applied to instances of these collections. A collection can be a stand-alone persistent object, embedded as a member of a class, or created as a collection literal in an OQL expression. When a collection is embedded as member of a class, it does not have identity. The OQL specification refers to such a collection as a collection *literal* or *value*. Stand-alone persistent collections are referred to as collection *objects*.

OQL Collection	C++ Name	Element Characteristics
set	d_Set<T>	Unordered, no duplicates
bag	d_Bag<T>	Unordered, duplicates allowed
list	d_List<T>	Ordered, duplicates allowed
array	d_Varray<T>	Ordered, duplicates allowed
dictionary	d_Dictionary<K,V>	Unordered, no duplicates

Table 11.9 OQL collections and their C++ equivalents.

11.3.1 Construction of Collection Literals

A collection literal can be created in a query. It is transient and cannot be inserted into the database. It does not have object identity. A set, bag, list, and array collection literal can be created in OQL. As of ODMG 2.0, no syntax is defined for creating a dictionary literal.

11.3.1.1 set

Given expressions $expr_1$, $expr_2$, ..., $expr_n$ of type T, the expression

```
set(expr1, expr2, ... , exprn)
```

defines a set that contains the elements defined by the $expr_i$ expressions.

11.3.1.2 bag

Given expressions $expr_1$, $expr_2$, ..., $expr_n$ of type T, the expression

```
bag(expr1, expr2, ... , exprn)
```

defines a bag that contains the elements defined by the $expr_i$ expressions.

11.3.1.3 list

Given expressions $expr_1$, $expr_2$, ..., $expr_n$ of type T, the two expressions

```
list(expr1, expr2, ... , exprn)
(expr1, expr2, ... , exprn)
```

define a list that contains the elements defined by the $expr_i$ expressions.

If min and max are two expressions of type integer or character and min < max, then the two expressions

```
list(min .. max)                and        (min .. max)
```

define a list that contains the values

```
list(min, min+1, ..., max-1, max )
```

In the following, for example, the expressions on the left are shorthand expressions for the lists on the right.

```
list(5 .. 9)                    list(5, 6, 7, 8, 9)
(1 .. 3)                        list(1, 2, 3)
list('a' .. 'e')                list('a', 'b', 'c', 'd', 'e')
```

11.3.1.4 array

Given the expressions $expr_1$, $expr_2$, ..., $expr_n$ of type T, the expression

```
array(expr₁, expr₂, ... , exprₙ)
```

defines an array that contains the elements defined by the $expr_i$ expressions.

11.3.2 Operations on All Collections

There are operations that can be performed on all collection expressions. Some of them deal with the collection's cardinality, which is the number of elements in the collection. A collection with no elements is referred to as the *empty set* or *null set*. A collection with only a single element is referred to as a *singleton*. In the list of supported collection operations in Table 11.10, coll represents a collection expression that contains elements expr of type T. The operation element raises an exception if the operand is not a singleton collection.

The following query determines whether the smartest employee in the company works in the Network Architecture department.

```
smartest in Network_Architecture.employees
```

Recall that these are both named objects.

Expression	Result Type	Result Value
exists(coll)	Boolean	True if coll contains at least one element
unique(coll)	Boolean	True if coll contains only one element (singleton)
element(coll)	T instance	The single element expr in coll, if coll is a singleton
expr in coll	Boolean	True if expr is an element in coll
distinct(coll)	See below	A collection with coll's duplicate elements removed
count(coll)	Integer	The number of elements in coll

Table 11.10 Collection operations.

The following two queries use the `count` operation.

```
count(Depts)
count(Network_Architecture.employees)
```

The first query reports the number of departments, and the second one returns the number of employees in the Network Architecture department.

When `distinct` is applied to a `set<T>` or `bag<T>`, the type of the result is a `set<T>`. Because a `set<T>` does not have duplicates, the result of applying `distinct` to a `set<T>` is the same set contents. When `distinct` is applied to an ordered collection, such as `list<T>` or `array<T>`, the result is the same type as the operand. The ordering of the elements in the `list<T>` or `array<T>` operand is preserved, duplicates are removed, and the result contains the first occurrence of each value in the operand.

For example,

```
distinct( list(1,2,3,4,5,4,3,2,1) )
```

results in

```
list(1,2,3,4,5)
```

11.3.2.1 Aggregate Operators

Aggregate operators can be applied to a collection that contains elements of a numeric type (integer, float). Assuming that `coll` is a collection expression that contains elements of type integer or float, the operations in Table 11.11 are supported.

Expression	Result Type	Result Value
`min(coll)`	Instance of T	The minimum value in coll
`max(coll)`	Instance of T	The maximum value in coll
`sum(coll)`	Instance of T	The sum of all elements in coll
`avg(coll)`	Float	The computed average of all values in coll

Table 11.11 Aggregate operators.

11.3.3   Operations Specific to Sets and Bags

This section discusses operations that can be applied to sets and bags.

11.3.3.1   Binary Set Operations

OQL supports the set operations union, intersection, and difference, which are formally defined in section 7.4.2. Given expressions $coll_1$ and $coll_2$ that are either a `set<T>` or `bag<T>` instance, you can perform the set operations in Table 11.12.

Operation	Description
$coll_1$ `union` $coll_2$	Union of $coll_1$ and $coll_2$
$coll_1$ `intersect` $coll_2$	Intersection of $coll_1$ and $coll_2$
$coll_1$ `except` $coll_2$	The difference, $coll_1 - coll_2$

Table 11.12 Set operations.

If one of the collections is a `bag` and the other one is a `set`, the `set` is logically converted to a `bag` before the operation is applied. If both $coll_1$ and $coll_2$ are of type `set<T>`, the result of the set operation is a `set<T>`. If either $coll_1$ or $coll_2$ is a `bag`, the result is a `bag`. The intersection of two bags is a bag that contains the minimum quantity of each of the multiple values.

The following expressions produce the result specified to the right.

```
set(1,2,3) union set(3,4,5)                  set(1,2,3,4,5)
set(1,2,3) union bag(3,4,5)                  bag(1,2,3,3,4,5)
bag(1,2,2,3,4) except bag(1,2,3,4)           bag(2)
bag(1,2,2,3,4,4) intersect bag(1,1,2,4,4,4)  bag(1,2,4,4)
```

11.3.3.2   Subset and Superset Operations

Given expressions $coll_1$ and $coll_2$ that denote either sets or bags, it is possible to determine whether one of them is a subset or superset of the other. These operations are formally defined in section 7.4.1. If one of $coll_1$ or $coll_2$ is a bag, the other is logically converted to a `bag` before the operation is applied. The expressions in Table 11.13 produce a Boolean result indicating whether the expression is true or false. A collection $coll_1$ is a proper subset of a collection $coll_2$ only if $coll_2$ contains all the elements in $coll_1$ and if $coll_1$ is not equal to $coll_2$—that is, $coll_2$ has additional elements. The word *proper* implies that the collections are not equal.

Expression	Description
$coll_1$ < $coll_2$	True if $coll_1$ is a proper subset of $coll_2$
$coll_1$ <= $coll_2$	True if $coll_1$ is a subset of $coll_2$
$coll_1$ > $coll_2$	True if $coll_1$ is a proper superset of $coll_2$
$coll_1$ >= $coll_2$	True if $coll_1$ is a superset of $coll_2$

Table 11.13 Subset and superset operations on sets and bags.

The following expressions produce the Boolean result on the right.

```
set(1,2)      <    set(1,2)           false
set(1,2)      <    set(1,2,3)         true
set(1,2)      <=   set(1,2)           true
bag(1,2,3)    >    bag(1,2)           true
bag(1,2,3)    >    bag(5,6)           false
```

11.3.4 Operations Specific to Indexed Collections (list and array)

Certain operations can be applied to `list` and `array` indexed collections. The first element of an indexed collection has an index value of 0.

Assume that $coll_1$, $coll_2$, and $coll_3$ are expressions that denote indexed collections (list<T> or array<T>) containing elements of type T and assume that i and j are integer expressions. The concatenation operator + can be used only on collections of the same type; both $coll_1$ and $coll_2$ must be arrays or lists. The operations in Table 11.14 are provided. The syntax and semantics for some of these operations are the same when they are used with strings, as defined in Table 11.7. Table 11.15 lists examples of these expressions and their results.

11.3.5 Dictionary Operations

Given that collection expression dict is a dictionary with a key type of T_1 and a value type of T_2, and given an expression expr of type T_1, then the expression

```
dict[expr]
```

is an expression of type T_2 with the value that is associated with expr in dict.

Expression	Result Type	Result Value
first(coll$_1$)	Instance of T	First element of coll$_1$
last(coll$_1$)	Instance of T	Last element of coll$_1$
coll$_1$[i]	Instance of T	Element at index position i of coll$_1$
coll$_1$[i:j]	coll$_3$	The subcollection of coll$_1$ starting at index i and ending at index j, where i < j
coll$_1$ + coll$_2$	coll$_3$	The concatenation of coll$_1$ and coll$_2$

Table 11.14 Operations on indexed collections.

Query Expression	Result Value
first(list(1,2,3))	1
last(list(1,2,3))	3
list(1,3,5)[1]	3
array(1,3,5,7,11)[1:3]	array(3,5,7)
array(2,4,6) + array(3,5,7)	array(2,4,6,3,5,7)

Table 11.15 Uses of operations on indexed collections.

11.3.6 Collection Conversions

Several operations are available to convert from one type of collection to another. They are useful when the schema has defined a collection to be of one type of collection but the query needs a different type. They also can be used to convert the result of a query expression from one collection type to another.

11.3.6.1 Conversions between Collection Objects and Collection Literals

It is possible to convert from a collection object to a collection literal and from a collection literal to a collection object. This conversion is necessary when you're trying to compare collection objects in the database with collection literals created in the OQL query.

Given an expression $coll_1$ representing a stand-alone, persistent collection object with identity, the expression

```
*coll₁
```

uses the dereference operation to convert the collection object into a collection literal value equivalent to the collection literals described in section 11.3.1. This dereference expression is required when you're testing the equality of a collection object with a collection literal, which is discussed more fully in section 11.4.

Alternatively, you can convert a collection literal into a collection object. If T is the name of a collection type defined in the application and $coll_2$ is a collection literal compatible with T, then

```
T(coll₂)
```

creates a collection object from the collection literal. OQL does not support the template syntax found in C++, so the following expression is not valid OQL.

```
d_Set<int>( set(1,2,3) )
```

To create a collection object in OQL of type d_Set<int>, you must specify the following typedef in C++.

```
typedef d_Set<int> SetOfIntegers;
```

This type name can then be used in an OQL expression

```
SetOfIntegers( set(1,2,3) )
```

to create a collection object of type SetOfIntegers, which is the same type as d_Set<int>. This is how you convert a collection literal into a collection object.

11.3.6.2 Converting a List to a Set

Table 11.10 showed that distinct can be used to convert a bag into a set. Given a list expression list containing elements of type T, the expression

```
listtoset(list)
```

creates a set containing the elements of list with duplicates removed.

11.3.6.3   Converting to a List

A collection can be converted to a list. But a list is an ordered collection, so the order among the elements must be defined. You can convert a collection to a list by using the `order by` clause, which is covered in section 12.5.

11.3.6.4   Flattening a Collection

Given a collection-valued expression coll that contains elements that are themselves collections of some type T, (in other words, coll is of type $coll_1<coll_2<T>>$), the expression

```
flatten(coll)
```

converts coll into a collection of elements of type T. This flatten operation operates only one level deep even if the collection elements are nested more levels. (But you could nest `flatten` operations to deal with more deeply nested collections.) The types of $coll_1$ and $coll_2$ can be any one of the collection types (set, bag, list, or array). The result type and value of the expression `flatten(coll)` depend on the specific collection type of $coll_1$ and $coll_2$. Table 11.16 indicates the result type and value for every combination of collections. The first column indicates the type of $coll_1$, and the second column indicates the type of $coll_2$. An entry in the first column of $coll_1$ implies that any one of the specific collection types can be substituted. For example, in the first row it states that if $coll_2$ is a set, the result type is a set regardless of the collection type of $coll_1$. The table assumes that we have an expression coll that is of type $coll_1<coll_2<T>>$. If the result type of a `flatten` operation is a set, duplicate values are removed.

$coll_1$	$coll_2$	Result Type	Result Value of $\texttt{flatten}(coll_1 <coll_2 <T>>)$
$coll_1$	set	set<T>	Union of all $coll_2$<T> in $coll_1$
$coll_1$	bag	bag<T>	Union of all $coll_2$<T> in $coll_1$
list	list	list<T>	Concatenation of all $coll_2$<T> based on their order in $coll_1$
array	list	list<T>	Concatenation of all $coll_2$<T> based on their order in $coll_1$
array	array	array<T>	Concatenation of all $coll_2$<T> based on their order in $coll_1$
list	array	array<T>	Concatenation of all $coll_2$<T> based on their order in $coll_1$
set	list or array	set<T>	Each $coll_2$<T> is converted into a set<T> and a union of the sets is performed
bag	list or array	bag<T>	Each $coll_2$<T> is converted into a bag<T> and a union of the bags is performed

Table 11.16 Result type and value of $\texttt{flatten}$ operator.

Assume the collections in Table 11.17 have the specified elements.

Collection	Elements	Collection	Elements
set_1	1 2 3 4	bag_1	1 2 1
set_2	2 4 6 8	bag_2	2 4 5
set_3	1 3 5 7	bag_3	3 5 5
$list_1$	1 2 3	$array_1$	2 4 6 8
$list_2$	2 4 6	$array_2$	1 2 2 4
$list_3$	1 3 3		

Table 11.17 Collections and their elements for $\texttt{flatten}$ examples.

Flatten Expression	Result
flatten(list(set$_1$, set$_2$, set$_3$))	set(1,2,3,4,5,6,7,8)
flatten(bag(set$_1$, set$_2$, set$_3$))	set(1,2,3,4,5,6,7,8)
flatten(set(bag$_1$, bag$_2$, bag$_3$))	bag(1,1,2,2,4,5,5,5,3)
flatten(array(bag$_1$, bag$_2$, bag$_3$))	bag(1,1,2,2,4,5,5,5,3)
flatten(array(list$_1$, list$_2$))	list(1,2,3,2,4,6)
flatten(list(list$_1$, list$_2$, list$_3$))	list(1,2,3,2,4,6,1,3,3)
flatten(set(list$_1$, list$_2$, list$_3$))	set(1,2,3,4,6)
flatten(list(array$_1$, array$_2$))	array(2,4,6,8,1,2,2,4)
flatten(set(array$_1$, array$_2$))	set(1,2,4,6,8)
flatten(bag(array$_1$, array$_2$))	bag(2,2,2,1,4,4,6,8)

Table 11.18 Examples using the flatten operator.

The examples in Table 11.18 use the flatten operator to produce their result.

11.4 Equality

It is possible to perform equality and inequality operations on expressions that are either object references or values of an arbitrary type. Given expressions ref$_1$ and ref$_2$ that are references to objects of compatible types and given expressions expr$_1$ and expr$_2$ that denote values of compatible types, the Boolean equality expressions in Table 11.19 are supported.

The expressions expr$_1$ and expr$_2$ of compatible primitive domain types are equal if their values are equal. If expr$_1$ and expr$_2$ are query expressions that denote structures of the same form, with each member of the same type, respectively, they are equal if the respective members of the two structures are equal. This operation is applied recursively if there is further nesting of the structures.

The expressions expr$_1$ and expr$_2$ of compatible primitive domain types are equal if their values are equal. If expr$_1$ and expr$_2$ are query expressions that denote structures of the same form, with each member of the same type, respec-

Expression	Value
$ref_1 = ref_2$	True if ref_1 and ref_2 reference the same object
$ref_1 \; != \; ref_2$	True if ref_1 and ref_2 do not reference the same object
$expr_1 = expr_2$	True if $expr_1$ and $expr_2$ are equal
$expr_1 \; != \; expr_2$	True if $expr_1$ and $expr_2$ are not equal

Table 11.19 Equality and inequality operators for object references and object values.

tively, they are equal if the respective members of the two structures are equal. This operation is applied recursively if there is further nesting of the structures.

Similarly, the equality of two expressions denoting object values is determined by evaluating the equality of the respective data members of the object. This implies that their implementation values—and not their abstraction values—are compared. OQL does not use any equality operators that may have been defined for the type T in C++. However, the OQL implementation can allow methods and functions to be called. An application could then define an equality operation for this purpose. It can be either a member function or a stand-alone function and can be made available for use in the OQL environment. A query user would need to invoke the function instead of using the equality operator. This would allow an equality operation to be used based on an object's abstraction value instead of its implementation value.

The following query determines whether the highest paid employee is also the smartest.

```
highest_paid = smartest
```

These are named objects. To evaluate the query, the names are used to obtain a reference to the objects and then the object references are compared. The actual objects are not examined.

The keyword nil can be used to check whether an object reference ref has a null value. Thus, an expression of the form

```
ref != nil
```

can be used in a Boolean expression to determine whether a reference is null. Any attempt to dereference a reference that has the value nil throws a d_Error_-RefNull exception.

Given an expression ref that references an object of type T, the expression *ref dereferences the reference, which results in the value of the referenced T instance. Thus, the expression

$$*ref_1 = *ref_2$$

evaluates the equality of the referenced objects. The expression

$$*ref = expr$$

tests whether the value referenced by ref is equal to the object value expr.

A stand-alone persistent collection object has object identity. A collection that is embedded as an attribute of a persistent object does not have identity and is treated in OQL as a literal collection value. Given expressions $coll_1$ and $coll_2$ that denote stand-alone persistent collection objects, the expression

$$coll_1 = coll_2$$

performs identity equality, which is similar to the comparison of two references. To test the equality of the collection value, which is based on the equality of the elements, you must use this expression:

$$*coll_1 = *coll_2$$

But if the collection expressions $coll_1$ and $coll_2$ were embedded attributes (and thus without object identity), the expression

$$coll_1 = coll_2$$

would test whether the collection values are equal. The embedded collections are treated as if they were collection literals.

If you had a collection object expression $coll_1$ and a collection literal value expression $coll_2$, the value equality of these expressions would be expressed by

$$*coll_1 = coll_2$$

For example, suppose coll is a collection object expression that contains the integers 1, 2, and 3. To test whether coll is a set containing integers 1, 2, and 3, you dereference coll and compare it with a collection literal.

```
*coll = set(1,2,3)
```

Given two collection value expressions that are sets of element type T, they are equal if they contain the same element values. Two dictionary collections are equal if they have the same key and value associations. Two bags are equal if they contain the same element values with the same number of occurrences. Two lists or two arrays are equal if they contain the same element values in the same order. These rules for collection equality are the same as those defined for the collections in C++.

11.5 Functions

Given a function named func of return type T that requires zero or more arguments of type T_i and given expressions $expr_i$ of type T_i or of a type compatible with T_i, then

$$func() \qquad or \qquad func(expr_1, \ expr_2, \ \ldots \ , \ expr_n)$$

are expressions of type T that invoke the function func. The function is called by OQL, and it returns a value of type T. The type of the $expr_i$ expressions depends on the type of the arguments declared for the function func. If the function func does not return a value—return type of void in C++—the return value is nil. OQL does not dictate in what language func is written. But the OQL environment must be able to invoke the function, pass arguments, and return a value.

OQL's ability to invoke functions or object operations (section 11.1.5) makes it a very extensible query language. Functionality specific to the object model and application domain can be provided within the query language framework. The return type and the argument types can be either single scalar values (such as an integer, string, or object reference) or a collection (such as a set of references to instances of some class T). An application can define new aggregate operations similar to min, max, and avg. For example, if an application requires that the median of a set of integers be computed, the function could be written in C++ and then linked into the OQL environment. A function could also be written to provide an initial "entry point" object that would be used as the starting point for navigation in a query.

11.6 Operator Precedence

Table 11.20 lists the OQL operators and their relative precedence.

Operators (in Order of Precedence)						
( )	[ ]	.	->			
not	– (unary)	+ (unary)				
in						
*	/	mod	intersect			
+	–	union	except	||		
<	>	<=	>=	<some	<any	<all
=	!=	like				
and	exists	for all				
or						
..	:					
,						
(identifier)						
order by						
having						
group by						
where						
from						
select						

Table 11.20 Precedence of OQL operators.

Some of these operators will be described in Chapter 12. The rows of the table are ordered from highest to lowest precedence. Operators in the same row have the same precedence and group left-to-right. The operators <some, <any, and <all are called *composite predicates* and are covered in section 12.2.3. There are corresponding operators for the other comparison operators (=, !=, <=, >, and >=). They have the same precedence as the corresponding operators in the table (<some and so on). They are grouped left-to-right in the same order shown in the table.

Chapter 12
Predicates and Collection Queries

Chapter 11 introduced most of the basic query expressions and operators of OQL. They can be used to compose either simple or elaborate query expressions. This chapter discusses predicates and their use in filtering elements of a collection.

The `select from where` construct is familiar to those who use SQL. OQL provides a similar `select` clause but with significant enhancements that extend the facility far beyond the capabilities found in SQL.

12.1 Iterator Variables

To iterate over a collection, a query expression uses an *iterator variable* to reference the current element of iteration. An iterator variable is declared in the `from` clause of a `select` query or within a *universal* or *existential quantification* predicate, each described later. An iterator variable has the same type as that of the elements of the collection with which it is associated. Many of the query expressions described in this chapter use iterator variables.

12.2 Predicates

A *predicate* is a Boolean expression that constrains the elements in the result of another query expression. It is used to filter out elements for which the predicate is not true. The `where` clause of SQL and OQL contains a Boolean predicate discussed in section 12.3. An iterator variable is used within a predicate to reference the current element.

You can combine Boolean expressions to compose arbitrarily complex Boolean expressions by using the Boolean operators and, or, and not, which are discussed in section 11.2.4. You can use parentheses to group related Boolean expressions, override operator precedence, and simplify the expressions.

12.2.1 Universal Quantification

Universal quantification is a Boolean expression that is true only if a provided predicate is true for *all* the elements of a collection. If the predicate is false for one or more elements, the universal quantification expression is false.

Given a variable var, a collection expression coll, and a predicate expression predicate, the OQL Boolean expression

```
for all var in coll : predicate
```

is true only if predicate is true for all the elements of coll. Otherwise, it is false. For example, the following query determines whether all the employees in the Network Architecture department have a salary greater than 50,000.

```
for all e in Network_Architecture->employees :
    e->_salary > 50000
```

In this query expression, e is an iterator variable used in the predicate to reference the current element. Because the member employees in Department is of type d_Set<d_Ref<Employee>>, e is also of type d_Ref<Employee>. The evaluation of this expression can complete and return false as soon as an employee is found who makes $50,000 or less.

12.2.2 Existential Quantification

Existential quantification is a Boolean expression that is true if *at least one* element of a collection is true for the given predicate. In other words, it is true if there exists an element in the collection for which the predicate is true.

Given an iterator variable var, a collection expression coll, and a Boolean predicate expression predicate, the Boolean expression

```
exists var in coll : predicate
```

is true if at least one element of coll is true for the predicate predicate. If the predicate is false for all the elements, the existential quantification expression is false. For example, the following query determines whether any department in the company has more than 250 employees.

```
exists d in Depts : count(d.employees) > 250
```

The implementation of this expression does not need to access all the elements of the collection. It can stop processing elements and return true as soon as it encounters the first element that is true for the predicate. Appropriately placed indexes may allow the query to be evaluated more efficiently by reducing the number of elements that must be examined.

12.2.3 Composite Predicates

OQL provides a syntactical variation of universal and existential quantification that uses the comparison operators (=, !=, <, <=, >, and >=). Given an expression coll denoting a collection of elements of type T, an expression expr denoting a value of type T, and a comparison operator $\otimes$ from the set (=, !=, <, <=, >, >=), the Boolean *composite predicates* in Table 12.1 are supported. The predicates some and any are synonyms and have equivalent behavior. The following composite predicates are true.

```
20 = some list(10, 20, 30, 40)
100 < some list(2, 300)
"blue" = any array("red", "blue", "green")
100 > all set(25, 50, 75)
```

Composite Predicate	Equivalent Expression
expr $\otimes$ some coll	exists var in coll : expr $\otimes$ var
expr $\otimes$ any coll	exists var in coll : expr $\otimes$ var
expr $\otimes$ all coll	for all var in coll : expr $\otimes$ var

Table 12.1 Composite predicates.

The following composite predicates are false.

```
20 = some list(1, 2, 3, 4)
100 > some set(2, 45)
5 != all bag(3, 1, 5)
```

12.3   select ... from ... where ...

Given expressions $coll_i$ denoting collections containing elements of type T_i, iterator variables v_i, a Boolean predicate predicate, ordering expression ord, and a projection projection, then the following is a query expression.

```
select   [distinct]   projection
from                  coll₁ as v₁, coll₂ as v₂, ... , collₙ as vₙ
[ where               predicate ]
[ order by            ord ]
```

The square brackets indicate optional keywords or clauses. There are also `group by` and `having` clauses, which are discussed in section 12.4.

The result of a `select` query expression is a collection of elements whose type is determined by the projection projection. The type of the collection itself is determined by the form of the query and whether the `distinct` keyword or `order by` clause is present (see Table 12.2). The `distinct` keyword causes duplicates to be removed. If `distinct` is not specified, the query may or may not have duplicate values. It depends on whether duplicate values are in the database and query result.

order by	distinct	Result Collection	Duplicates Removed
✔	✔	list	yes
✔		list	no
	✔	set	yes
		bag	no

Table 12.2 Type of collection result for `select`.

Conceptually, the following steps are taken to evaluate a `select` query expression.

1. The *cartesian product* of the collections $coll_i$ specified in the `from` clause is formed. Logically, each collection is treated as a `bag` of values of type T_i (`bag<`T_i`>`) even though the collection may actually be a `set`, `list`, or `array`. The result of the cartesian product is a `bag` of the following type:

$$\texttt{bag< struct(}v_1\texttt{:}T_1\texttt{, } v_2\texttt{:}T_2\texttt{, } \ldots \texttt{ , } v_n\texttt{:}T_n\texttt{) >}$$

   The elements collectively represent every possible combination of values from each collection $coll_i$.

2. The cartesian product is filtered by removing the elements from it that evaluate `false` for the Boolean predicate `predicate` in the `where` clause. If the `where` clause is omitted, no elements are filtered from the result. Having no `where` clause is equivalent to having a Boolean predicate `predicate` that is true for every element of the cartesian product.

3. If the `order by` clause is present, the result of step 2 is transformed into a `list` that is ordered based on the ordering expression `ord`. The `order by` clause is discussed in section 12.5.

4. The projection `projection` is applied to the filtered result of step 3.

5. If the `distinct` keyword is present, duplicate projection values are removed.

If you're unfamiliar with a cartesian product, consider the following example. Suppose the following three collections are used:

```
set< d_Ref<T> > c₁ = (objid₁, objid₂, objid₃)
list<d_String>  c₂ = ("red", "blue", "green")
array<int>      c₃ = (7, 11)
```

Following are the elements of the cartesian product formed by c_1, c_2, and c_3.

$objid_1$	"red"	7
$objid_1$	"red"	11
$objid_1$	"blue"	7
$objid_1$	"blue"	11
$objid_1$	"green"	7
$objid_1$	"green"	11

objid$_2$	"red"	7
objid$_2$	"red"	11
objid$_2$	"blue"	7
objid$_2$	"blue"	11
objid$_2$	"green"	7
objid$_2$	"green"	11
objid$_3$	"red"	7
objid$_3$	"red"	11
objid$_3$	"blue"	7
objid$_3$	"blue"	11
objid$_3$	"green"	7
objid$_3$	"green"	11

It contains each possible combination of values from the collections.

The cardinality of a cartesian product is the product of the collection cardinalities. It can become extremely large. Suppose there are three collections in the cartesian product with cardinalities of 1,000, 100,000, and 100. These are reasonable sizes if the collections represent all the instances of a type. The cardinality of this cartesian product is 10 billion elements! Minimizing the cardinalities of the collection expressions coll$_i$ can reduce the amount of processing required to compute the cartesian product formed by the `from` clause.

For practical reasons, implementations perform some filtering before generating the cartesian product. In most query implementations, the cartesian product is never explicitly generated, but the result must reflect the mathematical equivalent of the cartesian product.

12.3.1   The `from` Clause

The `from` clause specifies the collections to use in forming the cartesian product. Both SQL and OQL support the `from` clause, but there are several differences. The collection expressions coll$_i$ specified in the `from` clause of OQL are not simple extent names, similar to the table names that are specified in SQL. Any query expression whose result is a collection can be used as a collection expression in an OQL `from` clause. This includes the following expressions:

- Extent

- Named collection

- Literal collection (section 11.3.1)

- Collection attribute embedded as a member of a class

- Stand-alone collection that is referenced
- Collection returned by an object method or function
- Result of a binary set operation: union, intersection, or difference (section 11.3.3.1)
- Result of a subcollection or concatenation operation (section 11.3.4)
- Result of a collection conversion operation: `listtoset` or `flatten` (section 11.3.6)
- Another `select` query expression (subquery)

SQL allows views to be specified in the `from` clause, and they sometimes perform equivalent operations.

Each $coll_i$ denotes a collection of elements of some type T_i. The collection can be any type supported by the OQL environment, including a `set`, `bag`, `list`, or `array`. An OQL implementation should support every collection type that is also supported in the C++ interface. An element in a $coll_i$ is a *single value* of type T_i.

With a SQL relational database, a component in the `from` clause is a *table*. A table contains *tuples*, which, in general, have multiple columns. In other words, a tuple potentially has *multiple values*. From a C++ and OQL perspective, a tuple is like a `struct` with a data member corresponding to each column of a table. In SQL the `from` clause can contain only tables or views, which are computed tables.

The element type of the collections in OQL can be any type T supported in the schema. OQL provides much more flexibility in the types of data supported, letting you use function composition more effectively. The result of a `select` query can serve as an operand of an operation that expects a collection with elements of the type expressed in the `select`'s projection.

SQL is based on *tuple relational calculus*, which requires that the components of the cartesian product be of type tuple. OQL is based on *domain relational calculus*, and the components of the cartesian products can be of any domain type; it is not limited to tuples. Domain relational calculus is therefore more general and offers a higher degree of type flexibility than tuple relational calculus. Thus, OQL provides a richer typing environment than SQL for expressing database queries.

The OQL `from` clause specifies a comma-separated set of collections to use in forming the cartesian product. An iterator variable can be associated with each collection so that the "current" collection element value can be referenced in other parts of the query. The following expression is used to associate an iterator variable with a collection expression.

```
coll_i as v_i
```

The as keyword is optional; the expression can simply be stated as

```
coll_i v_i
```

For example, the following query uses the collection named Depts to access the names of all the departments in the company.

```
select   d.name()
from     Depts as d
```

This can also be written without the keyword as.

```
select   d.name()
from     Depts d
```

The iterator variable v_i can be omitted, in which case the collection expression $coll_i$ is used as the variable name to reference the current collection element in other parts of the query. But queries are easier to express and understand when an iterator variable is used.

In the $from$ clause, the expression

```
v_i in coll_i
```

can also be used, but this is old OQL syntax that has been kept for backward compatibility. To be more compatible with SQL, OQL adopted the membership operator in in ODMG-93 release 1.2, specified in Table 11.10. The SQL in operator is used as a membership operator, which has a different meaning from the original OQL meaning. Thus, the OQL in operator has one of two meanings depending on whether it is used in a $from$ clause or as the membership operator. Avoiding the use of the in operator in the OQL $from$ clause—instead using the syntaxes described earlier—will lead to queries that are more similar to SQL. You will also reduce confusion if you use the in operator only as the membership operator, as adopted from SQL.

A collection expression $coll_j$ in the $from$ clause can be based on another iterator variable v_i where $i < j$. (This restriction prevents circular definitions of iterator variables, which would result in an ill-formed query.) This technique provides a clear and efficient navigational means of expressing the set of related objects required. It allows a more precise designation of the collections $coll_i$ to be processed in a query. You can specify the expressions in *one* place: the $from$ clause.

For example, the following query gets the first and last name of the children whose parents work in any Human Resources department.

```
select   c._fname, c._lname
from     Depts d, d.employees e, e._children c
where    d._name = "Human Resources"
```

All the departments that have the name Human Resources are directly accessed via the iterator variable d. The employees in those departments are accessed directly from the employees member of Department and are referenced by e. The children of each of those employees are accessed via the _children member. This query directly navigates among objects that are statically related in the database. No join or search processing is required of either an Employee or a Person extent. Specifying an iterator variable based on the value of another iterator variable can provide a significant performance advantage. The cartesian product result of the from clause is restricted to a much smaller set of values, approaching the cardinality of the final query result.

With a relational SQL database, a join condition is specified in the where clause to establish relationships among tuples in the tables. The following SQL query is equivalent to the previous OQL example:

```
select   c._fname, c._lname
from     Department d, Employee e, Children c
where    d.name = "Human Resources" and
         d.deptID = e.deptID and
         c.parentID = e.empID
```

The join conditions are intermixed with all other Boolean constraints in a query. This arrangement results in a where clause that contains a mixture of expressions serving different roles in constraining the results of a query. The cartesian product ends up with a much larger cardinality. Without extensive optimization, the SQL cartesian product can have a much larger cardinality and require much more filter processing in the from clause than an equivalent OQL query.

The OQL version of this query can traverse known static relationships among the departments and their employees and among the employees and their children. Only the objects that are needed are accessed. In SQL, join processing must be performed to process the query. And hopefully, indexes are present so that the number of tuples that are searched can be minimized.

12.3.2 The where Clause

The where clause contains a Boolean predicate predicate that is logically evaluated for each element of the cartesian product formed by the from clause. (Use of optimizations such as indexes can reduce the number of elements of the cartesian product.) The iterator variables specified in the from clause can be used by expressions in the predicate to reference the components of the cartesian product. Many of the OQL operators return a Boolean value that can be used to express constraints in the `where` clause. Only the cartesian product elements that are true for the Boolean predicate are retained in the query result; those that are false are discarded.

12.3.3 The `select` Clause

A `select` query returns a collection. The type of the collection itself is determined by the form of the query as defined in Table 12.2. The type of the elements is determined by the projection projection in the `select` clause. Conceptually, the projection step of query evaluation receives as input a collection of elements that result from applying all the other clauses of the query. The type of these elements is as follows:

$$\texttt{struct}(v_1:T_1, \ v_2:T_2, \ \dots \ , \ v_n:T_n)$$

Each v_i is the iterator variable defined in the `from` clause of the query. These structures contain the values from the cartesian product that remain after all other filtering has been performed. The projection projection is a single query expression that uses the values contained in the structures to produce a final result. It can contain expressions that use the iterator variables v_i to refer to the values of the current element.

An element of the collection returned by a `select` query is a single value of a given type. The element type may be any of the following:

- An object reference

- An object value (including the actual attribute values)

- A `struct`

- A primitive type (like `int`, `float`, `string`)

- A collection

It can be any type supported in OQL.

The following queries illustrate some of the possibilities. The immediately following query accesses the budget of every department.

```
select  d._budget
from    Depts d
```

Because this query involves a single class, the iterator variable can be removed without ambiguity. The scope rules for names are covered in section 12.9. The following queries return a bag with elements of type integer.

```
select  _budget
from    Depts
```

The functional nature of OQL allows a query such as this to be used directly as an operand of another query expression. For example, the following query obtains the total budget of all departments.

```
sum( select _budget from Depts )
```

The return type of the query

```
select  d
from    Depts d
where   d._budget > 1000000
```

is a `bag` of `Department` references; the references refer to `Department` instances that have a budget greater than one million. To access the name and budget of each department, you must form a `struct` result.

```
select  struct(name: d->_name, budget: d->_budget)
from    Depts d
where   d._budget > 1000000
```

The `struct` member names (`name`, `budget`) are specified on the left side of the colons; the type and value of each `struct` member is determined by the query expression on the right side of the colon. The specification of a `struct` is covered in section 11.1.7. The following query shows how to return the actual `Depart-`ment instance value as the result of the query.

```
select  *d
from    Depts d
where   d._budget > 1000000
```

The type of this result is a `struct`, with a member for each attribute of `Department`, including its embedded collections that contain references to other objects. This includes the `employees` and `projects` members.

In these examples the expressions in the `select` clause simply access attributes. But they can be expressions of arbitrary complexity. You can use any valid query expression, including an expression that performs another `select`.

In OQL the result type is arbitrary, whereas SQL always returns a table of tuples. This is another outcome of OQL being based on domain relational calculus instead of tuple relational calculus. OQL can return the equivalent of a tuple if you construct a `struct` in the projection. The earlier query that returned the name and budget of departments returned a `struct` equivalent to a tuple.

If the projection projection is the single character `*`, the result of the query is a collection of `struct` in which each member positionally corresponds to an iterator variable declared in the `from` clause.

```
struct(v_1:T_1, v_2:T_2, ... , v_n:T_n)
```

As a syntactical convenience and to provide compatibility with SQL, you can also specify a comma-separated list of projection expressions. Each projection should be in one of the following forms:

- expression as identifier
- identifier : expression
- expression

An identifier must exist for each projection expression. This last form is valid only if an identifier name can be inferred from the expression—for example, if it corresponds to an attribute name. A list of n projection expressions creates a type defined as

```
struct( identifier_1 : type_of_expression_1,
        identifier_2 : type_of_expression_2,

   ...

        identifier_n : type_of_expression_n );
```

The type of each structure member is inferred from the type of the projection expression. For example, in the following query the structure consists of a string and an integer.

```
select  d._name, d._budget
from    Depts d
```

To return multiple values for each element in a `select` clause, the projection must be a `struct`. Use of the comma-separated list of expressions serves as a syntactical abbreviation for the more comprehensive specification of the `struct` defined by the projection.

12.4 **The `group by` and `having` Clauses**

OQL supports a `group by` clause similar to the one provided in SQL. It allows the elements of the cartesian product to be partitioned into separate groups based on specified criteria. Given a `select` query select_query as defined in section 12.3, a structure expression partition_attributes, and a group predicate group_predicate, the syntax of a `group by` expression is

>   select_query `group by` partition_attributes

or

>   select_query `group by` partition_attributes `having` group_predicate

The *partition attributes* define the basis for partitioning the elements of the cartesian product into groups. A partition attribute can be an expression of any type. A group is defined for each unique set of partition attribute values. Each element of the cartesian product will be associated with one group based on its values for the partition attributes.

Each element of the select_query is evaluated with respect to the partition attributes. Elements with the same values for all the partition attributes are placed in the same group. After this grouping is performed, the result is transformed (and potentially collapsed) into a set of structures. Each structure contains a value for each partition attribute and a bag containing each of the elements of the select_query that had the same values for the partition attributes.

The iterator variables v_i of a select_query are associated with collection expressions $coll_i$ that contain elements of type T_i (for i=1,n). The `group by` clause introduces partition attributes pa_j of type PT_j (j=1,m) for m partition attributes. The result type of the `group by` is defined as follows:

```
set <    struct( pa₁ : PT₁, pa₂ : PT₂, ... , paₘ : PTₘ,
                 partition : bag<struct(v₁:T₁, v₂:T₂, ..., vₙ:Tₙ)> )
     >
```

The set will contain a structure element for each unique set of partition attribute values. Each structure element contains a data member that contains the value of the partition attribute. It also contains a bag called `partition` whose elements are the iterator values of the select_query that have the same partition attribute values. Each element that resulted from the select_query is referenced in the `partition` of one and only one `struct` of the preceding `set`.

Consider the following query.

```
select      state, city,
                avg(select p.e._salary from partition p)
from        Depts d, d.employees e
where       d._budget > 10000000
group by    state: e._address.state, city: e._address.city
```

The `from` and `where` clauses obtain all the departments with budgets greater than 10 million along with their employees. Suppose the departments shown in Table 12.3 have large enough budgets.

Department	
ObjectID	name
dept$_1$	"Network Performance"
dept$_2$	"Switching Architecture"
dept$_3$	"Operations Engineering"

Table 12.3 Departments with budgets greater than 10 million.

The employees in Table 12.4 work in those departments. The intermediate result is a bag of structures. Each `struct` contains an `Employee` and `Department` reference, which corresponds to the first two columns in Table 12.4.

This bag is then grouped based on the names of the employee's state and city. The intermediate result of this step is a set described next. Its elements are of type `struct`, with a member for each partition attribute (`state` and `city`) and also a bag called `partition` that contains the elements of the cartesian product that have the same partition attribute values. They are contained in a `struct` and consist of the values of the iterator variables `e` and `d`, which become the names of the members of the `struct` in `partition`.

```
set<struct( state : char *, city : d_String,
            partition : bag<struct( d : d_Ref<Department>,
                                    e : d_Ref<Employee>)>
    )
>
```

Employee				
ObjectID	DeptID	_address.state	_address.city	_salary
emp_1	$dept_1$	"OH"	"Gahanna"	78000
emp_2	$dept_1$	"NJ"	"Holmdel"	89000
emp_3	$dept_1$	"IL"	"Naperville"	81000
emp_4	$dept_1$	"OH"	"Reynoldsburg"	75000
emp_5	$dept_1$	"NJ"	"Holmdel"	87000
emp_6	$dept_1$	"OH"	"Gahanna"	77000
emp_7	$dept_1$	"IL"	"Naperville"	83000
emp_8	$dept_1$	"OH"	"Reynoldsburg"	77000
emp_9	$dept_2$	"NJ"	"Holmdel"	85000
emp_{10}	$dept_2$	"NJ"	"Red Bank"	83000
emp_{11}	$dept_2$	"NJ"	"Red Bank"	85000
emp_{12}	$dept_2$	"IL"	"Naperville"	81500
emp_{13}	$dept_2$	"IL"	"Indian Hill"	85000
emp_{14}	$dept_2$	"IL"	"Naperville"	82500
emp_{15}	$dept_3$	"OH"	"Gahanna"	79000
emp_{16}	$dept_3$	"NJ"	"Red Bank"	84000
emp_{17}	$dept_3$	"OH"	"New Albany"	84000
emp_{18}	$dept_3$	"NJ"	"Murray Hill"	96000
emp_{19}	$dept_3$	"NJ"	"Murray Hill"	94000
emp_{20}	$dept_3$	"OH"	"New Albany"	80000

Table 12.4 Employees in big budget departments.

For the example data, the following set is produced.

```
set(
    struct("IL", "Indian Hill", bag(struct(dept₂, emp₁₃))),
    struct("IL", "Naperville",  bag(struct(dept₁, emp₃),
                                    struct(dept₁, emp₇),
                                    struct(dept₂, emp₁₂),
                                    struct(dept₂, emp₁₄))),
    struct("NJ", "Holmdel",     bag(struct(dept₁, emp₂),
                                    struct(dept₁, emp₅),
                                    struct(dept₂, emp₉))),
    struct("NJ", "Murray Hill", bag(struct(dept₃, emp₁₈),
                                    struct(dept₃, emp₁₉))),
    struct("NJ", "Red Bank",    bag(struct(dept₂, emp₁₀),
```

```
                                                       struct(dept_2, emp_11),
                                                       struct(dept_3, emp_16))),
          struct("OH",  "Gahanna",        bag(struct(dept_1, emp_1),
                                                       struct(dept_1, emp_6),
                                                       struct(dept_3, emp_15))),
          struct("OH",  "New Albany",     bag(struct(dept_3, emp_17),
                                                       struct(dept_3, emp_20))),
          struct("OH",  "Reynoldsburg",bag(struct(dept_1, emp_4),
                                                       struct(dept_1, emp_8)))
      )
```

The `select` clause produces a final query result that consists of the following:

- The name of a state (by using the partition attribute name `state`)
- The name of a city (by using the partition attribute name `city`)
- The average salary of the employees that live in the same city

To compute an average salary, the `partition` is converted from a bag of `struct` into a collection of integers (salaries). A query is performed on the partition, and the structure member `e` is used to access the salary of each employee in the partition. (Note that a query also has the option of returning the partition itself as a component of the final query result.) The final result of the query is the following:

```
      bag(
          struct("IL",  "Indian Hill",     85000),
          struct("IL",  "Naperville",      82000),
          struct("NJ",  "Holmdel",         87000),
          struct("NJ",  "Murray Hill",     95000),
          struct("NJ",  "Red Bank",        84000),
          struct("OH",  "Gahanna",         78000),
          struct("OH",  "New Albany",      82000),
          struct("OH",  "Reynoldsburg",    76000)
      )
```

Even though the intermediate result of the `group by` clause is a set, the final result is a bag. The projection in the `select` clause may have expressions that result in duplicate values. If the application needs each element to be unique, the `distinct` keyword should be used.

Some implementations may produce results in sorted order. They may use sorted data structures internally to improve performance. But the application should not rely on this side effect. If the final result must be sorted, the `order by` clause should be used.

Once `group by` has split the data into groups, the `having` clause can be used to filter entire groups from the query result. The `having` clause defines a Boolean group_predicate that is evaluated for each element of the set constructed by the `group by` operation. It filters the set before processing the projection in the `select` clause. A group in the set is included in the final query result only if the group_predicate evaluates to `true`.

The group_predicate can contain expressions that use the partition attributes and the `partition` bag. Because `partition` is a `bag`, any query expressions that can be performed on a bag can be applied to `partition` in either the `having` or the `select` clause. The previous query example is enhanced to remove the cities where the average employee salary is less than or equal to 82,500. The number of employees in each group is also retrieved.

```
select      state, city,
            avg(select p.e._salary from partition p),
            count(partition)
from        Depts d, d.employees e
where       d._budget > 10000000
group by    state: e._address.state, city: e._address.city
having      avg(select p.e._salary from partition p) > 82000
```

With this query the result is as follows:

```
bag(
    struct("IL", "Indian Hill", 85000, 1),
    struct("NJ", "Holmdel",     87000, 3),
    struct("NJ", "Murray Hill", 95000, 2),
    struct("NJ", "Red Bank",    84000, 3)
)
```

The `having` clause is similar to the `where` clause. The `where` clause has a predicate to filter elements from the cartesian product of the `from` clause. The `group by` clause uses the result of the `where` clause as input and groups the elements based on the specification of partition attributes. The `having` clause then uses a predicate to filter out groups produced by the `group by` clause. Thus, both the `where` and the `group by` clauses filter out elements from their input source.

12.5 The order by Clause

The results of a query can be ordered. Given a select_query of the form

```
select projection from Cᵢ [where predicate]
[group by partition_attributes [having group_predicate]]
```

(the brackets imply optional clauses) and expressions $expr_i$, then

```
select_query order by expr₁, expr₂, ... , exprₙ
```

returns the elements of select_query as a list ordered based on the expressions $expr_i$. The elements are first ordered based on the expression $expr_1$; then all elements with equal value for $expr_1$ are ordered based on $expr_2$ and so on for all $expr_i$. Each expression $expr_i$ can be followed by the keyword asc or desc (ascending or descending order). If no keyword (asc or desc) is provided for a given $expr_i$, the ordering is based on the ordering of the previous expression, $expr_{i-1}$. The default ordering for $expr_1$ is ascending.

The following query returns all the employees in the Network Architecture department sorted from highest paid to lowest and, for those making the same salary, alphabetically based on their last name and first name.

```
select      e._lname, e._fname
from        Network_Architecture.employees e
order by    e._salary desc, e._lname asc, e._fname
```

If any employees in the department have the same last name, their first names are used to determine the order.

12.6 Joins

A collection expression defined in the from clause can be derived from a path expression using an iterator variable for another collection in the from clause. This approach lets you use known relationships among objects to constrain the cartesian product to include only the related objects required in the query. In this way, an implementation can perform efficient navigational access to related objects by constraining the cardinality and computation of the cartesian product. But sometimes an application needs to establish a relationship among objects dynamically at run time, often by expression value constraints among the attributes of the objects.

A *join condition* is a Boolean expression that defines value constraints among the elements of the cartesian product. Elements for which the constraint is not true are removed from the result. The join conditions are specified in the `where` clause. Join conditions are the only means of establishing relationships in SQL. They can also be specified in an OQL query.

Given the named collection Depts containing all the departments and a named collection Projects containing all the projects in the company, the following query returns the name of all departments that have the same name as a project within another department.

```
select distinct p.name, d._name
from    Depts d, Projects p
where   d != p->department and d._name = p.name
order by p.name
```

Traversing a relationship that exists in the schema by using path expressions or defining one iterator variable in terms of another is preferred over using a join condition. But if the relationship does not explicitly exist in the schema and it can be established dynamically with a value-based association, then it is appropriate to use a join condition in the `where` clause.

12.7 Named Query Definition

Because OQL supports function composition, you can specify elaborate queries that contain an arbitrary nesting of operands. A large query can become complex. To simplify it, you can associate a name with a query expression and use the name in place of the query expression as a component within a larger one. Query expressions can be defined once and reused in other query expressions.

Given an identifier name (denoted here by name) and a query expression (denoted here by query_expr), then

```
define [query] name(x_1, x_2, ..., x_n) as query_expr
```

is a *query definition expression* that associates the name name with the query query_expr, with query variables x_i used in query_expr. The word `query` is optional. A query definition cannot be recursive.

If the query definition does not require any parameters, it can be defined as follows:

```
define name as query_expr
```

When a named query with no parameters is used, the parentheses are optional.

For example, the following query definition expression returns all the employees who have a first name of Bryce.

```
define all_emps_named_bryce as
    select  e
    from    Employees e
    where   e._fname = "Bryce"
```

Once this query definition has been defined, using the name substitutes the query associated with it into the query.

```
all_emps_named_bryce
```

The result of this query is a bag of references to employees whose first name's are Bryce. The following query definition returns all the employees with a specified last name living in a particular city.

```
define emp_name_in_city(n,c) as
    select  e
    from    Employees e
    where   e._lname = n and e._address.city = c
```

Once this has been defined, the following query is valid.

```
emp_name_in_city("Mathie", "Louisville")
```

You cannot overload the name name by varying the number of arguments. The name of a query expression cannot be the same as a named object in the database, the name of a class method or function, or a class name. Reuse of a name is not allowed, because it leads to ambiguities.

Each time a function expression is encountered in query evaluation, an attempt is first made to bind it to a schema-defined function or method. If this fails and a query definition exists with the right name and number of parameters, the query expression (query_expr) and its variables are substituted appropriately. The following query definition produces a Boolean result that is true if the manager of the Network Architecture department makes no less than any other employee in the department.

```
define NetArchMgrPaidMost as
    Network_Architecture->_manager._salary =
    max(select distinct e._salary
        from Network_Architecture->employees e)
```

A query definition is stored in the database. It remains active until it is replaced by a new query definition of the same name or when it is deleted by this command:

```
delete definition name
```

A previous query definition is deleted by the following statement:

```
delete emp_name_in_city
```

12.8 Subqueries

Because OQL is based on functional composition, a subquery is natural and straightforward. A query expression consists of an operator with a set of operands. Each operand can itself be an arbitrary query expression. Consequently, any operand of a query expression can itself be a subquery. Any query expression that expects a collection expression as an operand can use a `select` query to construct the collection expression. Query definitions can also be used as an effective mechanism for simplifying the specification of more complicated, nested queries.

For example, the query definition

```
define all_brookes as
    select  e
    from    Employees e
    where   e._fname = "Brooke"
```

can then be used in the specification of the following query:

```
define highly_paid_brookes as
    select  struct( fname: b._fname,
                    lname: b._lname, sal: b.salary)
    from    all_brookes b
    order by b.salary desc
```

Because the `order by` clause is used in this query, the result collection is a list of structures ordered from highest to lowest salary. The preceding query is equivalent to the following query, which does not use a query definition.

```
select  struct( fname: b._fname,
                lname: b._lname, sal: b.salary)
from    (   select e from Employees e
            where e._fname = "Brooke") b
order by b.salary desc
```

The following query would return the last name of the highest-paid employee with a first name of Brooke.

```
define highest_paid_brooke as
      first(highly_paid_brookes).lname
```

Because `highly_paid_brookes` is already ordered based on salary, accessing the first element of the list gets the highest-paid employee named Brooke.

12.9 Scope Rules for Names

When query users specify a complicated query with nested query expressions and multiple `select` clauses, it is important that they understand the scope of names used in the query. A query user may assume that a name is in one scope when it is actually in another scope much broader than anticipated. A misunderstanding about the scope of a name can lead to an incorrect query result and a confused query user.

A `select` query may involve several collections with elements of different types. A collection's element type may have an attribute with a name that is unique across all the collections in the `from` clause. In this case, there is no ambiguity about which collection element is being used, so the name can be used by itself without its associated iterator variable. But if an attribute name is associated with more than one of the collections in a `select` clause, the iterator variable is required. Otherwise, it would be ambiguous as to which collection element is being referred to. For clarity and ease of comprehension, it is recommended that iterator variables always be used.

12.9.1 Iterator Variable Names

Implicit and explicit names for iterator variables are introduced in a `from` clause. If a collection in the `from` clause does not have an iterator variable, the name of the collection itself serves implicitly as the iterator variable name. The scope of these names includes all parts of the corresponding `select` query, including all nested query expressions.

12.9.2 Partition Names

When a `group by` clause is used in a query, the name `partition` is introduced as well as any specified partition attribute names. These names are in a scope that includes the `having` and `select` clauses associated with the `group by` clause along with all nested query expressions within those clauses.

12.9.3 Name Lookup

When a name appears in a query, it is looked up in the following order:

1. A variable in the current scope
2. A named query, introduced by the `define` expression
3. A named object
4. An attribute or operation name of an iterator variable in the current scope when there is no ambiguity

12.10 Summary

This chapter concludes our coverage of OQL. The functional nature of the language allows the expression of elaborate queries. This chapter discussed predicates and the `select` clause, which is familiar to those who have used SQL. We noted the few differences between an OQL `select` and an SQL `select`—in particular, OQL's additional type flexibility and the ability to express navigation efficiently in the `from` clause. Chapter 13 discusses how to embed OQL queries in C++ applications.

Chapter 13
OQL Execution Environments

This chapter focuses primarily on C++ interfaces for issuing OQL queries. A query can be submitted on a collection or database basis. Each implementation that supports OQL provides a C++ interface and an interactive interface; the interactive interfaces differ with each product. Queries are either entered in an interactive shell environment or placed in a file that is read by a query program. This chapter concludes with a discussion of the implications of a query implementation in an object database architecture.

13.1 Collection Queries in C++

Four functions are provided in `d_Collection<T>` to retrieve the elements that are true for an OQL query predicate. The predicate can be any Boolean query expression. The query executes as if it were a complete OQL query that performed a `select` on the one collection and contained a `where` clause that consisted of the provided Boolean predicate. The `this` keyword can be used in the predicate to refer to the current element of iteration as if the keyword were the name of the iterator variable associated with the collection in the `from` clause.

The function `exists_element` returns a Boolean value of true if an element exists in the collection that is true for the predicate; otherwise, it returns false. Assume that the collection is represented by coll and the OQL Boolean predicate is represented by predicate. The `exists_element` member function is equivalent to the following stand-alone OQL query.

```
exists this in coll : predicate
```

Suppose we want to determine whether any of the employees in the Network Architecture department have a salary greater than 100,000. Recall that the name "Network_Architecture" is associated with a `Department` instance. The following code obtains the result.

```
d_Database db; // assume this is set to an open database

int result = 0; // boolean indicating if query is true

d_Ref<Department> dept = db.lookup_object(
                                "Network_Architecture");
if( !dept.is_null() ){
    result = dept->employees.exists_element(
                            "this->_salary > 100000");
}
```

The variable `result` will contain a true value if such an employee exists in the Network Architecture department. The variable `this` refers to the current element in the iteration.

The `select_element` function returns the value of the first element found that satisfies the Boolean predicate. The following code accesses the first `Employee` instance with a salary greater than 100,000. Assume that `dept` has been initialized to reference the department.

```
d_Ref<Employee> emp;

emp = dept->employees.select_element(
                            "this->_salary > 100000");
```

The `query` function populates a collection provided by the caller with all the elements that satisfy the predicate. Assume that the collection is represented by coll and the OQL Boolean predicate is represented by predicate. The `query` member function is equivalent to the following stand-alone OQL query.

```
select  this
from    coll this
where   predicate
```

The following query returns a set containing all the employees in the Network Architecture department with a last name of Kirsh. Assume again that dept is set to reference the department.

```
d_Set<d_Ref<Employee> > kirshs;

dept->employees.query(kirshs,
                "this->_last_name = \"Kirsh\"");
```

Once the query is evaluated, an iterator can be used to iterate through all the Employee references in the result. Because the return value is another collection, other collection operations, including another query, could be performed on the result.

The select member function returns an iterator so that the application can iterate over the elements that satisfy the predicate. The preceding code could be replaced with this alternative:

```
d_Iterator<d_Ref<Employee> > iter;
iter = dept->select(kirshs, "this->_last_name = \"Kirsh\"");
```

The iterator can then be used to access each of the elements in the result. This approach eliminates the need to form the collection result explicitly, something that can be important if the cardinality of the result is quite large.

13.2 Queries on d_Extent<T>

An extent facility, introduced in ODMG 2.0, supports the same query functions for extents.

Suppose an extent is defined for the Employee class. The following code will return all the Employee instances who live in New Albany.

```
d_Database *db; // assume this is set to point to an open DB
d_Iterator<d_Ref<Employee> > iter;
d_Ref<Employee> emp;
d_Extent<Employee> Emps(db);

iter = Emps.select("this->_address.city = \"New Albany\"");
while( iter.next(emp) ){
    // do something with the Employee referenced by emp
}
```

13.3 Database Queries in C++

A C++ application can also submit an arbitrary OQL query to the database. This facility must be used if a query is not being performed on a single collection. Constructed using the d_OQL_Query class, a query can be executed multiple times with different parameter values.

When a query is initially executed, the query string is parsed, compiled, and optimized. In some implementations, subsequent calls to execute the query with different parameters may not incur the costs of these initial processing steps.

An instance of d_OQL_Query contains the query specification. Once a query is constructed, it is passed as the first parameter to the function d_oql_execute. The second parameter of this template function defines the expected result type. It is a reference parameter in which the result of the query is placed. If the type of the query result is not the same as that of the second parameter or if any parameters used in the construction of the query have the wrong type, a d_Error_QueryParameterTypeInvalid exception is thrown.

Before it can be executed, a query must be constructed. Appendix B contains a complete description of the d_OQL_Query interface. An instance can be initialized with a character array, a d_String, or another d_OQL_Query object. The left shift operator << has been overloaded with several types to allow you to append values to the end of the query. The set of types supported is found in Appendix B. These functions allow progressive construction of the query specification.

A query can have parameters whose values are provided when the query is executed. They are designated by a substring of the form $i, where i is a number referring to the operand of the ith subsequent invocation of the << operator. The first operand has the symbol $1. A d_Error_QueryParameterCountInvalid exception is thrown if any of the $i query parameters does not have a corresponding value supplied when the query is executed. If a query parameter has the wrong type, a d_Error_QueryParameterTypeInvalid exception is thrown.

The original query specification in a d_OQL_Query instance remains intact when it is passed repeatedly to d_oql_execute. But the query parameters are cleared and must be provided again for each subsequent execution.

For example, the following query returns the set of employees in the company who work alone on a project.

```
d_OQL_Query query("distinct(select e from Depts d,\
        d.projects p, p.members e where unique(p.members))");

d_Set<d_Ref<Employee> > work_alone;
d_oql_execute(query, work_alone);
```

After this query executes, an iterator can be created from `work_alone` to iterate through each `Employee` who works alone on a project.

The preceding query did not have any parameters. Suppose a function is written to print the first names of all employees with a specified last name who work on a project that costs less than a specified amount. This query uses the object named Depts that contains a reference to every instance of `Department`.

```
void
print_employee_first_names(long cost,
                             const char *last_name)
{
    d_Set<d_Ref<Employee> > emps;
    d_Iterator<d_Ref<Employee> > iter;
    d_Ref<Employee> e;

static  d_OQL_Query q("select unique e from Depts d,\
              d.projects p, p.members e\
              where p.cost < $1 and e._last_name = $2");
    q << cost;
    q << last_name;
    d_oql_execute(q, emps);
    iter = emps.create_iterator();
    while( iter.next(e) ){
        cout << e->first_name() << endl;
    }
}
```

When `d_oql_execute` is called, it does not return until all the elements in the query result have been placed in the `d_Set` instance named `emps`. If a query has a large number of elements in the result, the population of the result in a collection can introduce a lot of unnecessary overhead, especially if the application iterates only forward through the result. ODMG 2.0 introduced a new `d_oql_-execute` function that returns a `d_Iterator` to iterate over the elements of the query result. The preceding code would be changed to use this function by replacing the lines

```
        d_oql_execute(q, emps);
        iter = emps.create_iterator();
```

with

```
        d_oql_execute(q, iter);
```

With this function, you need not construct a collection, and you can transfer the query results to the application in smaller batches on an as-needed basis as the iterator advances. One benefit is that the `d_oql_execute` function returns to the application faster. Moreover, if the application decides to end the iteration before it is complete, the remaining elements of the query result need not be transferred to the application, and that reduces processing overhead. This function is commonly referred to as a database cursor facility.

13.4 Query Engine Architectural Decisions

Designers must make numerous architectural decisions when implementing a query language for an object database. Most object database implementations are based on a client-server architecture, but, in contrast to a relational database, they place significant functionality in the client. Where does query processing execute? It can be performed in the server, the client, or a combination of both. The location differs among current implementations.

If the query implementation intends to provide an object interface that corresponds to the abstractions defined by the application's C++ classes, it must be able to execute operations (C++ member functions) that have been defined for the objects. Important architectural issues are involved in supporting this capability.

13.4.1 Query Processing Location

If query processing occurs in the server, it can perform all the necessary lookup processing and transfer only results to the client. This arrangement minimizes the amount of client-server communications overhead. A drawback of the approach is that it places the total query demands of all the database users on a single database server environment. Lack of multiprocessing or multithreading of query requests may place a significant load on the server and result in slower response times to clients in a multiuser system environment.

Query processing in the client shifts more of the overhead to the client machine. This means that the server has less processing to perform for each client, allowing it to service more clients. The clients may be on separate machines, so the total query processing costs are spread across many machine environments. The disadvantage of this approach is that evaluation of the query requires the transfer of database contents from the server to the client, substantially increasing the client-server communications overhead when compared with performing all query processing in the server. Partitioning of functionality often has the positive effect of increasing concurrency and the negative effect of increasing communications costs.

13.4.2   Execution of Operations

If the query facility allows object operations, they need to be accessible and callable when the query is evaluated. Typically, only a subset of the member functions is made available; the schema designer must specify which member functions are to be included and linked with the query engine. A separate step is required to build the query process executable program that includes the application-specific member functions. The approach used to support the calling of operations in the query language depends on whether query processing is performed on the client or the server.

Vendors generally do not allow users to link their C++ application code to the database server process. Errant pointers from user code could corrupt the database cache. If the query execution is performed in a client process, the operations could be linked directly with the query engine. This approach is the easiest one to implement and does not introduce any database integrity issues.

If query processing is performed in the server, another alternative is to place the operations in a separate process and have the server invoke them via remote procedure calls. The object must be transferred to the process and then have its operation invoked. In this way, the process evaluating the query need not be directly linked with the application software. Both approaches have been used in implementations.

Part III:
Architecture

Chapter 14
Object Database Architectures

An object database architecture has many components. Each vendor has made numerous decisions about these components and their interaction in order to construct a complete database environment. Each implementation establishes certain interrelationships among the components of its architecture. All design decisions involve trade-offs chosen to optimize specific features in a vendor's architecture, and these choices affect the suitability of an implementation for a particular application.

Application developers should understand an implementation's underlying architecture to determine whether it will meet their needs. This understanding should include the components and the alternative design choices and trade-offs.

14.1 Components

The components in an object database architecture fall into several categories. Each component handles data, processing, or communication among components (or all three). At a high level, these components include the following.

- Machine resources (networks, machines, processors, storage devices)

- Database server facilities (databases, database server processes, database server threads, database cache)

- Client application environment (processes, threads, client cache, application functionality)

The following figures illustrate the components and their interrelationships. A relationship between two components is drawn with a cardinality. A cardinality of "one" implies that at most one instance is involved in the relationship. A cardinality of "many" does not imply that multiple instances must be part of the relationship; it implies only that some architectures allow a cardinality greater than one. For some relationships a cardinality of one is the norm, but certain implementations allow more than one. The figures do not capture all the architectural configurations that may exist but serve as a basis for the discussions that follow.

Figure 14.1 shows the relationships among database groups, databases, storage volumes, and blocks on disk. ODMG addresses only the database component in Figure 14.1. A database group contains multiple databases, as discussed in Chapter 2. ODMG provides a naming facility for objects on a database basis. The scope of an object identifier is on a database or database group basis in implementations, whereas query processing is usually supported only within a single database.

All implementations have storage volumes and blocks, but ODMG does not address these lower-level implementation details, which do not usually affect the application interface. Most of the products have multiple storage volumes per database, although some of them allow only a single volume. A storage volume has multiple blocks, in which the objects are stored. Larger objects may span several blocks. Figure 14.3 provides an instance-level illustration of these components.

An application process can be connected to one or more database server processes. If multiple databases are being accessed by an application, a two-phase commit transaction protocol is required.

The database software manages both a database cache in the database server process and a client cache in the client application process. The database server and application processes may be on the same or different machines. If they are on different machines that are based on different processors, the database software must be able to support heterogeneity. The database server and client application processes may or may not have multiple threads of execution (see Figure 14.2). Each vendor implementation has a unique configuration of these architectural components. Some implementations are flexible and support multiple configura-

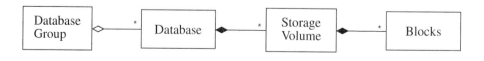

Figure 14.1 Database organization and storage.

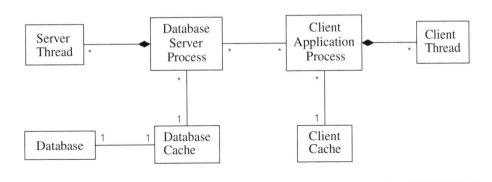

Figure 14.2 Database server and client application processes and caches.

tions, and we explore some of the alternative architectures later in this chapter. The top half of Figure 14.2 shows the processing elements in the architecture, and the bottom half illustrates the locations where data resides in the architecture. A primary function of each architecture is the movement of data between the database, the database cache, and the client cache. The following sections discuss each of these components and their relationships with one another.

14.2 Database Organization

A database has a physical organization in which objects are stored on disk in the database. An application, on the other hand, typically accesses database objects based on logical relationships. An object is usually a part of multiple logical groupings, which are defined either statically or dynamically. The mapping of the object model to the physical organization of the database can have a great impact on an application's overall performance.

The physical and logical organizations of the data take the form of multilevel hierarchies. Figure 14.1 illustrated the physical storage hierarchy, and several examples of logical hierarchies are discussed next.

14.2.1 Logical Organization and Access

An application usually accesses the database on an object basis. Chapter 6 enumerated the mechanisms for identifying objects: identifiers, names, and attribute values. An application usually accesses an instance of T via an object reference, d_Ref<T>.

Applications also access objects defined by group. Implementations often provide mechanisms for efficient transfer of groups of objects between the client and server. It is usually more efficient to access a group than to incur the overhead of a client-server transfer for each object.

By definition, a collection object contains a group of elements. When a collection object is instantiated in an application, its elements are also usually instantiated (although there are exceptions). The elements can be references to other objects. An implementation can implicitly instantiate the referenced objects when the collection object is activated in the application, or a mechanism can allow the application to explicitly instantiate all the objects referenced in the collection.

The instances of a class constitute a logical group of objects. An application may need to access every instance. The classes in an object model are arranged in a hierarchy, so access to all the instances of a class may consist of either instances of the specific class or instances of both the specific class and all its derived classes. A class hierarchy is one logical group that exists among the instances in the database.

A composite object represents another logical grouping of objects, and it often consists of a multilevel hierarchy of instances. Implementations do not have direct support for accessing all the instances associated with a composite object, but they sometimes provide the necessary low-level mechanisms so that the application can explicitly access the subobjects of a composite object efficiently.

Some implementations allow an application to access a particular object and all other objects it references. In some cases, the application can indicate a specific number of levels of dereferencing. This group is referred to as an *object closure*. A *complete closure* or *transitive closure* consists of every instance that is reachable transitively via references. In other words, if A refers to B, B refers to C, and C refers to D, then the complete closure of A would include A, B, C, and D.

A group of objects can be specified dynamically with a query that may or may not take into account static relationships among the objects. The application can issue an OQL query to return a set of references to objects that match a specified Boolean predicate. Implementations can support the activation of the referenced objects when the query result is returned. This approach minimizes the amount of client-server communications required.

14.2.2   Physical Storage

As illustrated in Figure 14.1, a physical storage hierarchy exists in an object database environment. Figure 14.3 illustrates the relationships among the storage

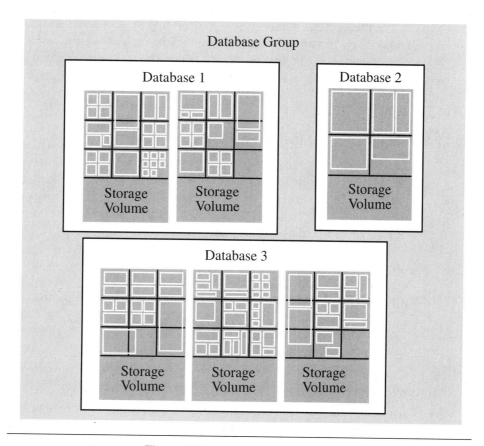

Figure 14.3 Physical storage hierarchy.

components with a specific example. At the outermost level of the hierarchy is a database group, which contains three databases. Each database consists of one or more segments, also called storage volumes. (The term *storage volume* is usually used to refer to the data on disk, and *segment* refers to the same data in memory.) A storage volume is usually associated with a single storage device. It contains a set of blocks, usually of a fixed size. The blocks are drawn here as boxes (outlined in black) within a storage volume. The size of a volume and the blocks within it can usually be set by the database administrator when the database is first initialized. Objects, depicted here as boxes outlined in white, are then placed in the blocks of storage. Objects vary in size and can span multiple blocks. Disk transfers are usually performed on a block basis. Larger blocks hold more objects, reducing the number of disk transfers required to access a given number of objects.

Some implementations use the operating system's virtual memory facilities and perform activation, transfers, and locking on a page basis. A page is treated as equivalent to a block, or a block will contain a fixed number of pages. To simplify our discussion, it is assumed that a block is the same size as the page in the application.

14.2.3   Mapping of Logical to Physical Organization

The object model provides natural groupings. During object analysis it is important to determine the logical groups that transactions will access and to understand the degree of concurrency that applications need. The granularity of lock acquisition should also be understood. This analysis is useful for determining how objects should be clustered or partitioned.

Figure 14.3 illustrates the physical storage hierarchy in which objects are placed. To maximize system throughput, objects used together in transactions should be clustered, whereas objects that may need to be accessed concurrently by different transactions should be partitioned. If locks are acquired on a physical basis, the granularity of locking should be taken into account when objects are placed in the storage hierarchy.

14.2.3.1   Cluster Objects

Clustering objects that will be used by the same transaction provides many benefits. It minimizes the number of disk blocks that must be transferred between the database cache and storage devices, increasing the use of the database cache. Objects can usually be clustered on a block, segment, or database basis. If locking is performed on a block basis, then clustering the objects in the same block also reduces the number of locks that need to be acquired.

Some implementations can perform clustering automatically. A common technique is to cluster all the instances of a class. The elements of a collection are often clustered to allow faster access of all the collection elements. The database software may automatically cluster objects that are interrelated, because an application typically traverses among related objects. Objects that are interrelated and created in the same transaction may get clustered automatically, an approach that is fairly easy to implement because the database must decide where to place the objects when they are first created. Filling a new, empty block with objects is simpler and requires less concurrency control than accessing blocks that may be accessed by other transactions. Objects that are created together in one transaction often are later accessed together by another transaction.

Usually, an application can also specify how objects should be clustered. If there is a collection of object references and the referenced objects are typically accessed with the collection, the referenced objects should be clustered near the collection. Subobjects are usually clustered with their associated composite object. A composite object may contain multiple groups of subobjects, but a transaction may access only one of these groups. It may make sense to cluster the subobjects within a group but partition each group.

Sometimes the automatic clustering provided by the database does not match the application's clustering needs and must be circumvented by using explicit clustering. Typically, this is necessary if the objects being clustered are needed by different transactions and locking is preventing concurrent access. One of the new operators defined for the d_Object class provides clustering capabilities.

14.2.3.2 Clustering versus Partitioning of Objects in Multiple Databases

In a multidatabase environment, you need to decide whether objects should be clustered into the same database or placed in separate databases. A multidatabase configuration offers many benefits. By partitioning objects and application processing, for example, you can place databases on either the same or different machines. A goal is to maximize the effective use of the system resources in a large multimachine environment. Partitioning objects into separate databases allows those databases to reside on different resources. Using different disk drives for each database eliminates disk contention among multiple applications accessing different databases. Spreading the processing across machines lets you use more processors to handle the computational load.

Objects may require different levels of concurrency, integrity, and robustness. Objects that serve as read-only reference resources have different database requirements than those that experience a high insertion rate or intense concurrent updates. Some data may require 24x7 access and other fault-tolerant characteristics, whereas other data may not have the same stringent availability requirements. Variables that affect the concurrency, integrity, and robustness capabilities of a database are administered on a database basis. The database may provide parameters to allow the application to customize the level of reliability, resulting in faster operation when the reliability requirements are more relaxed. In this way, separate databases with different operational characteristics can be used to provide the appropriate level of capabilities.

Databases can be clustered or partitioned based on the machine resources available and the anticipated amount of processing against each database. It is usually more efficient to cluster an object on the same machine environment in which most of the object access will occur and thereby minimize communication costs. If a set of objects is rarely accessed by an application, the application and objects may be candidates for partitioning onto separate machine resources. Partitioning objects onto different databases will affect the application depending on the degree of distributed query processing and distributed transaction management supported by the implementation. Whenever objects are being partitioned across multiple databases, you need to take into account the costs of client-server communications.

14.3 Client-Server Architecture

As illustrated in Figure 14.2, most implementations support a client-server architecture, which provides the flexibility of using a single machine environment or distributing the processing load over multiple machines. A server process can provide services for one or more client processes while a client interacts with multiple servers. A process may play the role of a server in one context and the role of a client in another context. Often, multiple communications mechanisms are available to the client and server.

Every process runs on a particular machine. Each machine has a particular processor architecture, which often determines the binary representation of data managed on that machine. The size of an integer word and the ordering of bytes within a word differ across processors. The client process and server process may be executing on machines having different processor architectures, something that is allowed by a system that supports client-server heterogeneity. Current object database implementations provide varying degrees of support for client-server heterogeneity. Some of the early implementations did not support it at all, and adding this capability has been difficult, although it has been achieved in most cases.

Not only does the binary representation of an object differ across processors, but also C++ compilers, even in the same machine environment, can have different representations. For example, the layout of data members can differ. Most implementations are affected by the compiler used by the application. Database software usually has some parts that are compiler-specific. Product configuration depends on the machine, operating system, and compiler used by the client application.

Some machine environments have multiple processors, an arrangement that is likely to become even more common. Multiple processors allow client and server processes to execute simultaneously on the same machine. In the past, some applications used a distributed architecture to take advantage of multiple single-processor machines. The advent of multiple processors on a single machine increases concurrent execution without increasing communication costs to the extent found in a distributed environment.

Another trend is the use of multiple threads of execution in a single process. The threads share the same process address space, allowing efficient communication and switching among threads. A server process can associate a thread with each of its clients. Database products have employed multithreaded servers for several years, and now we're seeing the use of threads in client applications. A transaction is associated with the process, or each thread can have its own transaction.

Figure 14.4 illustrates a typical object database client-server architecture. Usually, a single database cache is associated with a particular database. All database server processes manipulating a given database use the same database cache. The various configurations of database servers and caches are discussed later. The database software also maintains a client cache in the application process and takes responsibility for moving objects between the two caches. The application need not allocate and deallocate objects accessed from the database; this chore is handled automatically by the database software.

The granularity of data that is transferred between the client and server and between the database cache and storage devices varies among implementations. Data is usually transferred between the database cache and the storage volumes on a block or segment basis. Application software accesses data on a logical level, at the granularity of an object or group of objects. Somewhere in the architecture between the application access of objects and the manipulation of physical disk blocks, a transition is made from accessing data on a logical basis to accessing it

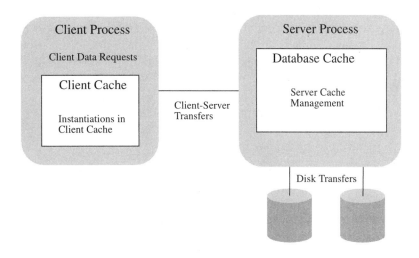

Figure 14.4 Object database client-server architecture.

on a physical basis. The granularity of data that is transferred between the client and server processes is often derived from the granularity used in the respective caches. Some implementations transfer data at several units of granularity, and others support only a single granularity. Transfers typically occur on the basis of an object, a group of objects, or a page.

14.3.1 Database Cache and Server Process

The database server process is responsible for maintaining the database cache. It performs transaction management and concurrency control. It also orchestrates the movement of data between the database cache and the storage volumes on disk and between the database cache and client processes.

The database cache must maintain all the information required to service the clients accessing the database. Its contents include the following.

- Blocks containing the database contents from disk
- Index information used to locate objects
- Information about each transaction and client
- Locking information
- Transaction logging information

14.3.1.1 Configurations

A database server process accesses the database cache directly. In Figure 14.2 the cardinality between the database cache and the database server process is one-to-many. Some implementations have a single server process that manages a database cache that is local and private to the server process, as shown in Figure

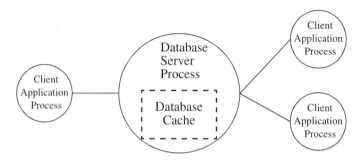

Figure 14.5 Single database server maintaining database cache and serving multiple clients.

14.5. The database server process handles requests from multiple clients accessing the same database. Without support for multiple threads within a process, the server must handle one client request at a time, limiting the degree of concurrency. A multithreaded server can be crucial in a database environment. If an operation is waiting on a reply from an external resource—such as waiting for a synchronous disk or network I/O request—it is advantageous for the server process to switch to another thread and continue processing. Threads can greatly increase the use of the CPU for a process. Some server implementations defined their own thread-like mechanisms before operating systems supported threads.

Other implementations allow a shared database cache to be accessed by multiple server processes (see Figure 14.6), often by using the shared memory facilities provided by the operating system. In a typical implementation, each database server process attaches to a region of shared memory that is directly addressable by all the database server processes. When an application opens the database, a server process is started that attaches to this common shared memory region. On multiprocessor architectures each server process can run on its own processor, avoiding contention for processor resources.

Some coordination and concurrency control must be employed as changes are made to the shared database cache. The internal locks used to control access to a shared cache are commonly referred to as *latches* to distinguish them from the locks acquired for application processes. Latches are usually associated with resources managed in the database cache. The granularity of latching in the database cache affects the degree of concurrency the server processes can attain. A single latch controlling access to the whole cache is too restrictive, severely limiting the degree of concurrency. Reducing the scope of control of a latch increases the level of concurrency.

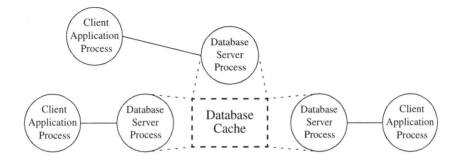

Figure 14.6 Multiple database servers access a shared database cache, each serving one client.

With the architecture in Figure 14.6, each client application process connects to its own database server process. Several communication mechanisms allow these two processes to communicate. When using TCP/IP, the client and server processes can be on the same or on different machines. When they're on the same machine, several other options are more efficient than using a networking protocol such as TCP/IP. For example, the two processes could use a shared memory region to transfer data.

In some implementations, the application software can be linked directly to libraries that contain the database server code, thereby creating a single application process (see Figure 14.7). This arrangement allows a data transfer between the database and client caches to be a direct memory copy, avoiding all client-server communication overhead. Such a database environment is less secure, because the application can potentially corrupt the database cache. But it provides efficient cache access with little client-server overhead.

An alternative architecture allows concurrent access to a shared database cache by adding threads to the single process model depicted in Figure 14.5. Some operating system environments allow you to run threads of a single process concurrently on multiple processors. This arrangement allows an architecture that begins to look a lot like the multiserver/shared cache architecture depicted in Figure 14.6. Figure 14.8 illustrates a single-server process that contains a thread for each client connection. Essentially, threads here access a database cache in a single process instead of multiple processes accessing a common region of shared memory. The process provides a common virtual memory address space shared by all the threads. A key factor here is the relative efficiency of context switching

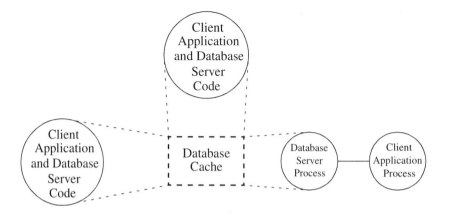

Figure 14.7 Monolithic processes access database cache.

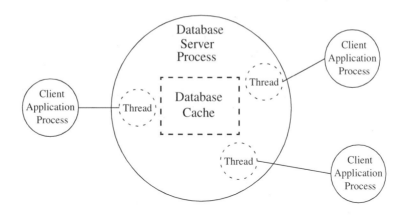

Figure 14.8 Multithreaded server architecture.

at a thread level versus the process level. Switching among threads is usually more efficient than switching among processes because of a reduced amount of operating system context that must be altered when the switch occurs.

14.3.1.2 Data Representation in the Database Cache

The database server process reads and writes blocks of data between the database cache and storage volumes on disk. The representation of data in both places is usually identical. Implementations vary significantly, however, in how the persistent objects are represented on disk. Client applications may be running on different processors and may have been compiled with different compilers. In a heterogeneous environment the server and client usually do not have the same binary representation of the objects. Some implementations support heterogeneity, and others have limited or no support.

There are nearly as many storage representations as there are vendors. The representation of data on secondary storage is often derived from the implementation's approach to client-server heterogeneity. The following approaches are currently being used.

1. In a strictly homogeneous client-server environment and implementation, the binary representation of the specific processor and compiler is used.

2. The object is stored in the binary representation used by the server, and mappings are performed at a binary level among the heterogeneous processor environments.

3. The object representation is based on the processor of the client application that originally created the object. In this case, the database server strictly manages binary pages with no interpretation of its contents. Binary conversions of data between heterogeneous processor environments are performed when the page is activated in the client.

4. A processor-neutral canonical form of the objects is stored, and specific client binary representations are established when objects are transferred between the client and server environments.

Some of these representations lend themselves to a higher degree of heterogeneity than others.

Some implementations have servers that are "object-aware"; others do not. Usually, if a server can operate on the individual objects in the database cache it can perform tasks such as locking, query processing, and client-server transfers on an object basis. When queries can be evaluated in the database server, only the final query result must be transferred to the client. Implementations whose servers cannot operate at an object level usually perform these activities only on a block basis. Queries are processed in a client process, potentially requiring that a greater amount of data be transferred to the client than would be necessary with server query processing.

14.3.1.3 Concurrency Control

The database cache services the needs of all the applications accessing the database. The database cache must contain information about each transaction in progress. It provides coordination of all access and must maintain lock information on an object, block, segment, or database basis. Some implementations support locking on a class or class hierarchy basis. Locking a class hierarchy implicitly locks all instances of the specified class and instances of all classes derived from that class.

Objects reside in both physical and logical hierarchies, which define various orthogonal groupings of objects at various levels of granularity. Locking is usually performed at one or more levels within one of these hierarchies. Some implementations acquire a lock at a level of granularity that is coarser than the application that is accessing data. The placement of data within the hierarchies is important when you're balancing the degree of concurrency versus the computational overhead of locking and avoiding deadlock situations.

Intention locks are used to coordinate locking at different levels of a hierarchy. Intention locks are usually acquired only by the database software and are used to implicitly lock nodes in a subtree of a hierarchy. When a transaction attempts to acquire a lock for a node in a hierarchy, its associated intention lock must first be acquired on its parent node. This rule is applied recursively up to the root of the tree. Attempts to acquire intention locks start at the root and progress down the hierarchy until the node being accessed is reached. Intention locks can minimize the chance of lock contention and deadlock.

Locking at a coarse unit of granularity implicitly locks all items contained at a finer granularity. Thus, it reduces the amount of locking required to lock the objects contained in the unit. But this also implies that all the objects in the unit are locked even if they are not needed by the application. To maximize the degree of concurrency, the goal is to lock only what the application is accessing.

Some implementations perform locking on a page basis, an approach that has advantages and disadvantages. Locking a page locks all the objects on that page. If most of these objects are accessed by the application or are not needed by other applications, this arrangement is fine. In fact, it is more efficient from the lock manager perspective, because only one lock is required for all the objects on the page. But the level of concurrency may be reduced. If two or more transactions are trying to update different objects that reside on the same page, only one transaction can run at a time. This concurrency issue becomes more problematic when locking is performed on a segment or database basis.

The database server must be able to detect deadlock situations. Deadlocks can occur whenever transactions are acquiring multiple incompatible locks. Suppose transactions A and B have opted to wait when there are lock conflicts. Consider the following progression of actions:

1. Transaction A acquires an exclusive lock on item 1.

2. Transaction B acquires an exclusive lock on item 2.

3. Transaction A attempts to acquire a lock on item 2. At this point there is lock contention, because A wants access to something locked by B. This is a common occurrence when transactions are concurrently accessing data. But consider the next step.

4. Transaction B attempts to acquire a lock on item 1.

This results in a deadlock situation. Transaction A is waiting for B to release a lock at the same time that B is waiting for A to release a lock. Neither transaction can continue. Unless the database server detects this situation, A and B will wait forever. One of the transactions must be aborted to allow the other to proceed.

14.3.2 Client Application Cache and Process

The database software automatically maintains a client cache for each application process. As persistent C++ objects are accessed, they are mapped into the client cache in the correct representation (based on the processor and compiler used). They have the same representation as other transient objects in the application. If an object is already in the cache, the database software simply returns a reference to the object. The database software also knows which objects are modified based on the application's calls to `mark_modified`. When the application commits a transaction, modified objects are automatically written back to the database. The application does not need to handle the mapping of C++ instances into the application cache when they are read, nor does it need to handle the mapping of objects back to the database at commit time. This greatly reduces the amount of development work for the application developer.

Client cache management is unique to object databases. Relational, hierarchical, and network databases do not provide an application cache. The client cache is one of the components in an object database that yield database transparency, a characteristic in which the database seems to disappear. The client cache serves as a view into the database. For the application, it seems as if the database is simply an extension of the application's virtual memory. Some object databases took this approach literally in their architecture. Coordination with the virtual memory subsystem of the operating system creates a seamless interface to the database.

14.3.2.1   Configurations

Even if a client is connected to multiple databases, it is processing a single transaction that involves updates to objects residing in any or all of the connected databases (see Figure 14.9). The client application process shown in Figure 14.9 has its own private client cache residing in its address space. It contains objects that have been retrieved from one or more databases, as shown.

Some application architectures need to share a cache among multiple application processes. Some implementations allow a single client cache to be shared by

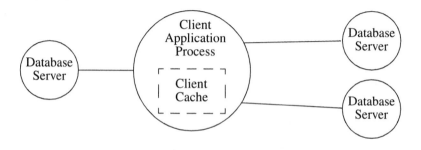

Figure 14.9 Client cache.

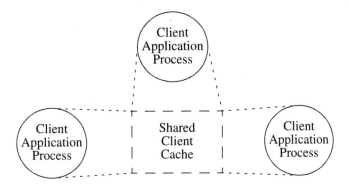

Figure 14.10 Shared client cache among multiple processes.

multiple application processes, as shown in Figure 14.10. Notice that this client architecture is essentially the same as the multiserver/shared cache architecture depicted in Figure 14.6. Obviously, some degree of coordination must be performed so that the client processes can safely modify shared cache resources.

Just as threads have been used in database server architectures, they also are employed in client applications. Object database vendors have only recently begun to support threaded clients (see Figure 14.11). The large circle in the center in Figure 14.11 is an application process that is connected to two databases, shown on the right. The two processes shown on the left are actually clients of the application process in the center. It has a thread associated with each of its clients and also a client cache that contains objects retrieved from the databases.

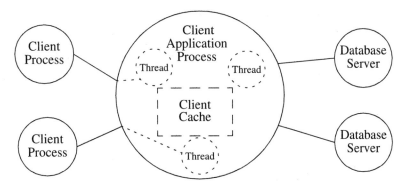

Figure 14.11 Multithreaded client.

Client applications employ threads for a variety of reasons. The object server process may be using the object database to provide persistence of the objects that it manages. This process is a client of the database server, but it is also operating as an object server for other clients. It is advantageous for the object server process to have a separate thread and transaction unit for each of its clients. This is a common scenario for object servers operating in a CORBA environment.

As object database vendors begin to support threaded client processes, another issue arises. Historically, there has only been a single transaction session per client application process. For some applications using threads, this arrangement may have been adequate. But if the application is acting as a server for its own set of client processes, does each of these other client processes need its own separate transaction? If the clients are performing multistep operations and expect to be isolated from the activities of other clients, the database client needs to have multiple concurrent transactions, one for each of its clients. The database server must accept the initiation of multiple transaction sessions from a single client process. Vendors have only recently begun to support this capability.

14.3.2.2   Allocation in the Cache

When an application attempts to access an object that is not in the cache, a request is made to the server. This is called an *object fault* or *cache fault*. The server will return the object, possibly with others. The granularity in which objects are transferred and activated in the client cache is transparent to the application.

Some implementations manage their cache on an object basis and can transfer a single object. Other implementations use the standard heap area that is managed by the `new` and `delete` operators in C++. Still others have their own separate large region of memory for the client cache in which memory is allocated to individual objects.

Other implementations manage the client cache on a physical basis and return a page of objects. The page corresponds to an operating system page. The block size either is equal to the page size or contains multiple pages.

14.3.2.3   Object Swapping

Some database implementations or application environments limit the size of the cache. Once it is filled with objects, an exception is typically thrown if an attempt is made to access another object. *Object swapping* allows a transaction to process more objects than will fit in the cache at any point in time. A least recently used (LRU) scheme is typically used to move objects from the cache to make room for new objects. The cache therefore has a virtual size larger than its actual size, and the application can manipulate more objects than will fit within the maximum cache size. For implementations that manage the cache on a page basis, this feature may be provided on a page basis.

Implementations that support swapping often associate a binary flag with each object indicating whether it is *pinned* in memory. Operations are provided to *pin* or *unpin* an object. Pinned objects cannot be swapped out, whereas unpinned objects are candidates to be swapped out. Implementations often have a default pin state for all objects, and it can be overridden by the application. It is up to the application to determine which objects should be candidates for swapping, based on performance requirements. Because a swapped object must be reread from the disk or server, it takes longer to access a swapped object than a cache-resident object. Objects that require fast access should be pinned.

With some implementations the application cannot rely on an object having the same virtual memory address for the lifetime of a transaction. An object that has been swapped can be placed at a different memory location when it is reactivated into the cache. Because some implementations allow objects to be moved or swapped during a transaction, applications must be careful in their use of pointers to objects. The pointer value will not be valid once the object is moved or swapped. In these environments, strictly using an object reference (d_Ref<T>) insulates the application from these address changes.

14.3.2.4 Cache Shuffling

Some object database implementations move objects around in the cache during a transaction to reduce cache fragmentation, thereby making larger regions of memory available for new objects entering the cache. In these environments, applications should not rely on an object's address, because it may change without any explicit notice to the application. Again, use of d_Ref<T> insulates the application from this movement. But the database implementation must not move objects that are still being referenced by a member function, because it depends on the memory address of the object contained in the this pointer.

14.3.3 Cache Coherency

At any point an object may reside in more than one cache. It may be in the database cache and also in multiple client caches. As a result, there is an issue of *cache coherency*. At most one client can acquire an exclusive write lock on an object and modify it. When an object is first modified in the client cache, the object gets out of sync with the copy in the database cache. When the client commits its transaction, the database cache will contain the new modified state of the object. But other applications may have accessed it (without acquiring a read lock) and have its previous state. Many implementations provide a means for refreshing the state of an object when another transaction has committed a modification to it.

Cache coherency is also an issue when query processing is performed. Assume that an application has accessed and modified some objects. The modified state of the objects is in the client cache, but the database cache still has the original object states. Suppose the application now performs a query on the database that involves the modified objects. If the query is evaluated on the server, it is evaluated with respect to the old state of the objects. If it is evaluated in the client, it is evaluated with respect to the new, modified state. The result of the query differs depending on where query processing is performed.

Some applications prefer that the query be based on the state of the objects before modification. Others need the current object state to be used. Implementations that perform query processing in the server sometimes provide a feature that flushes the modified objects back to the database cache before performing the query. This approach allows the application's current view of the objects' state to be used in the evaluation of the query.

14.4 Closing Comments on Architecture

There are many architectural differences among the object database implementations available in the marketplace. Before the specification of a common application interface by the ODMG, every implementation has also had a different programming interface. These proprietary interfaces will continue to exist as ODMG interfaces become available. The vendors will probably continue to support their own interfaces as long as their customer base requires it. The ODMG interface does not dictate a particular architecture in its implementation, so existing products will probably retain their architectures or make only minimal changes to better support the ODMG interfaces.

When vendors compete for use by a particular application, the architectures of the competing products often become a primary focus of both vendor and consumer. Architectural choices usually have associated benefits and drawbacks. Vendors are much more willing to point out the benefits of their products and the drawbacks of their competitors' offerings. It is important for database buyers to consider all the alternatives and weigh each product's suitability for the application's specific requirements.

Chapter 15
Performance

Many factors affect the overall performance of an application that uses a database management system. The architecture of the database system affects how well it uses computing resources, and section 15.1 discusses how an architecture's components affect performance.

It is also important for the application to use the capabilities of the database effectively. Object and relational databases have areas of strength; it is important to understand the application requirements and how each database technology meets them. The application data model and the transactions that manipulate the data govern which database technology will perform better.

Performance benchmarks assess the expected performance of a given set of transactions, databases, and computing environments. Although generic benchmarks exist, they rarely cover the spectrum of application demands. System designers can combine results from generic and application-specific benchmarks. Section 15.2 discusses performance benchmarking and monitoring.

Benchmarks can help you evaluate whether performance goals have been met and whether the database is operating efficiently and effectively. Examining some of the internal operational characteristics may reveal ineffective use of the database and suggest ways to alter configuration parameters and fine tune it. These same performance variables may give you insights into how to restructure the application to operate more efficiently with the database. Small changes in the application can change performance dramatically.

15.1 Database Architecture

The performance of an application is determined by the architecture of the database, the machine resources, and how the application is partitioned in a client-server environment. Database software must run in a variety of machine environments, and the effective use of the physical resources can help you attain optimal performance. The resources include memory, disks, network bandwidth, CPUs, and so on.

Consider the prototypical object database client-server architecture in Figure 15.1. Assume that a client application requests access to an object from the database (①). Assume that the object does not already reside in the client or server cache. The database server process must use the object identifier to locate the object on disk. It then reads the object from the disk (⑤) into the database cache (④), sends data from the server to the client process (③), and instantiates the object in the client cache (②). Excluding the overhead of concurrency control and locating the object on disk, much of the work involves the transfer of data: transfers between the disk and the database cache and between the server and client processes. There is almost no overhead if the object is already in the client cache. If the object is not in the client cache but is in the database cache, less overhead is involved than if the object resides only on disk. The speed at which the database dereferences an object reference and provides the object depends on where the object is and how many transfers are needed. Implementations that

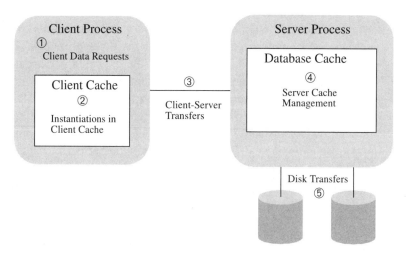

Figure 15.1 Typical database client-server architecture.

support heterogeneous environments also incur some overhead to convert an object to the binary representation required in the client cache. We'll discuss how cache use and transfer costs affect the overall performance of the database.

15.1.1 Effective Cache Use

A successful attempt to access an object in a particular cache is called a *cache hit*. If the object is not in the cache, it is referred to as a *cache miss*. Increasing the proportion of cache hits improves performance. If an object already resides in the client cache, there is no need to perform disk or client-server transfers and we have a *client cache hit*. If the object does not reside in the client cache but is in the database cache, it is a *database cache hit*. The object can be transferred from the database cache to the client cache without any disk transfer overhead.

The client and database caches are in memory. Three forms of memory are involved: client and database cache memory, virtual memory, and physical memory. Ideally, we would always have enough physical memory available to meet application demand, but this rarely happens. Virtual memory, provided by the operating system, is a cost-effective means of handling peak memory loads. The memory for the database and client caches resides in virtual memory pages, which may or may not be mapped into physical memory at a given time. Yet the purpose of these caches is to avoid the overhead of disk transfers. Having adequate amounts of physical memory for the caches is important for attaining optimal performance. Paging of cache memory should be minimized.

Some object database implementations can swap objects in the client or database cache out to disk based on application demands. The database software often has more knowledge than the operating system as to which objects and regions of memory are least critical and are the best candidates to be removed from memory.

Depending on the architecture, the database and client caches can contain extraneous objects. Transfers between the database cache and disk are usually performed on a block basis. Even when an application is accessing only a single object, the entire block may be placed in the database cache. If the objects that are needed by all applications are spread over a large number of disk blocks, more blocks will be required in the database cache. To maximize cache use, you should minimize the number of blocks by clustering objects that are frequently accessed in the same transaction. It also minimizes disk transfers.

The same principle applies to implementations that transfer physical pages or blocks to the client cache; memory is allocated in the client cache to objects that the application does not need and therefore is not available for other objects. Other implementations transfer to an application only the objects that have been explicitly requested.

Thus, an important issue when you're evaluating an object database architecture is whether the client cache contains an entire block (page) of objects or only the objects requested by the application. In the former case, clustering is crucial to maximize use of the client cache.

15.1.1.1 Cold and Hot Caches

A *cold cache* does not contain any objects. When a database is first accessed by an application, the database cache does not initially contain any objects. As applications begin to access objects, the database cache gradually acquires a set of blocks that contain objects. As the cache becomes full and more blocks are needed, blocks that are least recently used are candidates to be swapped out and replaced by blocks that are needed. If a block contains data that has only been read by applications, it can be discarded. If another request for the block is made, the database can simply retrieve the original contents from the database. If the block contains modified data, the database must save the modified block in a transaction log or a database swap area.

A *hot cache* contains a set of objects that have been recently accessed. A hot client cache contains the current working set of objects accessed by the application. A hot database cache contains data that has been accessed by all the applications accessing the database. A hot cache may already contain the objects that are needed, and a transfer is not required. But it may not contain a needed object. A goal is to have a hot cache that already contains the objects that are needed.

15.1.1.2 Adequate Sizing of the Cache

The application should be able to control the size of the cache. The needed cache size tends to vary among applications; it is best for the application to determine the size. Many implementations have configuration parameters that allow the application to control the initial, maximum, and growth increment sizes of the client and database caches.

15.1.1.3 Caching Objects across Transactions

Most object database implementations preserve the contents of the database cache across transaction boundaries. Many implementations allow an application to preserve the contents of the client cache across transaction boundaries. The function `commit` in the ODMG `d_Transaction` class releases all locks and removes all the objects from the cache. The next transaction starts with a clean slate—in other words, a cold client cache. The other option is to call `checkpoint`, which performs a commit but retains all the locks and objects in the cache. This technique allows a hot client cache across transaction boundaries.

Some vendors provide additional cache preservation options that allow an application to designate that all or some of the objects in the cache should be retained across transaction boundaries. This approach allows the application to avoid the overhead of reactivating the objects from the database at the start of each transaction.

This arrangement is extremely useful to an application that requires the same large set of objects—such as reference data—to be present in the cache with each subsequent transaction. Retaining these objects across transactions removes the overhead of activation and deactivation with each transaction. The application may also create or activate other objects during the transaction that are not needed across transaction boundaries. Being able to preserve a subset of the objects is useful to these applications.

15.1.1.4 Variables to Monitor Cache Use

Some implementations provide variables to monitor use of the database and client cache. Aspects of a vendor's architecture—such as the granularity that data is managed in the cache (an object or page basis)—affect which variables are provided.

Most of the following variables are provided for both the database and the client cache. The database cache parameters are often based on blocks. The client cache variables are based on either objects or blocks depending on the granularity data is managed in the client cache.

- Percentage of the cache in use
- Cache hit rate and miss rate (applications should check their relative values)
- Number of objects or blocks currently in the cache
- Number of objects or blocks read into the cache
- Number of objects or blocks written from the cache
- Number of objects or blocks in the cache that are marked for update
- Number of objects or blocks swapped out of the cache
- Number of blocks free or in use (database cache)
- Number of locks for each lock mode
- Number of bytes free or used in the cache

The number of objects in a client cache includes newly created objects that may not have been read. The number of objects or blocks in the cache may also be less than the number of objects or blocks read into the cache, because some objects or blocks may have been swapped out.

15.1.2 Disk Transfer Costs

An implementation uses disks to store the contents of the database, logging information, and objects or blocks that have been swapped out. The database contents include application objects, indexes, and information about the schema stored in a data dictionary.

Optimally, the storage should be spread among multiple disk drives. This arrangement allows for concurrent disk I/O, resulting in better performance. Some operating systems support disk striping, in which a logical volume is spread across drives. For reliability, the database and transaction logs must be placed on separate drives. It is impossible to recover the database from a failed disk drive if both are on the same failed device.

The operating system swap area should also be placed on a separate disk drive from the drives used by the database. Many applications that use an object database tend to manage a large number of objects in the client cache, and paging of virtual memory is more likely. Using a separate drive for paging helps minimize disk contention.

Most UNIX implementations allow the application to choose whether the database contents are stored in the file system or directly on a raw device. Often, a raw disk partition is more efficient than using an operating system file. With the UNIX file system, the database contents are first mapped from disk into the file buffer pools of the operating system and are then copied into the database cache. The use of raw devices avoids this dual copy. The operating system maintains the buffer pool so that multiple applications can access the file. But in a database environment there is usually a single database cache from which one or several database server processes access the data. One drawback of a raw device is that it usually implies a fixed allocation of disk space, whereas the UNIX file system offers the flexibility of dynamically sized files.

Determining an optimal block size for disk transfers is one means of optimizing performance. Most implementations support a block size that is a multiple of the block size used by the operating system, varying between 4K and 16K. The size of a block determines the number of objects that it can hold. Thus, the size of the objects and the number of objects that are both physically clustered and accessed together help determine an appropriate block size for an application.

The granularity of transaction logging varies among implementations; often it is per object, page, or block. The number of objects modified during a transaction affects the amount of logging activity, as does the number of concurrent transactions. Transactions that modify a large number of objects usually require larger transaction log buffers so that the number of disk transfers can be reduced.

Tunable parameters often exist to control the following.

- Whether logging is turned on or off
- Log buffer size
- Number of blocks in logging buffers
- Initial size of the log segment on disk
- Size of the growth increment of the log

Variables are often available to monitor the number of blocks or records written to the log.

15.1.3 Client-Server Transfers

The overhead of client-server transfers affects the overall performance of a database system, and the communications bandwidth between the server and client processes determines how fast data is transferred.

The granularity used by an application to access data also affects performance. It is usually more efficient to transfer many objects per request than to perform many requests for a single object. Another factor is the granularity that data is transferred to the application relative to the granularity that it is requested. Implementations may transfer an object or group of objects at a logical level or transfer a page or segment at a physical level.

Another factor is the ratio of the number of objects requested by the application versus the number of objects that get transferred. Implementations that perform page-level or segment-level transfers populate the application cache with all the objects from a physical block even if only a single object is needed. Clustering is important in these systems, both to maximize cache use and to minimize network transfer overhead.

15.1.3.1 Communication Mechanism between Client and Server

The client and server processes can be on the same or different machines. An environment often has multiple interprocess communication (IPC) and networking facilities that can be used for communication between the client and server processes. TCP/IP is often used when the two processes are on different machines. It can also be used when the client and server run on the same machine. Some implementations use shared memory to move data efficiently between processes. Some nonserver implementations use the Network File System (NFS) to access a remote database via the file system.

15.1.3.2   Tuning and Monitoring Variables

Some implementations have variables to monitor and tune the client-server traffic. The database server has message buffers to store messages being transmitted to and from clients. Some implementations allow the application to control the size and number of message buffers in the database cache. Server variables can be used to report the number of objects or bytes that are read and written to clients, seconds spent reading and writing to clients, and requests from clients. Client variables may be available to report the number of transfers to and from the server, bytes read or written to the server, and seconds spent reading and writing to the server. These variables can be used to assess whether client-server communication is introducing a bottleneck in the flow of data in the system.

15.1.4   Concurrency

If the database is accessed simultaneously by multiple applications, it is important to maximize the level of concurrency. Locks are acquired to coordinate access to the database, and how they are acquired affects concurrency. Ideally, only the objects needed by an application are locked. If locks are blocking access to other objects, the level of concurrency may be reduced.

You can use the following parameters to tune the level of concurrency.

- Turning locking on or off
- The length of time before a lock times out
- The maximum number of concurrent transactions

If the database is accessed only by a single application, some implementations let you turn off locking entirely. This approach reduces the overhead of acquiring locks and maintaining their state in the database cache.

Variables used to monitor the current level of concurrency may report the number of any of the following.

- Pages or objects that are locked, for each lock type
- Clients that are connected to the server
- Active transactions
- Transactions started, committed, and aborted
- Deadlocks that have occurred
- Time-outs waiting for locks
- Seconds a client has spent waiting for a lock
- Lock waits that have occurred
- Locks requested and granted

15.2 Performance Measurement and Benchmarks

It is important to assess whether a database can meet the performance constraints of an application. You should study published generic benchmarks and also implement a benchmark specific to your application. An application's performance depends on the object model and the kind of transactions that operate on the object model. An application may achieve different performance results with different object models. Some applications perform best with an object database, and others with a relational database. Similarly, one object database may be better suited than another for an application.

15.2.1 Generic Benchmarks

The two best-known object database benchmarks are the Cattell and OO7 benchmarks. Both use data models and transactions typical of computer-aided design (CAD) environments, but some of the transactions are general and applicable to a broad spectrum of application domains.

The Cattell benchmark obtains results for relational as well as object databases. Its designer, Rick G.G. Cattell, also founded and chairs the Object Database Management Group. The Cattell benchmark demonstrates that an object database can have significant performance advantages over a relational database for certain types of applications. It also shows the performance advantages of a hot client cache. With the relational implementation, SQL statements must be executed on the server for each transaction, so this system cannot take advantage of a hot client cache.

The OO7 benchmark was designed by Michael Carey, David DeWitt, and Jeffrey Naughton at the University of Wisconsin-Madison. A goal of the OO7 benchmark was to define a comprehensive set of tests for evaluating object database performance. No published implementations and results of OO7 yet exist for a relational database, and only some of the object database vendors have participated. A complete description of the OO7 benchmark and vendor results can be obtained from ftp.cs.wisc.edu/OO7.

15.2.2 Application-specific Benchmarks

Generic benchmarks rarely provide results that cover the requirements of every application. Applications almost always have unique transactions whose challenging performance criteria must be met.

If you have concerns about whether an implementation can meet specific performance objectives, you should implement and benchmark a prototype. The benchmark should realistically characterize the magnitude of the data and processing load that will be placed on the database. It must also account for the impact of architectural components such as the server and client caches and evaluate whether the database can meet the required level of concurrency. The public benchmarks mentioned earlier measured only single-user performance.

When performance of an object database is compared with that of a relational database, nondatabase application processing must also be taken into account. To provide a fair comparison, the overhead of mapping data from the relational database into appropriate application objects must be measured. Once objects are in memory, there may also be significant differences in the performance of the objects, something that also needs to be evaluated.

Many other aspects of an application affect performance. A slight performance variation among database products may not have much impact on overall system performance when these other things are taken into account.

The Cattell and OO7 benchmarks are strictly single-user benchmarks. Do not assume that single-user performance indicates the performance that can be attained in a multiuser environment. Object database architectures differ in how well they scale up to multiple users, and many aspects of a database architecture that affect performance do not exhibit themselves until the database is under a heavy multiuser load. Yet many project evaluations stop after single-user results are obtained. When the final system is put under a significant multiuser load, performance problems surface.

Basic benchmarks are often implemented during the prototype stage to demonstrate that performance will be sufficient. Unfortunately, performance often is not measured again before the software is shipped to the customer, especially if the project is behind schedule. But the final application software provides the specific functionality that the application needs, and measuring its performance provides the best information. It can determine whether enhancements should be incorporated in the next release.

There are not enough published benchmarks on object databases. Developers are encouraged to publish their results so that others can use the information. Unfortunately, the vendors often make it difficult, because it seems no vendor wants results published unless its product has the best performance.

15.2.3 Categories of Access

When you're evaluating the performance of an object database, you should take into account several categories of database access. It is important to understand the complete set of access demands that will be placed on the database.

All applications require transactions that modify the database, including insertion, removal, and modification of instances. For most C++ applications, efficient navigation of the objects in the application process is important.

The importance of query access varies among applications. For some object database application domains, such as CAD/CAM, query access was not very important in the past. These applications typically did not use ad hoc query languages such as SQL, and relational databases could not meet their performance requirements. They have historically used home-grown file system databases that did not support query access. The applications did not have the broad range of query requirements that their users now expect. As object databases begin to be applied to a broader spectrum of application domains, support of query access is becoming more crucial.

15.2.4 Factors Affecting Performance

Several primary factors affect the performance of an object database. They include the following.

- The size of the database
- The size of an extent
- The object size
- The collection size
- The indexes
- The use of a cold versus hot cache

These variables should be tested to assess their impact.

15.2.4.1 Database Size

Benchmarks should be run with several different database sizes, including sizes both larger and smaller than the size expected in the deployed application. Such tests will help you assess the scalability of the architecture to larger databases. The size of the database may affect the efficiency of mapping from an object reference to the actual instance, the index maintenance costs when updating indexed attributes, and the percentage of the database that resides in the cache. For object reference implementations that perform hashing and lookup, performance may vary based on the number of instances in the database. A small database can have a large percentage (or all) of the database in caches and have very fast access. As the database size increases, some of the blocks needed from disk will not fit in the database cache. To measure the efficiency of an implementation's cache management, you must force the database cache to handle more data than it can hold in memory at one time. A client cache may also require more objects than will fit in real memory. When more memory is needed than available, performance degrades, sometimes dramatically.

15.2.4.2 Extent Size

The number of instances of a class can affect the efficiency of mapping from an object identifier to the instance. If an application requires a large number of instances of a given type, it is recommended that benchmarks use at least the number of instances that are expected in a deployed application.

15.2.4.3 Object Size

The size of the objects in the application can also affect performance. For a given block size, larger objects imply fewer objects per block. In these situations it may be advantageous to increase the block size so that more objects can be read per disk transfer. Some implementations provide special data types to represent very large, variable-length data that will span many blocks. Others simply use a variable-length string object, which may not be adequate for storing many megabytes of data, such as MPEG-2 video.

Another factor is the number of attributes within an object. Some implementations remap the representation of an object during activation and deactivation to support heterogeneity. This approach requires attribute-level processing, so the number of attributes may affect performance.

15.2.4.4 Collection Size

The cardinality of collections and relationships affects performance. The underlying implementation of many collection abstractions is optimized for a collection of a certain magnitude in size. If an application uses collections whose cardinality differs by several orders of magnitude, performance may suffer. This can happen at both extremes. Requiring a collection to manage many more elements than it was designed to support will affect performance. But if only a small number of elements is placed in a collection that is optimized for a larger number of elements, the overhead per element may be high compared with that of a collection optimized for a smaller number.

15.2.4.5 Cold versus Hot Cache

Transfers among client, server, and disk introduce significant overhead that greatly affects overall database performance. It is important to measure both cold and hot cache situations. When an application is deployed, there are times when the caches will be cold. Obtaining a measure for only a cold or hot cache will result in misleading conclusions.

15.2.4.6 Indexes

Indexes can also affect performance. An object database relies much less on indexes than a relational database does. An index in an object database is usually placed on one of the following.

- An attribute containing a real-world user identifier for an object (such as a Social Security number in a `Person` object)

- Attributes that serve as secondary keys

- Attributes that are used frequently in associative lookups

Historically, object database applications have placed more emphasis on the efficiency of object references and collections, so vendors have put less effort than the relational vendors into index support. For example, some vendors allow an index only on a single attribute.

15.2.5 Application Access

Many C++ applications using an object database consider the C++ interface used to navigate among related objects as the primary interface to the database. This section examines the various database access facilities provided in a C++ interface that have been measured in published benchmarks. These transactions, found in the Cattell and OO7 benchmarks, represent a broad spectrum of access patterns. Not all of them are important to a given application.

15.2.5.1 Extent Access

Performing a sequential scan of all the instances of an extent is a common operation. It is performed when a class is searched to find all the instances that meet a query constraint and no indexes or other access mechanisms are available to reduce the scope of the search.

15.2.5.2 Instance Access

Several operations can be performed on a single instance of a class. The time it takes the database to create, update, and delete instances should be measured. Another operation is the mapping from an object name to an object reference; this operation occurs when `lookup_object` is called for the ODMG `d_Database` class.

The operation most often benchmarked is the efficiency of accessing an instance via its object reference, the most common means of accessing instances in a C++ object database. This operation occurs when the application invokes the operator-> or operator* of d_Ref<T>. The performance should be measured for each cache situation.

- The instance is already in the client cache
- The instance is not in the client cache but is in the database cache
- The instance is not in either cache and must be retrieved from disk

15.2.5.3   Large, Variable-length Objects

Many benchmarks measure the time it takes to access a large, variable-length object. The operations include the time required to sequentially scan the entire object and to read or write at the beginning, middle, and end of the data. The object's data is activated in the client cache in pieces, whose size varies among implementations, which affects the implementation's performance.

15.2.5.4   Attribute Access

Sometimes an object is accessed based on the values of its attributes. An index can be placed on the attribute(s) to improve lookup performance. Without an index, a sequential scan of the extent is necessary. Placing an index on an attribute may improve lookup performance, but it degrades overall performance when entries are added to the index or when an indexed attribute's value changes. Some implementations perform index lookups in the client, and others in the server. Client-side processing of large indexes can greatly increase the number of transfers between the client and server.

15.2.5.5   Collection Access

A C++ application uses collections extensively, so their performance has a significant impact. It is common to access all of a collection's elements. One approach is to visit each element individually using an iterator object such as the ODMG d_Iterator<T> class. Another means is to call a function provided by the collection that explicitly activates all the collection elements at once. If the collection contains elements of type d_Ref<T>, this operation may also have an option to activate the referenced objects. The implementations vary in the granularity of the collections and their elements that are transferred to the client. Invoking an operation that activates all the elements at once results in a single bulk transfer. This approach reduces the amount of communication traffic between the client and server and is more efficient. Both techniques for accessing elements should be evaluated.

Some collections have operations that access a specific element. The lookup depends on the collection abstraction. For example, a d_Varray<T> has an operation that looks up an object based on an index value. The d_Set<T> class has an efficient operation to determine whether a collection contains a particular value of type T. The d_map<K,V> class has an operation to look up a value of type V given a key of type K. The efficiency of these operations should be measured.

It is also important to measure insertion and removal of collection elements. Some collections allow an application to estimate the initial cardinality of the collection. The implementation can then preallocate the necessary storage, thereby avoiding the need to grow the collection incrementally, a practice that can be costly for some collections. The performance of an initial bulk insertion of many elements should be measured with and without preallocation.

In addition to measuring the removal of individual elements, the deletion of the collection object itself should be measured. It may be more efficient to delete an entire collection than to remove each element individually before deleting the collection object.

15.2.5.6 Composite Object Access

The Cattell and OO7 benchmarks emphasize the performance of accessing composite objects. A composite object infrastructure provides a means to measure several important factors.

- Dereferencing object references
- The effects of clustering
- Access of a large group of interrelated objects

Objects are often accessed as a group based on their relationships, so access of a composite object provides a natural unit to benchmark.

Both read and write access should be measured. Common scenarios include read access of all the subobjects in the composite, read access of all the subobjects and then modification to a subset, and read access and update of all the subobjects. Transactions that perform only read access do not incur the overhead of transferring modified objects back to the database when a transaction is committed. By first measuring the cost of reading the objects, you make it easier to determine the cost of updating the objects. Both hot and cold cache situations should be evaluated.

A composite object is usually traversed in depth-first order. A complete traversal, a dense traversal and a sparse traversal should be measured. A *complete traversal* accesses every subobject within the composite object. A *dense traversal* accesses a high percentage of the subobjects, and a *sparse traversal* accesses a small percentage of the subobjects. Subobjects are often clustered in a depth-first fashion so that subtrees in the hierarchy of the composite object are clustered. In this case, a depth-first dense traversal would take advantage of the clustering because there would be a high ratio of subobjects to blocks. But a sparse breadth-first traversal is much more likely to retrieve subobjects that are spread across more blocks. The performance of these operations depends on where subobjects are placed in the blocks. If the database interface can provide information about the block location of an object, it is beneficial to see how many blocks are involved and the degree of clustering that exists for the accessed subobjects.

15.2.6 Query Access

For applications that use a query language such as OQL it is important to measure its performance. Because most vendors have placed more emphasis on C++ navigational access than on query access, there may be significant differences in performance. If query performance is important to the application, the required types of queries should be benchmarked. The following sections discuss operations commonly measured. Some of them correspond to operations performed in C++.

15.2.6.1 Sequential Scan of Extent

The time required to sequentially scan a class's extent and access each instance should be measured. The query engine must do this whenever a query on a class does not have access mechanisms such as indexes or relationships to use in constraining the scope of the query.

15.2.6.2 Value-based Lookups

It is common to perform a query with a Boolean predicate that places constraints on the values of attributes. The required value-based lookups should guide the choice of attributes to index. The query processor should determine whether any indexes can be used to minimize the scope of the search. Performance tests should be run with and without indexes on the relevant attributes.

There are several types of value-based lookups. An *exact match* query determines whether any instances in a class have an attribute equal to a supplied value. Another common query is to find all the instances with an attribute whose value lies within a *range of values*. A *disjunctive query* involves use of the or operator, which can be used to test the query processor's effectiveness in choosing among several indexes on a class.

15.2.6.3 Join

A join is used to establish a dynamic relationship among instances based on defined value constraints that must exist among their attributes. Joins are not used very often with an object database. If this kind of query will be used often in the application, comparisons should be made with both an object and a relational database. Join processing has been a primary focus of optimization in relational databases, which may be a better choice if this operation is crucial to the application. But many joins performed in a relational database are better handled by object references and collections in an object database. The primary issue is whether the relationships are dynamic or static. Relational databases may perform better when joins are performed on relationships that must be established dynamically.

15.2.6.4 Relationship Traversal

The performance of navigational access should be measured by traversing relationships among objects. The number of levels of dereferencing performed in the final application should be determined and measured.

There may be transactions that traverse relationships as well as determine whether the object at the end of the navigation has attributes with specific values. These are referred to as *path queries*. If the implementation supports path indexes, the operation should be benchmarked with and without a path index.

15.3 Application Object Model and Access Patterns

Establishing the appropriate object model that supports the access patterns needed by the applications that will access the database is critical to the design of a high-performance schema and application. An object database is ideally suited for object models that have many interrelationships among objects that are used as the primary means of access. Very fast performance can be attained in these situations. An object database has efficient physical mechanisms for traversing static relationships that exist among objects in the database.

Application developers should define an object model that accurately models the real-world abstractions. The access patterns of the applications should also be taken into account when an object database schema is designed.

With a C++ object database, the schema consists of a set of C++ classes that are used by all the applications as the in-memory representation of the object model. It is therefore important to take into account the processing requirements of every application that will access the database. This approach helps guide schema design decisions. For example, collection abstractions differ in their ability to access, insert, and remove elements efficiently. Some applications may require only forward iteration of a collection, whereas others may require efficient lookup of a specific value in the collection or may require bidirectional iteration. If the schema does not provide a representation that can be used by an application, application developers are likely to construct their own in-memory access structures. This practice increases application development and maintenance costs and run-time processing overhead, and it defeats the purpose of using an object database.

It is important to determine the modeling constructs needed to represent the application object model. Some modeling constructs—such as collections, templates, and multiple inheritance—and some physical access mechanisms, such as keys and indexes, have varying support from the vendors.

An object database schema embodies the information that describes the conceptual and logical model used by the applications. This logical information is usually mapped directly to physical representations that provide efficient access to data. The direct support of the logical model at the physical level leads to high performance.

In contrast, with a relational database there is no direct knowledge of the application object model. Foreign keys are typically used to represent object references, and indexes can be used to provide faster access to elements of a collection. But the data must be dynamically associated based on the values in columns. The relational data model provides a lot of flexibility in establishing arbitrary relationships among data, but this flexibility comes at a cost. The flexibility is not always needed, and many of the relationships that must be established dynamically are actually static relationships that are known when the schema is designed.

The costs in relational databases include lookups in indexes, comparisons of attribute values, and access of rows that may be scattered among many disk blocks. The relational rows then must be mapped to a C++ representation. This process may involve populating collections, incurring insertion overhead, which can be expensive for some collections. Ordered collections will require a sorting operation in either SQL or the application.

Object databases are optimized to represent collections efficiently. Because the object database implementation provides the representation used both on disk and in memory, it can make design choices that allow an efficient representation and transfer. Collections can be transferred into the application "prebuilt"; collections that are ordered or that require access structures to be populated can avoid much of the overhead of construction when they are activated in an application cache. Clustering related objects also provides performance benefits.

Chapter 16
Database Schemas

The database management system maintains a description of all the objects (data types) stored in a database. This description, referred to as a *schema*, is typically stored in an area of the database called the *data dictionary*. The database implementation and facilities such as query tools, report writers, and forms tools use the schema information to manipulate the data stored in the database.

Some object-oriented programming languages and environments have a set of objects referred to as *metaobjects* or *metaclasses*. These metaclasses provide descriptions of the classes declared in the application. Unfortunately, C++ does not have a standard representation for metaclass information.

A database's data dictionary and an object-oriented programming environment's metaclasses provide nearly the same information, because the object database schema is derived from the application's class declarations. The schema must define a complete description of each type that has instances stored in the database. Most of the information found in the C++ declarations of types is maintained.

Database technologies that aren't based on objects don't need the amount of information necessary to characterize the application's representation of a rich object model. Because of the extensive modeling information that can be declared in an object-oriented programming language, the schema information in an object database is usually more extensive than the information found in other database technologies such as relational databases.

Application programs can derive many benefits from having access to the schema information. Third-party tool providers can develop tools that are schema-independent. Developers can write database browsers to interact with database objects without having details about the application classes hard-wired into the software.

ODMG release 2.0 has defined a set of classes that provides access to the schema information in an object database. The depth and breadth of the information varies among the implementations. This chapter describes the ODMG meta-classes, and Appendix C provides a complete definition of each one. Implementations of these classes were not available at this writing, so no working examples are provided, although other schema characteristics provided by implementations are mentioned. Refer to an implementation's documentation for a description of the exact information provided. We also cover the various forms of schema modification that are supported. The chapter concludes with a discussion of the migration of databases and their objects from one version of a schema to another.

16.1 Schema Acquisition

Basing the schema definition on the C++ class declarations introduces a lot of complexity for object database vendors. The implementation must acquire the type information discussed in this chapter, often by parsing the C++ application header files. Each database vendor must have C++ parsing expertise and must develop parsing software. This places a burden on database developers who must have expertise in C++ language processing in addition to database expertise.

Most vendors have licensed the *cfront* C++ translator technology from AT&T and have modified it to capture the needed schema information. But cfront is no longer being kept up-to-date with the enhancements to the C++ language. Many vendors are using the symbol table information provided by other available compilers. But each compiler has a proprietary representation of C++ type declarations, and implementations are dependent on each compiler used. Compilers differ in several areas.

- The layout of class members within an object
- The approach used to support polymorphism
- The approach used to support multiple inheritance

Each of these aspects affects the layout and representation of objects in memory.

As C++ has evolved and increased in complexity, the database vendors have also enhanced their schema capture and representation facilities. Inconsistencies among C++ compilers have placed a significant burden on the object database vendors, because they must modify their tools for each compiler implementation. Probably the biggest source of trouble has been C++ templates. In the past, there have been many areas of ambiguity in the definition of C++ templates; compiler vendors have implemented their own interpretations. These ambiguous areas are mostly resolved now because of the efforts of the C++ standards committee, but compiler implementations and user communities are not yet up-to-date with the standard.

Object database and other tool vendors would greatly benefit from a standard metaclass representation for C++. The lack of such a standard has been a major burden. Unfortunately, the ISO/ANSI C++ committee has not defined a standard representation. The run-time type information feature in C++ is not sufficient. If metaclass information were standardized and supported by all the compiler vendors, then object database vendors and others could place less effort in language parsing and devote more resources to their primary technology. Not only would it simplify object database implementations, but also it would lead to a much higher degree of portability for all software tools that must understand the definition of a C++ class.

Implementations provide a schema capture utility so that the data dictionary can be populated with a description of the application classes. Vendors use several approaches.

- A schema definition language generates both the schema and the C++ header files

- A preprocessor examines original C++ header files, capturing the schema and sometimes producing new header files to be used by the application

- A postprocessor examines the symbol table information produced by the compiler, eliminating the need to parse C++ source code

Each vendor uses at least one of these approaches in its ODMG and proprietary implementations; some vendors support several of them.

With each schema capture approach, a set of header files and implementation files is produced (by tool or programmer) that serves as input to a C++ compiler. The capture tool often generates additional source code for each class, and the source code must be compiled and linked with the application. This code provides functionality to support the run-time management of the objects in the application cache. The executable application includes database libraries along with these additional object files specific to the application schema.

The first approach to schema capture is the simplest to implement. A schema definition language, such as the ODMG Object Definition Language (ODL), is used to specify the schema. A similar approach is to specify a schema via a graphical user interface. ODL statements are used as input to a tool that generates both C++ header files and a corresponding schema. The mapping from ODL to

C++ is not defined by the ODMG, so the C++ class declarations generated by each vendor are likely to be different. The application software is dependent on these class declarations and will therefore not be portable across implementations.

The tool that generates the C++ class declarations has complete control of the coding style, but many C++ programmers prefer to control the style of class declarations. In addition, many C++ constructs that developers need are not supported in ODL. At this time, most of the vendors do not plan to use ODL as the basis for schema definition.

A preprocessor examines the original C++ header files defined by the application programmer. It captures the schema information directly from the C++ class declarations. This approach is used by implementations that expect standard C++ syntax and also by those that have extensions to the language. If the implementation uses nonstandard C++ extensions, this preprocessor approach must be used. The language extensions are translated into equivalent standard C++ syntax to serve as input to a C++ compiler.

Some implementations perform schema capture by using a postprocessor utility that examines the symbol table information contained in the object files produced by the compiler. The information about the C++ class declarations is derived from this information. Symbol table representations vary among compilers, so a postprocessor is specific to a compiler and is dependent on its level of detail about a class.

16.2   Schema Access

ODMG release 2.0 provides a set of metaclasses that allows an application to access the schema of a database. The schema information is represented by a set of interrelated metaobjects that describe the types stored in the database. Implementations may have a physical representation of the schema that differs from the ODMG metaclasses described here. These metaclasses are not required to be persistence-capable objects that are stored directly in the database.

Instead of providing direct access to collections of related metaobjects, functions are provided to access related objects. If a metaclass A has a to-one relationship with another metaclass B, a function is provided that returns a reference to the related B metaobject. If a to-many relationship exists between metaclasses A and B, then A has two functions that return iterators that reference B instances. One function returns an iterator positioned at the first element; its name has a suffix of _begin. The other function's name has a suffix of _end and is positioned past the last element. In Figures 16.1–16.12 these relationships are named with the name that precedes the _begin and _end suffixes. These begin and end functions and the iterators they return follow the interface conventions of the Standard Template Library (STL). Appendix C has a description of the iterators' operations and the `begin` and `end` functions provided for each metaclass.

16.2.1 Name Scopes

The schema is based on the application's type system. Each component of the schema has a name that resides in a particular name scope. Many different meta-classes are used to describe various types that can be defined in an application. Each such metaclass is derived from a base class called `d_Meta_Object`. Each `d_Meta_Object` instance has a unique name relative to its containing scope. The class provides a function called `name` that returns an instance's name relative to its containing scope. The scope of a `d_Meta_Object` instance is accessed by calling `defined_in`. The scope is represented by the metaclass `d_Scope`. A one-to-many relationship exists between `d_Scope` and `d_Meta_Object` (see Figure 16.1). Class `d_Scope` provides a function called `resolve` that returns a reference to the `d_Meta_Object` with a particular name. Class `d_Scope` has functions that return STL-style iterators to access the `d_Meta_Object` instances defined in a particular scope.

Some of the metaclasses derived from `d_Meta_Object` introduce a new scope. These classes are also derived from `d_Scope` to provide a namespace for their metaobject components. These metaclasses include the following.

- `d_Structure`
- `d_Class`
- `d_Enumeration_Type`
- `d_Operation`
- `d_Module`

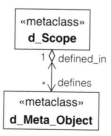

Figure 16.1 Scopes and metaobjects.

Because some d_Meta_Object instances can themselves also be d_Scope instances, a hierarchy of name scopes can be created in the schema. This corresponds to the ability to nest scopes in an object-oriented programming language.

16.2.2 Modules

A *module* manages a set of types in the dictionary and is used to represent a specific version of a schema. The d_Module class represents a module in the dictionary. For implementations that support multiple versions of a schema, each schema version would be represented by an instance of d_Module. A d_Module instance is a metaobject and introduces a scope, so it is derived from both d_Scope and d_Meta_Object, as illustrated in Figure 16.2. A hierarchy of d_Module instances can be constructed. Class d_Module has a static function called top_level that returns a reference to the d_Module instance at the top of a database's metaobject hierarchy. This function is used as the entry point into the web of interrelated metaobjects in the dictionary.

A d_Module contains collections of other metaobjects. Class d_Constant represents constant values that must be stored in the dictionary. Each of the metaclasses used to represent a specific kind of type is derived from d_Type. Operations are represented by an instance of d_Operation. An operation that is global and not contained in the scope of a class is associated with a d_Module instance.

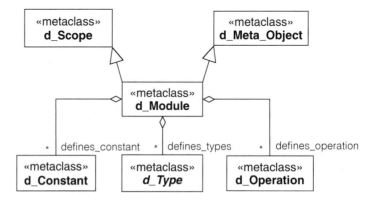

Figure 16.2 Module inheritance.

16.2.3 Operations

An operation is either a global function or a member function of a class. Class d_Operation represents an operation and is derived from both d_Meta_Object and d_Scope (see Figure 16.3). An operation has a name, which is accessed by a call to the name function inherited from d_Meta_Object. An operation has a list of parameters, a return type, and a set of exceptions that it might throw. A function is_static returns true if the operation is a static member function of a class. An operation also has an access specifier indicating whether the operation is public, private, or protected when it is associated with a class. A d_Parameter instance has a name, which is defined in the scope of its associated d_Operation. A function called parameter_type returns a reference to the d_Type instance that represents the type of the parameter.

Class d_Exception represents an exception. An exception can be thrown by multiple operations, and an operation can throw multiple exceptions. Therefore, there is a many-to-many relationship between metaclasses d_Operation and d_Exception. A d_Exception instance has a name within the scope of its d_Module. Exceptions are represented by types in the programming language, and class d_Exception has a function called exception_type that returns a reference to the d_Type instance representing its type.

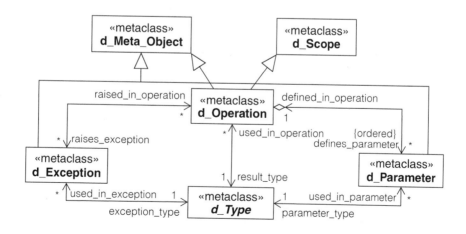

Figure 16.3 Operation.

16.2.4 Domains

Metaclass d_Primitive_Type represents the primitive types of C++; it is derived from d_Type, as shown in Figure 16.4. An enumeration called d_TypeId is defined within the class and has an identifier for each type. A value of this enumeration is returned by the member function type_id.

16.2.5 References

Pointers and instances of d_Ref<T> are represented by the d_Ref_Type metaclass. An enumeration called d_Ref_Kind is defined by the class and is returned by a function to indicate whether the reference is a pointer or d_Ref<T>. A function is also provided that returns a reference to the d_Type instance that represents the type of the referenced data, as shown in Figure 16.4.

16.2.6 Collections

The metaclass d_Collection_Type is used to represent the type of a collection. An enumeration called d_Kind is defined in the class and is used to indicate the kind of collection. A function is provided to return the type of the elements contained in the collection.

A metaclass called d_Keyed_Collection_Type is derived from d_Collection_Type to represent a keyed collection, including collections of type

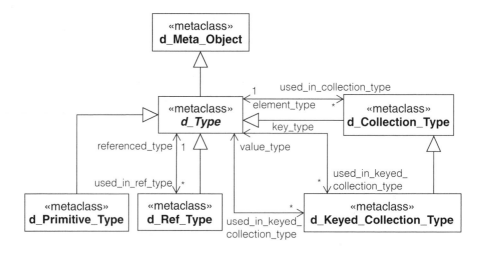

Figure 16.4 Primitives, references and collections.

d_Dictionary<K,V>, d_map, and d_multimap. This metaclass and its relationships with other metaclasses is shown in Figure 16.4. Functions are provided to return the types of the keyed collection's key and value. The type of the element returned by the base class d_Collection_Type is a d_Association of the key and value types.

16.2.7 Properties

Structures and classes have properties; a property has a name and a type. The metaclass d_Property represents these properties; it is derived from d_Meta_- Object (see Figure 16.5). The function type_of returns a reference to the d_Type instance representing the type of the property. Because a type may be used by multiple properties, there is a one-to-many relationship from d_Type to d_Property. The name function inherited from d_Meta_Object returns the name of the property. The access of the attribute (public, private, or protected) is returned by the function access_kind.

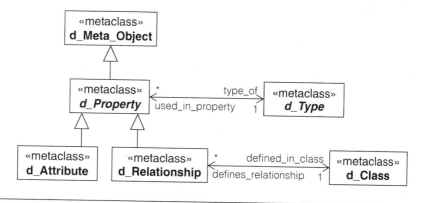

Figure 16.5 Properties

16.2.8 Attributes

The d_Attribute class is used to represent the members of a structure or class. It inherits its name and type characteristics from its base class, d_Property. If the attribute is actually a built-in array of values, the function dimension returns a nonzero value indicating the size of the array. The function is_read_only returns true if the attribute is declared to be const. A function is_static returns true if the attribute is a static data member of a class.

Implementations' proprietary interfaces often provide the following additional information.

- Relative offset of the attribute within an instance while in memory (this is both machine- and compiler-specific)

- Relative storage offset in the database

- Whether it is a transient attribute or is persistent

These characteristics of attributes are required by the implementation, but are not necessarily important to the application. Some of them are required by implementations when an instance is activated in the application cache.

16.2.9 Structures

A structure is a type that has a set of attributes. The d_Structure_Type class is derived from both d_Type and d_Scope, and an instance has a collection of d_Attribute instances that define the type's attributes (see Figure 16.6).

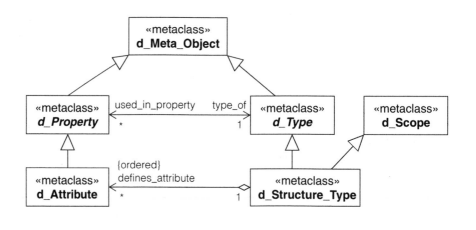

Figure 16.6 d_Structure_Type.

16.2.10 Classes

A class is a type that introduces a scope for its members. It is represented by an instance of the metaclass d_Class, which is derived from both d_Type and d_Scope. Figure 16.7 illustrates the metaclasses that have instances defined

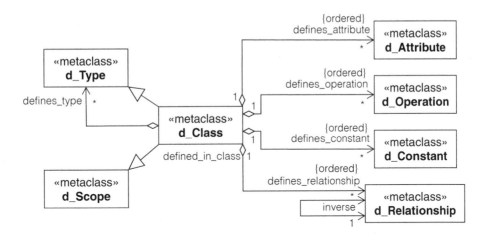

Figure 16.7 d_Class.

within the scope of a d_Class instance. As with all the other metaclasses, the name of the class is accessed by calling the name function inherited from d_Meta_Object.

Implementations may provide other information, including the following.

- The namespace in which the class is contained (each C++ namespace may be represented by a different d_Module)
- For a parameterized class, a list of its template parameters
- A Boolean flag indicating whether the class has any virtual functions
- A Boolean flag indicating whether the class is capable of persistence

16.2.11 Relationships

A bidirectional relationship between two classes A and B is represented by instances of d_Rel_Ref, d_Rel_List, or d_Rel_Set in A and B that refer to each other, as described in Chapter 8. Each declaration of a relationship member in a class is represented in the schema by an instance of d_Relationship associated with its corresponding d_Class instance. The member function inverse is used to access the inverse member of the relationship. An enumeration indicates the type of the relationship member.

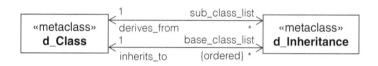

Figure 16.8 Inheritance.

16.2.12 Inheritance

Classes can be involved in inheritance relationships, which are represented by instances of the metaclass d_Inheritance. The metaclass d_Class has collections of d_Inheritance objects that represent their base and derived classes (subclasses). A d_Inheritance instance has a derives_from and a inherits_to relationship with two instances of d_Class (see Figure 16.8). The d_Inheritance class provides functions that indicate the access of the base class (d_Access_Kind) and whether it is virtual.

Consider the class hierarchy with single and multiple inheritance shown in Figure 16.9. This is represented in C++ by the following class declarations.

```
class A { ... };
class B : public virtual A { ... };
class C : public virtual A { ... };
class D : public B, public C { ... };
```

Figure 16.10 shows the instances of d_Class and d_Inheritance that would represent the inheritance relationships among these classes. The arrows illustrate the inverse members of the relationships between d_Class and d_Inheritance. The relationships and accessor functions return references to the d_Class and d_Inheritance instances and not to the inverse members.

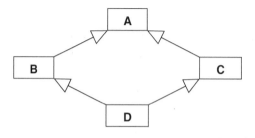

Figure 16.9 Class inheritance example.

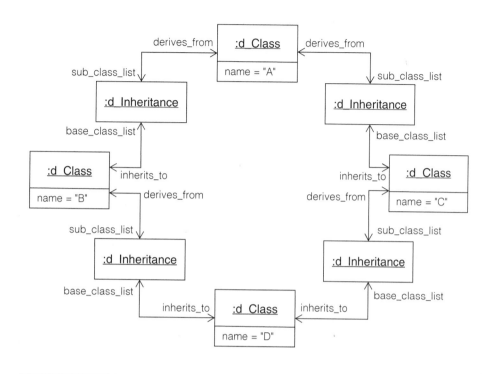

Figure 16.10 d_Class and d_Inheritance instances to model a class hierarchy.

16.2.13 Enumerations

The d_Enumeration_Type metaclass describes a type whose instances consist of a set of identifiers. It introduces a scope in which instances of d_Constant are named (see Figure 16.11). It is derived from d_Primitive_Type and d_Scope.

Each of the d_Constant instances associated with a particular d_Enumeration_Type instance must be of the same type. The enumeration identifiers are obtained by a call to the function name. For example, the d_Date class contains an enumeration called Month. It has identifiers for each month of the year: January, February, March, and so on. An instance of d_Enu-meration_Type with the name "Month" would be defined in the scope of a d_Class instance with the name "d_Date". There would be 12 d_Constant instances associated with this d_Enumeration_Type instance; their names would be "January", "February", "March", and so on. They would reference an instance of d_Primitive_Type that represented an integer. They would have the values 1, 2, ..., 12.

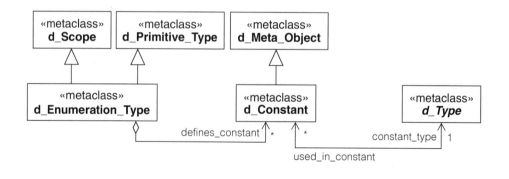

Figure 16.11 d_Enumeration_Type.

16.2.14 Type Aliases

A type alias introduces a new type, which in turn introduces a new name for an existing type. The typedef facility in C++ lets you define a type alias. It is often used to obtain a simple name for a type with a rather lengthy and complex type name. The metaclass d_Alias_Type represents a type alias. The name of the type alias is acquired by a call to name, which is inherited from d_Meta_Object. The class has a function called alias_type that returns a reference to the d_Type instance for which it provides an alternative name (see Figure 16.12).

16.3 Schema Modifications

A class evolves over time; its design and development are iterative processes. Some implementations maintain multiple versions of a schema. Those that allow the migration of an instance from one schema version to another must maintain a complete history so that an instance can be upgraded. Implementations often allow the application software to traverse through all the schema versions stored

Figure 16.12 d_Alias_Type.

in the database. The following sections cover the modifications that application developers can make to their database schemas.

Changes to a class in the schema should be made to the original source used as input to schema capture. They should not be made to the software generated by the schema capture tool. There are two reasons for this. You will need to run the schema capture again to acquire the new definition of a class, and changes made to files generated by a schema capture tool are not easily incorporated into new versions of the file.

The schema capture tool can determine which changes have been made to a class, and the tool registers any new types in the data dictionary. Differences in the class are evaluated to determine whether instances can be migrated from their old form to the new class definition.

16.3.1 Class-level Modifications

Class-level schema modifications include the following.

- Creating a new class

- Changing a class from concrete to abstract

- Renaming a class

- Removing a class

Creating a new class introduces little overhead when the database is upgraded, because there are no existing instances to be modified. When you convert a concrete class into an abstract base class, you must convert any existing instances into instances of a new derived, concrete class. Renaming a class does not have much overhead during schema migration, but it affects the C++ applications that use the old class name.

Several issues must be addressed when a class is removed. You must remove the instances from the database, and you must alter any other classes that contain embedded instances of the class. If any instances to be removed are referenced by other objects, you have several options depending on the implementation of object identifiers and references in the database. One option is to find all such references and set them to null. Another is to simply let the references refer to the removed instances. When an attempt is made to use the reference, a check can determine that the object has been deleted and a `d_Error_RefInvalid` exception can be thrown. This approach works only if object identifiers are not reused. Another technique is to prohibit the removal of an instance until all references to it have been removed from the database.

16.3.1.1 Attribute Modifications

Several schema modifications can be made to attributes, including the following.

- Adding an attribute (a default value is needed)
- Removing an attribute
- Changing the declaration order of data attributes

Changing the order in which data members are declared causes their in-memory offset to change. Several changes can be made to an individual attribute of a class.

- Changing the name
- Changing the type
- Changing the access (`public`, `private`, `protected`)
- Changing whether it is `const`
- Changing whether it is transient

16.3.1.2 Static Members

Static members are class-specific and do not affect the individual instances of the class. Supported modifications include the following.

- Adding or removing static members, including functions and data
- Changing the type of a static data member
- Changing the return type or signature (parameter types) of a static function

16.3.2 Inheritance Changes

A class can be involved in inheritance relationships with other classes. A change to an inheritance relationship can alter the representation and layout of many classes. Some of the changes are listed next.

- Inheriting from a new or existing class
- Removing a base class from the inheritance relationship
- Changing the order in which base classes are declared
- Changing whether a base class is `virtual`
- Reclassifying an instance

Changing the declaration order of base classes changes the physical layout of instances. Reclassifying an instance states that it should be an instance of a different class, often a base class or derived class of its existing class. When an instance is reclassified to a derived class, members in the derived class must be initialized to a default value.

16.3.3 Collections

Several schema changes can be made to collections.

- Changing the element type
- Changing the collection abstraction (for example, from a `d_List` to a `d_Varray`)
- Converting to or from a C++ array

16.3.4 Operations

The following lists some of the schema modifications that can be made to operations.

- Adding, removing, or renaming an operation
- Adding the first virtual function or removing the only virtual function of a class
- Changing the return type
- Adding or removing an argument
- Changing the type of an argument
- Modifying the implementation of an operation
- Changing the access of the operation

If a class has at least one virtual function, an instance has an embedded vtbl pointer. Its existence affects the object's layout and the procedure used when the instance is activated.

16.3.5 Multistep Changes

Usually, several schema changes are performed as a group. They should be treated as an atomic transaction; either all or none of the changes should be made, because interdependencies often exist among the changes. Migrating to a new schema version may require that the changes be performed in a particular sequence, or a change may require that others be performed first.

In isolation, a schema change may violate certain schema consistency constraints. As a result, the context of the other schema changes being applied is often required. It may be impossible to validate an individual schema change; instead, you may need to apply validation once for the set of changes.

16.4   Instance Migration

The migration of instances from one schema version to another requires the initialization of any new components and conversions of values from one type to another. One goal is to migrate as much as possible of the old object state to the new object state.

New data members require initialization. Many implementations simply initialize new primitive data members to binary zero values. For user-defined classes, some implementations allow the default (null) constructor to be executed for new members that are embedded in an object.

16.4.1   Conversions

A member can often be converted from one type to another. This section discusses various conversions commonly performed on instances migrated from one schema version to another.

16.4.1.1   Class-level

When a class is modified, you must alter both the direct instances as well as each instance of every derived class. A change to an inheritance relationship usually requires the upgrading of all the instances in the class hierarchy.

16.4.1.2   Attributes

An attribute can be converted from one type to another. For example, the numeric types can often be initialized from one another. A `short` can be converted to a `long` without any loss of data. But when an integer is converted to a smaller size, there is the potential for an overflow because of the loss of precision. Implementations probably vary in how this is handled; either the conversion is made without any check for overflow, or an exception is thrown.

A constructor or assignment operator may have been defined to set an instance of a new type with a value from the old type. If this operator is available, it should be used during schema migration. But many implementations do not support this.

If an attribute consists of a nesting of objects or structures, migration should be applied recursively to each nested component.

16.4.1.3   Problematic Conversions

Some conversions are not feasible, including conversions from a structure to a primitive literal, a structure to a collection, and a collection to a structure. No straightforward general conversions make sense in these cases. Some vendors allow the application to define *transformation functions* to convert from one type to another.

16.4.1.4 References

A reference to an instance of T_1, d_Ref<T_1>, can be changed to refer to an instance of another type T_2. If T_2 is a base class of T_1, the same instance can be referenced because it is also an instance of the base class. Otherwise, the reference should be set to null.

The implementation of object identifiers and references affects the migration of references during schema changes. If the object identifier contains physical location information and the referenced instance is changed so that it must be relocated, then the object identifier will change for the object. Thus, all the references to the object would need to be altered to reflect the object's new identifier.

16.4.1.5 Collections

Either a collection object itself or its element type can be changed. If the element type is changed, an attempt is made to convert the elements to their new type. Some collections can be mapped to another collection abstraction; if a conversion is not feasible, the new collection will be empty.

16.4.1.6 Transformation Functions

Some implementations let the schema designer associate a transformation function with each class that must be changed. The function uses attribute values from the old instance to initialize the new instance. This approach gives the designer complete control over the conversion.

Sometimes the type of an attribute must be changed and no default conversion can be performed automatically. In this case, you can use the following process to perform the conversion:

1. Add the new attribute with the right type but with a different name.

2. Write a routine to initialize the new attribute by using the old attribute.

3. Delete the original attribute.

4. Rename the new attribute with the original name.

16.5 Database Migration

You must upgrade three things when you change a database schema.

- The schema
- The instances
- The applications

A schema changes when you import a new definition of the classes into the database. You can convert instances immediately or defer it until they are accessed by an application.

The C++ applications have been compiled with a specific definition of each class. Because the database and application share the same type system, the applications must have the same representation as that of instances acquired from the database. Not all the applications may get converted at the same time as the database. Some of them may be based on an old schema definition, and they may encounter an instance that is based on a newer version of the schema. When this occurs, a `d_Error_DatabaseClassMismatch` exception is thrown.

16.5.1 Immediate Conversion

When instances are converted immediately, all the instances are accessed by the database software and upgraded to the new schema. An advantage of immediate conversion is that once all the instances have been converted, the run-time performance of applications is not affected by the overhead of migrating instances dynamically. But it can significantly degrade performance if it is done while the database is running. Some implementations support immediate conversion only if the database is taken off-line during the process.

16.5.2 Deferred Conversion

Some implementations let you defer the conversion of instances until they are accessed by an application. A database may undergo multiple schema changes before an instance is accessed, so the database maintains a history of all the class definitions and changes that have been made. In this way, an instance of any version of a class can be converted to the latest definition. The database software successively applies the schema changes from the instance's current version through each version to the latest version of the class.

With deferred conversion, the processing is amortized over time based on when instances are accessed. This approach lets you make schema changes without taking the database off-line or significantly affecting performance during modification. Most implementations that support this approach let you make the schema changes while the system is operational. This feature is important in applications that require high availability. Converting a large database could take hours or days, too long a time for the database to be off-line.

16.5.3 Indexes and Clustering

Indexes and clustering directives can be affected by schema modifications. Following are some of the schema changes that affect them.

- Removing a class that has an index
- Removing an attribute that is a component of an index
- Changing the type of an attribute in an index
- Changing the inheritance hierarchy, causing classes to be added or removed from an index

You may need to rebuild or redefine an index after the schema and database conversion is complete. If you use a deferred conversion, rebuilding an index may instead immediately convert all the instances associated with the index.

Part IV:
Retrospective

Chapter 17
Some Comparisons between Object and Relational Database Technology

Relational database technology currently dominates the database market for new application development. Products have been available from major vendors for more than a decade. A sizeable industry of third-party tools has evolved to support the technology.

Relational database technology was developed before the widespread market acceptance of object technology. Yet object concepts (which originated in the class construct in Simula-67) and the relational model (Codd's original proposal) date to the late 1960s. Only recently have attempts been made by the ANSI X3H2 SQL committee to combine the two technologies in SQL3. The SQL3 committee must maintain backward compatibility with existing legacy SQL software, and that has constrained its ability to add objects to SQL. Vendors of relational databases are also adding proprietary extensions to their SQL products to support objects. Does this imply that a development project can stay with relational technology and reap the benefits of both approaches? Developers must understand the fundamental differences between the technologies and the advantages each offers.

If relational vendors had adopted objects a decade ago, their database technology and associated applications would probably be quite different and more sophisticated today. SQL is only one of several languages that have been used to interface to a relational database. Another language better suited for objects may have fared better in the marketplace if the database community had adopted objects sooner.

What are the fundamental differences between relational and object database technology? How do application developers determine which technology is best suited for their application? This chapter addresses these questions, concluding with a discussion of SQL3.

The two database technologies serve the needs of different applications in the marketplace. Many development managers see SQL and relational databases as a safe choice because of the technology's maturity, market dominance, and level of standardization. But an object database would often be a better choice based on the application requirements. Conversely, in some situations an object database is chosen even though a relational database would be a better choice.

17.1 Models, Type Systems, and Languages

The primary differences between object and relational databases center on models, type systems, and languages, and how these elements are used in a client-server environment. The application's information model and its representation in a software architecture are significantly affected by the choices made with respect to these three components.

17.1.1 The Relational Model and Environment

The relational data model is based on the concept of a table. A *table* is defined for each entity modeled by the application. A *row* in a table corresponds to an instance of the entity. A table also has a set of *columns*, which correspond to the attributes of the entity being modeled. Each column has a particular data type, called a domain. The intersection of a row and a column is a *cell*. Each cell of a table has either a value of the domain or a null value.

The relational database implementation provides the types to use as domains. The domain type system is fixed; only the vendor's supplied types are supported. The set of operations that can be performed on a domain instance is determined by SQL and the vendor implementation. A schema is in first-normal form if every domain is atomic, meaning that it cannot contain a collection of values. The element of a collection must be represented by a row in a table.

A table is the only data type that an application can define. The application's information model is cast into the form of tables. But the operations that can be performed on a table are determined by the relational model and SQL. All interaction with the data in the database is done in SQL. The primitive read operations supported are *select*, *project*, and *join*. You establish a relationship among tables dynamically by specifying a join condition, which defines constraints that must exist among the columns of the tables. Boolean predicates are specified in a where clause to select the rows of interest. Expressions in the select clause are used to project values from the table's columns to form the final result of a query.

The relational type system representation and functionality are wholly contained in the database server. From the relational database's perspective, there is one model, one type system, and one language that it dictates. Applications must accept that model and must provide mappings between their representation and the one provided by the database.

SQL is used to express functionality to be executed in the relational database server. SQL can express elaborate constraints to control which data is processed. The application can control the amount of data that must be sent from the server to the application. Simple transactions can be expressed completely in SQL and can be executed entirely in the relational database server. Data can be updated without the need to make a round trip from the server to the client, with updates propagated from the client back to the server.

17.1.2 An Application in a Relational Environment

An application is usually written in a third-generation programming language (3GL) such as C, C++, Cobol, or Fortran. Or it is written in a higher-level fourth-generation language (4GL), such as PowerBuilder, which provides a rapid prototyping environment for building a form interface to the database. A typical 4GL type system is nearly a copy of the database's, providing a high degree of integration for simple applications. But applications requiring more-sophisticated functionality must be written in a 3GL.

The application and relational database have separate type systems. The data types and functionality that can be expressed differ dramatically. The database vendor often provides an interface between the values of column types and the values of the built-in types of the programming language. In SQL, all interaction between the database and the application occurs on a column basis, and no direct mapping is provided at a table level. Thus, no interface is provided at the level of abstraction of the entities in the application domain.

In object technology, the entity types are the focus of modeling. Relational tables correspond to the objects of the object model, but no interface is provided at this level. As a result, the object model must have two representations: the relational database schema and the application's classes. A mapping between the two models must be defined and implemented. The developers and the end users who interact with the database via SQL must understand both models and the mapping between them. In addition to the complexity this requirement introduces, implementing the mapping takes a significant amount of development work.

The relational database's architecture has no role in the representation or management of the application cache. The application is responsible for instantiating all the object instances and keeping track of all modifications to objects. Collections and relationships in the object model require join processing on the tables in the database. The application's cache should not contain multiple instantiations of the same instance; as the application accesses an object, it must make sure that the data has not already been instantiated. With queries that do not involve access of a specific row by key, the application will not know whether the object is already activated until it has received the object from the database. This arrangement results in significant unnecessary overhead.

Because the relational database's type system and execution environment are entirely independent of the application programming language, it can support multiple application languages better than an object database can. A minimalist approach has been taken for the type system, providing only a least common denominator. Most of the programming languages supported by relational databases have not been object-oriented. But with object technology, new programming languages have been introduced that allow application developers to define much richer data models and type systems. Developers want the semantics of their object models to be available in both the application and database environments.

17.1.3 Object Support

Object technology focuses on specifying abstractions and models and implementing them in the type system of a programming language. An underlying premise of the object paradigm is the need for an extensible typing system.

Application developers who were designing complex information models readily accepted object technology because of its ability to reduce complexity. The objects of a complex information model usually have many interrelationships, and applications often access a large number of the interrelated objects in a transaction. The needed computations exceed the expressability of SQL, resulting in the need to instantiate the objects in the application. The application's object model gets defined using the rich type environment of the object-oriented programming language, and the relational database becomes a simplistic, back-end storage mechanism.

A relational database lacks the object paradigm's modeling constructs: encapsulation, inheritance, and polymorphism. Encapsulation lets you specify a set of operations that defines all the functionality that can be performed on object instances. Each column of a row in a relational table, on the other hand, can be directly accessed. No representation is provided at a table level, where encapsulation is often needed. Inheritance relationships among the entities in the application domain cannot be represented, nor can polymorphism be used. An application must always specify the specific tables to use in a query. Although the object modeling constructs are quite useful in the application, they cannot be used in the relational database environment.

Some applications have fairly simple information models that can be represented and manipulated adequately with SQL. These applications benefit from the abundance of third-party tools that provide productive environments for building interfaces to the simple data models relational databases support well.

17.1.4 The Object Implementation Language

Defining an object involves specifying a set of operations, which must be implemented in a language. Their implementations are a part of a type's definition, and type systems are language-specific. For an instance of a type in a process to be manipulated directly, the type system and type implementation must be present.

If an object abstraction is to be fully supported in multiple programming languages, the operations must be specified in each language. Furthermore, the types used in the object implementation must be supported by both languages, something that rarely occurs. Developers do not have the time or resources to fully implement all their object abstractions in multiple languages. When multiple languages are being used, the complete definition of a type (all the operations) is usually defined only in one language. Other languages get a simpler, data-only representation.

In some situations, an object request broker architecture is used to execute operations remotely on an object instantiated in a server somewhere on the network. An object request broker architecture is often adopted in multilanguage application environments. The object implementation is defined in one language, and an interface is made available for applications written in other languages to invoke operations remotely on the objects.

17.1.5 In Contrast: C++ Object Databases

The emphasis in object database products has been on a tight integration with the application programming language, which is used to define the semantics of the objects. C++ object databases directly support the type system of the C++ application. One type system and object model is shared by the database and application, and the application's use of encapsulation, inheritance, and polymorphism is supported by the database.

With a C++ object database, the object functionality executes only in the client application. Although some implementations have domain types whose data representations can be manipulated in the database server, this capability is usually very limited. And the available functionality is fixed, as with relational databases. C++ object databases are client-centric, whereas relational databases are server-centric.

The OQL language supports the object model abstractions defined in the programming language. OQL allows the object's operations to be invoked, providing an interface that corresponds to the object abstraction. One area of weakness, however, is the lack of access control; the private members of a class are accessible. The encapsulation established in C++ is removed in the query environment. When a query needs to place constraints on data attributes, application programs should be able to issue such queries. Access control facilities should probably be added so that an interactive query interface could correspond more closely to the abstractions defined in the object model.

17.1.6 Normalization

Advocates of relational databases argue that this technology is superior because of its theoretical foundation—in particular, its normalization theory—and because it is based on relational calculus. SQL is based on tuple relational calculus. As discussed earlier, OQL is based on domain relational calculus, a more general form of relational calculus than SQL provides.

The relational normal forms include the following.

1. A relation is in first-normal form (1NF) only if all the underlying domains contain only atomic values.

2. A relation is in second-normal form (2NF) only if it is in 1NF and every nonkey attribute is fully dependent on the primary key.

3. A relation is in third-normal form (3NF) only if it is in 2NF and every nonkey attribute is nontransitively dependent on the primary key.

An object should represent a single abstraction. The underlying implementation may involve non-atomic aggregations, but the object interface should represent a single abstraction. Objects can be used to represent atomic abstraction values even though their underlying representation is not atomic.

In an object database, the identifier of an object serves a role analogous to a unique key in a relational database. Both the second- and third-normal forms deal with the modeling concern that the attributes be associated with the appropriate object abstraction. These normalization rules represent good modeling principles that should be applied in the design of object models and database schemas. They are not specific to relational databases and should also be applied in an object database environment. Neither object nor relational schema design enforces these design principles; they are applied by designers using either database technology.

Normalization often leads to a model in which many separate tables must be joined to represent a complex application object. The join processing required to bring together all the related rows can create a performance issue with a relational database, something that is an outcome more of the access mechanisms available than of the fact that the data is normalized. When performance degrades, application developers often denormalize the schema to avoid some of the join processing, but this technique can introduce update anomolies.

An object database schema is often normalized to the same extent as a relational database. The designer of an object database schema can embed an object as a member of a persistent object instead of referencing it. But applications still need to access and aggregate data when using an object database. The difference is that the relationships among objects in an object database are stated explicitly at a logical level and are implemented efficiently at the physical level. Using an object identifier to refer to an object is faster than performing a join in a relational database. Join performance degrades with an increase in the number of tables and the number of rows in the joined tables. With an object database, the efficiency of object identifiers stays relatively constant as the number of instances increases.

17.2 Data Access

All access to a relational database is performed via SQL on a table basis. A query involves specifying one or more tables in the `from` clause to use as initial input to the query. The `from` clause defines a cartesian product. Relationships among tables are established by specifying join conditions that establish constraints on the values in columns. The `where` clause selects a subset of the rows in the cartesian product of the tables to be rows in the final table result. The final query result is also a table. Expressions in the `select` clause are used to determine the columns of the final table result. An `order by` clause orders the rows of the final table result, and a `group by` clause establishes a grouping of the rows; the final table result has a single row for each group.

A specific set of tables is specified in the `from` clause of a query, preventing polymorphic access of instances in the database. With an object database, references (`d_Ref<B>`) can refer to instances of any class derived from a common base class `B`. A polymorphic reference can be embedded as a member of an object or can be contained as an element in a collection. Both C++ and OQL can use this reference to access an instance without knowing its actual type.

In OQL any collection expression can be a component in the `from` clause (see section 12.3.1). The collection can contain references to a small percentage of the instances of a class or even the specific objects required in the query. With SQL, the entire table is the starting point of query evaluation, and the cardinality of the table has a significant impact on the performance of the query. The number of rows is reduced by evaluating the Boolean predicate in the `where` clause, so a potentially much larger set of data must be processed with SQL than with OQL.

Relationships are established among tables dynamically based on the values of table columns. This operation is referred to as a relational *join*. The relational model has a lot of flexibility in establishing arbitrary relationships based on column values. Historically, object databases have not provided the same level of flexibility in establishing such dynamic relationships. OQL supports joins, and several vendors also provide SQL access with join support. Relational databases rely on join processing as their only means for establishing a relationship, and significant resources have been devoted to the optimization of joins. Relational databases can be expected to provide better, more efficient support for join processing. Object databases have focused on providing efficient support of static relationships among objects. OQL allows such relationships to be used in a query without the need to compute a join. Developers should determine whether the relationships in their schema are primarily static or dynamic. This aspect of the application model is a significant factor in the database decision process.

In addition to establishing relationships, the `where` clause can be used to reduce the query result by specifying constraints on the column values. This operation is referred to as the relational *select*. For a row in the cartesian product defined by the `from` clause to be included in the final result, the Boolean predicate in the `where` clause must be true. Relational SQL implementations allow a potentially huge volume of data to be examined and sifted by query constraints in the database server. Only the result of the query need be transferred from the server to the client.

An application that uses navigational access with an object database often evaluates such constraints in the C++ application software. This approach requires that the data be transferred into the client address space. Some implementations perform all query processing in the client application process. The ability and sophistication of server query processing varies widely among object database implementations. If server-based query facilities are not available and such a query is performed on all of the instances of a class, every instance must be transferred from the database server to the client application. For applications that require this type of access, it can be extremely important to understand how much query processing an implementation can perform in its database server.

The `select` clause of a SQL query determines the columns of the table in the final result. This operator is referred to as the relational *project*. A query essentially defines a view: a new table derived from the contents of one or more tables in the database. The result can be a simple, direct mapping of each column of a single table, but queries are often based on multiple tables, with the columns in the final result based on expressions involving only a subset of the original tables' columns. For example, a table `Employee` may be accessed to retrieve only a few of the columns in the table (`last_name` and `salary`).

An application that uses an object database typically uses an object reference to access an object. A dereference operation is performed, and the *entire* object is activated in the application cache. The C++ class definition specifies the form of an instance in application memory. A class implementation is not designed to work with a subset of its attributes.

Relational interfaces operate at the attribute level, whereas object databases provide interfaces at the entity level. Developers should determine whether their applications require access of entire objects or whether they must instead compute projection views based on expressions involving a subset of an object's attributes.

An index is used in a relational database for several things. One or more columns of a table usually serve as the primary key that contains a unique identifier for a row. For efficient row lookup, an index is usually placed on a primary key. A foreign key models a reference to a row, and an index on a foreign key allows quick location of the rows that contain a particular foreign key value. Once primary and foreign keys have been indexed, other columns that are often used in query predicates are indexed.

Object identifiers, relationships, and collections are used in an object database to access related objects efficiently. An index is reserved for cases when an object is accessed based on a user-specified identifier or attribute values. Indexes are used much less often in object databases than they are in relational databases, because more efficient navigational mechanisms are available in object databases.

17.3 Execution

With a relational database, all database processing executes in the database server. No assumptions are made about the execution facilities of a client application. The functionality executed in the database server is expressed in SQL, and elaborate query constraints can be specified. A relational database is server-centric.

A C++ object database has a tight integration with the programming language, and it provides facilities for managing an application cache. Many database access operations are initiated by performing operations on objects residing in the client cache. Object databases tend to be client-centric.

Some applications have simple information models and transaction requirements. The data definition and manipulation facilities of SQL may be adequate for these applications. Other applications execute a significant amount of functionality in the client application and may require that the data reside in the application's address space. A given application architecture may be better suited to either client or server processing. You should take this into account when evaluating the database technologies.

17.4   SQL3 Support for Objects

The ANSI SQL committee is defining SQL3, the next major version of the SQL language. Object technology is a primary new feature of SQL3. The specification is projected to be complete in 1998 or 1999; at this writing, most of the components in the standard are in the draft stage, including the SQL Persistent Stored Modules (PSM) language used for defining functions (object methods). Additional work remains before the standard is declared final. The information in this section is based on the 1996 draft SQL3 specification.

The design of SQL3 has a fundamental constraint: it must remain compatible with ANSI SQL-92, the previous version of SQL. The SQL language contains the inherent assumption that it processes tables as input and produces a table as output. This assumption has prevented extensions to support objects at a table level, a significant restriction that is discussed in the assessment in section 17.4.4.

Why add objects to SQL? How should objects be added? Application domains increasingly must support new data types, which need support for operations to define their behavior. To support new data types in applications, the industry has adopted object technology. Several approaches are being pursued to add objects to relational database technology. For example, database vendors can supply implementations of new data types. This approach is limiting, because the vendor can never meet the demands of the varied application domains that use the database. Several applications may need the same data type, but each one requires different semantics. Another approach is to add a layer of object semantics on top of the relational database. But with this approach the query language interface lacks the object semantics, raising concerns about the resulting performance.

The approach chosen by the SQL3 committee is to allow the database to be extended with user-supplied data types. This arrangement provides a high level of integration, extensibility, and performance. The SQL execution environment contains the complete specification and definition of the object semantics and can execute operations directly on instances of user-defined types.

17.4.1 Abstract Data Types for Column Domains

SQL3 allows user-defined abstract data types (ADTs) to be specified in the definition of a schema. The data type of a table column can be an ADT, and each cell (row and column combination) of a table contains an instance of the ADT. ADT instances are not persistence-capable on their own but attain persistence by residing in table cells. SQL3 ADTs also lack object identity.

17.4.1.1 Encapsulation

SQL3 ADTs support encapsulation. Only the set of functions defined with a type are allowed to access the attributes of the type. For example, the following type can be defined in SQL3.

```
create type Address (
        street          char(25),
        city            char(20),
        state           char(2),
        zip             integer,
function    is_rural(Address) returns integer
);
```

Each ADT attribute has a name and a type. The name must be unique within the type. The type can be any existing type, including other ADTs. The attributes, such as `street` or `city`, are not directly accessible, providing a level of encapsulation.

Observer and mutator functions are automatically generated for each attribute, something that reduces the level of encapsulation. For example, in the following code the first line declares the accessor function and the second line declares the mutator function for the `street` attribute of `Address`.

```
street(Address)                 returns char(25)
street(Address, char(25))       returns Address
```

The following syntactical variations are supported for convenience.

```
DECLARE a Address;

a..street           is equivalent to      street(a)
a..street = '1234 Elm Avenue' is equivalent to
            street(a,'1234 Elm Avenue')
```

SQL3 uses a double-dot notation to access the attribute of an ADT. (The single dot is already used for other SQL mechanisms.) The system generates a null constructor that sets all the attributes to a null value.

17.4.1.2 Inheritance

SQL3 ADTs can use both single and multiple inheritance. All the stored attributes and behaviors of the supertypes are inherited. An instance of a subtype can be used wherever an instance of a supertype is expected.

17.4.1.3 Polymorphism

SQL3 supports polymorphism. A subtype can overload any function defined on a supertype. But when a function is invoked, the function called is determined by the types of *all* the arguments and not just the primary argument. This form of polymorphism is found in CLOS. But in object-oriented languages such as C++, Smalltalk, and Java, polymorphism is based on the primary object on which an operation is invoked.

17.4.2 SQL Persistent Stored Modules

The SQL PSM provides a means for application developers to define stored modules, procedures, and functions that are accessible within the SQL environment. These routines can be written in a third-generation programming language or directly in an extended SQL.

Functions can be implemented with any 3GL that has an SQL binding, including Ada, C, Cobol, Fortran, Pascal, and PL/I. This arrangement allows SQL to leverage existing libraries, but it does not provide a very integrated environment. An impedance mismatch exists between the SQL language and the application programming language, and there are concerns about security and performance.

SQL/PSM also defines a computationally complete programming language that is fully integrated with the SQL language, providing complete support for the type system available in the SQL environment. A key drawback currently is the lack of implementations of the PSM language. The language includes the following constructs (among others).

- `call` / `return`
- `begin` / `end`
- `if` / `then` / `else` / `endif`
- `case` / `end case`
- `loop` / `end loop`

- while / end while
- repeat / until / end
- for / end for

These facilities can be used to define functions that are executed in the SQL environment.

SQL/PSM supports function overloading; the same name can be used for different functions. All the function arguments are used in function resolution. The specific function to be executed is chosen at run time based on a best match of the actual types of the arguments passed. Static function dispatch is supported only if one of the following is true.

- No argument is an ADT.
- None of the ADT arguments has subtypes.
- Only a single applicable function applies for all possible combinations of ADT arguments.

All ADTs are passed by reference to a function.

17.4.3 Named Row Types and Reference Types

SQL3 allows *named row types* to be defined. A named row type consists of a sequence of pairs of field name and data type. Instances of named row types can be either rows in base tables, views, or query results. Functions can be defined on named row types, but there is no encapsulation of the data. Type checking is based only on structural equivalence; two different tables can be considered the same row type if their sequences of field names and types are identical.

Reference types allow direct references to instances of named row types. These types are similar to object references in an object database. They are strongly typed but do not support referential constraints. They must reference an instance in a specific table, so no polymorphism is supported. They can be used to specify path expressions using the new -> operator in SQL.

```
select  e.last_name
from    Employee e
where   e.office_mate->address..city = 'Columbus'
```

17.4.4 Assessment of SQL3

SQL3 adds object support to SQL, but the objects serve only as the domain types of columns. The entities of the application domain must continue to be mapped into a tabular form, without support for the object-oriented constructs: encapsulation, inheritance, and polymorphism. Only the entity attributes will have these capabilities, something that is not likely to be readily accepted by the object-oriented development community. Current object-oriented design methodologies place most of their emphasis on the design of objects to represent the entities of the application domain. Attributes play a secondary role, usually hidden underneath the object interface. One possible approach is to have tables with a single column that contains an ADT. But it is not clear how well implementations would then allow things such as joins to be performed on ADT components in different tables.

SQL3 is based on a generalized object model in which the dynamic binding of functions is based on the types of all the function arguments and not on the type of a single object argument. Most people in the object-oriented development community are much more familiar with the conventional classical object model. The form of dynamic binding in SQL will seem strange to most object developers, who are accustomed to the polymorphism provided by most object programming languages. Dynamic binding based on all the arguments increases the complexity of the software and is less efficient to implement.

The SQL3 objects are defined within the type system of SQL, and the object semantics are executed within the SQL environment. The objects defined in SQL3 are not usable within an application written in an object-oriented language such as C++. Many C++ development groups have been told by vendors of relational databases that they should not buy an object database and wait for SQL3, which will provide them with objects. Yet SQL3 does not provide any better support for C++ object models than SQL-92 does.

SQL3 is suitable for applications written in non-object-oriented languages that define higher-level semantics for their data and are willing for that functionality to be available only within the SQL server environment. This approach is suitable for some applications but not all of them. With SQL3, the application continues to contend with multiple models and type systems.

SQL3 is an evolving draft standard. Relational vendors are not waiting for the standard to be completed. They are releasing new database products with proprietary support for objects that differs from that of SQL3. These products are being referred to as object-relational databases, and each one supports objects differently. As a result, the relational database market will probably lack the level of standardization it once had. A similar lack of standardization slowed market acceptance of object databases. Support of the ODMG standard by the object database vendors may result in their having a higher level of standardization than the object-relational products.

Chapter 18
In Closing

C++ developers who need database support should seriously consider using object database technology. C++ object databases have been commercially available since 1987. The interfaces are now being standardized by the ODMG, and the technology is maturing.

The development effort required to use an object database is substantially less than that of using a relational database. This translates into less code to test and maintain, shortening other stages of the project life cycle. A further consequence is a reduction in project costs and time to market. The common type system and application cache management facilities lead to a database interface that is fairly transparent and not intrusive. Application developers can focus on defining and implementing their object models instead of dealing with discrepancies between the modeling capabilities of the application language and those of the database.

C++ is the dominant object-oriented programming language. It has also been the primary language supported by the object database vendors. But a new language contender—Java—has entered the marketplace. Java has some language characteristics that make it a superior language from a database perspective. It solves some problems that relational and object database technologies have struggled with for years and will have a significant impact on both kinds of databases. If leading relational vendors begin supporting Java in their client and server environments, Java will also have a negative impact on the acceptance of the SQL3 standard.

18.1 Type Categories

Several categories of types have been introduced. These categories borrow from entity-relationship modeling and database theory in general. The types representing the entities of application domains require support of both persistence and identity. The domain category represents the most primitive types, which serve as the types for the attributes of entities. Entities consist of an aggregation of attributes, each of a domain type. Composite objects represent abstractions that require an aggregation of entity objects.

The types in each category contain an aggregation of components of more primitive types. You should use encapsulation when defining types to hide the complexity of the aggregations in the type implementation. Each type should represent a single atomic abstraction, and encapsulation should be used to hide the underlying implementation and provide an interface that embodies the abstraction.

18.2 Dual Interfaces

Object databases provide both navigational and declarative query access to a database. C++ classes are provided by the database implementation to represent references, collections, and relationships among objects. These classes give applications seamless access to objects from the database. Lower-level database accesses are hidden within the methods of these vendor-provided database classes.

Object databases initially did not place much emphasis on query support. Most applications preferred to have efficient navigational access within C++. Many of the initial application domains that adopted object database technology had previously used more primitive file system mechanisms that did not provide any query support, so these applications initially had lower expectations and demand for this support.

More application domains are beginning to use object databases. Systems using the technology are now in deployment to end users who have become accustomed to having a query language such as SQL. OQL is a sophisticated object-oriented query language that provides a simple syntax for specifying navigational access of static relationships and defining dynamic relationships via join predicates, as commonly found in SQL queries. Although C++ applications primarily use the C++-level navigational interface, the application can also initiate OQL queries.

18.3   **Paradigm Shifts**

Database schema designers and application developers confront several paradigm shifts with the introduction of object database technology. Although some of these changes require fundamental shifts in the way developers use databases, they also significantly reduce development complexity.

People who are unfamiliar with object technology must make the paradigm shift associated with learning how to model the world with objects. On the other hand, many developers who decide to use a C++ object database have already become familiar with object modeling in C++ and have a smaller learning curve to overcome. In fact, they discover that there are fewer modeling issues than if a relational database had been used.

For those who have used C++ with relational databases, the shared type system of a C++ object database is a welcomed paradigm shift that reduces the overall complexity of the system architecture. Having all the applications using the same object model also increases object reuse, reducing development costs. With a relational database, developers often end up working more independently, resulting in redundant development of the same objects across applications. Having the database and applications using a common object model forces a higher degree of reuse.

Having the database provide sophisticated application cache management represents another paradigm shift. Both the cache mechanisms and the common type system lead to another fundamental paradigm shift known as database transparency. Application cache management results in a substantial reduction in development costs. With a relational database, a considerable amount of code is often dedicated to the mapping of objects to and from their representation in the database. The object database also takes care of automatically writing modified objects back to the database at transaction commit, a step that the developer must implement when writing an application for a relational database. Although tools are available that provide these application facilities on top of a relational database, the query language user must interface at the relational level and must deal with the underlying representation.

Relational databases are server-centric and need manage data only for a fixed set of simple types. But objects involve operations as well as data, introducing a new level of implementation complexity. The operations must be implemented in a particular programming language, and that reduces the ability to support multiple languages effectively. Aspects of C++, such as the use of pointers to directly reference memory, has led C++ object databases to be more client-centric. Vendors have been unwilling to let application C++ code run in their servers.

18.4 Standardization

Several factors have affected the level of acceptance of object databases in the market. The leading object database vendors are small compared with their relational database counterparts. Each object database vendor has a unique interface, leading to much less portability than can be attained with an SQL relational database. There are also significant architectural differences among the object database products.

The market for object databases has been extremely competitive. To convince customers that their product is superior, many vendors have used marketing tactics that consist of claims that their competitors' products have fundamental flaws. This strategy has been self-defeating for the technology and its overall market acceptance. When users talk to several vendors, they end up hearing much more bad news than good news about the technology, reducing their confidence that they can make the right decision. To protect their market share, vendors of relational databases also criticize the object database product offerings. Development managers often conclude that choosing an object database vendor and using the technology are too risky.

The Object Database Management Group has defined an initial standard for interfacing to object databases. This book has described the ODMG C++ and OQL interfaces. Standardization of the interfaces supported by the vendors provides some degree of application portability. Vendors claim that market interest in their products is rising in anticipation that standardization and maturation of the technology are near.

Developers should demand support of the ODMG standard from the vendors. Vendors are not required to implement all components of the standard. Developers should determine which components they require and expect those components from the vendors they are working with. Those who write C++ applications, for example, should demand the C++ binding. Those requiring query language support should demand support of OQL.

Some object databases support SQL, and that allows them to leverage the third-party tools based on SQL and ODBC. The database schemas are defined in C++ and not SQL. And the mapping of object models into SQL differs among vendors, resulting in a lack of query portability for the same C++ object model. Thus, having SQL does not imply portability.

OQL is based on the same ODMG object model that is used in the C++ binding, so OQL will provide a much higher degree of portability among ODMG implementations than SQL provides for object databases.

18.5 Object and Relational Databases

Object and relational databases serve different application requirements; both kinds of databases will continue to have a role in the marketplace. Object databases are tightly integrated with an object-oriented programming language, providing an object model and type system shared by the application and the database. Relational databases are independent of the application programming language and provide an interface and type system that can uniformly support applications written in multiple programming languages. Even as SQL3 incorporates objects, the object type system used in the database environment will be different and separate from the type system used in the applications.

Object databases provide much more efficient support for static relationships that are used to navigate among interrelated objects. Relational databases excel in the specification of dynamic relationships, using join conditions among tables to specify the relationships based on the values of columns. Application developers should have a clear understanding of the data modeling and transaction needs of their applications before choosing a database technology.

18.6 Future Directions

The year 1996 was a significant turning point for object support in databases. Initial implementations of the ODMG-93 standard were released. Two leading object database vendors had their initial public offering of stock. The vendors experienced increased sales and market acceptance. Object database technology is moving from the "early adopter" to the "early majority" phase of technology acceptance. In 1996, the ANSI SQL3 committee revealed its intention to standardize SQL support of objects.

During the latter part of the 1990s, object and relational database technologies will incorporate each other's features and functionality. Relational databases will add object features, probably emphasizing server support of objects along with better client-side support. For their part, the object database vendors will expand their level of standardization and support for query language access. Deciding among the alternatives will probably become more confusing rather than less confusing.

18.7 Java

Java will have a major impact on relational and object database technologies. The speed of its acceptance has reached levels unprecedented in the computer industry. The language is highly regarded even by veterans and supporters of competing object programming languages, such as C++ and Smalltalk. Libraries are being developed for the language at a record pace. In many cases, vendors are leveraging their existing investments in C++.

JavaSoft, the division of Sun responsible for the Java language and libraries, has defined a Java interface called JDBC, modeled somewhat after the ODBC interface but with better integration with the Java language. ODBC provides SQL column-level access to the database. Several vendors are also developing object (entity) level access to relational databases for Java. ODMG 2.0 defines a Java binding for object databases, and object database vendors are already providing Java interfaces. Several relational vendors are considering using Java instead of (or in addition to) the SQL3 PSM language to support object semantics in their SQL environments. Java has many advantages over the SQL3 PSM language. Java is a general-purpose programming language and will always have much stronger industry support than a language focused only on database management.

Relational vendors are already offering object solutions that are not based on SQL3. Some relational vendors will use Java as a database server language, and several have announced support for this. The relational market rally around Java instead of SQL3 PSM will fragment the market, affecting the level of standardization in the relational database industry. The relational vendors are heading in different directions in their pursuit of objects, a move that will probably hurt chances of market acceptance.

Java offers many benefits to a database environment. It provides platform independence and has minimal installation and administration costs. A fundamental characteristic of Java is its lack of pointers; Java applications cannot directly access memory. Java source code is compiled in bytecode form. A Java Virtual Machine provides an execution environment in which Java bytecodes are interpreted. When the Java Virtual Machine dynamically links a class into the environment, it performs checks to make sure that the software cannot directly access memory or outside resources for which it has not been authorized. This feature provides a higher level of robustness and security than C++ provides.

Database vendors are more willing to incorporate the Java Virtual Machine and execute Java bytecodes in their server processes than they are to use C++. The vendors are concerned that errant C++ pointers will corrupt server memory. The database vendors allow C++ application objects to execute only in the address space of the client application process.

Vendors that support some degree of query processing in their servers limit the functionality executable to the capabilities of the primitive data types. The semantics of application objects exist only in the client environment, reducing the seamlessness of the type support in the database environment. It compromises the performance gains that could be attained if object semantics were included in the query constraints evaluated in the server. As a result, more objects are transferred to a client than necessary.

A database could include a Java Virtual Machine implementation in the database server, where Java classes could execute without corrupting the server memory. The same Java types can be used in the database server or the client application. Applications written in Java and queries written in a language such as OQL or SQL could share the same type system and have the complete functionality of the objects available. The type system would not be running in a client-centric or server-centric environment but instead would run seamlessly in both environments. The application could then use both the client and the server execution environments most effectively. Object and relational database vendors are planning to offer Java as a server language. Java classes will be able to execute in both the client and the server.

Although Java is attaining unprecedented market acceptance, it will be a few years before the various database offerings for Java become established in the marketplace. C++ will continue to be the best choice for object database applications that require high performance. Current Java just-in-time (JIT) compilers produce object code that performs slower than C++ (garbage collection is usually slower than explicit deletion). The performance advantage of C++ object databases has been a key factor in the adoption of the technology by the initial application domains using object databases (CAD/CAM, CASE, and telecommunications). C++ will continue to dominate these markets for the next few years, and other application domains will also begin using the technology.

Appendix A:
Example Schema

The object model in Figure A.1 illustrates the example schema used in the book. The thick gray bar represents an ISA relationship between `Person` and `Employee`.

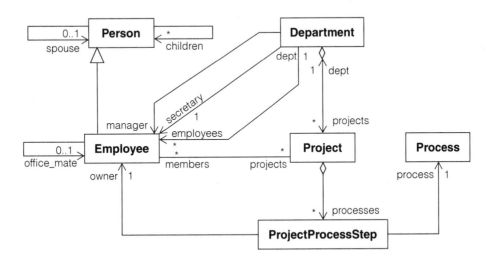

Figure A.1 Example schema.

The following C++ header file represents the database schema.

```
class ostream;
class istream;

struct  Address {
                                        Address(const char *s, const char *c,
                                                const char *st, const char *z);
                                        Address();
                                        Address(const struct Address &);
            d_String                    street;
            d_String                    city;
            char                        state[3];
            char                        zip_code[6];
friend  ostream &                       operator<<(ostream &, const Address &);
};


class   Person : public d_Object {
public:
                                        Person(const char *fn, const char *ln,
                                                const Address &, const d_Date &,
                                                const char *phone);
                                        Person(const char *fn, const char *ln);
                                        ~Person();
            const d_String &            first_name() const;
            const d_String &            last_name() const;
            const struct Address        address() const;
            void                        newAddress(const struct Address &);
            d_Date                      birth_date() const;
            d_UShort                    age() const;
            void                        d_activate();
            void                        d_deactivate();
friend  ostream &                       operator<<(ostream &, const Person &);
private:
            d_String                    _fname;
            d_String                    _lname;
            Address                     _address;
            char                        _phone_number[11];
            d_Date                      _birth_date;
            d_Ref<Person>               _spouse;
            d_Set<d_Ref<Person> >       _children;
};

class   Employee : public Person {
public:
                                        Employee(const char *fn, const char *ln,
                                                const Address &, const d_Date &,
                                                const char *phone,
                                                const d_Ref<Department>&d,
                                                const char *ophone,
                                                const char *email,
                                                d_ULong sal);
```

```
                                    Employee(const char *fn, const char *ln);
                                    ~Employee();
            d_Ref<Employee>         office_mate;
            d_Ref<Department>       dept;
            d_Set<d_Ref<Project> >  projects;
            const char *            office_phone() const;
            d_ULong                 salary() const;
            void                    d_activate();
            void                    d_deactivate();

    static  const char * const      extent_name;
    static  d_Set<d_Ref<Employee> > * Employees();
    friend  ostream &               operator<<(ostream &, const Employee &);
    static  d_Ref<Employee>         create_from_stream(istream &,
                                            const d_Ref<Department> &);
    private:
    static  d_Set<d_Ref<Employee> > *_extent;
            char                    _office_phone[11];
            d_String                _email_address;
            d_ULong                 _salary;
    };

    class   Department : public d_Object {
    public:
                                    Department(const char *n,
                                            const char *fax);
                                    ~Department();
            const d_String &        name() const;
            d_Set<d_Ref<Employee> > employees;
            d_List<d_Ref<Project> > projects;

            void                    addEmployees(istream&);
            Employee *              employee(const char *fn,
                                            const char *ln) const;
            Project *               project(const char *pn) const;
            Project *               addProject(const char *pn, d_ULong cost);
            int                     assign(const char *fn, const char *ln,
                                            const char *pn);
            Employee *              manager() const;
            void                    assignManager(Employee *);
            void                    assignSecretary(Employee *);
            void                    printEmployees(ostream &);
            void                    printProjects(ostream &);
    static  d_Ref<d_Set<d_Ref<Department> > > depts();
    friend  ostream &               operator<<(ostream &, const Department&);
    private:
            d_String                _name;
            d_Ref<Employee>         _manager;
            d_Ref<Employee>         _secretary;
            d_ULong                 _budget;
            char                    _fax[11];
    static d_Ref<d_Set<d_Ref<Department> > > _depts;
```

```
static  const char * const        depts_name;
};

class   Process : public d_Object {
public:
        d_String                  name;
};

class   ProjectProcessStep : public d_Object {
public:
                                  ProjectProcessStep();
                                  ProjectProcessStep(
                                  const ProjectProcessStep &);
                                  ~ProjectProcessStep();
        ProjectProcessStep&       operator=(const ProjectProcessStep &);
        void                      d_activate();
        void                      d_deactivate();
        d_Ref<Process>            process;
        d_Ref<Employee>           owner;
        d_Date                    projectedCompletion;
        d_Date                    actualCompletion;
        d_ULong                   staffHours;
};

class   Project : public d_Object {
public:
                                  Project(const char *pname,
                                      const d_Ref<Department> &,
                                      d_ULong c);
        void                      d_activate();
        void                      d_deactivate();
        d_String                  name;
        d_Ref<Department>         dept;
        d_Set<d_Ref<Employee> >   members;
        d_List<d_Ref<ProjectProcessStep> > processes;
        d_Date                    due_date;
        d_ULong                   cost;
friend  ostream &                 operator<<(ostream &, const Project &);
};
```

Appendix B:
ODMG C++ Classes

This appendix contains a complete description of the ODMG 2.0 classes and their member functions in the form of manual pages. One exception is the metaclasses introduced in ODMG 2.0, which are covered separately in Appendix C. These appendices are meant to serve as a reference both for this book and for an ODMG implementation. Unfortunately, the ODMG 2.0 specification does not include a complete description of the interface. I suggested that such material be added to the ODMG specification, but the group decided that such a manual page style would not mesh well with the rest of the ODMG book. So I have provided it here.

Boolean

Many functions in the ODMG interface return a Boolean value of true or false. The `bool` data type was not part of the C++ language when ODMG-93 was originally designed, nor is `bool` yet ubiquitous in C++ environments. In ODMG-93 release 1.2 these Boolean functions return an `int` value of 0 for false and a non-zero value for true. With ODMG release 2.0, the Boolean data type `d_Boolean` is used in the interface. The symbols `d_True` and `d_False` are defined to represent true and false. The manual pages in this book have been updated to reflect the release 2.0 interfaces. If you are using a release 1.2 implementation, you should be aware that the interface is based on the `int` data type. The application could define `d_True` and `d_False` to achieve portability with the ODMG 2.0 release in the interim.

Name   **Preprocessor Symbols**

In ODMG release 1.2 a preprocessor symbol is defined called `__ODMG_93__`, which can be used for conditional compilation. With ODMG release 2.0 the following symbol is defined.

```
#define __ODMG__ 20
```

The value of this symbol indicates the ODMG release of the implementation.

Name   **All Classes**

Figure B.1 shows the inheritance relationships that exist among all the ODMG classes (indicated by the lines) and categories in which the classes and other types belong (grouped into labeled gray boxes).

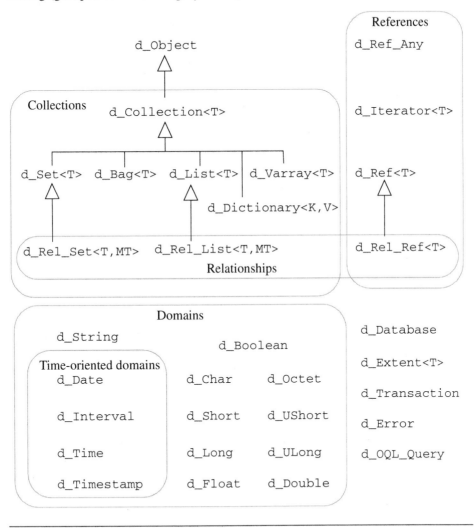

Figure B.1 ODMG C++ classes.

Name   d_Bag<T>

An unordered collection of elements of type T that allows duplicate values. The
union, intersection, and difference operations are described in section 7.4.2.

Synopsis

```
template <class T> class d_Bag : public d_Collection<T> {
public:
                              d_Bag();
                              d_Bag(const d_Bag<T> &b2);
                              ~d_Bag();
        d_Bag<T> &            operator=(const d_Bag<T> &b2);
        unsigned long         occurrences_of(const T &val) const;
        d_Bag<T> &            union_of(const d_Bag<T> &b1,
                                       const d_Bag<T> &b2);
        d_Bag<T> &            union_with(const d_Bag<T> &b2);
        d_Bag<T> &            operator+=(const d_Bag<T> &b2);
        d_Bag<T>              create_union(const d_Bag<T> &b2) const;
 friend d_Bag<T>              operator+(const d_Bag<T> &b1,
                                       const d_Bag<T> &b2);
        d_Bag<T> &            intersection_of(const d_Bag<T> &b1,
                                       const d_Bag<T> &b2);
        d_Bag<T> &            intersection_with(const d_Bag<T> &b2);
        d_Bag<T> &            operator*=(const d_Bag<T> &b2);
        d_Bag<T>              create_intersection(const d_Bag<T>&b2) const;
 friend d_Bag<T>              operator*(const d_Bag<T>&b1,const d_Bag<T>&b2);
        d_Bag<T> &            difference_of(const d_Bag<T> &b1,
                                       const d_Bag<T> &b2);
        d_Bag<T> &            difference_with(const d_Bag<T> &b2);
        d_Bag<T> &            operator-=(const d_Bag<T> &b2);
        d_Bag<T>              create_difference(const d_Bag<T> &b2) const;
 friend d_Bag<T>              operator-(const d_Bag<T>&b1,const d_Bag<T>&b2);
};
```

Description

```
d_Bag()
```
The null constructor initializes the bag with no elements.

d_Bag<T>

```
d_Bag(const d_Bag<T> &b2)
```

> The copy constructor initializes a new bag with a copy of the elements in the bag referenced by b2. For nonprimitive types, the copy constructor of T is called.

```
~d_Bag()
```

> The destructor uninitializes the bag. For nonprimitive types, the destructor for T is called for each element in the bag.

```
d_Bag<T> &
operator=(const d_Bag<T> &b2)
```

> The assignment operator assigns the contents of one bag (b2) to another bag. It returns a reference to the object, allowing a cascading of assignment operations. If an attempt is made to assign a bag to itself, no assignment operation is performed. If the bag being assigned to had elements before the assignment operation, they are first removed. The object will contain a copy of the elements in the bag referenced by b2.

```
unsigned long
occurrences_of(const T &val) const
```

> The number of elements in the bag that are equal to val is returned.

```
d_Bag<T> &
union_of(const d_Bag<T> &b1, const d_Bag<T> &b2)
```

> The union of the function arguments b1 and b2 is created and placed in the object. The original elements of the bag object before the operation are discarded, and the destructor (if it exists) is called for each of the original elements. The function returns a reference to the object.
>
> Example syntax:
>
> ```
> bag.union_of(bag1, bag2);
> ```

```
d_Bag<T> &
union_with(const d_Bag<T> &b2)
```

> A union is created of the bag object and the bag b2. The result of the union is placed in the original object. The function returns a reference to the object.
>
> Example syntax:
>
> ```
> bag.union_with(bag2);
> ```

```
d_Bag<T> &
operator+=(const d_Bag<T> &b2)
```

> This function performs the same operation as the preceding function union_-with. A union of the object and the bag b2 is computed and placed into the object. The function returns a reference to the object.
>
> Example syntax:
>
> ```
> bag += bag2;
> ```

```
d_Bag<T>
create_union(const d_Bag<T> &b2) const
```

> A union is created of the bag object and the bag b2. The original bag object is not altered, and the result is a new bag object returned by value.
>
> Example syntax:
>
> ```
> bagresult = bag.create_union(bag2);
> ```
>
> In this example the new bag object created by create_union is returned by value, and then the returned value is assigned to bagresult using the assignment operator defined for d_Bag<T>.

```
friend d_Bag<T>
operator+(const d_Bag<T> &b1, const d_Bag<T> &b2)
```

> A union is created of b1 and b2, and the resulting bag is returned by value.
>
> Example syntax:
>
> ```
> bagresult = bag1 + bag2
> ```
>
> In this example, the bag value returned by operator+ is then assigned to bagresult.

```
d_Bag<T> &
intersection_of(const d_Bag<T> &b1, const d_Bag<T> &b2)
```

> The intersection of b1 and b2 is created and placed in the object. The original elements that were in the bag object before the operation are discarded; the destructor (if defined for the type) is called for each element. The function returns a reference to the object.
>
> Example syntax:
>
> ```
> bag.intersection_of(bag1, bag2);
> ```

```
d_Bag<T> &
intersection_with(const d_Bag<T> &b2)
```

> An intersection is created of the bag object and the bag b2. The result of the intersection is placed in the original object. The function returns a reference to the object.
>
> Example syntax:
>
> ```
> bag.intersection_with(bag2);
> ```

```
d_Bag<T> &
operator*=(const d_Bag<T> &b2)
```

> This function performs the same operation as the function intersection_with. An intersection of the object and the bag b2 is computed and placed into the object. The function returns a reference to the object.
>
> Example syntax:
>
> ```
> bag *= bag2;
> ```

d_Bag<T>

```
d_Bag<T>
create_intersection(const d_Bag<T>&b2) const
```

>   An intersection is created of the object and the bag b2.
>
>   Example syntax:
>
>   ```
>   bagresult = bag.create_intersection(bag2);
>   ```
>
>   The original bag object is not altered, and a new result bag object is returned by value, which is then assigned to bagresult using the d_Bag<T> assignment operator.

```
friend d_Bag<T>
operator*(const d_Bag<T> &b1, const d_Bag<T> &b2)
```

>   The intersection of b1 and b2 is created. The result is a bag returned by value.
>
>   Example syntax:
>
>   ```
>   bagresult = bag1 * bag2
>   ```
>
>   In the example the resulting bag is then assigned to bagresult.

```
d_Bag<T> &
difference_of(const d_Bag<T> &b1, const d_Bag<T> &b2)
```

>   The difference of b1 and b2 (b1 - b2) is created and placed in the object. The bag's original elements before the operation are discarded; if defined for the type T, the destructor is called for each element. The function returns a reference to the object.
>
>   Example syntax:
>
>   ```
>   bag.difference_of(bag1, bag2);
>   ```
>
>   In the example, the return value of the call to difference_of is a reference to bag.

```
d_Bag<T> &
difference_with(const d_Bag<T> &b2)
```

>   The difference of the bag object and the bag b2 is created and placed in the object. The function returns a reference to the object.
>
>   Example syntax:
>
>   ```
>   bag.difference_with(bag2);
>   ```

```
d_Bag<T> &
operator-=(const d_Bag<T> &b2)
```

>   This function performs the same operation as the preceding function difference_with. The difference of the object and the bag b2 is computed and placed into the object. The function returns a reference to the object.
>
>   Example syntax:
>
>   ```
>   bag -= bag2;
>   ```

```
d_Bag<T>
create_difference(const d_Bag<T> &b2) const
```

The difference of the object and the bag b2 is created. The original bag object is not altered, and the result is a new bag object returned by value.

Example syntax:

```
bagresult = bag.create_difference(bag2);
```

```
friend d_Bag<T>
operator-(const d_Bag<T> &b1, const d_Bag<T> &b2)
```

The difference of b1 and b2 is computed, and a new result bag is returned by value.

Example syntax:

```
bag3 = bag1 - bag2
```

Name   d_Collection<T>

This is the abstract base class for each ODMG collection class; instances of this class cannot be created. This class is derived from d_Object, so instances of any derived collection classes are persistence-capable. Some of the member functions may be pure virtual functions; it is up to each implementation to decide which functions are virtual or pure virtual functions.

The element type T must support the following operations.

```
class T {
public:
                T();
                T(const T&);
                ~T();
    T &         operator=(const T &);
    d_Boolean   operator==(const T&, const T&);
    };
```

In other words, the type T must be able to be initialized both without a value and with another value of the same type. It must also be possible to assign another instance of T to a T instance. It must be possible to compare two T instances for equality. Finally, it must be possible to destroy an instance of T.

Synopsis

```
template <class T> class d_Collection : public d_Object {
public:
virtual                 ~d_Collection();
        d_Collection<T> & assign_from(const d_Collection<T> &c2);
friend d_Boolean        operator==(const d_Collection<T> &c1,
                                   const d_Collection<T> &c2);
friend d_Boolean        operator!=(const d_Collection<T> &c1,
                                   const d_Collection<T> &c2);
        unsigned long   cardinality() const;
        d_Boolean       is_empty() const;
        d_Boolean       is_ordered() const;
        d_Boolean       allows_duplicates() const;
        d_Boolean       contains_element(const T &val) const;
        void            insert_element(const T &val);
```

```
        void                remove_element(const T &val);
        void                remove_all();
        void                remove_all(const T &val);
        d_Iterator<T>       create_iterator() const;
        d_Iterator<T>       begin() const;
        d_Iterator<T>       end() const;
        T                   select_element(const char *OQL_pred) const;
        d_Iterator<T>       select(const char *OQL_pred) const;
        int                 query(d_Collection<T> &c,
                                  const char *OQL_pred) const;
        d_Boolean           exists_element(const char*OQL_pred) const;
protected:

                            d_Collection(const d_Collection<T> &c2);
    d_Collection<T> &       operator=(const d_Collection<T> &c2);
                            d_Collection();
    };
```

Description

```
~d_Collection()
```

>   The virtual destructor. All elements of the collection are removed. If the element type T has a destructor, it is called for each element.

```
d_Collection<T> &
assign_from(const d_Collection<T> &c2)
```

>   This function assigns the elements of c2 to the object. The elements that were in the collection before the operation are removed. After the operation the object contains the same elements as c2. A reference to the object is returned.
>
>   Each type of collection derived from d_Collection<T>, such as d_Set<T> and d_List<T>, provides an assignment operator to assign one instance of the collection type to another instance of the same collection type (set1 = set2). The function assign_from is used to perform assignment between different collection types, such as d_Set<T> and d_List<T>.

```
friend d_Boolean
operator==(const d_Collection<T> c1&,const d_Collection<T> &c2)
```

>   The equality operator returns true if collections c1 and c2 are equal; otherwise, it returns false.

```
friend d_Boolean
operator!=(const d_Collection<T> &c1,const d_Collection<T> &c2)
```

> The inequality operator returns true if collections c1 and c2 are not equal. If the collections are equal, it returns false.

```
unsigned long
cardinality() const
```

> This function returns the number of elements in the collection.

```
d_Boolean
is_empty() const
```

> If the collection is empty this function returns true; otherwise, it returns false.

```
d_Boolean
is_ordered() const
```

> If this is an ordered collection, d_List<T> and d_Varray<T>, this function returns true. Otherwise, it returns false.

```
d_Boolean
allows_duplicates() const
```

> This function returns true if this collection allows elements with duplicate values; otherwise, it returns false. The d_Bag<T>, d_List<T>, and d_Varray<T> classes allow duplicate values.

```
d_Boolean
contains_element(const T &val) const
```

> This function returns true if the collection contains an element with the value val. Otherwise, it returns false.

```
void
insert_element(const T &val)
```

> This function inserts a new element with the value val into the collection. If the collection is a d_Set<T>, the set will not be altered if it already contains an element with value val. If the collection is a d_List<T>, the new element will be placed at the end of the list. If the collection is a d_Varray<T>, the size of the array will be increased by 1 and the new element will be placed in the newly created last position.

```
void
remove_element(const T &val)
```

> This function removes one element equal to val from the collection. For ordered collections, the element removed is the first element that is reached if a forward iteration of the collection is being performed.

```
void
remove_all()
```

This function removes all the elements from the collection. After this operation is complete, the collection is empty.

```
void
remove_all(const T &val)
```

All the elements that are equal to `val` are removed from the collection. This function was added in ODMG 2.0.

```
d_Iterator<T>
create_iterator() const
```

This function returns a `d_Iterator<T>` positioned at the first element of iteration.

```
d_Iterator<T>
begin() const
```

This function returns a `d_Iterator<T>` positioned at the first element of iteration. This function is required for STL iterator compatibility. It returns the same value as `create_iterator`.

```
d_Iterator<T>
end() const
```

This function returns a `d_Iterator<T>` positioned just past the last element of iteration. This function is required for STL iterator compatibility.

```
T
select_element(const char *OQL_pred) const
```

This function applies the OQL predicate to the elements of the collection and returns the value of the first element for which the predicate evaluates to true. In ODMG-93 1.2, this function had a return type of `const T &`. It was changed to `T` in release 2.0.

```
d_Iterator<T>
select(const char *OQL_pred) const
```

This function returns an iterator that iterates over all the elements of the collection for which the OQL predicate evaluates to true.

```
int
query(d_Collection<T> &c, const char *OQL_pred) const
```

This function places in the return collection `c` all the elements that evaluate to true for the OQL predicate. If an error occurs, a nonzero value is returned indicating the error. The error values have not yet been standardized.

d_Collection<T>

```
d_Boolean
exists_element(const char *OQL_pred) const
```

> This Boolean function performs existential quantification. It returns true if at least one element evaluates to true for the OQL predicate. Otherwise, it returns false.

```
d_Collection(const d_Collection<T> &c2)
```

> The copy constructor is made available only to the concrete derived classes.

```
d_Collection<T> &
operator=(const d_Collection<T> &c2)
```

> The `protected` assignment operator is made available only to the concrete derived classes.

```
d_Collection()
```

> The `protected` null constructor is made available only to the concrete derived classes. It is not possible to create an instance of this abstract class.

Name   d_Database

The class representing the interface to a database.

Synopsis

```
class d_Database {
public:
static d_Database * const transient_memory;
        enum access_status { not_open, read_write, read_only, exclusive};
                            d_Database();
        void                open(const char *db_name,
                                        access_status access=read_write);
        void                close();
        void                set_object_name(const d_Ref_Any &objref,
                                        const char *name);
        void                rename_object(const char *oldName,
                                        const char *newName);
        d_Ref_Any           lookup_object(const char *name) const;
private:
                            d_Database(const d_Database &);
        d_Database &        operator=(const d_Database &);
};
```

Description

```
static d_Database *const transient_memory
```

This pointer is used with the new operator of d_Object to indicate that an object should be placed in transient memory. It allows a single uniform interface to the new operator for the creation of both persistent and transient objects. There is no actual "database" associated with transient memory. In ODMG-93 1.2, this variable was declared as

```
static const d_Database *const transient_memory
```

The type was changed in release 2.0.

```
enum access_status;
```

This enumeration defines the possible levels of access when a database is opened.

```
d_Database()
```

The null constructor initializes the database object.

```
void
open(const char *db_name, access_status access)
```

> This function is used to open the database named db_name with access level access. The function locates and establishes a connection with the database. A database must be opened before objects within it can be accessed. An attempt to open a database that has already been opened throws a d_Error_DatabaseOpen exception.

```
void
close()
```

> This function closes the connection with the database. Any attempts to access a database object after the database has been closed throws a d_Error_-DatabaseClosed exception.

```
void
set_object_name(const d_Ref_Any &objref, const char *name)
```

> This function establishes an association between the given object and a name. In ODMG-93 release 1.2, an object could have only a single name. With ODMG release 2.0, an object can have multiple names. In release 1.2, if the object already has a name it is changed to the new name. In release 2.0, the additional name is associated with the object. If the name specified is not unique in the database, a d_Error_NameNotUnique exception is thrown. In ODMG release 1.2, when an object is deleted its name entry is automatically removed. In ODMG 2.0, names are not removed automatically. All the names associated with an object can be removed by calling this function and passing 0 as the second argument.

```
void
rename_object(const char *oldName, const char *newName)
```

> This function changes the name oldName of an object to newName. If the new name is not unique, a d_Error_NameNotUnique exception is thrown and the object retains the old name. You can remove a name of an object by specifying 0 for newName.

```
d_Ref_Any
lookup_object(const char *name) const
```

> This function attempts to find an object with the given name and returns a reference to the object. If there is no object with the given name, the reference returned has a null value.

```
d_Database(const d_Database &)
```

```
d_Database &
operator=(const d_Database &)
```

> These are private. They cannot be performed with a d_Database object.

Name   d_Date

A class representing a date, consisting of a year, month, and day.

Synopsis

```
class d_Date {
public:
        enum Weekday {      Sunday = 0, Monday = 1, Tuesday = 2,
                            Wednesday = 3, Thursday = 4, Friday = 5,
                            Saturday = 6 };
        enum Month {        January = 1, February = 2, March = 3,
                            April = 4, May = 5, June = 6, July = 7,
                            August = 8, September = 9, October = 10,
                            November = 11, December = 12 };
                            d_Date();    // sets to current date
                            d_Date(unsigned short year,
                                        unsigned short day_of_year);
                            d_Date(unsigned short year,
                                        unsigned short month,
                                        unsigned short day);
                            d_Date(const d_Date &d2);
                            d_Date(const d_Timestamp &ts);
        d_Date &            operator=(const d_Date &d2);
        d_Date &            operator=(const d_Timestamp &ts);
        unsigned short      year() const;
        unsigned short      month() const;
        unsigned short      day() const;
        unsigned short      day_of_year() const;
        Weekday             day_of_week() const;
        Month               month_of_year() const;
        d_Boolean           is_leap_year() const;
 static d_Boolean           is_leap_year(unsigned short year);
 static d_Date              current();
        d_Date &            next(Weekday wd);
        d_Date &            previous(Weekday wd);
        d_Date &            operator+=(const d_Interval &i);
        d_Date &            operator+=(int ndays);
        d_Date &            operator++();
        d_Date              operator++(int);
```

```
        d_Date &        operator-=(const d_Interval &i);
        d_Date &        operator-=(int ndays);
        d_Date &        operator--();
        d_Date          operator--(int);
 friend d_Date          operator+ (const d_Date &d,
                                  const d_Interval &i);
 friend d_Date          operator+ (const d_Interval &i,
                                  const d_Date &d);
 friend d_Interval      operator- (const d_Date &d1, const d_Date &d2);
 friend d_Date          operator- (const d_Date &d,
                                  const d_Interval &i);
 friend d_Boolean       operator==(const d_Date &d1, const d_Date &d2);
 friend d_Boolean       operator!=(const d_Date &d1, const d_Date &d2);
 friend d_Boolean       operator< (const d_Date &d1, const d_Date &d2);
 friend d_Boolean       operator<=(const d_Date &d1, const d_Date &d2);
 friend d_Boolean       operator> (const d_Date &d1, const d_Date &d2);
 friend d_Boolean       operator>=(const d_Date &d1, const d_Date &d2);
        d_Boolean       is_between(const d_Date &d2, const d_Date &d3)
                                  const;
 friend d_Boolean       overlaps(const d_Date &sL, const d_Date &eL,
                                  const d_Date &sR,
                                  const d_Date &eR);
 friend d_Boolean       overlaps(const d_Timestamp &sL,
                                  const d_Timestamp &eL,
                                  const d_Date &sR,
                                  const d_Date &eR);
 friend d_Boolean       overlaps(const d_Date &sL, const d_Date &eL,
                                  const d_Timestamp &sR,
                                  const d_Timestamp &eR);
 static int             days_in_year(unsigned short year);
        int             days_in_year() const;
 static int             days_in_month(unsigned short year,
                                  unsigned short month);
        int             days_in_month() const;
 static d_Boolean       is_valid_date(unsigned short year,
                                  unsigned short month,
                                  unsigned short day);

};
```

Description

enum Weekday

> This enumeration represents the days of the week.

enum Month

> This enumeration represents the months of the year.

d_Date()

> The null constructor initializes the object to the current date.

d_Date(unsigned short year, unsigned short day_of_year)

> This constructor initializes the object to the given year and day of year. The full four-digit year must be specified (such as 2001). The day_of_year should be a value from 1 to 366 (for a leap year).

d_Date(unsigned short year, unsigned short month,
        unsigned short day);

> This constructor initializes the object based on the specified year, month, and day. The full four-digit year must be specified (such as 2001). The month should be a value from 1 through 12, and the day should be a value from 1 through 31.

d_Date(const d_Date &d2)

> The copy constructor initializes the object to the same date as d2.

d_Date(const d_Timestamp &ts)

> This constructor initializes the object with the year, month, and day components of ts.

d_Date &
operator=(const d_Date &d2)

> This assignment operator assigns the date value of d2 to the object and returns a reference to the object.

d_Date &
operator=(const d_Timestamp &ts)

> This assignment operator assigns the year, month, and day components of ts to the object, returning a reference to the object.

unsigned short
year() const

> The date's four-digit year value is returned, such as 2001.

```
unsigned short
month() const
```

The integer month value is returned (1–12). The integer value of each month is defined by the enumerator `Month`.

```
unsigned short
day() const
```

The day value (within the month) is returned.

```
unsigned short
day_of_year() const
```

The day within the year is returned.

```
Weekday
day_of_week() const
```

The `Weekday` enumeration value representing the day of the week is returned.

```
Month
month_of_year() const;
```

The `Month` enumeration value representing the month is returned.

```
d_Boolean
is_leap_year() const
```

This Boolean function returns true if the date is in a leap year; otherwise, it returns false.

```
static d_Boolean
is_leap_year(unsigned short year)
```

This static Boolean member function returns true if the given year is a leap year. Otherwise, it returns false.

```
static d_Date
current()
```

This static function returns a `d_Date` object value containing the current date.

```
d_Date &
next(Weekday wd)
```

This function advances the date value to the value corresponding to the subsequent day in which the day of the week is `wd`. The function returns a reference to the updated object. For example, repeatedly calling `next` and passing `Date::Monday` will advance the date value to the subsequent Monday with each iteration.

```
d_Date &
previous(Weekday wd)
```

This function decrements the date value to the previous date with the given weekday wd. A reference to the object is returned.

```
d_Date &
operator+=(const d_Interval &i)
```

This function adds the number of days specified by i (i.day()) to the date value and returns a reference to the object. A positive value returned by i.day() moves the date forward; a negative value moves the date back.

```
d_Date &
operator+=(int ndays)
```

This function adds the value ndays to the date and returns a reference to the object. If ndays is positive, the date is moved forward; a negative ndays value moves the date back.

```
d_Date &
operator++()
```

This pre-increment operator advances the date value by one day and returns a reference to the object.

```
d_Date
operator++(int)
```

This post-increment operator advances the date value by one day and returns the original value of the d_Date object by value.

```
d_Date &
operator-=(const d_Interval &i)
```

This function subtracts the number of days specified by i (i.day()) from the date and returns a reference to the object.

```
d_Date &
operator-=(int ndays)
```

This function subtracts ndays days from the date and returns a reference to the object. If ndays is positive, the date is moved back; if ndays is negative, the date is moved forward.

```
d_Date &
operator--()
```

This predecrement operator moves the date value back one day and returns a reference to the object.

```
d_Date
operator--(int)
```

This postdecrement operator moves the date value back one day and returns the original date value.

```
friend d_Date
operator+(const d_Date &d, const d_Interval &i)
```

```
friend d_Date
operator+(const d_Interval &i, const d_Date &d)
```

These operators are used to add `i.day()` days to the `d_Date` d, returning a new `d_Date` object by value.

```
friend d_Interval
operator-(const d_Date &d1, const d_Date &d2)
```

The interval of time between date d1 and d2 is returned (d1 - d2). If the date d1 falls before the date d2, the result will be negative. This function was added in ODMG 2.0.

```
friend d_Date
operator-(const d_Date &d, const d_Interval &i)
```

This operator is used to subtract `i.day()` days from the date d, returning a new date value.

```
friend d_Boolean
operator==(const d_Date &d1, const d_Date &d2)
```

This Boolean equality operator returns true if the two `d_Date` objects represent the same day; otherwise, it returns false.

```
friend d_Boolean
operator!=(const d_Date &d1, const d_Date &d2)
```

This Boolean inequality operator returns true if the two `d_Date` objects do not represent the same day; otherwise, false is returned.

```
friend d_Boolean
operator<(const d_Date &d1, const d_Date &d2)
```

This Boolean less-than operator returns true if the date d1 falls before the date d2. Otherwise, it returns false.

```
friend d_Boolean
operator<=(const d_Date &d1, const d_Date &d2)
```

This Boolean less-than-or-equal operator returns true if the date d1 is the same day or falls before the date d2. Otherwise, it returns false.

```
friend d_Boolean
operator>(const d_Date &d1, const d_Date &d2)
```

> This Boolean greater-than operator returns true if the date d1 falls after the date d2. Otherwise, it returns false.

```
friend d_Boolean
operator>=(const d_Date &d1, const d_Date &d2)
```

> This Boolean greater-than-or-equal operator returns true if the date d1 is the same day or falls after the date d2. Otherwise, it returns false.

```
d_Boolean
is_between(const d_Date &d1, const d_Date &d2) const
```

> This Boolean function returns true if the object's date value lies between the dates d1 and d2; otherwise, it returns false. The function returns true if the value of the object is equal to either d1 or d2.
>
> If d1 <= d2, then the expression
>
> > d.is_between(d1, d2)
>
> is equivalent to the expression
>
> > (d >= d1) && (d <= d2)
>
> If d1 >= d2, then the expression is equivalent to
>
> > (d >= d2) && (d <= d1)

```
friend d_Boolean
overlaps(const d_Date &sL, const d_Date &eL,
         const d_Date &sR,const d_Date &eR)
```

> This Boolean friend function returns true if the period of time L (bounded by the time between sL and eL) has any period of time in common with the period R (bounded by the time between sR and eR). Otherwise, it returns false.

```
friend d_Boolean
overlaps(const d_Timestamp &sL, const d_Timestamp &eL,
         const d_Date &sR, const d_Date &eR)
```

> This Boolean friend function returns true if the period of time L (bounded by the time between sL and eL) has any period of time in common with the period R (bounded by the time between sR and eR). Otherwise, it returns false.

```
friend d_Boolean
overlaps(const d_Date &sL, const d_Date &eL,
         const d_Timestamp &sR, const d_Timestamp &eR)
```

> This Boolean friend function returns true if the period of time L (bounded by the time between sL and eL) has any period of time in common with the period R (bounded by the time between sR and eR). Otherwise, it returns false.

d_Date

```
static int
days_in_year(unsigned short year)
```

>   This static function returns the number of days in the year `year`.

```
int
days_in_year() const
```

>   This member function returns the number of days in the year based on the year
>   value in the object.

```
static int
days_in_month(unsigned short year, unsigned short month)
```

>   This static member function returns the number of days in a given month for a
>   given year.

```
int
days_in_month() const
```

>   The member function returns the number of days in the month based on the
>   current month and year of the object.

```
static d_Boolean
is_valid_date(unsigned short year,
              unsigned short month, unsigned short day)
```

>   The function returns true if the given year, month, and day represent a valid date
>   value. Otherwise, it returns false.

Name   **d_Dictionary<K,V>**

An unordered collection of associations of a key with a value. The key and value can be of arbitrary types. Only one association can have a particular key value. The d_Dictionary class is derived from d_Collection where the element type is d_Association. Element-based operations inherited from d_Collection are performed with instances of d_Association. The iterators returned by the functions inherited from d_Collection return instances of d_Association.

When the inherited function insert_element is called, if the dictionary contains a d_Association with the key value passed to the function, the d_Association is replaced, causing the new value to be associated with the key. If the key is not found in the dictionary, a new d_Association is added to the dictionary.

When remove_element is called, the key and value of the d_Association parameter must be equal for the element to be removed. If the dictionary does not contain an element with a key and value equal to the d_Association parameter, a d_Error_ElementNotFound exception is thrown. Similarly, contains_element returns true only if the dictionary contains a d_Association that has a key and value equal to the d_Association passed as the parameter.

The d_Dictionary class is a new collection added in ODMG release 2.0.

Synopsis

```
template <class K, class V> class d_Association
{
public:
        K               key;
        V               value;
                        d_Association(const K &k, const V &v)
                                : key(k), value(v) { }
};

template <class K, class V>
class d_Dictionary : public d_Collection<d_Association<K,V> > {
public:
                        d_Dictionary();
                        d_Dictionary(const d_Dictionary<K,V> &dict);
                        ~d_Dictionary();
        d_Dictionary<K,V>&  operator=(const d_Dictionary<K,V> &dict);
```

```
        void              bind(const K &k, const V &v);
        void              unbind(const K &k);
        V                 lookup(const K &k) const;
        d_Boolean         contains_key(const K &k) const;
};
```

Description

d_Dictionary()

> The null constructor initializes an instance with no elements.

d_Dictionary(const d_Dictionary<K,V> &dict)

> The copy constructor initializes the dictionary to contain a copy of the same associations that are in dict.

~d_Dictionary()

> The destructor uninitializes the dictionary, deleting each of the associations it contains.

d_Dictionary<K,V> &
operator=(const d_Dictionary<K,V> &dict)

> The assignment operator removes the dictionary's current elements, replacing them with a copy of the same associations in dict.

void
bind(const K &k, const V &v)

> This function establishes an association of the key k with the value v in the dictionary. An association is added to the dictionary if an association does not already exist with a key of k. If the dictionary already contains a d_Association with key k, its value is changed to v.

void
unbind(const K &k)

> If the dictionary contains a d_Association with the value k, it is removed from the dictionary.

V
lookup(const K &k) const

> An attempt is made to access a d_Association element in the dictionary with a key equal to k. If the dictionary does not contain such an element, a d_Error_-ElementNotFound exception is thrown.

d_Boolean
contains_key(const K &k) const

> This function returns true if the dictionary contains a key equal to k.

Name   d_Error

The d_Error class is used to represent ODMG exceptions. It is derived from the
C++ class exception defined in the ANSI/ISO C++ standard.

Synopsis

```
class d_Error : public exception {
public:
        typedef d_Long      kind;
                            d_Error();
                            d_Error(const d_Error &e2);
                            d_Error(kind the_kind);
                            ~d_Error();
        kind                get_kind();
        void                set_kind(kind the_kind);
        const char *        what() const throw();

        d_Error &           operator<<(d_Char d);
        d_Error &           operator<<(d_Short s);
        d_Error &           operator<<(d_UShort us);
        d_Error &           operator<<(d_Long L);
        d_Error &           operator<<(d_ULong UL);
        d_Error &           operator<<(d_Float f);
        d_Error &           operator<<(d_Double d);
        d_Error &           operator<<(const char *s);
        d_Error &           operator<<(const d_String &s);
        d_Error &           operator<<(const d_Error &e2);
};
```

Description

typedef d_Long kind

The type kind represents the identifier indicating a specific error that has
occurred. A list of the possible values for kind is provided at the end of this
manual page.

d_Error()

The null constructor initializes the object, and the kind is set to d_Error_None.

```
d_Error(const d_Error &e2)
```

> The copy constructor initializes the object to the same value as e2.

```
d_Error(kind the_kind)
```

> This constructor initializes the error object with the value the_kind.

```
~d_Error()
```

> The destructor uninitializes the object, freeing the error string if any.

```
kind
get_kind()
```

> This function returns the kind of error.

```
void
set_kind(kind the_kind)
```

> This function is used to set the kind of error.

```
const char *
what() const throw()
```

> This virtual function is inherited from the base class exception and is used to access a string that describes the error. The d_Error object is responsible for releasing the string returned by what.

```
d_Error &
operator<<(d_Char c)
```

> This function appends an ASCII character to the end of the error string that gets returned by what.

```
d_Error &
operator<<(d_Short s)
```

> This function appends an ASCII representation of a short integer to the end of the error string that gets returned by what.

```
d_Error &
operator<<(d_UShort us)
```

> This function appends an ASCII representation of an unsigned short integer to the end of the error string that gets returned by what.

```
d_Error &
operator<<(d_Long L)
```

> This function appends an ASCII representation of a long integer to the end of the error string that gets returned by what.

d_Error

```
d_Error &
operator<<(d_ULong UL)
```

> This function appends an ASCII representation of an unsigned long integer to the end of the error string that gets returned by `what`.

```
d_Error &
operator<<(d_Float f)
```

> This function appends an ASCII representation of a floating-point number to the end of the error string that gets returned by `what`.

```
d_Error &
operator<<(d_Double d)
```

> This function appends an ASCII representation of a double floating-point number to the end of the error string that gets returned by `what`.

```
d_Error &
operator<<(const char *s)
```

> This function appends a character string to the end of the error string that gets returned by `what`.

```
d_Error &
operator<<(const d_String &s)
```

> This function appends a `d_String` to the end of the error string that gets returned by `what`.

```
d_Error &
operator<<(const d_Error &e2)
```

> This function appends the contents of another `d_Error` e2 to the end of the error string that gets returned by `what`.

Error Kinds

`d_Error_None`

> No error has occurred.

`d_Error_DatabaseClassMismatch`

> The definition of a class in the application does not match the class definition in the database.

`d_Error_DatabaseClassUndefined`

> The database does not have schema information about a particular class.

d_Error_DatabaseClosed

> An attempt has been made to close a database that is already closed (it is not open). Or an attempt has been made to access an object and the database is closed.

d_Error_DatabaseOpen

> An attempt has been made to open a database that is already open.

d_Error_DateInvalid

> An attempt has been made to set a d_Date object to an invalid date value.

d_Error_ElementNotFound

> An attempt has been made to access an element that is not in the collection.

d_Error_IteratorDifferentCollections

> An attempt has been made to use an iterator with a collection that the iterator is not associated with.

d_Error_IteratorExhausted

> An attempt has been made to advance an iterator that has already reached the end of iteration.

d_Error_IteratorNotBackward

> An attempt has been made to iterate backward through either a d_Set<T> or a d_Bag<T>, which does not support backward iteration.

d_Error_MemberIsOfInvalidType

> The second template argument (MT) in the declaration of a d_Rel_Ref<T,MT>, d_Rel_Set<T,MT>, or d_Rel_List<T,MT> refers to a data member of T that is not of type d_Rel_Ref<T,MT>, d_Rel_Set<T,MT>, or d_Rel_List<T,MT>.

d_Error_MemberNotFound

> The second template argument (MT) in the declaration of a d_Rel_Ref<T,MT>, d_Rel_Set<T,MT>, or d_Rel_List<T,MT> contains a string that does not correspond to the name of any data member in the referenced class T.

d_Error_NameNotUnique

> An attempt has been made to give an object a name that is already associated with an object.

d_Error_PositionOutOfRange

> A position has been supplied as an index into a collection that is not within the range of valid values. This error was added in ODMG release 2.0.

d_Error_QueryParameterCountInvalid

> The number of arguments used to build a query with a d_OQL_Query object does not equal the number of arguments supplied in the query string.

`d_Error_QueryParameterTypeInvalid`

Either the type of a query parameter or the return value is invalid for the given query based on the types known by the database.

`d_Error_RefInvalid`

An attempt was made to dereference a `d_Ref<T>` that is referencing an object that does not exist (the object may have been deleted).

`d_Error_RefNull`

An attempt was made to dereference a null `d_Ref`.

`d_Error_TimeInvalid`

An attempt was made to set a `d_Time` object to an invalid time value.

`d_Error_TimestampInvalid`

An attempt was made to set a `d_Timestamp` object to an invalid timestamp value.

`d_Error_TransactionNotOpen`

A call has been made to `commit`, `abort`, or `checkpoint` without an initial call to `begin`. This exception was added in ODMG release 2.0.

`d_Error_TransactionOpen`

The function `d_Transaction::begin` has been called multiple times on the same object without intervening calls to `commit` or `abort`.

`d_Error_TypeInvalid`

An attempt has been made to initialize a `d_Ref<T>` with a reference to an object that is not of type `T` or a class publicly derived from `T`.

Name   d_Extent<T>

d_Extent<T> provides an interface to the extent of class T. The extent contains all the instances of T in the database. It is maintained automatically as instances are created and deleted. This is a new class introduced in ODMG release 2.0.

Synopsis

```
template <class T> class d_Extent {
public:
                          d_Extent(const d_Database *db,
                                   d_Boolean inc_subclasses =d_True);
        virtual           ~d_Extent();
        unsigned long     cardinality() const;
        d_Boolean         is_empty() const;
        d_Boolean         allows_duplicates() const;
        d_Boolean         is_ordered() const;
        d_Iterator<T>     create_iterator() const;
        d_Iterator<T>     begin() const;
        d_Iterator<T>     end() const;
        d_Ref<T>          select_element(const char *OQL_pred) const;
        d_Iterator<T>     select(const char *OQL_pred) const;
        int               query(d_Collection<d_Ref<T> > &c,
                                const char*OQL_pred) const;
        d_Boolean         exists_element(const char *OQL_pred) const;
protected:
                          d_Extent(const d_Extent<T> &e2);
        d_Extent<T> &     operator=(const d_Extent<T> &e2);
};
```

Description

```
d_Extent(const d_Database *db,
                d_Boolean inc_subclasses = d_True)
```

This constructor associates the object with the extent of class T in database db. The second parameter indicates whether the subclasses of T should be included.

```
~d_Extent()
```

The destructor uninitializes the object. The actual extent in the database is not removed.

```
unsigned long
cardinality() const
```

> The number of T instances in the extent is returned.

```
d_Boolean
is_empty() const
```

> This function returns true if there are no T instances in the extent; otherwise, it returns false.

```
d_Boolean
allows_duplicates() const
```

> This function always returns false. There are never duplicate elements in an extent.

```
d_Boolean
is_ordered() const
```

> This function always returns false. The instances of T in the extent are not returned in any particular order.

```
d_Iterator<T>
create_iterator() const
```

> This function returns an iterator used to iterate over the instances of T in the extent.

```
d_Iterator<T>
begin() const
```

> This function returns an iterator positioned at the "beginning" instance of T in the extent. Note that the elements of extents do not have any inherent ordering.

```
d_Iterator<T>
end() const
```

> This function returns an iterator positioned past the end of the extent.

```
d_Ref<T>
select_element(const char *OQL_pred) const
```

> The OQL Boolean predicate specified in OQL_pred is evaluated, and a reference to the instance is returned. This function is meant for query predicates that result in only a single instance of T.

```
d_Iterator<T>
select(const char *OQL_pred) const
```

> The OQL Boolean predicate specified in OQL_pred is evaluated, and an iterator is returned that can be used to iterate over the T instances that are true for the given predicate.

d_Extent<T>

```
int
query(d_Collection<d_Ref<T> > &c, const char *OQL_pred) const
```

> The OQL Boolean predicate specified in `OQL_pred` is evaluated, and the collection `c` is populated with references to the `T` instances that are true for the predicate.

```
d_Boolean
exists_element(const char * OQL_pred) const
```

> This function returns true if there is an instance of `T` in the extent that is true for the OQL Boolean predicate `OQL_pred`.

```
d_Extent(const d_Extent<T> &)
```

```
d_Extent<T> &
operator=(const d_Extent<T> &)
```

> It is not possible to make a copy of an extent or assign one extent to another.

Name   d_Interval

This class represents a duration of time. This class accepts non-normalized input but normalizes the time component values when accessed. For example, suppose that you initialize the object with 130 minutes. The object would then return 2 hours and 10 minutes when calling the access functions. The fact that the interval components are normalized implies that hour returns a value in the range [−23, +23] and that minute and second return a value in the range [−59,+59]. Also, the component integer values will all be zero, all negative, or all positive; in other words, the components will not have a mix of positive and negative values.

Synopsis

```
class d_Interval {
public:
                            d_Interval(int days = 0, int hours = 0,
                                       int mins = 0, float secs = 0.0f);
                            d_Interval(const d_Interval &i2);
        d_Interval &        operator=(const d_Interval &i2);
        int                 day() const;
        int                 hour() const;
        int                 minute() const;
        float               second() const;
        d_Boolean           is_zero() const;
        d_Interval &        operator+=(const d_Interval &i2);
        d_Interval &        operator-=(const d_Interval &i2);
        d_Interval &        operator*=(int i);
        d_Interval &        operator/=(int i);
        d_Interval          operator-() const;
 friend d_Interval          operator+(const d_Interval &i1,
                                      const d_Interval &i2);
 friend d_Interval          operator-(const d_Interval &i1,
                                      const d_Interval &i2);
 friend d_Interval          operator*(const d_Interval &i1, int i);
 friend d_Interval          operator*(int i, const d_Interval &i2);
 friend d_Interval          operator/(const d_Interval &i1, int i);
 friend d_Boolean           operator==(const d_Interval &i1,
                                       const d_Interval &i2);
 friend d_Boolean           operator!=(const d_Interval &i1,
                                       const d_Interval &i2);
```

d_Interval

```
friend  d_Boolean            operator< (const d_Interval &i1,
                                         const d_Interval &i2);
friend  d_Boolean            operator<=(const d_Interval &i1,
                                         const d_Interval &i2);
friend  d_Boolean            operator> (const d_Interval &i1,
                                         const d_Interval &i2);
friend  d_Boolean            operator>=(const d_Interval &i1,
                                         const d_Interval &i2);
};
```

Description

`d_Interval(int days=0, int hours=0, int mins=0,float secs=0.0f)`

> The constructor initializes the interval object with the given number of days, hours, minutes, and seconds.

`d_Interval(const d_Interval &i2)`

> The copy constructor initializes the `d_Interval` object with the value of `i2`.

`d_Interval &`
`operator=(const d_Interval &i2)`

> The assignment operator assigns the value of `i2` to the object.

`int`
`day() const`

> The number of days in the interval is returned.

`int`
`hour() const`

> The number of hours in the interval is returned.

`int`
`minute() const`

> The number of minutes in the interval is returned.

`float`
`second() const`

> The number of seconds in the interval is returned.

`d_Boolean`
`is_zero() const`

> If the value of all the components in the interval is zero, this function returns true. If any time components are nonzero, this function returns false.

```
d_Interval &
operator+=(const d_Interval &i2)
```

> The value of `i2` is added to the interval object. A reference to the object is returned.

```
d_Interval &
operator-=(const d_Interval &i2)
```

> The interval `i2` value is subtracted from the interval object. A reference to the object is returned.

```
d_Interval &
operator*=(int i)
```

> The interval value is multiplied by the given factor `i`. A reference to the object is returned.

```
d_Interval &
operator/=(int i)
```

> The interval value is divided by the divisor `i`. A reference to the object is returned.

```
d_Interval
operator-() const
```

> The interval value is negated and returned by value.

```
friend d_Interval
operator+(const d_Interval &i1, const d_Interval &i2)
```

> This function adds the intervals `i1` and `i2` and returns their sum in a new `d_Interval` object.

```
friend d_Interval
operator-(const d_Interval &i1,const d_Interval &i2)
```

> This function subtracts `i1` from `i2` and returns the result by value.

```
friend d_Interval
operator*(const d_Interval &i1, int i)
```

> This function multiplies the interval `i1` by `i` and returns the result by value.

```
friend d_Interval
operator*(int i, const d_Interval &i2)
```

> This function multiplies the interval `i2` by `i` and returns the result by value.

```
friend d_Interval
operator/(const d_Interval &i1, int i)
```

> This function divides the interval `i1` by `i` and returns the result by value.

```
friend d_Boolean
operator==(const d_Interval &i1, const d_Interval &i2)
```

> If the intervals `i1` and `i2` are equal, true is returned; otherwise, false is returned.

```
friend d_Boolean
operator!=(const d_Interval &i1, const d_Interval &i2)
```

    If i1 and i2 are not equal, true is returned; otherwise, false is returned.

```
friend d_Boolean
operator<(const d_Interval &i1, const d_Interval &i2)
```

    If i1 is less than i2, this function returns true; otherwise, it returns false.

```
friend d_Boolean
operator<=(const d_Interval &i1, const d_Interval &i2)
```

    If i1 is less than or equal to i2, this function returns true; otherwise, it returns false.

```
friend d_Boolean
operator>(const d_Interval &i1, const d_Interval &i1)
```

    If i1 is greater than i2, this function returns true; otherwise, it returns false.

```
friend d_Boolean
operator>=(const d_Interval &i1, const d_Interval &i2)
```

    If i1 is greater than or equal to i2, this function returns true; otherwise, it returns false.

Name   **d_Iterator<T>**

The class used for iterating over the elements of a collection. The d_Collection<T> class has functions create_iterator, begin, and end, which return instances of d_Iterator<T>. Both create_iterator and begin return iterators positioned at the first element. The function end returns an iterator value that is positioned logically past the last element, and this value is used to determine that the end of iteration has been reached.

Synopsis

```
template <class T> class d_Iterator {
public:
                            d_Iterator();
                            d_Iterator(const d_Iterator<T> &i2);
                            ~d_Iterator();
        d_Iterator<T> &     operator=(const d_Iterator<T> &i2);
friend d_Boolean            operator==(const d_Iterator<T> &i1,
                                    const d_Iterator<T> &i2);
friend d_Boolean            operator!=(const d_Iterator<T> &i1,
                                    const d_Iterator<T> &i2);
        void                reset();
        d_Boolean           not_done() const;
        void                advance();
        d_Iterator<T> &     operator++();
        d_Iterator<T>       operator++(int);
        d_Iterator<T> &     operator--();
        d_Iterator<T>       operator--(int);
        T                   get_element() const;
        T                   operator*() const;
        void                replace_element(const T &val);
        d_Boolean           next(T &val);
};
```

Description

```
d_Iterator()
```

The null constructor initializes the object. The object cannot yet be used for iteration, because it does not reference a collection. An iterator associated with a collection must be assigned to the object before it can be used. This function is required for STL iterator compatibility.

```
d_Iterator(const d_Iterator<T> &i2)
```

The copy constructor initializes the iterator to the same value as iterator i2. This function is required for STL iterator compatibility.

```
~d_Iterator()
```

The destructor.

```
d_Iterator<T> &
operator=(const d_Iterator<T> &i2)
```

The assignment operator is used to assign one iterator to another. This function is required for STL iterator compatibility.

```
friend d_Boolean
operator==(const d_Iterator<T> &i1,const d_Iterator<T> &i2)
```

If the two iterators are equal—that is, they refer to the same element in the same collection—this Boolean equality operator returns true; otherwise, it returns false. This function is required for STL iterator compatibility. If an attempt is made to compare the equality of iterators from different collections, the d_Error_-IteratorDifferentCollections exception is thrown.

```
friend d_Boolean
operator!=(const d_Iterator<T> &i1,const d_Iterator<T> &i2)
```

If the two iterators are not equal—that is, they refer to different elements—this Boolean equality operator returns true; otherwise, it returns false. This function is required for STL iterator compatibility. If an attempt is made to compare the equality of two iterators from different collections, the d_Error_Iterator-DifferentCollections exception is thrown.

```
void
reset()
```

The reset function is used to reset an iterator to the beginning element of iteration for the collection.

```
d_Boolean
not_done() const
```

This Boolean function can be called to determine whether iteration is incomplete. It returns true if there are more elements to visit in the iteration.

```
void
advance()
```

This function advances the iterator to the next element of iteration.

```
d_Iterator<T> &
operator++()
```

> The prefix increment operator advances the iterator to the next element of iteration. It returns a reference to the iterator object. If the iterator has reached the end of iteration and this function is called, a d_Error_IteratorExhausted exception is thrown. This function is required for STL iterator compatibility.

```
d_Iterator<T>
operator++(int)
```

> The postfix increment operator advances the iterator to the next element of iteration. It returns the original iterator value that existed before the increment operation. If the iterator has reached the end of iteration and this function is called, a d_Error_IteratorExhausted exception is thrown. This function is required for STL iterator compatibility.

```
d_Iterator<T> &
operator--()
```

> The prefix decrement operator moves the iterator to the previous element of iteration. It moves the iterator back one position and returns a reference to the iterator object. If the iterator has reached the end of backward iteration (iterator positioned at first element) and this function is called, a d_Error_Iterator-Exhausted exception is thrown. This function is required for STL iterator compatibility.
>
> This function cannot be called for iterators on unordered collections (such as d_Set<T> or d_Bag<T>). An attempt to do so will throw a d_Error_Itera-torNotBackward exception.

```
d_Iterator<T>
operator--(int)
```

> The postfix decrement operator moves the iterator to the previous element of iteration. It returns the original iterator value that existed before the operation. If the iterator has reached the end of iteration and this function is called, a d_Error_IteratorExhausted exception is thrown. This function is required for STL iterator compatibility.
>
> This function cannot be called for iterators on unordered collections (such as d_Set<T> or d_Bag<T>). An attempt to do so will throw a d_Error_Itera-torNotBackward exception.

```
T
get_element() const
```

> The function returns the current element of iteration by value. A d_Error_-IteratorExhausted exception is thrown if there is no current element when this function is called.

```
T
operator*() const
```

> The function returns by value the current element of iteration. This function is required for STL iterator compatibility. This function is equivalent to `get_element`. If there is no current element, a `d_Error_IteratorExhausted` exception is thrown.

```
void
replace_element(const T &val)
```

> This function replaces the current element value with `val`. This function can be used only with a `d_List<T>` or `d_Varray<T>` collection.

```
d_Boolean
next(T &val)
```

> This function can be used to check for the end of iteration and return the current element (if there is one) into `val`. If the iterator is positioned past the last element of iteration, the function simply returns false. Otherwise, the function assigns the current element value to the parameter `val`, advances the iterator, and returns true.

Name   d_List<T>

An ordered collection of elements of type T that allows duplicate values. The
beginning index value is 0.

Synopsis

```
template <class T> class d_List : public d_Collection<T> {
public:
                              d_List();
                              d_List(const d_List<T> &L2);
                              ~d_List();
        d_List<T> &           operator=(const d_List<T> &L2);
        T                     retrieve_first_element() const;
        T                     retrieve_last_element() const;
        void                  remove_first_element();
        void                  remove_last_element();
        T                     operator[ ](unsigned long pos) const;
        d_Boolean             find_element(const T &val, unsigned long &pos)
                                      const;
        T                     retrieve_element_at(unsigned long pos) const;
        void                  remove_element_at(unsigned long pos);
        void                  replace_element_at(const T &val,
                                      unsigned long pos);
        void                  insert_element(const T &val); // inherited
        void                  insert_element_first(const T &val);
        void                  insert_element_last(const T &val);
        void                  insert_element_after(const T & val,
                                      unsigned long pos);
        void                  insert_element_before(const T &val,
                                      unsigned long pos);
        d_List<T>             concat(const d_List<T> &L2) const;
 friend  d_List<T>            operator+(const d_List<T> &L1,
                                      const d_List<T> &L2);
        d_List<T> &           append(const d_List<T> &L2);
        d_List<T> &           operator+=(const d_List<T> &L2);
};
```

Description

d_List()

>   The null constructor initializes the list with no elements.

d_List(const d_List<T> &L2)

>   The copy constructor initializes the object using the values of the elements in the
>   list L2. The elements in the initialized object are in the same order as in L2. The
>   copy constructor of T is used to copy the elements.

~d_List()

>   The destructor uninitializes the list, removing all the elements. If the element type
>   has a destructor, it is called for each element.

d_List<T> &
operator=(const d_List<T> &L2)

>   The assignment operator removes the original elements from the object and
>   initializes the object with the elements in L2. The elements in the initialized object
>   are in the same order as in L2.

T
retrieve_first_element() const

>   This function returns the value of the first element in the list.

T
retrieve_last_element() const

>   This function returns the value of the last element in the list.

void
remove_first_element()

>   The first element of the list is removed.

void
remove_last_element()

>   The last element of the list is removed.

T
operator[](unsigned long pos) const

>   The value of the element at position pos is returned. This function performs the
>   same operation as retrieve_element_at.

d_Boolean
find_element(const T &val, unsigned long &pos) const

>   This Boolean function attempts to find an element with value val. It returns true
>   if it finds an element that equals val; otherwise, it returns false. If an element is
>   found, its position is returned via the parameter pos.

```
T
retrieve_element_at(unsigned long pos) const
```

> The value of the element at position `pos` is returned. This function performs the same operation as `operator[]`.

```
void
remove_element_at(unsigned long pos)
```

> This function removes the element at position `pos`.

```
void
replace_element_at(const T &val, unsigned long pos)
```

> This function replaces the value of the element at position `pos` with the value `val`.

```
void
insert_element(const T &val)
```

> The value `val` is inserted at the end of the list.

```
void
insert_element_first(const T &val)
```

> This function inserts an element at the beginning of the list with the value `val`.

```
void
insert_element_last(const T &val)
```

> This function inserts an element at the end of the list with the value `val`.

```
void
insert_element_after(const T &val, unsigned long pos)
```

> This function inserts a new element with the value `val` after the element at position `pos`.

```
void
insert_element_before(const T &val, unsigned long pos)
```

> This function inserts a new element with the value `val` before the element at position `pos`.

```
d_List<T>
concat(const d_List<T> &L2) const
```

> This function creates and returns a new `d_List<T>` object by value that is a concatenation containing copies of the element values of the list object followed by the elements of the list `L2`. The `operator+` function performs the same operation.
>
> Example syntax:

```
        list3 = list1.concat(list2)
```

```
friend d_List<T>
operator+(const d_List<T> &L1, const d_List<T> &L2)
```

> This function creates and returns a new d_List<T> object by value that is a concatenation of L2 onto the end of L1. Copies of the element values contained in L1 and L2 are placed in the result list. The function performs the same operation as concat.
>
> Example syntax:
>
> ```
> list3 = list1 + list2
> ```

```
d_List<T> &
append(const d_List<T> &L2)
```

> This function appends copies of the element values of L2 onto the end of the object and returns a reference to the list object. This function performs the same functionality as operator+=.
>
> Example syntax:
>
> ```
> list1.append(list2);
> ```

```
d_List<T> &
operator+=(const d_List<T> &L2)
```

> Copies of the element values of L2 are appended to the end of the list object, and a reference to the object is returned. This function performs the same operation as append.
>
> Example syntax:
>
> ```
> list1 += list2;
> ```

Name   d_Object

This base class is necessary to make a class persistence-capable.

Synopsis

```
class d_Object {
public:
                          d_Object();
                          d_Object(const d_Object &obj);
virtual                   ~d_Object();
        d_Object &        operator=(const d_Object &obj);
        void              mark_modified();
        void *            operator new(size_t size);
        void *            operator new(size_t size,
                                  const d_Ref_Any &clusterObj,
                                  const char *typename);
        void *            operator new(size_t size, d_Database *db,
                                  const char *typename);
        void              operator delete(void *);
virtual void              d_activate();
virtual void              d_deactivate();
};
```

Description

```
d_Object()
```
The null constructor initializes the object.

```
d_Object(const d_Object &obj)
```
The copy constructor initializes the object with the value of obj.

```
virtual ~d_Object()
```
The destructor removes the object from the client cache and the database.

```
d_Object &
operator=(const d_Object &obj)
```
The assignment operator assigns the value of obj to the object.

```
void
mark_modified()
```
This function should be called *before* any modification of an object to indicate that the object will be changed. The database implementation uses this informa-

tion to acquire necessary locks and to commit the modified object to the database at transaction commit. Calling this function on a transient object has no effect.

```
void *
operator new(size_t size)
```

This new operator is used to create a transient instance of a class derived from d_Object. For example, assume that a class Department exists with a null constructor.

```
Department *dept = new Department();
```

```
void *
operator new(size_t size, const d_Ref_Any &clusterObj,
                const char *typename)
```

This new operator creates a persistence instance of a class of name typename that should be clustered near the object referenced by clusterObj.

```
void *
operator new(size_t size, d_Database *db, const char *type)
```

This new operator creates an instance of class typename in the database db. If the db argument supplied is d_Database::transient_memory, the instance will be transient. Otherwise, it will be a persistent object in the database db.

```
void
operator delete(void *)
```

The delete operator is used to delete the object from the database, subject to transaction commit.

```
virtual void
d_activate()
```

The virtual function d_activate is called whenever an object enters the application cache. An application can define this function in a class derived from d_Object to perform any initialization of the object. If the application does not define this virtual function, no operation is performed.

```
virtual void
d_deactivate()
```

The virtual function d_deactivate is called whenever an object exits the application cache. An application can define this function in a class derived from d_Object to perform any cleanup of the object. If the application does not define this virtual function, no operation is performed.

Name   d_OQL_Query

This class is used for constructing OQL queries and executing them from within a C++ program. The shift operator << has been overloaded to allow both incremental construction of a query and the passing of argument values to the query. Two of the constructors accept a string argument, which should contain a query. The query in the string may contain parameters of the form $i, where i is a number referring to the ith subsequent right operand of a call to the left shift operator <<. The value passed in the first call to the left shift operator would replace all instances of $1 in the string. If d_oql_execute is called and there are any $i in the query string that do not have a corresponding initialization via a left shift operation, a d_Error_QueryParameterCountInvalid exception is thrown. If an argument has the wrong type, a d_Error_QueryParameter-TypeInvalid exception is thrown. The initial query string is retained after a call to d_oql_execute, but the operands must be resupplied.

Synopsis

```
class d_OQL_Query {
public:
                            d_OQL_Query();
                            d_OQL_Query(const char *s);
                            d_OQL_Query(const d_String &s);
                            d_OQL_Query(const d_OQL_Query &q2);
                            ~d_OQL_Query();
        d_OQL_Query &       operator=(const d_OQL_Query &q2);
        void                clear(); // ODMG 2.0 addition

friend d_OQL_Query &        operator<<(d_OQL_Query &q, const char *s);
friend d_OQL_Query &        operator<<(d_OQL_Query &q, const d_String &s);
friend d_OQL_Query &        operator<<(d_OQL_Query &q, d_Char c);
friend d_OQL_Query &        operator<<(d_OQL_Query &q, d_Octet o);
friend d_OQL_Query &        operator<<(d_OQL_Query &q, d_Short s);
friend d_OQL_Query &        operator<<(d_OQL_Query &q, d_UShort us);
friend d_OQL_Query &        operator<<(d_OQL_Query &q, int i);
friend d_OQL_Query &        operator<<(d_OQL_Query &q, unsigned int ui);
friend d_OQL_Query &        operator<<(d_OQL_Query &q, d_Long L);
friend d_OQL_Query &        operator<<(d_OQL_Query &q, d_ULong UL);
friend d_OQL_Query &        operator<<(d_OQL_Query &q, d_Float f);
friend d_OQL_Query &        operator<<(d_OQL_Query &q, d_Double d);
```

d_OQL_Query

```
friend  d_OQL_Query  &        operator<<(d_OQL_Query &q, const d_Date &d);
friend  d_OQL_Query  &        operator<<(d_OQL_Query &q, const d_Time &t);
friend  d_OQL_Query  &        operator<<(d_OQL_Query &q,
                                              const d_Timestamp &ts);
friend  d_OQL_Query  &        operator<<(d_OQL_Query &q,
                                              const d_Interval &i);
template<class T>
friend  d_OQL_Query  &        operator<<(d_OQL_Query &q, const d_Ref<T> &r);
template<class T>
friend  d_OQL_Query  &        operator<<(d_OQL_Query &q,
                                              const d_Collection<T> &c);

};


template<class T> void d_oql_execute(d_OQL_Query &q, T &r);
template<class T> void d_oql_execute(d_OQL_Query &q, d_Iterator<T> &r);
```

Description

d_OQL_Query()

> The null constructor initializes the query object.

d_OQL_Query(const char *s)

> The string argument s contains an OQL query that initializes the query object.

d_OQL_Query(const d_String &s)

> The string contained in s is a query that is used to initialize the query object.

d_OQL_Query(const d_OQL_Query &q)

> The copy contructor initializes the query object with the state of the query object parameter q.

~d_OQL_Query()

> The destructor uninitializes the query object, freeing all secondary data structures.

d_OQL_Query &
operator=(const d_OQL_Query &q)

> The assignment operator assigns the state of the query object q to the object.

void
clear()

> This function clears any query parameters that have been supplied via the << operators and places the query object into a state to accept the first query argument. This member function was added in ODMG release 2.0.

```
friend d_OQL_Query &
operator<<(d_OQL_Query &q, const char *s)
```

> The string s is substituted for the next uninitialized query parameter specified in the query, if there is one. A reference to the query object q is returned.

```
friend d_OQL_Query &
operator<<(d_OQL_Query &q, const d_String &s)
```

> The d_String s is substituted for the next uninitialized query parameter specified in the query, if there is one. A reference to the query object q is returned.

```
friend d_OQL_Query &
operator<<(d_OQL_Query &q, d_Char c)
```

> The character c is substituted for the next uninitialized query parameter specified in the query, if there is one. A reference to the query object q is returned.

```
friend d_OQL_Query &
operator<<(d_OQL_Query &q, d_Octet o)
```

> The d_Octet is substituted for the next uninitialized query parameter specified in the query, if there is one. A reference to the query object q is returned.

```
friend d_OQL_Query &
operator<<(d_OQL_Query &q, d_Short s)
```

> The short integer s is substituted for the next uninitialized query parameter specified in the query, if there is one. A reference to the query object q is returned.

```
friend d_OQL_Query &
operator<<(d_OQL_Query &q, d_UShort us)
```

> The unsigned short integer us is substituted for the next uninitialized query parameter specified in the query, if there is one. A reference to the query object q is returned.

```
friend d_OQL_Query &
operator<<(d_OQL_Query &q, int i)
```

> The integer i is substituted for the next uninitialized query parameter specified in the query, if there is one. A reference to the query object q is returned.

```
friend d_OQL_Query &
operator<<(d_OQL_Query &q, unsigned int ui)
```

> The unsigned integer ui is substituted for the next uninitialized query parameter specified in the query, if there is one. A reference to the query object q is returned.

```
friend d_OQL_Query &
operator<<(d_OQL_Query &q, d_Long L)
```

> The long integer L is substituted for the next uninitialized query parameter specified in the query, if there is one. A reference to the query object q is returned.

d_OQL_Query

```
friend d_OQL_Query &
operator<<(d_OQL_Query &q, d_ULong UL)
```

>   The unsigned long integer `UL` is substituted for the next uninitialized query parameter specified in the query, if there is one. A reference to the query object `q` is returned.

```
friend d_OQL_Query &
operator<<(d_OQL_Query &q, d_Float f)
```

>   The float `f` is substituted for the next uninitialized query parameter specified in the query, if there is one. A reference to the query object `q` is returned.

```
friend d_OQL_Query &
operator<<(d_OQL_Query &q, d_Double d)
```

>   The double `d` is substituted for the next uninitialized query parameter specified in the query, if there is one. A reference to the query object `q` is returned.

```
friend d_OQL_Query &
operator<<(d_OQL_Query &q, const d_Date &d)
```

>   The `d_Date` d is substituted for the next uninitialized query parameter specified in the query, if there is one. A reference to the query object `q` is returned.

```
friend d_OQL_Query &
operator<<(d_OQL_Query &q, const d_Time &t)
```

>   The `d_Time` t is substituted for the next uninitialized query parameter specified in the query, if there is one. A reference to the query object `q` is returned.

```
friend d_OQL_Query &
operator<<(d_OQL_Query &q, const d_Timestamp &ts)
```

>   The `d_Timestamp` ts is substituted for the next uninitialized query parameter specified in the query, if there is one. A reference to the query object `q` is returned.

```
friend d_OQL_Query &
operator<<(d_OQL_Query &q, const d_Interval &i)
```

>   The `d_Interval` time interval `i` is substituted for the next uninitialized query parameter specified in the query, if there is one. A reference to the query object `q` is returned.

```
friend template<class T> d_OQL_Query &
operator<<(d_OQL_Query &q, const d_Ref<T> &r)
```

>   A reference `r` to an object of type `T` is substituted for the next uninitialized query parameter specified in the query, if there is one. A reference to the query object `q` is returned.

```
friend template<class T> d_OQL_Query &
operator<<(d_OQL_Query &q, const d_Collection<T> &c)
```

A reference, ref, to a collection of elements of type T is substituted for the next uninitialized query parameter specified in the query, if there is one. A reference to the query object q is returned.

```
template<class T>
void d_oql_execute(d_OQL_Query &q, T &r)
```

The query q is executed, and the result is placed in the result parameter r. If the query executes successfully, the query parameters are cleared. If an error condition occurs and the query does not execute successfully or an exception is raised, the query parameters are not cleared. The application can call the function clear to provide new query parameters.

```
template<class T>
void d_oql_execute(d_OQL_Query &q, d_Iterator<T> &r)
```

The query q is executed. Instead of the complete result being placed in the result r, as is the case with the previous function, the iterator referenced by r is initialized to reference the first element of the result. The application can then iterate over each element in the result. This function provides a database cursor-like facility and, unlike the previous function, does not require that the complete result be instantiated as a complete collection. This function allows the results to be transferred to the application in smaller batches based on application demand.

d_OQL_Query

Name   d_Ref<T>

A reference to an instance of the persistence-capable class T.

Synopsis

```
template <class T> class d_Ref {
public:
                        d_Ref();
                        d_Ref(T *p);
                        d_Ref(const d_Ref<T> &r2);
                        d_Ref(const d_Ref_Any &r2);
                        ~d_Ref();
                        operator d_Ref_Any() const;
        d_Ref<T> &      operator=(T *p);
        d_Ref<T> &      operator=(const d_Ref<T> &r2);
        void            clear();
        T *             operator->() const;
        T &             operator*() const;
        T *             ptr() const;
        void            delete_object();
// Boolean predicates to check reference
        d_Boolean       operator!() const;
        d_Boolean       is_null() const;
// do these d_Refs and pointers refer to the same objects?
    friend d_Boolean        operator==(const d_Ref<T> &r1,
                                    const d_Ref<T> &r2);
    friend d_Boolean        operator==(const d_Ref<T> &r1, const T *p);
    friend d_Boolean        operator==(const T *p, const d_Ref<T> &r2);
    friend d_Boolean        operator==(const d_Ref<T> &r1,
                                    const d_Ref_Any &r2);
    friend d_Boolean        operator!=(const d_Ref<T> &r1,
                                    const d_Ref<T> &r2);
    friend d_Boolean        operator!=(const d_Ref<T> &r1, const T *p);
    friend d_Boolean        operator!=(const T *p, const d_Ref<T> &r1);
    friend d_Boolean        operator!=(const d_Ref<T> &r1,
                                    const d_Ref_Any &r2);
};
```

Description

`d_Ref()`

> The null constructor initializes the reference to a null value.

`d_Ref(T *p)`

> The reference is initialized to refer to the instance of `T` pointed to by `p`. The value 0 is treated as a null reference.

`d_Ref(const d_Ref<T> &r2)`

> The copy constructor initializes the reference to the same value as reference `r2`.

`d_Ref(const d_Ref_Any &r2)`

> The copy constructor initializes the reference to the same value as reference `r2`. If `r2` does not refer to an instance of `T` or to any class publicly derived from `T`, a `d_Error_TypeInvalid` exception is thrown.

`~d_Ref()`

> The destructor uninitializes the reference; the referenced object is not removed.

`operator d_Ref_Any() const`

> This function converts the `d_Ref<T>` to a `d_Ref_Any`.

`d_Ref<T> &`
`operator=(T *p)`

> The reference is assigned a value to represent a reference to the instance pointed to by `p`. It returns a reference to the `d_Ref<T>` object. This function is used to convert a pointer (`T *`) into a reference (`d_Ref<T>`) to an object. See section 6.1.1.

`d_Ref<T> &`
`operator=(const d_Ref<T> &r2)`

> This assignment operator assigns the reference value of `r2` to this reference and returns a reference to the object. See section 6.1.1.

`void`
`clear()`

> This function clears the reference, setting it to a null value.

`T *`
`operator->() const`

> This function returns a pointer to the referenced instance of `T`. The pointer is valid until the completion of the transaction, or until the `d_Ref<T>` or referenced object is deleted. If the reference is null when this operation is performed, a `d_Error_RefNull` exception is thrown.

```
T &
operator*() const
```

> This function returns a C++ reference to the referenced instance of T. The return value is valid until the completion of the transaction or when either the d_Ref<T> or referenced object is deleted. If the reference is null when this operation is performed, a d_Error_RefNull exception is thrown.

```
T *
ptr() const
```

> This function converts the reference to a pointer to T. The pointer is valid until the completion of the transaction or until the object is deleted. If the reference is null when this operation is performed, a d_Error_RefNull exception is thrown.

```
void
delete_object()
```

> This function deletes the referenced object. If the reference is null when this operation is performed, a d_Error_RefNull exception is thrown.

```
d_Boolean
operator!() const
```

> This Boolean function returns true if the reference has a null value. If the reference refers to an instance, it returns false.

```
d_Boolean
is_null() const
```

> If the reference is null, this Boolean function returns true. If the reference refers to an object, it returns false.

```
friend d_Boolean
operator==(const d_Ref<T> &r1, const d_Ref<T> &r2)

friend d_Boolean
operator==(const d_Ref<T> &r1, const T *p)

friend d_Boolean
operator==(const T *p, const d_Ref<T> &r2)

friend d_Boolean
operator==(const d_Ref<T> &r1,const d_Ref_Any &r2)
```

> These Boolean equality operators return true if the two operands are equal—that is, they refer to the same instance or are both null. Otherwise, the operators return false.

```
friend d_Boolean
operator!=(const d_Ref<T> &r1, const d_Ref<T> &r2)

friend d_Boolean
operator!=(const d_Ref<T> &r1, const T *p)

friend d_Boolean
operator!=(const T *p, const d_Ref<T> &r2)

friend d_Boolean
operator!=(const d_Ref<T> &r1, const d_Ref_Any &r2)
```

These Boolean inequality operators return true if the operands refer to different instances or if only one of the operands is null. Otherwise, the operators return false.

Name   **d_Ref_Any**

A *generic* reference to an instance of any persistence-capable class, any class
derived from d_Object.

Synopsis

```
class d_Ref_Any {
public:
                        d_Ref_Any();
                        d_Ref_Any(const d_Ref_Any &r2);
                        d_Ref_Any(d_Object *p);
                        ~d_Ref_Any();
        d_Ref_Any &     operator=(const d_Ref_Any &r2);
        d_Ref_Any &     operator=(d_Object *p);
        void            clear();
        void            delete_object();

// Boolean predicates checking to see if value is null or not
        d_Boolean       operator!() const;
        d_Boolean       is_null() const;

friend d_Boolean        operator==(const d_Ref_Any &r1,
                                   const d_Ref_Any &r2);
friend d_Boolean        operator==(const d_Ref_Any &r1,
                                   const d_Object *p);
friend d_Boolean        operator==(const d_Object *p,
                                   const d_Ref_Any &r2);
friend d_Boolean        operator!=(const d_Ref_Any &r1,
                                   const d_Ref_Any &r2);
friend d_Boolean        operator!=(const d_Ref_Any &r1,
                                   const d_Object *p);
friend d_Boolean        operator!=(const d_Object *p,
                                   const d_Ref_Any &r2);
};
```

Description

d_Ref_Any()

> The null constructor initializes the reference object to a null value.

d_Ref_Any(const d_Ref_Any &r2)

> The copy constructor initializes the object to the same value as r2. It refers to either an instance of a class derived from d_Object or is null.

d_Ref_Any(d_Object *p)

> This constructor initializes the object to refer to the same object pointed to by p. A pointer value of 0 initializes the reference to null.

~d_Ref_Any()

> The destructor uninitializes the d_Ref_Any; the referenced object is not removed.

d_Ref_Any &
operator=(const d_Ref_Any &r2)

> The assignment operator assigns the value of r2 to the object.

d_Ref_Any &
operator=(d_Object *p)

> The assignment operator assigns to the object the value of a reference to the object pointed to by p.

void
clear()

> This function sets the object to a null reference value.

void
delete_object()

> This function deletes the referenced object.

d_Boolean
operator!() const

> If the reference has a null value, this Boolean function returns true. If the reference object refers to an instance, it returns false.

d_Boolean
is_null() const

> If the reference is null, this Boolean function returns true. If the reference refers to an object, it returns false.

```
friend d_Boolean
operator==(const d_Ref_Any &r1, const d_Ref_Any &r2)
friend d_Boolean
operator==(const d_Ref_Any &r1, const d_Object *p)
friend d_Boolean
operator==(const d_Object *p, const d_Ref_Any &r2)
```

These Boolean equality operators return true if the two operands are equal—that is, they refer to the same instance or are both null; otherwise, the operators return false.

```
friend d_Boolean
operator!=(const d_Ref_Any &r1, const d_Ref_Any &r2)
friend d_Boolean
operator!=(const d_Ref_Any &r1, const d_Object *p)
friend d_Boolean
operator!=(const d_Object *p, const d_Ref_Any &r2)
```

These Boolean inequality operators return true if either the operands refer to different instances or only one of the operands is null. Otherwise, the operators return false.

Name　　d_Rel_List<T, MT>

This template class represents a positional to-many bidirectional relationship between the classes S and T. An instance of d_Rel_List<T, MT> is embedded in S. The persistent class T at the other end of the bidirectional relationship must have a member of type d_Rel_List<S,MS>, d_Rel_Set<S,MS>, or d_Rel_Ref<S,MS>. The second template parameter MT is a const char *, and the name of a character string variable must be specified. It must be a string variable and not a string literal. The string variable must contain the name of the member in class T that references class S. Similarly, the member in T should have a second template parameter that refers to the member in class S.

Example header file:

```
extern const char _listT[], _refS[];

class S {
    d_Rel_List<T,_refS>   listT;
};
class T {
    d_Rel_X<S,_listT>     refS; // X can be Ref, List, or Set
};
```

Example code file:

```
const char _refS[] = "refS";
const char _listT[] = "listT";
```

The member at each end of the relationship references the member at the other end.

This class inherits its interface from the base class d_List<d_Ref<T>>.

Synopsis

```
template <class T, const char *MT> class d_Rel_List :
                        public d_List<d_Ref<T> >
{
public:
                        d_Rel_List();
                        d_Rel_List(const d_List<d_Ref<T> > &L2);
                        ~d_Rel_List();
```

```
          d_Rel_List<T,MT> & operator=(const d_List<d_Ref<T> > &L2);
          d_Ref<T>          retrieve_first_element() const;
          d_Ref<T>          retrieve_last_element() const;
          void              remove_first_element();
          void              remove_last_element();
          d_Ref<T>          operator[](unsigned long pos) const;
          d_Boolean         find_element(const d_Ref<T> &val,
                                         unsigned long &pos) const;
          d_Ref<T>          retrieve_element_at(unsigned long pos) const;
          void              remove_element_at(unsigned long pos);
          void              replace_element_at(const d_Ref<T> &val,
                                         unsigned long pos);
          void              insert_element_first(const d_Ref<T> &val);
          void              insert_element_last(const d_Ref<T> &val);
          void              insert_element_after(const d_Ref<T> &val,
                                         unsigned long pos);
          void              insert_element_before(const d_Ref<T> &val,
                                         unsigned long pos);
          d_List<d_Ref<T> > concat(const d_List<d_Ref<T> > &L2) const;
   friend d_List<d_Ref<T> > operator+(const d_Rel_List<T,MT> &L1,
                                         const d_Rel_List<T,MT> &L2);
          d_Rel_List<T,MT> & append(const d_List<d_Ref<T> > &L2);
          d_Rel_List<T,MT> & operator+=(const d_List<d_Ref<T> > &L2);
   };
```

Description

d_Rel_List()

> The null constructor initializes the list with no elements.

d_Rel_List(const d_Rel_List<d_Ref<T> > &L2)

> The copy constructor initializes the relationship list object using the references to T contained in the list L2. The elements in the initialized object are in the same order as they existed in refList. Each instance of T that is referenced in L2 has its inverse relationship member modified to add a reference to the instance of S that contains this object.

~d_Rel_List()

> The destructor uninitializes the list, removing all the elements. Because instances of d_Rel_List can be embedded only in a persistence-capable class, this

function can be called only when the containing persistent object of type S is deleted. For each element in the list, the instance of T referenced will have its member (identified by the template parameter MT) altered to remove the reference to the instance of S containing this object.

```
d_Rel_List<T, MT> &
operator=(const d_List<d_Ref<T> > &L2)
```

The assignment operator removes the current elements from the list object and initializes the object with the elements in L2. The elements in the initialized object are in the same order as in L2. For each of the original elements that is removed, the member of the instance of T (identified by MT) is altered to remove the reference to the instance of S that contains this object. When the elements of L2 are added to the object, the instance of T referenced by the element has its member (identified by MT) altered to refer to the instance of S containing this object.

```
d_Ref<T>
retrieve_first_element() const
```

This function returns the first element of the list.

```
d_Ref<T>
retrieve_last_element() const
```

This function returns the last element of the list.

```
void
remove_first_element()
```

The first element of the list is removed. The instance of T referred to by the removed element has its member (identified by MT) altered to remove the reference to the instance of S that contains this object.

```
void
remove_last_element()
```

The last element of the list is removed. The instance of T referred to by the removed element has its member (identified by MT) altered to remove the reference to the instance of S that contains this object.

```
d_Ref<T>
operator[](unsigned long pos) const
```

A reference to the element at position pos is returned.

```
d_Boolean
find_element(const d_Ref<T> &val, unsigned long &pos) const
```

This Boolean function attempts to find an element with value val. It returns true if it finds an element that equals val; otherwise, it returns false. If an element is found, the position of the element is returned via the parameter pos.

d_Rel_List<T, MT>

```
d_Ref<T>
retrieve_element_at(unsigned long pos) const
```

This function returns a reference to the element at position pos.

```
void
remove_element_at(unsigned long pos)
```

This function removes the element at position pos. The instance of T referred to by the removed element has its member (identified by MT) altered to remove the reference to the instance of S that contains this object.

```
void
replace_element_at(const d_Ref<T> &val, unsigned long pos)
```

This function replaces the value of the element at position pos with the value val. The instance of T referred to by the replaced element has its member (identified by MT) altered to remove the reference to the instance of S that contains this object. The instance of T referred to by the parameter val has its member (identified by MT) altered to add a reference to the instance of S that contains this object.

```
void
insert_element_first(const d_Ref<T> &val)
```

This function inserts a reference to an instance T at the beginning of the list. The instance of T has its member (identified by MT) altered to add a reference to the instance of S that contains this object.

```
void
insert_element_last(const d_Ref<T> &val)
```

This function inserts a reference to an instance T at the end of the list. The instance of T has its member (identified by MT) altered to add a reference to the instance of S that contains this object.

```
void
insert_element_after(const d_Ref<T> &val, unsigned long pos)
```

This function inserts a reference to an instance T after position pos in the list. The instance of T has its member (identified by MT) altered to add a reference to the instance of S that contains this object.

```
void
insert_element_before(const d_Ref<T> &val,unsigned long pos)
```

This function inserts a reference to an instance of T before position pos in the list. The instance of T has its member (identified by MT) altered to add a reference to the instance of S that contains this object.

```
d_List<d_Ref<T> >
concat(const d_List<d_Ref<T> > &L2) const
```

> This function creates and returns a new d_List<d_Ref<T>> object by value. The list contains a concatenation of the elements of the list object followed by the elements of the list L2. No alterations are made to the instances involved in the bidirectional relationship.
> Example syntax:

```
        list1.concat(list2)
```

```
friend d_List<d_Ref<T> >
operator+(const d_Rel_List<T,MT> &L1, const d_Rel_List<T,MT> &L2)
```

> These functions use operator+ to create and return a new d_List<d_Ref<T>> object by value that is a concatenation of L2 onto the end of L1. No alterations are made to the instances involved in the bidirectional relationship.

```
d_Rel_List<T, MT> &
append(const d_List<d_Ref<T> > &L2)
```

> This function appends the elements of L2 onto the end of the object and returns a reference to the list object. For each instance of T referred to by an element in L2, the member of T (identified by MT) is altered to add a reference to the instance of S that contains this object.

```
d_Rel_List<T, MT> &
operator+=(const d_List<d_Ref<T> > &L2)
```

> This function performs the same operation as append. The elements of L2 are appended to the end of the list object, and a reference to the object is returned. For each instance of T referred to by an element in L2, the member of T (identified by MT) is altered to add a reference to the instance of S that contains this object.

d_Rel_List<T, MT>

Name   **d_Rel_Ref<T, MT>**

This template class represents a to-one bidirectional relationship between a class S (in which an instance of d_Rel_Ref<T, MT> is embedded) and the class T. The class T at the other end of the bidirectional relationship must have a member that is of type d_Rel_List<S, MS>, d_Rel_Set<S, MS>, or d_Rel_Ref<S, MS>. The second template parameter MT must be a character string variable that contains the name of the member in class T that references class S. Similarly, the member in T should have a second template parameter, MS, that refers to the member in class S that is the instance of this class d_Rel_Ref<T, MT>.

Example header file:

```
extern const char _refT[], _refS[];

class S {
    d_Rel_Ref<T,_refS>     refT;
};
class T {
    d_Rel_X<S,_refT>       refS; // X can be Ref, List, or Set
};
```

Example code file:

```
const char _refS[] = "refS";
const char _refT[] = "refT";
```

Because this class inherits its interface from the base class d_Ref<T>, its interface is provided here noting the additional behavior provided. Some of the functions are simply inherited but are specified here for completeness. Functionality that alters the references has additional behavior to maintain the bidirectional relationship.

Synopsis

```
template <class T, const char *MT> class d_Rel_Ref : public d_Ref<T>
{
public:
                        d_Rel_Ref();
                        d_Rel_Ref(T *p);
                        d_Rel_Ref(const d_Ref<T> &r2);
```

d_Rel_Ref<T, MT>

```
                                        d_Rel_Ref(const d_Ref_Any &r2);
                                        d_Rel_Ref(const d_Rel_Ref<T,MT> &r2);
                                        ~d_Rel_Ref();
                                        operator d_Ref_Any() const;
                 d_Rel_Ref<T,MT> &      operator=(T *p);
                 d_Rel_Ref<T,MT> &      operator=(const d_Ref<T> &r2);
                 d_Rel_Ref<T,MT> &      operator=(const d_Rel_Ref<T,MT> &r2);
                 void                   clear();
                 T *                    operator->() const;
                 T &                    operator*() const;
                 T *                    ptr() const;
                 void                   delete_object();
// Boolean predicates to check reference
                 d_Boolean              operator!() const;
                 d_Boolean              is_null() const;
// do these d_Refs and pointers refer to the same objects?
     friend d_Boolean                   operator==(const d_Rel_Ref<T,MT> &r1,
                                                   const d_Rel_Ref<T,MT> &r2);
     friend d_Boolean                   operator==(const d_Rel_Ref<T,MT> &r1,
                                                   const T *p);
     friend d_Boolean                   operator==(const T *p,
                                                   const d_Rel_Ref<T,MT> &r2);
     friend d_Boolean                   operator==(const d_Rel_Ref<T,MT> &r1,
                                                   const d_Ref_Any &r2);
     friend d_Boolean                   operator==(const d_Ref_Any &r1,
                                                   const d_Rel_Ref<T,MT> &r2);
     friend d_Boolean                   operator!=(const d_Rel_Ref<T,MT> &r1,
                                                   const d_Rel_Ref<T,MT> &r2);
     friend d_Boolean                   operator!=(const d_Rel_Ref<T,MT> &r1,
                                                   const T *p);
     friend d_Boolean                   operator!=(const T *p,
                                                   const d_Rel_Ref<T,MT> &r2);
     friend d_Boolean                   operator!=(const d_Rel_Ref<T,MT> &r1,
                                                   const d_Ref_Any &r2);
     friend d_Boolean                   operator!=(const d_Ref_Any &r1,
                                                   const d_Rel_Ref<T,MT> &r2);

     };
```

d_Rel_Ref<T,MT>

Description

d_Rel_Ref()

> The null constructor initializes the reference to a null value.

d_Rel_Ref(T *p)

> The reference is initialized to refer to the instance of T pointed to by p. The member in the instance of T, specified by MT, is altered to include a reference to the instance of S that contains this object.

d_Ref(const d_Ref<T> &r2)

> The copy constructor initializes the reference to the same value as reference r2. The member in T (assuming the reference is not null), specified by MT, is altered to include a reference to the instance of S that contains this object.

d_Ref(const d_Ref_Any &r2)

> The copy constructor initializes the reference to the same value as reference r2. The member in T, specified by MT, is altered to include a reference to the instance of S that contains this object. If r2 does not refer to an instance of T, a d_Error_TypeInvalid exception is thrown.

~d_Rel_Ref()

> Because an instance of this class must be embedded in a persistent object, this destructor gets called when the containing object is deleted. The member of the T instance, specified by MT, is altered to remove the reference to the instance of S that contains this object.

operator d_Ref_Any() const

> This function converts the d_Rel_Ref<T, MT> to a d_Ref_Any. No bidirectional relationship functionality is performed.

d_Rel_Ref<T, MT> &
operator=(T *p)

> This assignment operator assigns to the object the reference value of the object pointed to by p. It returns a reference to the object. This function performs two bidirectional relationship actions. If the object was referring to an instance of T before the operation—that is, it was not null—then the member in the referenced instance of T is altered to remove the reference to the instance of S that contains this object. Then, assuming that ptrT is not null, the member in the instance of T pointed to by p is altered to include a reference to the instance of S that contains this object.

```
d_Rel_Ref<T, MT> &
operator=(const d_Ref<T> &r2)
```

> This assignment operator assigns to the object the reference value of r2 and returns a reference to the object. This function performs two bidirectional relationship actions. If the object was referring to an instance of T before the operation—that is, it was not null—then the member in the referenced instance of T, specified by MT, is altered to remove the reference to the instance of S that contains this object. Then, assuming that r2 is not null, the member in the instance of T pointed to by r2, identified by MT, is altered to include a reference to the instance of S that contains this object.

```
void
clear()
```

> This function clears the reference, setting it to a null value. If the reference referred to an instance of T, then the member in the instance of T, specified by MT, is altered to remove the reference to the instance of S that contains this object.

```
T *
operator->() const
```

> This function inherits its behavior from d_Ref<T>. No bidirectional relationship functionality is performed.

```
T &
operator*() const
```

> This function inherits its behavior from d_Ref<T>. No bidirectional relationship functionality is performed.

```
T *
ptr() const
```

> This function inherits its behavior from d_Ref<T>. No bidirectional relationship functionality is performed.

```
void
delete_object()
```

> This function deletes the referenced object. Note that the member in the instance of T, identified by MT, that contains a reference to the instance of S that contains this object will be removed as a result of deleting the instance of T. When the instance of T is deleted, all of the objects involved in a bidirectional relationship with the T instance must be updated to remove their reference to the T instance. If the reference is null when this operation is performed, a d_Error_RefNull exception is thrown.

d_Rel_Ref<T, MT>

```
d_Boolean
operator!() const
```

> This function inherits its behavior from d_Ref<T>. No bidirectional relationship functionality is performed.

```
d_Boolean
is_null() const
```

> This function inherits its behavior from d_Ref<T>. No bidirectional relationship functionality is performed. Because d_Rel_Ref<T,MT> is publicly derived from d_Ref<T>, the following equality and inequality operators defined for d_Ref<T> can be used with instances of d_Rel_Ref<T,MT> or d_Ref<T>.

```
friend d_Boolean
operator==(const d_Rel_Ref<T,MT> &r1, const d_Rel_Ref<T,MT> &r2)
```

> This Boolean equality operator returns true if the references are either referring to the same instance or are both null. Otherwise, it returns false.

```
friend d_Boolean
operator==(const d_Rel_Ref<T,MT> &r1, const T *p)
friend d_Boolean
operator==(const T *p, const d_Rel_Ref<T> &r2)
friend d_Boolean
operator==(const d_Rel_Ref<T,MT> &r1, const d_Ref_Any &r2)
friend d_Boolean
operator==(const d_Ref_Any &r1,const d_Rel_Ref<T,MT> &r2)
```

> These Boolean equality operators return true if the references are either referring to the same instance or are both null; otherwise, they return false.

```
friend d_Boolean
operator!=(const d_Rel_Ref<T,MT> &r1, const d_Rel_Ref<T,MT> &r2)
```

> This Boolean inequality operator returns true if the two references are not referring to the same instance. If the references refer to the same instance or both are null, it returns false.

```
friend d_Boolean
operator!=(const d_Rel_Ref<T,MT> &r1, const T *p)
friend d_Boolean
operator!=(const T *p, const d_Rel_Ref<T,MT> &r2)
friend d_Boolean
operator!=(const d_Rel_Ref<T,MT> &r1, const d_Ref_Any &r2)
friend d_Boolean
operator!=(const d_Ref_Any &r1, const d_Rel_Ref<T,MT> &r2)
```

> These Boolean inequality operators return true if the references are not referring to the same instance. Otherwise, they return false.

Name   **d_Rel_Set<T, MT>**

This template class represents an unordered to-many bidirectional relationship between the class S (in which an instance of d_Rel_Set<T,MT> is embedded) and the class T. The persistent class T at the other end of the bidirectional relationship must have a member that is of type d_Rel_List<S,MS>, d_Rel_Set<S,MS>, or d_Rel_Ref<S,MS>. The second template parameter MT must be a character string variable that contains the name of the member in class T that references class S. Similarly, the member in T should have a second template parameter that refers to the member in class S.

Example header file:

```
extern const char _refS[], _setT[];

class S {
    d_Rel_Set<T,_refS>    setT;
};
class T {
    d_Rel_X<S,_setT>      refS; // X can be Ref, List, or Set
};
```

Example code file:

```
const char _refS[] = "refS";
const char _setT[] = "setT";
```

This class inherits its interface from the base class d_Set<d_Ref<T>>.

Synopsis

```
template <class T, const char *MT> class d_Rel_Set :
                    public d_Set<d_Ref<T> >
{
public:
                            d_Rel_Set();
                            d_Rel_Set(const d_Set<d_Ref<T> > &s2);
                            ~d_Rel_Set();
        d_Rel_Set<T,MT> &   operator=(const d_Set<d_Ref<T> > &s2);
        d_Rel_Set<T,MT> &   union_of(const d_Set<d_Ref<T> > &s1,
                                const d_Set<d_Ref<T> > &s2);
```

```
         d_Rel_Set<T,MT> &     union_with(const d_Set<d_Ref<T> > &s2);
         d_Rel_Set<T,MT> &     operator+=(const d_Set<d_Ref<T> > &s2);
         d_Set<d_Ref<T> >      create_union(const d_Set<d_Ref<T> >&s2)const;
  friend d_Set<d_Ref<T> >      operator+(const d_Set<d_Ref<T> > &s1,
                                         const d_Set<d_Ref<T> > &s2);

         d_Rel_Set<T,MT> &     intersection_of(const d_Set<d_Ref<T> > &s1,
                                         const d_Set<d_Ref<T> > &s2);
         d_Rel_Set<T,MT> &     intersection_with(const d_Set<d_Ref<T> >&s2);
         d_Rel_Set<T,MT> &     operator*=(const d_Set<d_Ref<T> > &s2);
         d_Set<d_Ref<T> >      create_intersection(
                                         const d_Set<d_Ref<T> > &s2)const;
  friend d_Set<d_Ref<T> >      operator*(const d_Set<d_Ref<T> > &s1,
                                         const d_Set<d_Ref<T> > &s2);

         d_Rel_Set<T,MT> &     difference_of(const d_Set<d_Ref<T> > &s1,
                                         const d_Set<d_Ref<T> > &s1);
         d_Rel_Set<T,MT> &     difference_with(const d_Set<d_Ref<T> > &s2);
         d_Rel_Set<T,MT> &     operator-=(const d_Set<d_Ref<T> >&s2);
         d_Set<d_Ref<T> >      create_difference(
                                         const d_Set<d_Ref<T> > &s2)const;
  friend  d_Set<d_Ref<T> >     operator-(const d_Set<d_Ref<T> > &s1,
                                         const d_Set<d_Ref<T> > &s2);
         d_Boolean            is_subset_of(const d_Set<d_Ref<T> >&s2)const;
         d_Boolean            is_proper_subset_of(
                                         const d_Set<d_Ref<T> > &s2) const;
         d_Boolean            is_superset_of(
                                         const d_Set<d_Ref<T> > &s2) const;
         d_Boolean            is_proper_superset_of(
                                         const d_Set<d_Ref<T> > &s2) const;
};
```

Description

d_Rel_Set()

> The set object is initialized with no elements.

d_Rel_Set(const d_Set<d_Ref<T> > &s2)

> The copy constructor initializes the object to contain the same elements as s2. For each element of s2, the member in the referenced instance of T, identified by MT, is altered to add a reference to the instance of S that contains this object.

~d_Rel_Set()

> The destructor uninitializes the object, removing all the elements from the set. For each element of the set, the member in the referenced instance of T, identified by MT, is altered to remove the reference to the instance of S that contains this object.

d_Rel_Set<T, MT> &
operator=(const d_Set<d_Ref<T> > &s2)

> The assignment operator is used to assign the contents of one set to another. If the object had elements before the assignment operation, they are first removed. For each of the removed elements, the member in the referenced instance of T, identified by MT, is altered to remove the reference to the instance of S that contains this object.

> The object will contain a copy of the elements in the set referenced by s2. For each element of set s2 that is copied into the object, the member in the referenced instance of T, identified by MT, is altered to add a reference to the instance of S that contains this object. The function returns a reference to the object, allowing a cascading of the assignment operation.

d_Rel_Set<T, MT> &
union_of(const d_Set<d_Ref<T> > &s1, const d_Set<d_Ref<T> > &s2)

> The union of sets s1 and s2 is created and placed in the object. The original elements in the set object before the operation are discarded. For each of the removed elements, the member in the referenced instance of T, identified by MT, is altered to remove the reference to the instance of S that contains this object. For each member that is in the union result, the member in the referenced instance of T, identified by MT, is altered to add a reference to the instance of S that contains this object.

> Example syntax:

```
aset.union_of(set1, set2);
```

> The function returns a reference to the object.

d_Rel_Set<T, MT> &
union_with(const d_Set<d_Ref<T> > &s2)

> A union is created of the set object and the set s2. The result of the union is placed in the original object. For each of the additional elements added from s2, the member in the referenced instance of T, identified by MT, is altered to add a reference to the instance of S that contains this object.

> Example syntax:

```
aset.union_with(set2);
```

> The function returns a reference to the object.

d_Rel_Set<T, MT>

```
d_Rel_Set<T, MT> &
operator+=(const d_Set<d_Ref<T> > &s2)
```

> This function uses `operator+=` to perform the same operation as the preceding function `union_with`. A union of the object and `s2` is computed and placed into the object. For each of the additional elements added to the set object from `s2`, the member in the referenced instance of `T`, identified by `MT`, is altered to add a reference to the instance of `S` that contains this object.
>
> Example syntax:
>
> ```
> aset += set2;
> ```
>
> The function returns a reference to the object.

```
d_Set<d_Ref<T> >
create_union(const d_Set<d_Ref<T> > &s2) const
```

> A union is created of the set object and the set `s2`.
>
> Example syntax:
>
> ```
> setresult = set.create_union(set2);
> ```
>
> The original set object is not altered, and the result is a new set object returned by value. Because the result of this operation is a new stand-alone set object, no bidirectional relationship processing is performed.

```
friend d_Set<d_Ref<T> >
operator+(const d_Set<d_Ref<T> > &s1,
          const d_Set<d_Ref<T> > &s2)
```

> A union is created of `s1` and `s2`, and the result set is returned by value. Because the result of this operation is a new stand-alone set object, no bidirectional relationship processing is necessary.
>
> Example syntax:
>
> ```
> set1 + set2
> ```
>
> The result is a set returned by value.

```
d_Rel_Set<T, MT> &
intersection_of(const d_Set<d_Ref<T> > &s1,
                const d_Set<d_Ref<T> > &s2)
```

> The intersection of `s1` and `s2` is created and placed in the object. The original elements in the set object before the operation are discarded. For each of the original elements that is discarded, the member in the referenced instance of `T`, identified by `MT`, is altered to remove the reference to the instance of `S` that contains this object. For each element in the intersection result, the member in the referenced instance of `T`, identified by `MT`, is altered to include a reference to the instance of `S` that contains this object.

Example syntax:

```
aset.intersection_of(set1, set2);
```

The function returns a reference to the object.

```
d_Rel_Set<T, MT> &
intersection_with(const d_Set<d_Ref<T> > &s2)
```

An intersection is created of the set object and the set s2. The result of the intersection is placed in the original object. Because an intersection consists of all the elements in both sets, no elements will be added to the object. However, all the elements that were in the original set object that are not in the set s2 must be removed. For each of these elements removed from the object, the member in the referenced instance of T, identified by MT, is altered to remove the reference to the instance of S that contains this object.

Example syntax:

```
aset.intersection_with(set2);
```

The function returns a reference to the object.

```
d_Rel_Set<T, MT> &
operator*=(const d_Set<d_Ref<T> > &s2)
```

This function performs the same operation as the function intersection_with.
Example syntax:

```
aset *= set2;
```

The function returns a reference to the object.

```
d_Set<d_Ref<T> >
create_intersection(const d_Set<d_Ref<T> > &s2) const
```

An intersection is created of the object and the set s2.
Example syntax:

```
setresult = set.create_intersection(set2);
```

The original set object is not altered, and the result is a new set object returned by value. Because the result is a new d_Set<d_Ref<T>> object returned by value, no bidirectional relationship processing is necessary.

```
friend d_Set<d_Ref<T> >
operator*(const d_Set<d_Ref<T> > &s1,
          const d_Set<d_Ref<T> > &s2)
```

An intersection is created of s1 and s2.
Example syntax:

```
set1 * set2
```

The result is a set returned by value. Because the result is a new set object returned by value, no bidirectional relationship processing is necessary.

d_Rel_Set<T, MT>

```
d_Rel_Set<T, MT> &
difference_of(const d_Set<d_Ref<T> > &s1,
              const d_Set<d_Ref<T> > &s2)
```

The difference of s1 and s2 (s1 – s2) is created and placed in the object. The original elements in the set object before the operation are discarded. For each of the original elements of the object that is removed, the member in the referenced instance of T, identified by MT, is altered to remove the reference to the instance of S that contains this object.

Example syntax:

```
aset.difference_of(set1, set2);
```

The function returns a reference to the object.

```
d_Rel_Set<T, MT> &
difference_with(const d_Set<d_Ref<T> > &s2)
```

The difference of the set object and the set s2 is created. The result of the difference is placed in the original object. In computing the difference, for each element value that is contained in set s2, it is removed (if it is an element) from the set object. For each of the elements removed from the set object, the member in the referenced instance of T, identified by MT, is altered to remove the reference to the instance of S that contains this object.

Example syntax:

```
aset.difference_with(set2);// (aset - set2)
```

The function returns a reference to the object.

```
d_Rel_Set<T, MT> &
operator-=(const d_Set<d_Ref<T> > &s2)
```

This function performs the same operation as the function difference_with. The difference of the object and the set s2 is computed and placed into the object. In computing the difference, for each element value that is contained in set s2, it is removed (if it is an element) from the set object. For each of the elements removed from the set object, the member in the referenced instance of T, identified by MT, is altered to remove the reference to the instance of S that contains this object.

Example syntax:

```
set -= set2;
```

The function returns a reference to the object.

```
d_Set<d_Ref<T> >
create_difference(const d_Set<d_Ref<T> > &s2) const
```

The difference of the object and the set s2 is created.

Example syntax:

```
setresult = aset.create_difference(set2);
```

The original set object is not altered, and the result is a new set object returned by value. Because a new set object is returned by value, no bidirectional relationship processing is necessary.

```
friend d_Set<d_Ref<T> >
operator-(const d_Set<d_Ref<T> > &set1,
             const d_Set<d_Ref<T> > &set2)
```

The difference of s1 and s2 is computed, and the result set is returned by value. Because a new set object is returned by value, no bidirectional relationship processing is necessary.

Example syntax:

```
set1 - set2
```

```
d_Boolean
is_subset_of(const d_Set<d_Ref<T> > &s2) const
```

If the set is a subset of set s2, this Boolean function returns true; otherwise, it returns false.

```
d_Boolean
is_proper_subset_of(const d_Set<d_Ref<T> > &s2) const
```

If the set is a proper subset of set s2, this Boolean function returns true; otherwise, it returns false.

```
d_Boolean
is_superset_of(const d_Set<d_Ref<T> > &s2) const
```

If the set is a superset of set s2, this Boolean function returns true; otherwise, it returns false.

```
d_Boolean
is_proper_superset_of(const d_Set<d_Ref<T> > &s2) const
```

If the set is a proper superset of set s2, this Boolean function returns true; otherwise, it returns false.

d_Rel_Set<T, MT>

Name   d_Set<T>

An unordered collection of elements of type T; no duplicates are allowed. The
union, intersection, and difference operations on sets are described in section
7.4.2.

Synopsis

```
template <class T> class d_Set : public d_Collection<T> {
public:
                        d_Set();
                        d_Set(const d_Set<T> &s2);
                        ~d_Set();
        d_Set<T> &      operator=(const d_Set<T> &s2);
        d_Set<T> &      union_of(const d_Set<T> &s1,
                                const d_Set<T> &s2);
        d_Set<T> &      union_with(const d_Set<T> &s2);
        d_Set<T> &      operator+=(const d_Set<T> &s2);
        d_Set<T>        create_union(const d_Set<T> &s2) const;
friend  d_Set<T>        operator+(const d_Set<T> &s1,
                                const d_Set<T> &s2);
        d_Set<T> &      intersection_of(const d_Set<T> &s1,
                                const d_Set<T> &s2);
        d_Set<T> &      intersection_with(const d_Set<T> &s2);
        d_Set<T> &      operator*=(const d_Set<T> &s2);
        d_Set<T>        create_intersection(const d_Set<T> &s2) const;
friend  d_Set<T>        operator*(const d_Set<T> &s1,
                                const d_Set<T> &s2);
        d_Set<T> &      difference_of(const d_Set<T> &s1,
                                const d_Set<T> &s2);
        d_Set<T> &      difference_with(const d_Set<T> &s2);
        d_Set<T> &      operator-=(const d_Set<T> &s2);
        d_Set<T>        create_difference(const d_Set<T> &s1) const;
friend  d_Set<T>        operator-(const d_Set<T> &s1,
                                const d_Set<T> &s2);
        d_Boolean       is_subset_of(const d_Set<T> &s2) const;
        d_Boolean       is_proper_subset_of(const d_Set<T> &s2) const;
        d_Boolean       is_superset_of(const d_Set<T> &s2) const;
        d_Boolean       is_proper_superset_of(const d_Set<T> &s2)const;
};
```

Description

d_Set()

> The set object is initialized and contains no elements.

d_Set(const d_Set<T> &s2)

> The copy constructor initializes the object to contain the same element values as s2.

~d_Set()

> The destructor uninitializes the object, removing all the elements from the set. If the element type has a destructor, it is called for each element.

d_Set<T> &
operator=(const d_Set<T> &s2)

> The assignment operator is used to assign the contents of one set to another. It returns a reference to the object, allowing a cascading of the assignment operation. If the object had elements before the assignment operation, they are first removed. The object will contain a copy of the elements in set s2.

d_Set<T> &
union_of(const d_Set<T> &s1, const d_Set<T> &s2)

> The union of s1 and s2 is created and placed in the object. The original elements in the set object before the operation are discarded.
> Example syntax:
>
> ```
> aset.union_of(set1, set2);
> ```
>
> The function returns a reference to the object.

d_Set<T> &
union_with(const d_Set<T> &s2)

> A union is created of the set object and set s2. The result of the union is placed in the original object.
> Example syntax:
>
> ```
> aset.union_with(set2);
> ```
>
> The function returns a reference to the object.

d_Set<T> &
operator+=(const d_Set<T> &s2)

> This function uses operator+= to perform the same operation as the function union_with. A union of the object and s2 is computed and placed into the object. The function returns a reference to the object.
> Example syntax:
>
> ```
> aset += set2;
> ```

```
d_Set<T>
create_union(const d_Set<T> &s2) const
```

>   A union is created of the set object and the set s2.
>   Example syntax:
>
>   ```
>   setresult = set.create_union(set2);
>   ```
>
>   The original set object is not altered, and the result is a new set object returned by value.

```
friend d_Set<T>
operator+(const d_Set<T> &s1, const d_Set<T> &s2)
```

>   A union is created of s1 and s2, and the result set is returned by value.
>   Example syntax:
>
>   ```
>   setresult = set1 + set2
>   ```
>
>   The result is a set returned by value.

```
d_Set<T> &
intersection_of(const d_Set<T> &s1, const d_Set<T> &s2)
```

>   The intersection of s1 and s2 is created and placed in the object. The original elements in the set object before the operation are discarded.
>   Example syntax:
>
>   ```
>   aset.intersection_of(set1, set2);
>   ```
>
>   The function returns a reference to the object.

```
d_Set<T> &
intersection_with(const d_Set<T> &s2)
```

>   An intersection is created of the object and the set s2. The result of the intersection is placed in the original object.
>   Example syntax:
>
>   ```
>   aset.intersection_with(set2);
>   ```
>
>   The function returns a reference to the object.

```
d_Set<T> &
operator*=(const d_Set<T> &s2)
```

>   This function performs the same operation as the function intersection_with. An intersection of the object and the set s2 is computed and placed into the object.
>   Example syntax:
>
>   ```
>   aset *= set2;
>   ```
>
>   The function returns a reference to the object.

```
d_Set<T>
create_intersection(const d_Set<T> &s2) const
```

>   An intersection is created of the object and the set s2.

Example syntax:

```
setresult = set.create_intersection(set2);
```

The original set object is not altered, and the result is a new set returned by value.

```
friend d_Set<T>
operator*(const d_Set<T> &s1, const d_Set<T> &s2)
```

An intersection is created of s1 and s2.

Example syntax:

```
setresult = set1 * set2
```

The result is a new d_Set<T> object returned by value.

```
d_Set<T> &
difference_of(const d_Set<T> &s1, const d_Set<T> &s2)
```

The difference of s1 and s2 (s1 - s2) is created and placed in the object. The original elements in the set object before the operation are discarded.

Example syntax:

```
aset.difference_of(set1, set2);
```

The function returns a reference to the object.

```
d_Set<T> &
difference_with(const d_Set<T> &s2)
```

The difference of the object and the set s2 is created. The result of the difference is placed in the original object.

Example syntax:

```
aset.difference_with(set2);
```

The function returns a reference to the object.

```
d_Set<T> &
operator-=(const d_Set<T> &s2)
```

This function performs the same operation as the function difference_with. The difference of the object and the set s2 is computed and placed into the object.

Example syntax:

```
set -= set2;
```

A reference to the object is returned.

```
d_Set<T>
create_difference(const d_Set<T> &s2) const
```

The difference of the object and the set s2 is created.

Example syntax:

```
setresult = aset.create_difference(set2);
```

The original set object is not altered, and the result is a new set object returned by value.

```
friend d_Set<T>
operator-(const d_Set<T> &s1, const d_Set<T> &s2)
```

> The difference of s1 and s2 is computed, and the result set is returned by value.
> Example syntax:

```
        setresult = set1 - set2
```

```
d_Boolean
is_subset_of(const d_Set<T> &s2) const
```

> If the set is a subset of the set s2, this Boolean function returns true; otherwise, it returns false. See section 7.4.1.

```
d_Boolean
is_proper_subset_of(const d_Set<T> &s2) const
```

> If the set is a proper subset of the set s2, this Boolean function returns true; otherwise, it returns false. See section 7.4.1.

```
d_Boolean
is_superset_of(const d_Set<T> &s2) const
```

> If the set is a superset of the set s2, this Boolean function returns true; otherwise, it returns false. See section 7.4.1.

```
d_Boolean
is_proper_superset_of(const d_Set<T> &s2) const
```

> This Boolean function returns true if the set is a proper superset of the set s2; otherwise, it returns false. See section 7.4.1.

Name   d_String

A class used to represent a variable-length string.

Synopsis

```
class d_String {
public:
                              d_String();
                              d_String(const d_String &s2);
                              d_String(const char *s2);
                              ~d_String();
        d_String &            operator=(const d_String &s2);
        d_String &            operator=(const char *s2);
                              operator const char *() const;
        char &                operator[](unsigned long index);
        unsigned long         length() const;
    friend d_Boolean          operator==(const d_String &s1,
                                         const d_String &s2);
    friend d_Boolean          operator==(const d_String &s1, const char *s2);
    friend d_Boolean          operator==(const char *s1, const d_String &s2);
    friend d_Boolean          operator!=(const d_String &s1,
                                         const d_String &s2);
    friend d_Boolean          operator!=(const d_String &s1, const char *s2);
    friend d_Boolean          operator!=(const char *s1, const d_String &s2);
    friend d_Boolean          operator< (const d_String &s1,
                                         const d_String &s2);
    friend d_Boolean          operator< (const d_String &s1, const char *s2);
    friend d_Boolean          operator< (const char *s1, const d_String &s2);
    friend d_Boolean          operator<=(const d_String &s1,
                                         const d_String &s2);
    friend d_Boolean          operator<=(const d_String &s1, const char *s2);
    friend d_Boolean          operator<=(const char *s1, const d_String &s2);
    friend d_Boolean          operator> (const d_String &s1,
                                         const d_String &s2);
    friend d_Boolean          operator> (const d_String &s1, const char *s2);
    friend d_Boolean          operator> (const char *s1, const d_String &s2);
    friend d_Boolean          operator>=(const d_String &s1,
                                         const d_String &s2);
    friend d_Boolean          operator>=(const d_String &s1, const char *s2);
    friend d_Boolean          operator>=(const char *s1, const d_String &s2);
};
```

d_String

Description

d_String()

> The null constructor initializes the object to a null string value.

d_String(const d_String &s2)

> The copy constructor initializes the object to contain a copy of the same string value as s2.

d_String(const char *s2)

> This constructor initializes the object to contain a copy of the same string value as s2.

~d_String()

> The destructor uninitializes the string.

d_String &
operator=(const d_String &s2)

> The assignment operator assigns a copy of the string s2 to the object. It returns a reference to the object.

d_String &
operator=(const char *s2)

> The assignment operator assigns a copy of the string value of s2 to the object. A reference to the object is returned.

operator const char *() const

> This function converts the d_String to a null-terminated character array. The d_String object is responsible for releasing the returned value.

char &
operator[](unsigned long index)

> This function provides access to the character at position index in the string. The first character is at position 0.

unsigned long
length() const

> The length of the string is returned.

```
friend d_Boolean
operator==(const d_String &s1, const d_String &s2)

friend d_Boolean
operator==(const d_String &s1, const char *s2)

friend d_Boolean
operator==(const char *s1, const d_String &s2)
```

If the strings referenced by s1 and s2 are equal, these Boolean functions return true; otherwise, the functions return false.

```
friend d_Boolean
operator!=(const d_String &s1, const d_String &s2)

friend d_Boolean
operator!=(const d_String &s1, const char *s2)

friend d_Boolean
operator!=(const char *s1, const d_String &s2)
```

If the strings referenced by s1 and s2 are not equal, these Boolean functions return true; otherwise (if they are equal), the functions return false.

```
friend d_Boolean
operator<(const d_String &s1, const d_String &s2)

friend d_Boolean
operator<(const d_String &s1, const char *s2)

friend d_Boolean
operator<(const char *s1, const d_String &s2)
```

If the string referenced by s1 is lexicographically less than the string referenced by s2, these Boolean functions return true. Otherwise, they return false.

```
friend d_Boolean
operator<=(const d_String &s1, const d_String &s2)

friend d_Boolean
operator<=(const d_String &s1, const char *s2)

friend d_Boolean
operator<=(const char *s1, const d_String &s2)
```

If the string referenced by s1 is lexicographically less than or equal to the string referenced by s2, these Boolean functions return true. Otherwise, they return false.

d_String

```
friend d_Boolean
operator>(const d_String &s1, const d_String &s2)

friend d_Boolean
operator>(const d_String &s1, const char *s2)

friend d_Boolean
operator>(const char *s1, const d_String &s2)
```

If the string referenced by s1 is lexicographically greater than the string referenced by s2, these Boolean functions return true; otherwise, they return false.

```
friend d_Boolean
operator>=(const d_String &s1, const d_String &s2)

friend d_Boolean
operator>=(const d_String &s1, const char *s2)

friend d_Boolean
operator>=(const char *s1, const d_String &s2)
```

If the string referenced by s1 is lexicographically greater than or equal to the string referenced by s2, these Boolean functions return true; otherwise, they return false.

Name   d_Time

A class used to represent a specific time.

Synopsis

```
class d_Time {
public:
        enum Time_Zone {  GMT = 0, GMT12 = 12, GMT_12 = -12, GMT1 = 1,
                          GMT_1 = -1, GMT2 = 2, GMT_2 = -2, GMT3 = 3,
                          GMT_3 = -3, GMT4 = 4, GMT_4 = -4, GMT5 = 5,
                          GMT_5 = -5, GMT6 = 6, GMT_6 = -6, GMT7 = 7,
                          GMT_7 = -7, GMT8 = 8, GMT_8 = -8, GMT9 = 9,
                          GMT_9 = -9, GMT10 = 10, GMT_10 = -10,GMT11 =11,
                          GMT_11 = -11, USeastern = -5, UScentral = -6,
                          USmountain = -7,  USpacific = -8 };
    static void           set_default_Time_Zone(Time_Zone tz);
    static void           set_default_Time_Zone_to_local();
                          d_Time();
                          d_Time(unsigned short hour,
                                    unsigned short minute,
                                    float sec = 0.0f);
                          d_Time(unsigned short hour,
                                    unsigned short minute, float sec,
                                    short tzhour, short tzminute);
                          d_Time(const d_Time &t);
                          d_Time(const d_Timestamp &ts);
        d_Time &          operator=(const d_Time &t);
        d_Time &          operator=(const d_Timestamp &ts);
        unsigned short    hour() const;
        unsigned short    minute() const;
        float             second() const;
        Time_Zone         time_zone() const;
        short             tz_hour() const;
        short             tz_minute() const;
    static d_Time         current();
        d_Time &          operator+=(const d_Interval &i);
        d_Time &          operator-=(const d_Interval &i);
    friend d_Time         operator+(const d_Time &t,const d_Interval &i);
    friend d_Time         operator+ (const d_Interval &t,
```

```
                                       const d_Time &i);
friend d_Interval       operator- (const d_Time &t, const d_Time &t);
friend d_Time           operator- (const d_Time &t,
                                   const d_Interval &i);
friend d_Boolean        operator==(const d_Time &t1, const d_Time &t2);
friend d_Boolean        operator!=(const d_Time &t1, const d_Time &t2);
friend d_Boolean        operator< (const d_Time &t1, const d_Time &t2);
friend d_Boolean        operator<=(const d_Time &t1, const d_Time &t2);
friend d_Boolean        operator> (const d_Time &t1, const d_Time &t2);
friend d_Boolean        operator>=(const d_Time &t1, const d_Time &t2);
friend d_Boolean        overlaps(  const d_Time &sL,
                                   const d_Time &eL,
                                   const d_Time &sR,
                                   const d_Time &eR);
friend d_Boolean        overlaps(  const d_Timestamp &sL,
                                   const d_Timestamp &eL,
                                   const d_Time &sR,
                                   const d_Time &eR);
friend d_Boolean        overlaps(  const d_Time &sL,
                                   const d_Time &eL,
                                   const d_Timestamp &sR,
                                   const d_Timestamp &eR);
};
```

Description

```
enum Time_Zone
```

This enumeration represents time zone values.

```
static void
set_default_Time_Zone(Time_Zone)
```

This function alters the default time zone value.

```
static void
set_default_Time_Zone_to_local()
```

This function sets the time zone value used for the local time zone to be local to the time in the client application machine environment.

```
d_Time()
```

This constructor initializes the object to the current time.

```
d_Time(unsigned short hour,unsigned short minute,float sec = 0.0f)
```
The object is initialized with the given hour, minutes, and seconds, assuming the default time zone. The default value for the `sec` parameter was added in ODMG release 2.0.

```
d_Time(unsigned short hour, unsigned short minute, float sec,
              short tzhour, short tzminute)
```
The object is initialized with the given hour, minutes, and seconds. The parameters `tzhour` and `tzminute` indicate the number of hours and minutes Greenwich Mean Time (GMT).

```
d_Time(const d_Time &t)
```
The copy constructor initializes the object to the same value as `t`.

```
d_Time(const d_Timestamp &ts)
```
The object is initialized with the time component values of the timestamp `ts`.

```
d_Time &
operator=(const d_Time &t)
```
The assignment operator assigns `t` to the object and returns a reference to the object.

```
d_Time &
operator=(const d_Timestamp &ts)
```
This assignment operator assigns the time value of the timestamp `ts` to the object and returns a reference to the object.

```
unsigned short
hour() const
```
The number of hours is returned.

```
unsigned short
minute() const
```
The number of minutes is returned.

```
float
second() const
```
The number of seconds is returned.

```
Time_Zone
time_zone() const
```
The time zone is returned. This function was added in ODMG 2.0.

```
short
tz_hour() const
```
The number of hours relative to GMT is returned.

```
short
tz_minute() const
```

The number of minutes relative to GMT is returned.

```
static d_Time
current()
```

The current time is returned.

```
d_Time &
operator+=(const d_Interval &i)
```

The time is advanced based on the interval i, and a reference to the object is returned.

```
d_Time &
operator-=(const d_Interval &i)
```

The interval value i is subtracted from the d_Time object value, and a reference to the object is returned.

```
friend d_Time
operator+(const d_Time &t, const d_Interval &i)
```

```
friend d_Time
operator+(const d_Interval &i, const d_Time &t)
```

The time and interval objects t and i are added, and a new d_Time is returned by value.

```
friend d_Interval
operator-(const d_Time &t1, const d_Time &t2)
```

The difference of time between t1 and t2 (t1 - t2) is computed and returned as a d_Interval.

```
friend d_Time
operator-(const d_Time &t, const d_Interval &i)
```

The interval value is subtracted from the time, and a new d_Time value is returned.

```
friend d_Boolean
operator==(const d_Time &t1, const d_Time &t2)
```

If the time objects t1 and t2 are equal, this Boolean function returns true; otherwise, it returns false.

```
friend d_Boolean
operator!=(const d_Time &t1, const d_Time &t2)
```

If the time objects t1 and t2 are not equal, this Boolean function returns true. If they are equal, the function returns false.

```
friend d_Boolean
operator<(const d_Time &t1, const d_Time &t2)
```

If time `t1` is less than time `t2`, this Boolean function returns true. Otherwise, it returns false.

```
friend d_Boolean
operator<=(const d_Time &t1, const d_Time &t2)
```

If time `t1` is less than or equal to time `t2`, this Boolean function returns true. Otherwise, it returns false.

```
friend d_Boolean
operator>(const d_Time &t1, const d_Time &t2)
```

If time `t1` is greater than `t2`, this Boolean function returns true. Otherwise, it returns false.

```
friend d_Boolean
operator>=(const d_Time &t1, const d_Time &t2)
```

If time `t1` is greater than or equal to `t2`, this Boolean function returns true. Otherwise, it returns false.

```
friend d_Boolean
overlaps(const d_Time &sL, const d_Time &eL,
          const d_Time &sR, const d_Time &eR)
```

```
friend d_Boolean
overlaps(const d_Timestamp &sL, const d_Timestamp &eL,
          const d_Time &sR, const d_Time &eR)
```

```
friend d_Boolean
overlaps(const d_Time &sL, const d_Time &eL,
          const d_Timestamp &sR, const d_Timestamp &eR)
```

These Boolean friend functions return true if the period of time L (bounded by the time between `sL` and `eL`) has any period of time in common with the period R (bounded by the time between `sR` and `eR`). Otherwise, they return false.

Name   d_Timestamp

A class used to represent both a date and a time.

Synopsis

```
class d_Timestamp {
public:
                                d_Timestamp();
                                d_Timestamp( unsigned short year,
                                        unsigned short month = 1,
                                        unsigned short day = 1,
                                        unsigned short hour = 0,
                                        unsigned short minute = 0,
                                        float sec = 0.0f);
                                d_Timestamp(const d_Date &d);
                                d_Timestamp(const d_Date &d, const d_Time &t);
                                d_Timestamp(const d_Timestamp &ts);
        d_Timestamp &           operator=(const d_Timestamp &ts);
        d_Timestamp &           operator=(const d_Date &d);
        const d_Date &          date() const;
        const d_Time &          time() const;
        unsigned short          year() const;
        unsigned short          month() const;
        unsigned short          day() const;
        unsigned short          hour() const;
        unsigned short          minute() const;
        float                   second() const;
        short                   tz_hour() const;
        short                   tz_minute() const;

static  d_Timestamp             current();
        d_Timestamp &           operator+=(const d_Interval &i);
        d_Timestamp &           operator-=(const d_Interval &i);
friend  d_Timestamp             operator+ (const d_Timestamp &ts,
                                        const d_Interval &i);
friend  d_Timestamp             operator+ (const d_Interval &i,
                                        const d_Timestamp &ts);
friend  d_Interval              operator- (const d_Timestamp &ts1,
                                        const d_Timestamp &ts2);
```

```
friend d_Timestamp         operator- (const d_Timestamp &ts,
                                      const d_Interval &i);
friend d_Boolean           operator==(const d_Timestamp &ts1,
                                      const d_Timestamp &ts2);
friend d_Boolean           operator!=(const d_Timestamp &ts1,
                                      const d_Timestamp &ts2);
friend d_Boolean           operator< (const d_Timestamp &ts1,
                                      const d_Timestamp &ts2);
friend d_Boolean           operator<=(const d_Timestamp &ts1,
                                      const d_Timestamp &ts2);
friend d_Boolean           operator> (const d_Timestamp &ts1,
                                      const d_Timestamp &ts2);
friend d_Boolean           operator>=(const d_Timestamp &ts1,
                                      const d_Timestamp &ts2);
friend d_Boolean           overlaps(const d_Timestamp &sL,
                                    const d_Timestamp &eL,
                                    const d_Timestamp &sR,
                                    const d_Timestamp &eR);
friend d_Boolean           overlaps(const d_Timestamp &sL,
                                    const d_Timestamp &eL,
                                    const d_Date &sR,
                                    const d_Date &eR);
friend d_Boolean           overlaps(const d_Date &sL,
                                    const d_Date &eL,
                                    const d_Timestamp &sR,
                                    const d_Timestamp &eR);
friend d_Boolean           overlaps(const d_Timestamp &sL,
                                    const d_Timestamp &eL,
                                    const d_Time &sR,
                                    const d_Time &eR);
friend d_Boolean           overlaps(const d_Time &sL,
                                    const d_Time &eL,
                                    const d_Timestamp &sR,
                                    const d_Timestamp &eR);
};
```

d_Timestamp

Description

d_Timestamp()

> This constructor initializes the object to the current time.

d_Timestamp(unsigned short year, unsigned short month = 1,
            unsigned short day = 1, unsigned short hour = 0,
            unsigned short minute = 0, float sec = 0.0)

> This constructor initializes the object to the given year, month, day, hour, minute, and second.

d_Timestamp(const d_Date &d)

> This constructor initializes the object with the components of the date d.

d_Timestamp(const d_Date &d, const d_Time &t)

> This constructor initializes the object with the components of the date d and time t.

d_Timestamp(const d_Timestamp &ts)

> The copy constructor initializes the object with the value of ts.

d_Timestamp &
operator=(const d_Timestamp &ts)

> The assignment operator assigns the value of the timestamp ts to the object.

d_Timestamp &
operator=(const d_Date &d)

> This assignment operator assigns the value of the date d to the object. The time components (hours, minutes, seconds) are set to zero.

const d_Date &
date() const

> A constant reference to the d_Date component of the timestamp is returned.

const d_Time &
time() const

> A constant reference to the d_Time component of the timestamp is returned.

unsigned short
year() const

> The year is returned.

unsigned short
month() const

> The month is returned. Valid values are 1–12.

```
unsigned short
day() const
```

> The day is returned, valid values are 1–31.

```
unsigned short
hour() const
```

> The hour is returned. Valid values are 0–23.

```
unsigned short
minute() const
```

> The minutes are returned. Valid values are 0–59.

```
float
second() const
```

> The number of seconds is returned. Valid values are (0.0 <= value < 60.0).

```
short
tz_hour() const
```

> The number of hours relative to GMT is returned.

```
short
tz_minute() const
```

> The number of minutes GMT is returned.

```
static d_Timestamp
current()
```

> A timestamp of the current time is returned.

```
d_Timestamp &
operator+=(const d_Interval &i)
```

> The timestamp value is incremented by the given interval i, and a reference to the object is returned.

```
d_Timestamp &
operator-=(const d_Interval &i)
```

> The timestamp value is decremented by the given interval i, and a reference to the object is returned.

```
friend d_Timestamp
operator+(const d_Timestamp &ts, const d_Interval &i)

friend d_Timestamp
operator+(const d_Interval &i, const d_Timestamp &ts)
```

> The timestamp ts and interval i are added, and a new d_Timestamp value is returned.

```
friend d_Interval
operator-(const d_Timestamp &ts1, const d_Timestamp &ts2)
```

The timestamp `ts2` is subtracted from the timestamp `ts1` (ts1 − ts2), and the interval is returned.

```
friend d_Timestamp
operator-(const d_Timestamp &ts, const d_Interval &i)
```

The interval `intrvl` is subtracted from the value of the timestamp `ts`, and the new `d_Timestamp` value is returned.

```
friend d_Boolean
operator==(const d_Timestamp &tsL, const d_Timestamp &tsR)
```

If the timestamps `tsL` and `tsR` are equal, this Boolean function returns true; otherwise, it returns false.

```
friend d_Boolean
operator!=(const d_Timestamp &tsL, const d_Timestamp &tsR)
```

If the timestamps `tsL` and `tsR` are not equal, this Boolean function returns true. If they are equal, the function returns false.

```
friend d_Boolean
operator<(const d_Timestamp &tsL, const d_Timestamp &tsR)
```

If timestamp `tsL` is less than `tsR`, this Boolean function returns true; otherwise, it returns false.

```
friend d_Boolean
operator<=(const d_Timestamp &tsL, const d_Timestamp &tsR)
```

If timestamp `tsL` is less than or equal to `tsR`, this Boolean function returns true; otherwise, it returns false.

```
friend d_Boolean
operator>(const d_Timestamp &tsL, const d_Timestamp &tsR)
```

If timestamp `tsL` is greater than `tsR`, this Boolean function returns true; otherwise, it returns false.

```
friend d_Boolean
operator>=(const d_Timestamp &tsL, const d_Timestamp &tsR)
```

If timestamp `tsL` is greater than or equal to `tsR`, this Boolean function returns true; otherwise, it returns false.

d_Timestamp

```
friend d_Boolean
overlaps(const d_Timestamp &sL, const d_Timestamp &eL,
         const d_Timestamp &sR, const d_Timestamp &eR)
friend d_Boolean
overlaps(const d_Timestamp &sL, const d_Timestamp &eL,
         const d_Time &sR,const d_Time &eR)
friend d_Boolean
overlaps(const d_Date &sL, const d_Date &eL,
         const d_Timestamp &sR, const d_Timestamp &eR)
friend d_Boolean
overlaps(const d_Timestamp &sL, const d_Timestamp &eL,
         const d_Time &sR,const d_Time &eR)
friend d_Boolean
overlaps(const d_Time &sL, const d_Time &eL,
         const d_Timestamp &sR, const d_Timestamp &eR)
```

These Boolean friend functions return true if the period of time L (bounded by the time between sL and eL) has any period of time in common with the period R (bounded by the time between sR and eR). Otherwise, they return false.

Name   d_Transaction

This class is used to perform database transactions. All access, creation, modification, and deletion of persistent objects must be performed within a transaction. Transient objects are not subject to transaction semantics. Transient objects are not removed from memory when a transaction commits or aborts, and their prior state is not restored when a transaction aborts.

Synopsis

```
class d_Transaction {
public:
                            d_Transaction();
                            ~d_Transaction();
        void                begin();
        void                commit();
        void                abort();
        void                checkpoint();
        void                join();
        void                leave();
        d_Boolean           is_active() const;
static  d_Transaction *     current();
private:
                            d_Transaction(const d_Transaction &);
        d_Transaction &     operator=(const d_Transaction &);
};
```

A d_Transaction object cannot be copied or assigned to another instance of d_Transaction, and that is why the copy constructor and assignment operators are declared private.

Description

d_Transaction()

The null constructor initializes the transaction. It does *not* begin a transaction.

~d_Transaction()

The destructor aborts the transaction if it is active.

```
void
begin()
```

> This function starts a transaction. If this function is called multiple times without intervening calls to `commit` or `abort`, this function throws a `d_Error_-TransactionOpen` exception. This function implicitly joins the current thread to the transaction.

```
void
commit()
```

> This function commits all changes to the database that have been made during the transaction. These changes include creation, modification, and deletion of persistent objects. The function also releases any locks acquired by the transaction. Specific implementations may allow `d_Ref<T>` and `d_Ref_Any` reference objects to be valid across transaction boundaries. If a call is made to this function and a call has not been made to begin the transaction, a `d_Error_-TransactionNotOpen` exception is thrown.

```
void
abort()
```

> This function aborts the current transaction, releasing all locks that have been acquired by the transaction. None of the changes made to persistent objects by the transaction is applied to the database. Specific implementations may allow `d_Ref<T>` and `d_Ref_Any` reference objects to be valid across transaction boundaries. If a call is made to this function and a call has not been made to begin the transaction, a `d_Error_TransactionNotOpen` exception is thrown.

```
void
checkpoint()
```

> This function commits to the database all objects that have been modified since the last call to `checkpoint` or the beginning of the transaction. The original transaction continues, the objects remain in the cache, and all locks acquired are retained. All references, `d_Ref<T>`, `d_Ref_Any`, and pointers remain valid. If a call is made to this function and a call has not been made to begin the transaction, a `d_Error_TransactionNotOpen` exception is thrown.

```
void
join()
```

> This function associates the current thread with the transaction object. A thread can be associated with only one transaction at a time. If the thread was previously associated with another transaction, the thread is detached from that transaction.

d_Transaction

```
void
leave()
```

> This function detaches the current thread from the transaction. The thread is not automatically reassociated with another transaction.

```
d_Boolean
is_active() const
```

> This function returns true if the transaction is currently active—that is, a `begin` has been performed but the transaction has not been completed with an `abort` or `commit`.

```
static d_Transaction *
current()
```

> This function returns a pointer to the transaction object that the current thread is associated with.

Name   d_Varray<T>

A one-dimensional array of varying length containing elements of type T. This is an ordered collection based on the index (and not the element values). The starting index is 0. ODMG-93 1.2 had a function upper_bound, which has been removed in ODMG 2.0. Use the inherited function cardinality to determine the size of the array.

Synopsis

```
template <class T> class d_Varray : public d_Collection<T> {
public:
                            d_Varray();
                            d_Varray(unsigned long sz);
                            d_Varray(const d_Varray<T> &a2);
                            ~d_Varray();
    d_Varray<T> &           operator=(const d_Varray<T> &a2);
    void                    resize(unsigned long sz);
    T                       operator[](unsigned long pos) const;
    void                    insert_element(const T &val); // inherited
    d_Boolean               find_element(const T &val,
                                    unsigned long &pos ) const;
    T                       retrieve_element_at(unsigned long pos) const;
    void                    remove_element_at(unsigned long pos);
    void                    replace_element_at(const T &val,
                                    unsigned long pos);
};
```

Description

d_Varray()

> The null constructor creates an empty array.

d_Varray(unsigned long sz)

> This constructor creates an array with sz elements. The array elements will be set to a null value, depending on the element type.

d_Varray(const d_Varray<T> &a)

> The copy constructor initializes the array object with the d_Varray<T> argument a. The object will have the same element values as a in the same order.

~d_Varray()

>The destructor uninitializes the array, removing the elements. If the element type has a destructor, it is called for each element.

```
d_Varray<T> &
operator=(const d_Varray<T> &a)
```

>The assignment operator is used to assign the value of the argument a to the object. The original array elements are discarded.

```
void
resize(unsigned long sz)
```

>This function resizes the array to have sz elements.

```
T
operator[](unsigned long pos) const
```

>The value of the element at position pos is returned. The return type of this function was const T & in ODMG-93 1.2 but was changed to T in release 2.0.

```
void
insert_element(const T &val)
```

>The size of the array is increased by 1, and the value val is placed at the new last position in the array.

```
d_Boolean
find_element(const T &val, unsigned long &pos) const
```

>This Boolean function searches the array for an element with value val. If an element is found, the function returns true and the position of the element is returned in pos; otherwise, it returns false. This function provides an existential quantification facility.

```
T
retrieve_element_at(unsigned long pos) const
```

>The value of the element at position pos is returned. The return type of this function was const T & in ODMG-93 1.2 but was changed to T in release 2.0.

```
void
remove_element_at(unsigned long pos)
```

>This function removes the element at position pos.

```
void
replace_element_at(const T &val, unsigned long index)
```

>This function replaces the value of the element at position pos with the value val.

Name   **STL**

With ODMG release 2.0, a subset of the Standard Template Library (STL) collections is supported. Each collection has the ODMG prefix of d_, but supports the interface defined in STL. These collections include the following:

- d_set<T>
- d_multiset<T>
- d_vector<T>
- d_list<T>
- d_map<K,V>
- d_multimap<K,V>

Readers are encouraged to obtain a copy of one of the books dedicated to STL to understand the complete interface.

Appendix C:
ODMG Metaclasses

This appendix contains manual pages for the metaclasses that have been added to ODMG 2.0. An ODMG database schema is represented by a set of interrelated instances of these classes. An overview of these classes and their interrelationships can be found in section 16.2.

Name   Iterators

An iterator is used to traverse a one-to-many relationship that exists between two classes in the metamodel. Such relationships are not directly represented by collections, because implementations have their own metamodel representation. When a to-one relationship is involved, an accessor returns a reference to the related metamodel object. But metamodel objects that have a one-to-many relationship are accessed via iterators. An STL style of iteration has been adopted. Each end of a to-many relationship has two provided functions: one function returns an iterator positioned at the beginning of a virtual list of related objects, and the other function returns an iterator positioned just past the last object in the list. The function names have a suffix of `begin` or `end` that indicates their position. The iterators returned by the functions can be used to iterate over each metaobject involved in the relationship. The iterators are declared in the scope of the metaobject class in which they are used.

Synopsis

The following interface defines the generic operations each iterator type should support. This interface corresponds to the constant forward iterator type defined by STL.

```
class IterType {
public:
                              IterType();
                              IterType(const IterType &);
         IterType &           operator=(const IterType &);
         int                  operator==(const IterType &) const;
         int                  operator!=(const IterType &) const;
         IterType &           operator++();
         IterType             operator++(int);
         const  T &           operator*() const;
};
```

A class is represented by an instance of `d_Class`. An attribute of a class is represented by an instance of `d_Attribute`. An iterator type is declared within the scope of `d_Class` with the name `attribute_iterator` and is used to iterate over the attributes of the class. Its operations are as follows:

```
class attribute_iterator {
public:
                                attribute_iterator();
                                attribute_iterator(
                                 const attribute_iterator &);
        attribute_iterator & operator=(const attribute_iterator &);
        int                  operator==(const attribute_iterator &)
const;
        int                  operator!=(const attribute_iterator &)
const;
        attribute_iterator & operator++();
        attribute_iterator   operator++(int);
        const  d_Attribute & operator*() const;
};
```

The following code declares an instance of this type.

```
d_Class::attribute_iterator attrs;
```

The variable `attrs` can be used to iterate over the attributes of a class.

All metaclasses use a consistent iterator type name to access metaclass objects of a particular type. The iterator type names in Table C.1 are used.

Iterator Type Name	Element Type
alias_type_iterator	d_Alias_Type
attribute_iterator	d_Attribute
collection_type_iterator	d_Collection_Type
constant_iterator	d_Constant
exception_iterator	d_Exception
inheritance_iterator	d_Inheritance
keyed_collection_type_iterator	d_Keyed_Collection_Type
operation_iterator	d_Operation
parameter_iterator	d_Parameter
property_iterator	d_Property
ref_type_iterator	d_Ref_Type
relationship_iterator	d_Relationship
type_iterator	d_Type

Table C.1 Iterators for metaclass access.

Name   d_Access_Kind

This enumeration indicates the access specifier for a property, operation, or base class.

Synopsis

```
typedef enum {
       d_PUBLIC,
       d_PROTECTED,
       d_PRIVATE } d_Access_Kind;
```

Name   d_Alias_Type

An alias type defines an alternative name for a type. A `typedef` is used in C++ to create an alias type. The scope of the alias type is either a module or class. The method `defined_in` inherited from `d_Meta_Object` returns the metaobject that represents the scope of the alias type; it will be an instance of `d_Class` or `d_Module`.

Synopsis

```
class d_Alias_Type : public d_Type {
public:
        const d_Type &        alias_type() const;
};
```

Description

```
const d_Type &
alias_type() const
```
A reference to the actual type is returned.

Name   d_Attribute

A d_Attribute instance describes a data member of a class or structure. Each attribute has a name that is accessed by calling the function name inherited from d_Meta_Object. An attribute also has a type, which is accessed by calling type_of inherited from d_Property.

Synopsis

```
class d_Attribute : public d_Property {
public:
        d_Boolean              is_read_only() const;
        d_Boolean              is_static() const;
        unsigned long          dimension() const;
};
```

Description

```
d_Boolean
is_read_only() const
```

An attribute can be declared const in C++, in which case this function returns true.

```
d_Boolean
is_static() const
```

This function returns true if the attribute is a static data member of a class.

```
unsigned long
dimension() const
```

If the attribute is a single-dimensional array, this function returns the number of elements in the array. If the attribute is not an array, this function returns 0.

Name   **d_Class**

Every application-defined class that has instances stored in the database is represented by an instance of d_Class. A d_Inheritance instance is used to associate two classes involved in an inheritance relationship. It is possible to iterate over
the base and derived classes for each d_Class instance. Iterators are also provided to access the data and function members, the relationships with other
classes, and the constants and types defined within the class. The class is their
defining scope. Each of these components can also be accessed generically by
using the meta_object_iterator inherited from d_Meta_Object.

Synopsis

```
class d_Class : public d_Type, public d_Scope {
public:
/*      The following iterator types are defined in this class' scope.
        inheritance_iterator
        operation_iterator
        attribute_iterator
        relationship_iterator
        constant_iterator
        type_iterator
*/
        d_Boolean               persistent_capable() const;
        d_Boolean               has_extent() const;

        inheritance_iterator    sub_class_list_begin() const;
        inheritance_iterator    sub_class_list_end() const;
        inheritance_iterator    base_class_list_begin() const;
        inheritance_iterator    base_class_list_end() const;

        operation_iterator      defines_operation_begin() const;
        operation_iterator      defines_operation_end() const;
        const d_Operation &     resolve_operation(const char *name) const;

        attribute_iterator      defines_attribute_begin() const;
        attribute_iterator      defines_attribute_end() const;
        const d_Attribute &     resolve_attribute(const char *name) const;

        relationship_iterator   defines_relationship_begin() const;
```

```
relationship_iterator  defines_relationship_end() const;
const d_Relationship & resolve_relationship(
                          const char *name)const;


constant_iterator       defines_constant_begin() const;
constant_iterator       defines_constant_end() const;
const d_Constant &      resolve_constant(const char *name) const;


type_iterator           defines_type_begin() const;
type_iterator           defines_type_end() const;
const d_Type &          resolve_type(const char *name) const;
};
```

Description

```
d_Boolean
persistent_capable() const
```

> This function returns true if the class is persistence-capable—that is, it is derived from d_Object.

```
d_Boolean
has_extent() const
```

> This function returns true if the class has an extent.

```
inheritance_iterator
sub_class_list_begin() const
```

> This function returns an iterator positioned at the beginning of a collection of d_Inheritance instances that represent an inheritance relationship between this class and a subclass (derived class).

```
inheritance_iterator
sub_class_list_end() const
```

> This function returns an iterator positioned past the end of a collection of d_Inheritance instances that represent an inheritance relationship between this class and a subclass (derived class). Iteration is complete when the iterator returned by sub_class_list_begin is equal to the iterator returned by this function.

d_Class

```
inheritance_iterator
base_class_list_begin() const
```

> This function returns an iterator positioned at the beginning of a collection of d_Inheritance instances that represent an inheritance relationship between this class and a base class. They are returned in their declaration order.

```
inheritance_iterator
base_class_list_end() const
```

> This function returns an iterator positioned past the end of a collection of d_Inheritance instances that represent an inheritance relationship between this class and a base class. Iteration is complete when the iterator returned by base_class_list_begin is equal to the iterator returned by this function.

```
operation_iterator
defines_operation_begin() const
```

> This function returns an iterator positioned at the beginning of a collection of d_Operation instances that are the member functions defined for this class. They are returned in their declaration order.

```
operation_iterator
defines_operation_end() const
```

> This function returns an iterator positioned past the end of a collection of d_Operation instances. Iteration is complete when the iterator returned by defines_operation_begin is equal to the iterator returned by this function.

```
const d_Operation &
resolve_operation(const char *name) const
```

> A reference to the d_Operation instance with the specified name is returned. The instance is an element of the collection that is accessed by the iterators returned by the two previous functions.

```
attribute_iterator
defines_attribute_begin() const
```

> This function returns an iterator positioned at the beginning of a collection of d_Attribute instances that represent the data members defined for this class. They are returned in their declaration order.

```
attribute_iterator
defines_attribute_end() const
```

> This function returns an iterator positioned past the end of a collection of d_Attribute instances. Iteration is complete when the iterator returned by defines_attribute_begin is equal to the iterator returned by this function.

```
const d_Attribute &
resolve_attribute(const char *name) const
```

> A reference to the `d_Attribute` instance with the specified name is returned. The instance is an element of the collection that is accessed by the iterators returned by the two previous functions.

```
relationship_iterator
defines_relationship_begin() const
```

> This function returns an iterator positioned at the beginning of a collection of `d_Relationship` instances that represent the relationships this class has with other classes. They are returned in their declaration order.

```
relationship_iterator
defines_relationship_end() const
```

> This function returns an iterator positioned past the end of a collection of `d_Relationship` instances. Iteration is complete when the iterator returned by `defines_relationship_begin` is equal to the iterator returned by this function.

```
const d_Relationship &
resolve_relationship(const char *name)const
```

> A reference to the `d_Relationship` instance with the specified name is returned. The instance is an element of the collection that is accessed by the iterators returned by the two previous functions.

```
constant_iterator
defines_constant_begin() const
```

> This function returns an iterator positioned at the beginning of a collection of `d_Constant` instances that represent the constants associated with this class. They are returned in their declaration order.

```
constant_iterator
defines_constant_end() const
```

> This function returns an iterator positioned past the end of a collection of `d_Constant` instances. Iteration is complete when the iterator returned by `defines_constant_begin` is equal to the iterator returned by this function.

```
const d_Constant &
resolve_constant(const char *name) const
```

> A reference to the `d_Constant` instance with the specified name is returned. The instance is an element of the collection that is accessed by the iterators returned by the two previous functions.

d_Class

```
type_iterator
defines_type_begin() const
```

> This function returns an iterator positioned at the beginning of a collection of d_Type instances that represent the types associated with this class. They are returned in their declaration order.

```
type_iterator
defines_type_end() const
```

> This function returns an iterator positioned past the end of a collection of d_Type instances. Iteration is complete when the iterator returned by defines_type_begin is equal to the iterator returned by this function.

```
const d_Type &
resolve_type(const char *name) const
```

> A reference to the d_Type instance with the specified name is returned. The instance is an element of the collection that is accessed by the iterators returned by the two previous functions.

Name   d_Collection_Type

An instance of d_Collection_Type describes a specific collection type. An enumeration called d_Kind is declared in the class and is used to indicate the type of the collection.

Synopsis

```
class d_Collection_Type : public d_Type {
public:
        typedef enum {          LIST,
                                ARRAY,
                                BAG,
                                SET,
                                DICTIONARY,
                                STL_LIST,
                                STL_SET,
                                STL_MULTISET,
                                STL_VECTOR,
                                STL_MAP,
                                STL_MULTIMAP } d_Kind;

        d_Kind                  kind() const;
        const d_Type &          element_type() const;
};
```

Description

```
d_Kind
kind() const
```

This function indicates the type of the collection.

```
const d_Type &
element_type() const
```

A reference is returned to the d_Type instance representing the type of the collection's elements.

d_Collection_Type

Name   d_Constant

A `d_Constant` describes a constant value that has both a name and a type. The name of the constant is accessed by calling `name` inherited from `d_Meta_-Object`. A constant is declared in the scope of exactly one module or class, which can be accessed by calling the `defined_in` function inherited from `d_Meta_-Object`.

Synopsis

```
class d_Constant : public d_Meta_Object {
public:
        const d_Type &          constant_type() const;
        void *                  constant_value() const;
};
```

Description

```
const d_Type &
constant_type() const
```

A reference to the `d_Type` instance defining the type of the constant.

```
void *
constant_value() const
```

A generic pointer to the constant value is returned. This pointer must be cast to the appropriate type based on the type returned by `constant_type`. The value should not be changed.

Name   d_Enumeration_Type

A d_Enumeration_Type describes a type whose instances consist of a set of identifiers. This class is used to represent a C++ enum.

Synopsis

```
class d_Enumeration_Type : public d_Primitive_Type, public d_Scope {
public:
/*      The following iterator type is defined in this class's scope.
        constant_iterator
*/
        constant_iterator      defines_constant_begin() const;
        constant_iterator      defines_constant_end() const;
        const d_Constant &     resolve_constant(const char *name) const;
};
```

Description

```
constant_iterator
defines_constant_begin() const
```

This function returns an iterator positioned at the beginning of a collection of d_Constant instances that represent the constants associated with this enumeration. They are returned in the order in which they were declared in the enumeration.

```
constant_iterator
defines_constant_end() const
```

This function returns an iterator positioned past the end of a collection of d_Constant instances. Iteration is complete when the iterator returned by defines_constant_begin is equal to the iterator returned by this function.

```
const d_Constant &
resolve_constant(const char *name) const
```

A reference to the d_Constant instance with the specified name is returned. The instance is an element of the collection that is accessed by the iterators returned by the two previous functions.

d_Enumeration_Type

Name   **d_Exception**

A d_Exception instance describes an exception that can be raised by operations. Multiple operations can throw the exception.

Synopsis

```
class d_Exception : public d_Meta_Object {
public:
/*      The following iterator type is defined in this class's scope.
        operation_iterator
*/
        const d_Type &        exception_type() const;
        operation_iterator    raised_in_operation_begin() const;
        operation_iterator    raised_in_operation_end() const;
        const d_Module &      defined_in_module() const;
};
```

Description

```
const d_Type &
exception_type() const
```

A reference to the type of the exception is returned.

```
operation_iterator
raised_in_operation_begin() const
```

This function returns an iterator positioned at the beginning of a collection of d_Operation instances that represent the operations that can throw this exception.

```
operation_iterator
raised_in_operation_end() const
```

This function returns an iterator positioned past the end of a collection of d_Operation instances. Iteration is complete when the iterator returned by raised_in_operation_begin is equal to the iterator returned by this function.

```
const d_Module &
defined_in_module() const
```

This function returns a reference to the module that defines the scope of the exception.

Name   d_Inheritance

A d_Inheritance instance represents the relationship between a base class and one of its derived classes. An instance of d_Inheritance connects two instances of type d_Class.

Synopsis

```
class d_Inheritance {
public:
        const d_Class &        derives_from() const;
        const d_Class &        inherits_to() const;

        d_Access_Kind          access_kind() const;
        d_Boolean              is_virtual() const;
};
```

Description

```
const d_Class &
derives_from() const
```
> A reference to the base class is returned.

```
const d_Class &
inherits_to() const
```
> A reference to the derived class is returned.

```
d_Access_Kind
access_kind() const
```
> The accessibility (public, private, protected) of the base class is returned.

```
d_Boolean
is_virtual() const
```
> This function returns true if the base class is virtual.

d_Inheritance

Name   **d_Keyed_Collection_Type**

A d_Keyed_Collection_Type instance describes a collection whose elements are accessed via keys, including the d_Dictionary, d_map, and d_multimap classes. Most of its collection properties are inherited from d_Collection_-Type.

Synopsis

```
class d_Keyed_Collection_Type : public d_Collection_Type {
public:
        const d_Type &          key_type() const;
        const d_Type &          value_type() const;
};
```

Description

```
const d_Type &
key_type() const
```

A reference to the type of the collection's key is returned.

```
const d_Type &
value_type() const
```

A reference to the type of the collection's value is returned.

Name   d_Meta_Object

The d_Meta_Object class is the base class for all the classes that are used to represent the elements of the schema that are stored in the data dictionary. Each d_Meta_Object instance has a name that can be used to uniquely identify it within a given scope (d_Scope). Some instances of d_Meta_Object are derived from d_Scope, in which case they define a namespace in which other d_Meta_Object instances can be identified by name.

Synopsis

```
class d_Meta_Object {
public:
        const char *        name() const;
        const char *        comment() const;
        const d_Scope &     defined_in() const;
};
```

Description

```
const char *
name() const
```
    The name associated with this metaobject.

```
const char *
comment() const
```
    A comment that provides some description of the metaobject.

```
const d_Scope &
defined_in() const
```
    The scope in which the name of this metaobject is defined.

Name   **d_Module**

A `d_Module` instance manages a logical set of types in a data dictionary and represents a complete schema in the dictionary. It is used to group together a set of `d_Meta_Object` instances.

A hierarchy of `d_Module` instances represents subschemas or different versions of a schema. The static function `top_level` can be called to access the instance of `d_Module` at the root of the hierarchy. A `d_Module` is also an instance of `d_Scope`, allowing it to serve as a scope for names in the schema. A hierarchy of `d_Module` instances allows a naming hierarchy to be defined.

Synopsis

```
class d_Module : public d_Meta_Object, public d_Scope {
public:
/*      The following iterator types are defined in this class's scope.
        type_iterator
        constant_iterator
        operation_iterator
*/
static  const d_Module &        top_level(const d_Database &db);

        type_iterator           defines_types_begin() const;
        type_iterator           defines_types_end() const;

        constant_iterator       defines_constant_begin() const;
        constant_iterator       defines_constant_end() const;

        operation_iterator      defines_operation_begin() const;
        operation_iterator      defines_operation_end() const;
};
```

Description

```
static const d_Module &
top_level(const d_Database &db)
```

A reference to the `d_Module` instance at the top of the hierarchy for database `db` is returned.

```
type_iterator
defines_types_begin() const
```

> This function returns an iterator positioned at the beginning of a collection of d_Type instances that are associated with the module.

```
type_iterator
defines_types_end() const
```

> This function returns an iterator positioned past the end of a collection of d_Type instances. Iteration is complete when the iterator returned by defines_types_begin is equal to the iterator returned by this function.

```
constant_iterator
defines_constant_begin() const
```

> This function returns an iterator positioned at the beginning of a collection of d_Constant instances that are associated with the module.

```
constant_iterator
defines_constant_end() const
```

> This function returns an iterator positioned past the end of a collection of d_Constant instances. Iteration is complete when the iterator returned by defines_constant_begin is equal to the iterator returned by this function.

```
operation_iterator
defines_operation_begin() const
```

> This function returns an iterator positioned at the beginning of a collection of d_Operation instances that are associated with the module.

```
operation_iterator
defines_operation_end() const
```

> This function returns an iterator positioned past the end of a collection of d_Operation instances. Iteration is complete when the iterator returned by defines_operation_begin is equal to the iterator returned by this function.

d_Module

Name   **d_Operation**

A d_Operation instance describes the characteristics of an operation, including
its name, return type, and parameters as well as the exceptions it may throw. The
access characteristic is also specified.

Synopsis

```
class d_Operation : public d_Meta_Object, public d_Scope {
public:
/*      The following iterator types are defined in this class's scope.
        parameter_iterator
        exception_iterator
*/
        const d_Type &          result_type() const;
        d_Boolean               is_static() const;
        d_Access_Kind           access_kind() const;

        parameter_iterator      defines_parameter_begin() const;
        parameter_iterator      defines_parameter_end() const;
        const d_Parameter &     resolve_parameter(const char *name) const;

        exception_iterator      raises_exception_begin() const;
        exception_iterator      raises_exception_end() const;
};
```

Description

```
const d_Type &
result_type() const
```
The d_Type representing the type of the result is returned.

```
d_Boolean
is_static() const
```
This function returns true if the operation is a static member function of a class.

```
d_Access_Kind
access_kind() const
```

> This function returns a d_Access_Kind enumeration indicating whether the operation is public, private, or protected.

```
parameter_iterator
defines_parameter_begin() const
```

> This function returns an iterator positioned at the beginning of a collection of d_Parameter instances that are associated with the operation. These instances are the parameters to the operation and are returned in their declaration order.

```
parameter_iterator
defines_parameter_end() const
```

> This function returns an iterator positioned past the end of a collection of d_Parameter instances. Iteration is complete when the iterator returned by defines_parameter_begin is equal to the iterator returned by this function.

```
const d_Parameter &
resolve_parameter(const char *name) const
```

> A reference to the d_Parameter instance with the specified name is returned. The instance is an element of the collection that is accessed by the iterators returned by the two previous functions.

```
exception_iterator
raises_exception_begin() const
```

> This function returns an iterator positioned at the beginning of a collection of d_Exception instances that are associated with the operation. These instances are the exceptions that this operation may throw.

```
exception_iterator
raises_exception_end() const
```

> This function returns an iterator positioned past the end of a collection of d_Exception instances. Iteration is complete when the iterator returned by raises_exception_begin is equal to the iterator returned by this function.

d_Operation

Name   d_Parameter

An instance of d_Parameter describes a parameter of an operation. The name of
the parameter is returned by the function name inherited from d_Meta_Object.
An enumeration called d_Mode is defined in the class and is used to indicate
whether the parameter is used for input, output, or both.

Synopsis

```
class d_Parameter : public d_Meta_Object {
public:
        typedef enum { IN, OUT, INOUT } d_Mode;
        d_Mode              mode() const;
        const d_Type &      parameter_type() const;
        const d_Operation & defined_in_operation() const;
};
```

Description

```
d_Mode
mode() const
```

This function returns a d_Mode that indicates the purpose of the parameter in the
operation.

```
const d_Type &
parameter_type() const
```

The type of the parameter is returned, represented by an instance of d_Type.

```
const d_Operation &
defined_in_operation() const
```

The operation this parameter is associated with is returned.

d_Parameter

Name   **d_Primitive_Type**

An instance of d_Primitive_Type represents a primitive type. An enumeration called d_TypeId is specified to indicate the specific primitive type.

Synopsis

```
class d_Primitive_Type : public d_Type {
public:
        typedef enum {
                CHAR,
                SHORT,
                LONG,
                DOUBLE,
                FLOAT,
                USHORT,
                ULONG,
                OCTET,
                BOOLEAN,
                ENUMERATION } d_TypeId;

        d_TypeId                type_id() const;
};
```

Description

```
d_TypeId
type_id() const
```
This function returns a d_TypeId value indicating the primitive type.

Name   **d_Property**

The d_Property class is an abstract base class for classes d_Attribute and d_Relationship. A property has a name and a type. The name is accessed by calling the name function inherited from d_Meta_Object. Each property also has an access specifier.

Synopsis

```
class d_Property : public d_Meta_Object {
public:
        const d_Type &        type_of() const;
        d_Access_Kind         access_kind() const;
};
```

Description

```
const d_Type &
type_of() const
```

> The function returns the type of the property, represented by an instance of d_Type.

```
d_Access_Kind
access_kind() const
```

> An enumeration representing the access (public, private, or protected) of the property is returned.

Name   **d_Ref_Type**

A d_Ref_Type is used to represent a type that references an instance of a specified type T. It can represent either a pointer to T or the type d_Ref<T>; an enumeration called d_Ref_Kind is returned to indicate which form of reference is being used.

Synopsis

```
class d_Ref_Type : public d_Type {
public:
        typedef enum { REF, POINTER } d_Ref_Kind;
        d_Ref_Kind              ref_kind() const;
        const d_Type &          referenced_type() const;
};
```

Description

```
d_Ref_Kind
ref_kind() const
```

This function returns an enumeration that indicates the type of reference.

```
const d_Type &
referenced_type() const
```

This function returns a reference to the d_Type representing the type of the instance that is being referenced.

Name   d_Relationship

A d_Relationship represents a relationship between two classes. Each end of a relationship has a traversal member that is used to access the other end. The traversal member is represented by an instance of d_Relationship, so each relationship between two classes is represented by two instances of d_Relationship. Instances of d_Rel_Ref<T,MT>, d_Rel_List<T,MT>, and d_Rel_Set<T,MT> in the schema are represented by instances of d_Relationship. An enumeration called d_Rel_Kind indicates which of these relationship types is used. The defining scope of a relationship is a class, which is accessed by a call to defined_in_class.

Synopsis

```
class d_Relationship : public d_Property {
public:
        typedef enum { REL_REF, REL_SET, REL_LIST } d_Rel_Kind;
        d_Rel_Kind              rel_kind() const;
        const d_Relationship &  inverse() const;
        const d_Class &         defined_in_class() const;
};
```

Description

```
d_Rel_Kind
rel_kind() const
```

> This function returns a d_Rel_Kind enumeration indicating the kind of relationship.

```
const d_Relationship &
inverse() const
```

> This function returns the d_Relationship instance representing the inverse traveral member at the other end of the relationship.

```
const d_Class &
defined_in_class() const
```

> This function returns the d_Class representing the class that this end of the relationship is associated with.

Name   d_Scope

A d_Scope instance is used to form a hierarchy of metaobjects. It contains a collection of d_Meta_Object instances that are defined within the scope. Each instance has a unique name, with the namespace defined by the scope. All instances of classes derived from d_Meta_Object (except d_Module) are associated with one d_Scope instance.

Synopsis

```
class d_Scope {
public:
/*      The following iterator type is defined in this class's scope.
        meta_object_iterator
*/
        const d_Meta_Object &    resolve(const char *name) const;

        meta_object_iterator     defines_begin() const;
        meta_object_iterator     defines_end() const;
};
```

Description

```
const d_Meta_Object &
resolve(const char *name) const
```

This function is used to access the d_Meta_Object instance with the specified name.

```
meta_object_iterator
defines_begin() const
```

This function returns an iterator positioned at the beginning of a collection of d_Meta_Object instances that are associated with the d_Scope instance.

```
meta_object_iterator
defines_end() const
```

This function returns an iterator positioned past the end of a collection of d_Meta_Object instances. Iteration is complete when the iterator returned by defines_begin is equal to the iterator returned by this function.

d_Scope

Name   d_Structure_Type

A d_Structure_Type instance represents a struct defined by an application. It consists of a collection of attributes.

Synopsis

```
class d_Structure_Type : public d_Type, public d_Scope {
public:
/*      The following iterator type is defined in this class's scope.
        attribute_iterator
*/
        attribute_iterator    defines_attribute_begin() const;
        attribute_iterator    defines_attribute_end() const;
        const d_Attribute &   resolve_attribute(const char *name) const;
};
```

Description

```
attribute_iterator
defines_attribute_begin() const
```

This function returns an iterator positioned at the beginning of a collection of d_Attribute instances that are associated with the structure. They are returned in their declaration order.

```
attribute_iterator
defines_attribute_end() const
```

This function returns an iterator positioned past the end of a collection of d_Attribute instances. Iteration is complete when the iterator returned by defines_attribute_begin is equal to the iterator returned by this function.

```
const d_Attribute &
resolve_attribute(const char *name) const
```

This function is used to access the d_Attribute instance with the specified name.

d_Structure_Type

Name   d_Type

The class d_Type is a base class for each of the other metaclasses used to represent types in the data dictionary. Many of the metaclasses have references to types. The d_Type class provides iterators to access all the metaobjects that reference the type.

Synopsis

```
class d_Type : public d_Meta_Object {
public:
/*      The following iterator types are defined in this class's scope.
        alias_type_iterator
        collection_type_iterator
        keyed_collection_type_iterator
        ref_type_iterator
        property_iterator
        operation_iterator
        exception_iterator
        parameter_iterator
        constant_iterator
*/
        alias_type_iterator     used_in_alias_type_begin() const;
        alias_type_iterator     used_in_alias_type_end() const;

        collection_type_iterator
                                used_in_collection_type_begin() const;
        collection_type_iterator
                                used_in_collection_type_end() const;

        keyed_collection_type_iterator
                                used_in_keyed_collection_type_begin() const;
        keyed_collection_type_iterator
                                used_in_keyed_collection_type_end() const;

        ref_type_iterator       used_in_ref_type_begin() const;
        ref_type_iterator       used_in_ref_type_end() const;

        property_iterator       used_in_property_begin() const;
```

```
        property_iterator      used_in_property_end() const;

        operation_iterator     used_in_operation_begin() const;
        operation_iterator     used_in_operation_end() const;

        exception_iterator     used_in_exception_begin() const;
        exception_iterator     used_in_exception_end() const;

        parameter_iterator     used_in_parameter_begin() const;
        parameter_iterator     used_in_parameter_end() const;

        constant_iterator      used_in_constant_begin() const;
        constant_iterator      used_in_constant_end() const;
};
```

Description

```
alias_type_iterator
used_in_alias_type_begin() const
```

> This function returns an iterator positioned at the beginning of a collection of d_Alias_Type instances that reference this d_Type instance.

```
alias_type_iterator
used_in_alias_type_end() const
```

> This function returns an iterator positioned past the end of a collection of d_Alias_Type instances. Iteration is complete when the iterator returned by used_in_alias_type_begin is equal to the iterator returned by this function.

```
collection_type_iterator
used_in_collection_type_begin() const
```

> This function returns an iterator positioned at the beginning of a collection of d_Collection_Type instances that reference this d_Type instance.

```
collection_type_iterator
used_in_collection_type_end() const
```

> This function returns an iterator positioned past the end of a collection of d_Collection_Type instances. Iteration is complete when the iterator returned by used_in_collection_type_begin is equal to the iterator returned by this function.

d_Type

```
keyed_collection_type_iterator
used_in_keyed_collection_type_begin() const
```

> This function returns an iterator positioned at the beginning of a collection of d_Keyed_Collection_Type instances that reference this d_Type instance.

```
keyed_collection_type_iterator
used_in_keyed_collection_type_end() const
```

> This function returns an iterator positioned past the end of a collection of d_Keyed_Collection_Type instances. Iteration is complete when the iterator returned by used_in_keyed_collection_type_begin is equal to the iterator returned by this function.

```
ref_type_iterator
used_in_ref_type_begin() const
```

> This function returns an iterator positioned at the beginning of a collection of d_Ref_Type instances that reference this d_Type instance.

```
ref_type_iterator
used_in_ref_type_end() const
```

> This function returns an iterator positioned past the end of a collection of d_Ref_Type instances. Iteration is complete when the iterator returned by used_in_ref_type_begin is equal to the iterator returned by this function.

```
property_iterator
used_in_property_begin() const
```

> This function returns an iterator positioned at the beginning of a collection of d_Property instances that reference this d_Type instance.

```
property_iterator
used_in_property_end() const
```

> This function returns an iterator positioned past the end of a collection of d_Property instances. Iteration is complete when the iterator returned by used_in_property_begin is equal to the iterator returned by this function.

```
operation_iterator
used_in_operation_begin() const
```

> This function returns an iterator positioned at the beginning of a collection of d_Operation instances that reference this d_Type instance.

```
operation_iterator
used_in_operation_end() const
```

> This function returns an iterator positioned past the end of a collection of d_Operation instances. Iteration is complete when the iterator returned by used_in_operation_begin is equal to the iterator returned by this function.

d_Type

```
exception_iterator
used_in_exception_begin() const
```

This function returns an iterator positioned at the beginning of a collection of d_Exception instances that reference this d_Type instance.

```
exception_iterator
used_in_exception_end() const
```

This function returns an iterator positioned past the end of a collection of d_Exception instances. Iteration is complete when the iterator returned by used_in_exception_begin is equal to the iterator returned by this function.

```
parameter_iterator
used_in_parameter_begin() const
```

This function returns an iterator positioned at the beginning of a collection of d_Parameter instances that reference this d_Type instance.

```
parameter_iterator
used_in_parameter_end() const
```

This function returns an iterator positioned past the end of a collection of d_Parameter instances. Iteration is complete when the iterator returned by used_in_parameter_begin is equal to the iterator returned by this function.

```
constant_iterator
used_in_constant_begin() const
```

This function returns an iterator positioned at the beginning of a collection of d_Constant instances that reference this d_Type instance.

```
constant_iterator
used_in_constant_end() const
```

This function returns an iterator positioned past the end of a collection of d_Constant instances. Iteration is complete when the iterator returned by used_in_constant_begin is equal to the iterator returned by this function.

References

Douglas K. Barry, *The Object Database Handbook: How to Select, Implement, and Use Object-Oriented Databases*, John Wiley & Sons, Inc., 1996.

C. Batini, S. Ceri, and S. Navathe, *Conceptual Database Design: An Entity-Relationship Approach*, Benjamin/Cummings, 1992.

R.G.G. Cattell, *Object Data Management*, Addison-Wesley, 1994.

R.G.G. Cattell et al., *The Object Database Standard: ODMG-93 Release 1.2*, Morgan Kaufmann, 1996.

R.G.G. Cattell et al., *The Object Database Standard: ODMG 2.0*, Morgan Kaufmann, 1997.

P.P. Chen, "The Entity-Relationship Model: Toward a Unified View of Data." *ACM Transactions on Database Systems* 1, no. 1 (March 1976): 9–37.

P.P. Chen, "The Entity-Relationship Model: A Basis for the Enterprise View of Data." *Proceedings IFIPS NCC* 46, no. 46 (1977): 76–84.

C.J. Date, *An Introduction to Database Systems*, 3rd edition, Addison-Wesley, 1981.

Martin Fowler, *UML Distilled: Applying the Standard Object Modeling Language*, Addison-Wesley, 1997.

Peter Gray, *Logic, Algebra and Databases*, Ellis Horwood, 1984.

Barbara Liskov and John Guttag, *Abstraction and Specification in Program Development*, McGraw-Hill, 1986.

Mary E.S. Loomis, *Object Databases: The Essentials*, Addison-Wesley, 1995.

Jim Melton, "SQL3: Moving into the Future," *Proceedings of the Object/Relational Summit*, 1996.

Ronald Ross, *Entity Modeling: Techniques and Applications*, Database Research Group, 1987.

Index